Roger Bresnahan

Roger Bresnahan

A Baseball Life

John R. Husman

Foreword by John Thorn

McFarland & Company, Inc., Publishers
Jefferson, North Carolina

ISBN (print) 978-1-4766-9466-5
ISBN (ebook) 978-1-4766-5239-9

Library of Congress and British Library
cataloguing data are available

Library of Congress Control Number 2024012908

Front cover: New York Giants player Roger Bresnahan, 1903 (photograph by Carl Horner, courtesy of Roger M. Bresnahan)

Printed in the United States of America

McFarland & Company, Inc., Publishers
Box 611, Jefferson, North Carolina 28640
www.mcfarlandpub.com

Since I have known my wife Sandy, she has had a hand
in every good and meaningful thing I have accomplished.
This book is among them.

… no man, except perhaps Cobb, exerted so great an individual force in a ball game, either behind the bat, at the bat, or on the bases as Bresnahan.[1]

—John B. Sheridan, "Back of the Home Plate," *Sporting News*, February 11, 1926.

Table of Contents

Acknowledgments

Research for this work has been helped by many along the way. Without their collective contributions, this story would be an empty shell: Sue Baxter, Ben Beazley, Michael J. Bielawa, Cliff Blau, Dave Bresnahan, Veronica Buchanan, David Cameron, Steve Charter, Marian Bresnahan Childers, Donna Christian, Jill Clever, Ev Cope, Jim Dayboch, Ken Dixon, Stephen Evinsky, Mark Fedder, Mark Fimoff, Vicki Fitts, Fred Folger, Kurt Franck, Cappy Gagnon, Kathy Gardner, Steve Gietschier, Megan Goins-Diout, Shirley Green, Rex Hamann, Dan Henige, Jordie Henry, Ed Hill, John Horne, Art House, Reed Howard, Alex Huguelet, Ann Hurley, Mike Jones, Jack Kerin, Angela Kindig, John Kovach, Bill Lamb, Craig Lammers, Cassidy Lent, Ken Levin, John Lewis, Mike Lora, Clint Lowell, Sophia Marciniak, Jim Marshall, Irene Martin, Nellie Martin, John Matthew IV, Ann Mason, Bill Mason, Lynn McGuire, Judith Metz, Kit Moore, Bob Morris, Peter Morris, Dorothy Nowak, Nancy Oliver, Connie Panzariello, Jacob Pomrenke, Jack Puffenberger, Erica Powell, Carla Reczek, Matt Rothenberg, Tom Ruane, Wendy Rutkowski, Rhoda Segan, Anna Selfridge, Tom Shieber, Jim Silk, Dave Smith, Steve Steinberg, Beth Thieman, Joan Thomas, John Thorn, Stew Thornley, Jim Tootle, Scott Trostel, Joel Tschantz, Elizabeth Van Tuyl, Brittany Venturella, Laura Voelz, David Vincent, Don Williams and Miriam Wuwert.

Roger Michael Bresnahan graced me with Bresnahan family lore and willingly shared his collection of his great-uncle's memorabilia. No person aided my research more. The first to read my work and to offer ways to improve it was my wife, Sandy. She was followed by our professional wordsmith daughter Marianne Quellhorst who caught the many miscues her parents had missed. Then came reviews by career newspaper journalists Mike Jones and Mike Lackey. Lackey was doubly valuable as he is a knowledgeable devotee of Deadball Era baseball. My friend Mike Moore read and added his baseball expertise.

Besides these named individuals, institutions have been constant and invaluable throughout my research. The Society for American Baseball Research provides research sources the greatest of which is its members who so willingly share their individual knowledge. The Toledo-Lucas County Public Library, The National Baseball Hall of Fame and Library, the availability of digitized and searchable historical newspapers and of course, the internet have enabled a solitary individual to gather the information included in this work.

Foreword

by John Thorn

Over the past two decades baseball sophisticates have derided the voting patterns and special selections of the Baseball Hall of Fame as a measure of nothing except sentimentality, foolishness and cronyism. How did Rabbit Maranville get a plaque? Or Joe Tinker? Or Roger Bresnahan? Yet the Hall's purpose in honoring worthies of a bygone age, once famous if no longer so, has been to secure for them a sure pedestal in the pantheon, beyond challenge from future statistical savants or the mere forgetfulness of a later generation.

In a baseball pantheon, renown may endure beyond record. It may provide a valuable context for understanding.

That's what John R. Husman has done here for Bresnahan, who until now has been one of the few Hall of Famers without a book-length biography. In his day the Duke of Tralee, as he was mysteriously called, was famous as the favorite of McGraw and Mathewson and as the innovator of the catcher's shin guards. Yet he also played other positions and for a batter in the Deadball Era, his OPS+ (era-adjusted on base plus slugging) was 126, or 26 percent better than an average batsman, which was outstanding. Of the more than 20,000 major league players, that figure was the 245th best ever; in his seven years with the Giants, his mark was 139.

Even without benefit of advanced statistics, the Hall's electors of 1936 named Bresnahan on 20 percent of the ballots cast. (This was the election that created a "First Five" of Babe Ruth, Ty Cobb, Walter Johnson, Christy Mathewson, and Honus Wagner.) In the ensuing elections up to 1945, when Bresnahan was named, only Buck Ewing was inducted as a catcher. This was odd, as catcher had been, in the memory of some living electors, the most important position of all.

What made for stardom in that perhaps simpler time was not mere proficiency but courage—steadiness, endurance, bravery ... *character,* in short, which might provide a model for young fans. Like a pugilist who could not only dish it out but also take it, a catcher was admired for his pluck, especially in the days before mitt, mask, and mattress (let alone shin guards).

Before Jim Creighton introduced speed and Candy Cummings spin, the pitcher was not as admired as catchers Joe Leggett of the Brooklyn Excelsiors and Charles

DeBost of the New York Knickerbockers. The latter became famous for his "ground and lofty tumbling" in fearless pursuit of errant pitches or foul tips, a term borrowed from the acrobatics of the gymnasium.

Before the advent of the mask in 1877, when fouls caught on a bounce were still recorded as outs, catchers played 15 to 20 feet back of home plate unless runners were on base. Nat Hicks of the New York Mutuals once went into the game with his right eye almost knocked out of his head and his nose and the whole right side of his face swollen to three times their normal size. Yet, notwithstanding his injuries, batter after batter went down before his unfaltering nerve.

Playing the position steadily, day after day, was more important to a team than what a catcher could do with the bat. King Kelly and Ewing—and, more recently, Deacon White—would not have won their Hall of Fame plaques without their batting lines, but the weak-hitting Hicks—like Frank Flint, Bill Bergen, Chief Zimmer, Doug Allison, and Lou Criger—might be more appreciated if modern eyes could see them as their peers did.

It was into this tradition, when few men had caught 100 games in a season, that Bresnahan decided that he would enter. He transformed the position, especially in the media center of the nation, and went on to enjoy a long career in the game—especially in Toledo, Ohio, the author's hometown. Indeed, he and I first worked together in 1985 on a story he wrote about J. Lee Richmond who, after throwing the first perfect game in baseball history for Worcester in the National League of 1880, settled in Toledo.

It is delightful for me now to circle back with the pitcher's great-grandson, John Richmond Husman, to recommend his book to you, dear reader.

John Thorn *is the Official Historian for Major League Baseball. His most recent book is* Baseball in the Garden of Eden.

Preface

He was once a sensation in New York City but—even in his hometown of Toledo, Ohio—he is not remembered except by serious baseball fans. Roger Bresnahan was a baseball lifer. He played every position on the field and managed. He began his major league career in 1897 as an 18-year-old pitcher and ended it in 1915 as a Hall-of-Fame catcher who had introduced shin guards to his position. Following his playing days, he coached and was principal owner and president of the Toledo American Association franchise.

My friend Mike Lackey, a former newspaper writer and author of *Spitballing*, a prize-winning biography of Bresnahan contemporary Bob Ewing, once told me "Nobody really needs an Ewing book, but we need a Bresnahan book."[1] He was far too modest about his book but correct about a Bresnahan book. Lackey also told me that "Bresnahan was the most notable old-timer ... in the Hall of Fame who had never been the subject of a full-scale biography. It amazes me he's had to wait this long."[2]

I have been researching Roger Bresnahan for a long time. Looking back at a feature story about him that I wrote in 1987, I already had some solid biographical information, but I also discovered some factual errors. Those have been corrected but there may be more in this book. These are my responsibilities and hopefully they are few.

I recently read a book whose author expounded on "the many works of intimate history—memoirs, autobiographies, diaries—that I came across along the way."[3] I wish I could say something similar about my experience, but I cannot. My research sources were limited to newspapers, the writings of others, public records, a smattering of family lore and some other miscellaneous bits. I do, however, have a wonderful scrapbook made available to me by Roger's grandnephew, Roger M. Bresnahan. It proved to be a wonderful source of newspaper clippings and photographs. The clippings date from early in Roger's career through his years as a New York Giant with an emphasis on the 1905 World's Series.[4] For citation purposes I have titled it *Roger's Scrapbook* and designated Roger Bresnahan as its author. Each page is completely covered as a jigsaw puzzle. Neither sources nor dates are usually included. Nonetheless, it has proved to be an immensely valuable resource and has been a Rosetta Stone for solving several mysteries. The contemporary Roger has graciously allowed the

Toledo-Lucas County Public Library to scan the entire document and make it available for all to use.

My intention is to introduce Roger Bresnahan and tell the story of his life. I do not attempt to recount the major events of Roger's baseball career years or to retell the history of the Giants, Cardinals, or Cubs of the Deadball Era. That has already been done by others more capable than I. However, I show how Roger contributed to these teams and noteworthy events including the resurgence of the New York Giants under John McGraw, the 1905 World's Series, and baseball's tightest-ever pennant races of 1908. This book details his amateur, semi-professional and minor league experiences which have either been erroneously reported or neglected until now. Where and when he played during his early years has never been published correctly before. I tell the account of his on-field near-death experience. And this book reveals—for the first time—the story of his long-time dream to own a team which was realized. Featured are photographs—including some action images from 1905 as well as some which have never been published.

I do not try (with one minor exception) to rank or compare Roger Bresnahan to other players and particularly to other catchers over the century and a half of major league baseball. Despite modern analytical methods, which is an impossible task. Instead, my focus is on the opinions and impressions he made on his contemporaries. In the era in which he played; his ability was undeniable.

My work includes extensive use of primary sources and quotations from those who saw him doing what he did. These sources are chiefly newspapers, the only mass communication medium of his day. Newspapers of Bresnahan's day suffered from inaccuracies and sometimes outright fabrications. At best the printed word came from a reliable source but was filtered through a reporter and a newsroom staff. Nonetheless, newspapers are the best primary source we have. Sportswriters of that era used a very expressive style that was vastly more descriptive than today's. My hope is that the reader will enjoy the writing style and vocabulary of turn-of-the-twentieth-century sports writers as much as I do.

My overriding feeling is that I have left stones unturned and that there is much more to the story because research is always endless. After more than thirty-five years of investigation, though, it's time to tell his story.

One

"A High Fast One, on the Inside"[1]

The ball crashed into his head behind the left ear. The force of the collision propelled it "to first baseman [John] Ganzel, who caught it on the fly."[2] One of baseball's premier players and the outstanding catcher of his day lay in an unconscious heap near home plate. He had been struck by a pitched ball. A priest hurried from the stands and administered last rites. Roger Bresnahan was transported to a nearby hospital.

The next batter was also hit by a pitched ball, fracturing his right arm. Team Captain Dan McGann remained as a baserunner but then retired from the game.

The New York Giants, two years removed from the world championship, had won two-thirds of their games at that mid–June juncture of the 1907 National League season. The loss of two of their mainstays on that fateful day proved to be too much to overcome.

Cincinnati Reds pitcher Andy Coakley understood that he could not win the battle with the batter if he allowed him to be close to the plate.[3] Roger Bresnahan understood that he could effectively shrink the strike zone if he crowded the plate. Both were aggressive in attempting to gain an advantage. These tactics were and are an accepted part of the game but sometimes result in batters being unintentionally hit by a pitched ball.

By his approach, Roger Bresnahan invited being moved away from the plate. Sportswriter Harry Grayson explained, "Extremely aggressive, Bresnahan, a right-hand hitter, crowded the plate with a short, thick bat in his well-developed hands. His bat had the thick handle preferred by many players of his day. He always was a choke hitter, and his tremendous strength gave him distance in all directions. Bresnahan was absolutely fearless. Pitchers could not drive him away from the plate."[4]

Andy Coakley explained his view of the pitcher's role in the battle: "...it seems to me that hitting a player with a ball, whether the accident results seriously or not is much like shooting a man in battle—you worry about it for a moment, and then go about your business, shooting a few more, if necessary. Of course I feel exceedingly sorry for both Bresnahan and McGann, but that did not prevent me from shooting the ball with all of the speed at Bill Dahlen, who was the batsman to follow the two men I had placed on the hospital list.... But as for these or similar accidents taking a pitcher's nerve away, there isn't a chance, provided the pitcher has any nerve in the first place."[5]

These approaches to their roles define the issue—the pitcher and the batter each want to control home plate. One or the other always wins the battle.

* * *

On June 18, 1907, the New York Giants were nearing the end of a tour of the National League's western cities. They had played in Chicago, St. Louis, Pittsburg[6] and then were in Cincinnati for the second game of a three-set series. Lefty Hooks Wiltse was the starting pitcher for the Giants while veteran right-hander Andy Coakley got the call for the Reds. Completing the batteries were Bresnahan for the Giants and Admiral Schlei for the home team—both made news that day.

Neither team scored in the first inning. After Cy Seymour struck out leading off the second, Bresnahan singled to start a four-run outburst. Coakley did not give up another run on the day. Meanwhile Wiltse shut out the Reds through five innings. Cincinnati scored one in the sixth and two more in an exciting ninth but came up short in losing 4–3.

Reds' Catcher Admiral Schlei joined a growing list of backstops adopting protective shin guards when he came out for the ninth inning wearing pads.[7] It was the first he had appeared with covered shins. Bresnahan had worn the cricket-like devices on Opening Day and regularly ever since. He was maligned in the press for being soft and "later recalled receiving 'an awful razzing.... Fans called me everything from 'Sissie' to 'Cream Puff.'"[8] Nonetheless, the devices he led in popularizing soon came to universal use.

Though the Giants won the game, they suffered significant long-term losses due to events of the third inning. With one out Andy Coakley delivered a high inshoot[9] to Bresnahan. The *New York Times* described the at bat: "Bresnahan had been looking down toward third base and kidding Mike Mowery about the hit he had driven past him the previous inning. He told Mike that he was going to put another through just like it. Just then Coakley delivered the ball, a high fast one, on the inside. Bresnahan followed his usual habit of stepping forward and into the ball. When he saw that it was coming closer in than he thought he threw up his left arm to protect his head, but the ball glanced off his arm and struck him with full force behind the ear."[10] He "fell like a log" and lay unconscious on the ground.[11] Attempts to revive him by use of "cold water and a breast protector used as a fan failed...." After about 10 minutes, four Giants bore their fallen mate to the clubhouse.[12]

The game continued. Giants' Manager John McGraw inserted himself as the runner for Bresnahan.[13] McGann was then hit but Coakley got the next batter, Bill Dahlen, to hit into a double play to end the inning. McGann's injury was described as "not nearly so serious as Bresnahan's, but it was quite painful and will keep him out of the game for a few days. He was hit on the right wrist by a swift inshoot. Luckily, no bones were broken, but his arm last night was very stiff, and he cannot possibly throw a ball before the end of the week."[14] This assessment proved to be grossly inaccurate.

Among the 3,500 fans at the Palace of the Fans, the grandstand at League Park, were four physicians who had responded to umpire Cy Rigler's call for help. The team of doctors successfully revived the fallen ball player. Though accounts vary, Bresnahan may have been unconscious for as long as 30 minutes.

Once awake, Bresnahan asked for a priest. The doctors said "the injury was trivial, but Bresnahan begged so persistently…."[15] that his wish was granted. The Rev. Father John F. Hickey "rushed from the grandstand to comfort the injured man."[16] Hickey administered the sacrament of Extreme Unction. The stricken catcher again lapsed into unconsciousness and was then removed by ambulance to Seton Hospital.

Two

The Duke of ~~Tralee~~ Toledo

Roger Bresnahan lived falsehoods for most of his life.

From early in his major league baseball career, he was known by a nickname. At first it was Rajah or Duke but later and lastingly as The Duke of Tralee. Tralee is the largest city in County Kerry of southwestern Ireland. During Bresnahan's playing career and the years following, Tralee was widely known as his birthplace. We know he was born in Toledo, Ohio. How the Duke of Tralee's untruth originated is not known but Bresnahan did nothing to correct it. In his book on baseball nicknames, James Skipper wrote, "Bresnahan always maintained he was born in Tralee, Ireland."[1] Further, he had a hand in starting the misnomer. Explaining his refusal to appear in a vaudeville skit in late 1912, he told the press, "It's no business for a man from Tralee."[2]

Roger perpetrated a complementary lie. His middle name was long recognized and recorded as the popular Irish name Patrick. As with his birthplace the name was not factual but was allowed to prevail in place of his true name Philip. This, too, enhanced his Irishness and revealed his Irish pride. He delighted in being Irish and was "known to slip into a brogue when the moment struck him."[3]

Harvey T. Woodruff, sporting editor for the *Chicago Tribune*, wrote about Roger's birthplace and middle name, "Roger Patrick Bresnahan was born in Tralee, Ireland, on June 12, 1880, according to his own statement." Woodruff had the facts wrong because he took Roger's statement at face value, although he did question the given birth date: "Roger is generally regarded as older than the 32 years to which he confesses … but it is not the province of an interviewer to dispute the statement of an Irish born gentleman of Bresnahan's build."[4]

Roger was born on June 11, 1879. The date given in Woodruff's story is just a day short of being a year off and could be simply an error or as has long been a baseball practice, he could have misstated his birth year to appear younger than he was. Roger's confirmation of his fantasy middle name and birthplace reveals he was capable of self-promotion through deceit.

Roger's possible creating and certain nurturing of his nickname may have been done to enhance his popularity. There is some basis for the Tralee moniker as Roger's parents did hail from Tralee. Rightfully though, he should have been known as The Duke of Toledo.

* * *

Roger Bresnahan failed in his first two attempts to gain a lasting roster position at the major league level, but his third try was the charm. He stuck, this time in 1901, in the new American League with the also new Baltimore Orioles club, led by another Irishman, John McGraw. McGraw was building a team with a strong Irish core that would morph into the New York Giants beginning in 1902. Of course, the first criterion in making McGraw's new team was that the prospect could play but being Irish most probably gained him a favorable look. As told by David Fleitz in *The Irish in Baseball*, "Predictably, the new Orioles had a distinct Irish flavor, enhanced by young stars such as Roger Bresnahan."[5]

Though the number of Irish Americans playing major league baseball was declining as Bresnahan entered the picture, they still accounted for a quarter of the names on rosters during the first decade of the twentieth century.[6] Fleitz explained how the Irish influence on the game originated, especially because of second-generation Irish Americans such as Bresnahan: "As baseball grew in popularity, the influx of hundreds of thousands of young men from Ireland during this era created a new source of participants for the rapidly growing sport.... Baseball was an activity that the second-generation Irishman [as Bresnahan] could engage in to become a part of his new American community."[7]

John Thorn, Official Baseball Historian for Major League Baseball, said much the same: "baseball is an Americanising mechanism for immigrants."[8]

* * *

Both of Roger Bresnahan's parents were born in Ireland, but some of Roger's family lived in a London household headed by his mother Mary. The 1871 England and Wales census lists Mary Brusnehair, but the given names and ages of her children match the first four of Roger's siblings. The identity of the family is clinched as Mary's mother is included. The census reveals all four children were born in London.

It appears that the family's father, Michael, had gone ahead to the United States as he is not included 1871 English census. According to his naturalization affidavit and the 1910 United States census, he first arrived in the United States in January of 1867. Further, a man matching his personal data is found in the 1870 United States census living in New York City's lower east side. He shared a dwelling with eight others, two of them Bresnahans.

How Michael and Mary managed to assemble their family in the New World is not straightforward. Mary and some of the children crossed the Atlantic Ocean three times after Michael had landed in America. According to passenger lists she and their first three children arrived in New York on October 7, 1868. We do not know why or when they returned to England, but they did. Documents show that they left the United States prior to the 1870 census and arrived back in England before the 1871 English census. Mary returned to the United States on September 27, 1873, again with three children—but not the same three. John, who was in the first group, was replaced by Michael Jr. John remained in New York with his father. John's 1937 obituary revealed, "At the age of nine he came to the United States with his family, and they settled in New York City. Later they moved to Toledo."[9]

Michael makes his first appearance in a Toledo, Ohio, city directory in 1875 listed as a laborer living on Bancroft Street one door east of the Toledo & Detroit Railroad. Only the family head is listed.

The 1880 United States census enumerates, with ages and birth places, the family unit consisting of parents Michael and Mary and seven children.

* * *

Initially, St. Patrick's Roman Catholic Church, located just south of downtown Toledo was the Bresnahan family's home parish. St. Ann's, on Bancroft Street three blocks from the Bresnahan home, began serving the neighborhood and the Bresnahan family in 1898.

Michael Cornelius Bresnahan completed a years-long journey to his life's long-term home in Toledo's Auburndale neighborhood. He had left his native Ireland for England and spent a decade or so there before coming to America. He and his family spent some time in New York before the final leg of his trek to Toledo. He would never stray from the vicinity of his first Toledo address.

On arrival in Toledo, Michael either had the means or quickly acquired them to provide a permanent home where his children grew to adulthood. He moved his family several times, but never more than a few doors, before settling at 1434 West Bancroft Street in late 1881 or early 1882. At some point he purchased an adjacent lot but never built on it. That added space was large enough for casual play and a likely place for Michael Bresnahan's sons to have their first toss.

* * *

Biographies of Roger Bresnahan's birth family follow.

Father—Michael Cornelius Bresnahan was born in Tralee, County Kerry, Ireland about 1840 and died in Toledo in 1918. As a Toledoan he worked as a laborer, grinder, brick layer and teamster.

Mother—Mary O'Donohue Bresnahan was born in Cahersiveen, County Kerry, Ireland about 1841 and died in Toledo in 1925.[10] She gave birth to eight children who survived to adulthood and was a homemaker her entire life. Though their wedding date and place are not known, she and Michael were married for about 58 years.

Incorrect birth dates for both of Roger's parents resulted in the ages of both being overstated on their death certificates, in their obituary notices and on their grave markers—Michael by about 17 years and Mary by about 11 years.

Brother—John "Jack" was born in London, England in 1861 and died in Hartford City, Indiana, in 1937. He was a brick mason. He married Theresa Brunn in

Wabash, Indiana, in 1892. The couple established their home in Hartford City and raised three children.

Brother—Cornelius was born in 1862 in London, England and died in Toledo in 1913. He was a brick mason and married Ellen "Nellie" Martin in 1886. Martin, their oldest of four children, played professional baseball for six seasons.

Sister—Mary was born in London, England in 1864 and died in Toledo in 1942. She married James Welsh of Toledo in 1894 and raised four children.

Brother—Michael C. was born in London, England in 1871 and died in Toledo in 1931. He married Anna Haase in 1902. They had two sons, the first of whom died as an infant, before Anna's death in 1906 due to "stomach trouble."[11] He worked as a laborer, grinder, and machine hand, retiring as a supervisor in an automotive plant two years before his death from a self-inflicted gunshot wound.

Roger Bresnahan's parents, Mary O'Donohue Bresnahan (1841–1925) and Michael Cornelius Bresnahan (1840–1918), both hailed from County Kerry, Ireland and came to America via England. The couple raised eight children—the first four born in England; the others, including Roger, born in America (courtesy Roger M. Bresnahan).

Sister—Margaret H. was born in Toledo in 1874 and died in Toledo in 1954. She married Peter Henige around 1901 and was the mother of two. Margaret was especially close to her brother and accompanied his wife to Roger's hospital bedside when he was nearly killed as described in Chapter One.

Brother—James J. was born in 1876 in Toledo and died in Bedford, Virginia, in 1963. He married Emma Hunsberger in 1903. They had no children. Emma died in 1957 while the couple was living in Chicago. Jimmy was a top-flight amateur and semi-professional catcher and was often the battery mate of his younger brother Roger. A newspaper once noted the "star catcher should be gathered in by a league club."[12]

Self—Roger Philip was born in Toledo on June 11, 1879, and died in Toledo on December 4, 1944. We know nothing of his early years. He likely attended grade school at St. Patrick's Catholic Church School and the 1940 federal census reveals that he completed the seventh grade.[13] Baseball was his life's endeavor, and he is the subject of this work.

Brother—Philip Roger was born in Toledo in 1885 and died in Memphis, Tennessee, in 1942. He married Hazel Mettler around 1915 and the couple had two daughters. He was a good enough semi-professional catcher to earn trials with the Philadelphia Phillies[14] and the New York Giants. John McGraw invited Phil to spring training "in hope that the family that gave Roger to the baseball world would yield another son."[15] For several years, he was associated with his older brother Roger as business manager of the Toledo baseball club.[16]

Overall, the Bresnahan family appears to have been close-knit and most members remained geographically close to each other. The parents and five of their eight children, including Roger, remained in Toledo for their entire lives and 1434 Bancroft Street was always the family base.[17]

* * *

All three of Michael's American-born boys became accomplished baseball players. It was easy for them to get involved in the game as the baseball craze abounded in Toledo as in the rest of America. Roger entered the upper levels of Toledo's amateur game in 1896 at age 16. He followed his brother Jimmy who had become a regular catcher in the Toledo City League in 1895. Jimmy was the catcher for the Crescents 1896 and played for other teams as well. On one such occasion he was engaged to catch a May 23 game for Toledo's Outing Club. Completing the battery that day was Roger. The game was the first noted for Roger in the local press and is his first game of record. The opponent was the crack Toledo State Hospital team otherwise known as the Asylums. It was a disaster. The Asylum team knocked Roger out of the box with a seven-run second inning. The battery for the Outing Club was noted as "Bresnahan Brothers."[18]

Roger took on the Asylums, this time for the Toledo Grays, again on June 9 and lost 9–6. He went the distance but was hurt by his mates' nine errors.[19]Bresnahan and Bresnahan travelled with the Auburndale club to Bryan, Ohio, and defeated the town team there 19–15 on June 26. The game was described as "uninteresting throughout"[20] but was a win for Roger, nonetheless.

Roger did not appear in Toledo newspaper game accounts for more than a month. Then on July 28, pitching for yet another team, the Trumans, he won 13–12.[21]

In August, Roger joined his brother on the elite City League Crescents and pitched in relief in road games at Fremont and Norwalk, Ohio. Then he was retained by the Toledo State Hospital team that had roughed him up early in the season to pitch two games against the Orientals of the Toledo City League. The first resulted in a 12-inning tie with Roger going the route. The Asylum won the second, and the *Toledo Bee* headline over the game story read "Orientals Tried Two Batteries but Could Do Nothing with Bresnahan."[22]

Roger and brother, Catcher Jimmy, who was a fixture behind the plate, were both listed on the season-ending roster of the team managed by Joseph A. Starr. His gaining a roster spot on the Crescents club of the City League was no small feat for the young pitcher. Starr and the Bresnahan brothers would remain together going forward.

Three

"A Laurel to the Hibernian Brow of the Youngster" (1897)

Roger Bresnahan began the 1897 baseball season as a 17-year-old pitcher for his neighborhood Auburndale team in the Toledo City League of amateur clubs. The season opened on May 9 with Roger pitching and batting fourth. In seven innings of work, he gave up three hits, walked none and struck out 15.[1]

Three and a half months later, on August 27, Roger Bresnahan, now 18, made his major league debut. He pitched the Washington Senators past the St. Louis Browns 3–0.[2] He was the youngest man to have thrown a shutout in his major league debut and remained so until 1961 when Lew Krauss, younger by 25 days, did the same.[3]

Roger and his brother Jimmy were announced as the battery for Auburndale on May 16.[4] They did not appear, but Jimmy caught for the Bryan, Ohio, town team that day instead.[5] Bryan, located about 60 miles west of Toledo, was home to an independent semi-professional team managed by Joseph A. Starr.[6]

On May 23, the battery for Bryan was Bresnahan and Bresnahan for a game at South Bend, Indiana. Bryan prevailed over the locals 6–4 before 1,500 spectators. A Toledo newspaper headline proclaimed "'Kid' Bresnahan Struck Out 14 Men" and described his pitching as "phenomenal."[7] Four days later, with the same battery, Bryan bested the Defiance, Ohio, team 12–7.[8] "The work of pitcher Bresnahan especially pleased."[9]

Decoration Day was a day made for baseball, but the Bresnahans did not play anywhere, and oddly, the Bryan team was not even scheduled. The reason for both was found in a Lima, Ohio, newspaper on May 28 which reported of, "a proposition to move the Bryan baseball team in this city."[10] Starr would have had his players under contract so his players could not play elsewhere.

* * *

The new-to-Lima team made its debut on June 7. The Defiance team provided the opposition. Fifteen hundred spectators turned out at Faurot Park. When the game ended Manager Starr must have felt like the roof had fallen in as he lost not only the contest, 10–7, but also his only catcher and the team's ace pitcher. The catcher, Jimmy Bresnahan, was hurt in a collision at home plate and was out for over two weeks. Pitcher Eddie Mackey broke a finger in the first inning and was relieved by

Roger Bresnahan who went the rest of the way and took the loss. On June 16 Roger assumed the role as Lima's number-one starting pitcher. He won 14–1 at St. Marys, Ohio. His performance was, "a complete puzzle for the locals."[11] He followed up with a 7–4 win at Greenville, Ohio, three days later.[12]

Returning to Lima, he turned in a gem when he ambushed the Galion (Ohio) Indians with a no-hitter on June 20. He struck out nine and walked one in the 16–0 whitewashing. He also "made the first home run for the team this season."[13]

Roger's no-hitter was noticed by an Inter-State League team that tried to secure him but, "Bresnahan has refused an offer from the manager of the Dayton team."[14]

The next stop for the Limas was at nearby Wapakoneta, Ohio, with the Indians and their notable pitcher, Bob Ewing, on June 26. The rival cities were separated by just 16 miles of west central Ohio farmland. This may have been the first meeting between Ewing and Bresnahan. The pair would enjoy a friendship that continued until Roger's death in 1944. Ewing and the home team prevailed 7–4. The *Toledo Bee's* game report referred to the "Cyclonic Ewing" and commented that "Bresnahan pitched a fine game and with proper support should have won."[15]

Following the loss to Ewing, Roger reeled off four straight wins including a win over Ewing. His win streak ended when St. Marys clobbered him 15–1. A report said that Bresnahan pitched with "a very sore arm."[16]

The sore arm was rested for a week before both Bresnahan brothers went the distance in a 4–3, 13-inning loss at Urbana, Ohio, on July 22. Roger gave up just six hits in what was called "the finest game of the season played here."[17] The rest proved effective as he pitched nine times over the next 19 days.

On July 25, Toledo newspaper readers were given an update on their native son; "Young Roger Bresnahan, the star twirler of the Lima team, has pitched 29 games this season, and out of the 29 he has lost 4.... He is also a good hitter and fields his position like an old leaguer. Several Inter-State League managers have watched his work, and they have their eye on him."[18]

Roger and his Lima Crescents continued to do well until an August 9 contest against Wapakoneta and Ewing. According to the *Times-Democrat,* "It was a game that started nicely and was well-played on both sides up until the sixth inning, when the game was virtually given away. It was a game hard to lose, and not a few people were disgusted with the playing of Roger Bresnahan in the latter part of the game, when he became sulky and merely tossed the ball to the Indians, who smashed the ball for good clean hits." Roger was pouting because of a costly error committed behind him. He was roundly scolded in the game account which also noted that this was not the young pitcher's first such offense adding "Roger is a good pitcher and can play winning ball, but he should not so readily give vent to his feelings."[19]

Roger Bresnahan had proven that, at least on a pair of occasions and at the tender age of 18, he could control a baseball far better than he could control his emotions. He would not appear in a Lima uniform ever again.

* * *

Roger Bresnahan is reclining on the right with the 1897 Lima, Ohio, Crescents. As the team's pitcher, he is holding the ball as was customary in 19th-century team photographs. His older brother and catcher Jimmy is on the far left in the top row. Top row: Jim Bresnahan, Jim Delahanty, Jack Murray, Frank Sealts, Tim McCarthy. Middle row: Danny Burt, Bill Covert, Joe Starr (manager), Jack Hunter, Henry Machen. Bottom row: Eddie Mackey, Roger Bresnahan (courtesy the Allen County [Ohio] Historical Society).

Less than two days after being pulled from the mound because of his sulky behavior, Roger stepped aboard a train at 2 a.m. on August 11 and left Lima behind.[20]

He had received a telegram "from the manager of the Washington National League Club and asked if Roger would consider an offer from the Washington club, and for him to wire his answer immediately, stating his terms."[21]

Roger responded and his terms were accepted. The Washington response contained the agreed-upon terms, "Your terms are accepted. Will pay you $300 for the balance of the season, and transportation. Purchase ticket; will refund on your arrival. Report at once."[22]

The train that started his journey to the nation's capital took him to hometown Toledo where he connected that afternoon with another bound for the east. When he headed off on the final leg of his trip he was truly on his own and no longer following a path blazed by his older brother Jimmy.

Roger's hometown press followed him as he prepared to make his major league debut and reported that the *Washington Post* printed an "excellent likeness" of him and that "Roger Bresnahan is the youngest pitcher at present on the roll of any club in the big league."[23] Yet another bit reported his 18-year-old body as being five-feet-six-inches tall and weighing a slight 153 pounds.[24]

Manager Tom Brown seemed in no hurry to give Roger his first start and explained his reasoning when questioned, "Of course the Washington patrons of the game would like to see the new faces as soon as possible, but it would be folly for me to work any of the new men regularly while the team is winning.... I may give young Bresnahan a chance on the return of the Senators from Boston"[25]

Brown made good on that promise and on the August 27 debut day, Washington's *Evening Star* alerted its readers that: "...local enthusiasts will be given an opportunity to see whether the new pitcher, Roger Bresnehan,[26] will do for fast company. He has been coached by Farrell and McGuire and has all the curves necessary for a good pitcher. If Roger wins his game, he will be in a $45 suit of clothes, donated by a prominent citizen of Lima, Ohio."[27]

Roger also received instruction from Washington ace Win Mercer who willingly shared some secrets of his trade with the youngster. "Bresnahan was simply carried away with Winnie's slow teaser and asked for a few pointers on the floater. Mercer spent many an hour with Bresnahan to impart to him knowledge of delivering the slow one."[28]

This early image of Roger Bresnahan, with his name spelled Bresnehan, appeared in the *Washington Post* just before his major league debut with the Washington Senators of the National League on August 27, 1897.

Roger Bresnahan's major league baptism was all that he could have hoped for and one of the better games he had ever pitched. Headlines in the *Washington Post* told the story and spelled the new man's name incorrectly:

"KID PITCHER A WIZARD
Senators Shut St. Louis Out
on Bresnehan's Debut
ONLY SIX HITS FOR THE BROWNS
The Youngster Fielded His Position
in Sprightly Fashion"

The game story said in part Roger's debut "... 'twas one that brought a laurel to the Hibernian brow of the youngster.... He worked with the nerve and confidence of a seasoned veteran.... In fielding his position, Bresnehan also displayed agility, and he saved two hits by blocking hard-hit grounders that would have figured as safeties, had they eluded him."[29]

Roger was in control all the way. He scattered six hits, walked one and struck out another as his team prevailed 3–0. By any standard Bresnahan's first game was an impressive one but the accolades should be tempered a bit because of the quality of his opposition. Simply put, St. Louis was an awful team. The Browns finished the 1897 season at the bottom of the National League with a 29–102 record.

Bresnahan's next appearance was unscheduled and came on September 2 when he was summoned to relieve Win Mercer in the first inning of Washington's home contest against Pittsburg. Bresnahan, in what must have been a test of his nerves, was effective and allowed just two runs the rest of the way but Mercer took a 6–5 loss.[30] His second start came on September 6 in the nightcap of a doubleheader against Louisville with Honus Wagner at first base. A Labor Day crowd of 12,000—probably the most people Roger had ever seen—watched him win 7–3.[31] Roger was next assigned to complete a home twin bill on September 12 versus Cincinnati. He responded with a darkness-shortened seven-inning 8–4 win in which he chipped in three singles in three trips.[32]

Roger's first road experience came on September 18 at Brooklyn. It was a game he deserved to lose as Brooklyn scored in five of the first seven frames and held a seven-run lead heading into the eighth. But the Senators rallied with six runs in the eighth and three more in the ninth to pull out a 10–9 win. Roger was replaced by Mercer, who saved the win, with one out in the ninth because Bresnahan was a "trifle unsteady" due to razzing from the Brooklyn fans. As described the hazing may have affected the youngster more than a trifle, "a vociferous serenade ... fell on the ears of the pony Buckeye twirler with the shock of a boxing glove."[33]

Tom Brown was pushing the Senators toward the National League's first division and perhaps Bresnahan's awful outing against Brooklyn caused his manager not to trust him with another start. Roger sat for two weeks but got the call on the season's final day against the defending champion Baltimore Orioles. It was a meaningless game for Baltimore, but Washington needed a win to finish in the first division. Baltimore started four substitutes and Washington started Roger who gave up three runs in the second and was not allowed to come out for the third. Washington came back to win and finish sixth and took Roger off the hook again.[34]

That final game of 1897 provided the platform for the introduction of Roger Bresnahan and John McGraw. On the day they met, Roger retired his future mentor who was leading off the game but surrendered a base hit to him in the second inning and then promptly picked him off first base.[35]

The 1897 season ended on a high note for the Washington Senators and Roger Bresnahan's 4–0 record was a small contribution to the club's late season success. As Roger left for his Toledo home and a "winter position in a Toledo bicycle house"[36] his future as a pitching mainstay in the nation's capital appeared to be assured even despite his shaky season-ending performances.

* * *

Wood County, Ohio, adjacent to Toledo's Lucas County, was home to an eight-team amateur league in 1897. Two of its teams engaged in a five-game series following the regular season. The games were the result of a challenge issued by the North Baltimore club to its Bowling Green counterpart, "We hereby challenge you to play a series of five games for a purse of $200 and one half of all receipts."[37] Both teams fortified their rosters for the first game played at North Baltimore on October 6. North Baltimore brought in future Detroit star George Mullin to pitch. Bowling Green added Hall-of-Fame-bound Elmer Flick in center, Grant Johnson of the African American Page Fence Giants of Adrian, Michigan, at shortstop and the reunited Bresnahan brothers as battery. Roger was paid $15 for his day in the box. North Baltimore embarrassed him by amassing 24 hits in a 16–13 win.[38] Roger was not called on again to pitch in the series and ended his much traveled and overall, highly successful 1897 season on a sour note.

Four

"Bresnahan Was Very Wild" (1898)[1]

Roger Bresnahan was offered $2,000 by the Washington Senators[2] for the six months of work for the 1898 season. The still-18-year-old knew a tender was coming as the club had reserved him the previous fall.[3] One would guess, it would have been received favorably. The offer approached the unofficial National League maximum of $2,400 and was generous especially for such a young and untested player. But Roger did not immediately respond.

Roger's off-season routine, as published on March 3, told that the development of a slow teaser proved to be his focus, "Roger Bresnahan, the pony member of the Senatorial twirling staff, who is employed by a detective agency in Toledo, announces that he will be on hand next week, and that his twirling wing will be re-enforced by a slow ball, that Roger has been rehearsing in a Toledo 'gym' during the winter."[4]

Roger had accepted a position as a private detective. His employer was the Carew Detective Agency, a firm that provided "protection to large stores against petty thieves, shoplifting, etc."[5] He worked each winter as a "special detective" with Carew through the fall of 1908.[6] More than a half-dozen news clippings can be found in the Bresnahan scrapbook detailing some of his arrests of shoplifters.

The *Washington Post* stated on March 30 that "Bresnehen has neglected to report."[7] But three days later the same paper listed Washington holdouts or insurgents, as they were called, and Roger was not among them.[8] In fact, the same story indicated that Bresnahan was being counted on to contend for a regular spot in the rotation. Another reversal was published on April 9 when the *Post* labeled him a holdout and indicated that Manager Brown had decided to farm him out to a minor league club.[9] He was not on hand at the season's start and his status was a mystery until it was announced on May 11 that he was "unconditionally released yesterday by Earl Wagner because he failed to report for practice and has given no excuse for his absence."[10]

Sporting Life condemned young Roger for acting with "very little judgment" and that "Bresnehen was surrounded by a lot of old ball players, who gave him bad advice, and consequently Roger would not agree to Mr. Wagner's terms and the promising youngster will probably not be seen in the National League this year."[11] Another newspaper faulted "fool friends [who] kept Roger from signing." Some doubted that Bresnahan was offered $2,000 and the *Ohio State Journal,* in a dispatch carried by a Dayton, Ohio, newspaper, said so. "Bresnahan was offered considerably less than $1,000 for his services for the season. The *Dayton Evening Press* rejected the salary amount offered by the *Journal,* 'Bresnahan showed the *Press* baseball editor the contract mailed at Washington on the 18th of last February offering him 'twenty hundred dollars.'"[12]

Later, *Sporting Life* revealed that Washington may have promised to pay Bresnahan the maximum $2,400 but sent him a contract offering $2,000. Bresnahan could risk losing his deal with Washington as he had an ace in the hole. *Sporting Life* went on, "It is generally thought that manager [Charles] Strobel [of Toledo, Inter-State League] offered him more money than Washington did, and as Bresnahan is not in the business exclusively for honor, he secured his release from Washington, and accepted Strobel's proposition."[13]

Because of his refusal to sign with Washington the press suggested that Bresnahan "suffered from an inflated cranium" and "a forty-eight-inch chest."[14] But his refusal may well have been an early demonstration of his self-confidence and a genuine belief in his worth or simply his reaction to being treated in a manner he thought unfair or dishonest by the Washington management. The press generally stated that Roger was a fool and universally cited the influence of others as his reason for not accepting Washington's terms. Bill James, baseball historian, said the incident "... should give you an idea of Roger's temperament,...."[15]

Although contract dates and dollar amounts vary among sources, the results are clear. Bresnahan was the property of the Washington Senators, was offered a contract which he did not sign, was released, and then signed with Toledo.

* * *

Before Strobel signed Bresnahan he engaged him to pitch a trial game—a league match with Grand Rapids on May 20. He passed the test with a three-hit, complete game 6–2 win. He was excused for walking six, throwing a wild pitch and hitting two batters, "The Toledo boy was a puzzler to the Wolverines and but for the wildness which comes from lack of work would have shut 'em out."[16] The contract was then signed. The details are uncertain, but it was reported that his Toledo contract was about half the amount offered by Washington.[17]

Roger was immediately inserted into the Toledo rotation. Starting at Ft. Wayne on May 23 he was touched up for 15 hits, was again wild and beaten 8–0.[18] On May 27 he gave up 11 runs against Mansfield, was again wild, but won nonetheless as Toledo tallied 19 times. Roger helped his own cause with four hits.[19]

It was on to Dayton for a three-game series that included two games on Decoration Day. Toledo was protecting a slim lead in a tight five-team dog fight. Dayton won all three games and dropped Toledo from first to fourth place. Not only did Toledo lose its first-place standing—it lost Roger Bresnahan as well.

Roger started the afternoon holiday game. Trouble came "In the third... [Fred]

Frank picked out a nice one and slammed it right at Bresnahan. The little pitcher jumped in the air and turned around sideways, and the ball struck the fibula bone of his right leg. He took a step towards regaining the ball, but in a moment collapsed and fell to the ground in a heap. Drs. DuPuy and Salisbury, who were in the audience, gave the lad immediate attention. He was unconscious for a few moments and was frothing at the mouth. He was carried off the field and taken to his hotel."[20]

Another report stated Bresnahan "was removed from the Phillips House to the St. Elizabeth Hospital Tuesday. The surgeon said that it would be necessary to encase the knee in a plaster cast."[21]

Roger had received a severe injury and a significant setback that received surprisingly little mention by the press. Neither of the surviving Toledo papers mentioned the incident until a week later when a note in the *Toledo Daily Blade* reported, "Roger Bresnahan was out to see the game yesterday, hobbling about on crutches."[22]

* * *

History has not given us a diagnosis for Roger's May 30 injury, and we do not know the terms of his Toledo contract including provisions for his release due to his inability to play. But, two months later, a Minneapolis sports page announced, "Roger Bresnehan, the young pitcher just secured, will be on the slab for the Millers."[23] The Millers were the Minneapolis Millers of the Western League and Roger was scheduled to pitch for them against the Detroit Tigers a day later, July 25. He kept his new team in the game, but the Millers ultimately lost 7–6. The *Minneapolis Tribune* said of him, "Bresnehan, the young Twirler from Washington, for whom much is promised, pitched the first seven innings. He failed to have the best control but was not in good condition. An injured finger compelled him to leave...."[24] He was back on the mound five days later against Indianapolis and "the Indians hammered him at will"[25] and piled up 18 runs on 20 hits and seven bases on balls. It was not much better for his next game against the Milwaukee Brewers on August 2 when he was beaten 9–2 and he "was responsible for yesterday's defeat" according to the *Tribune*.[26]

Just as suddenly as Roger had appeared in Minneapolis he was gone. Following his third straight loss, *The Minneapolis Journal* reported, "The Axe Falls on Bresnahan,"[27] ending his three-and-out stay in Minnesota.

* * *

After his Minneapolis discomfiture the pitcher returned home to Toledo. Three weeks later, he was seen at Toledo's Armory Park, "in the grandstand and would have pitched but for too short notice...."[28] He did pitch for the Mud Hens the following day, August 26. The *Bee* headline over their game account provided a concise description of Bresnahan' ongoing problem, "BRESNAHAN WAS VERY WILD Eight Bases on Balls, Hit One Man and Two Wild Pitches His Record."[29] On the season Roger had pitched four games in May for Toledo, three for Minneapolis in late

July and early August and a late August game for Toledo. His composite record for the season was 2–6 with 49 bases on balls and six hit batters. Charlie Strobel had seen enough—Roger Bresnahan did not pitch again for him, or anybody else, in 1898.

The Toledo team journeyed to Wapakoneta for an exhibition game on August 29. Bob Ewing pitched. His catcher was Roger Bresnahan.[30]The impetus for installing a pitcher as a catcher is not known but proved to be prophetic. This is the first known instance of Roger playing behind the bat.

Roger Bresnahan's disappointing season had ended and there appeared to be no interest in his services going forward. But, in October, Ban Johnson announced that the Western League's Milwaukee Brewers had made a claim for him, giving rise to hope for another season.[31]

Five

"Speed Bresnahan" (1899–1900)[1]

The Milwaukee Brewers did not act upon their claim for Roger Bresnahan's services in 1899. A January report mentioned Roger "was injured last year," and had undergone "treatment for his arm."[2] Another said he was "now in excellent condition."[3] In spite of their earlier experience, Minneapolis came back into the picture and signed him for his third organized baseball season.

Bresnahan played in all three of the Millers preseason games. In the first, on April 13, he played shortstop against the University of Minnesota.[4] Two days later he played second base, batted cleanup and had four hits including a pair of doubles.[5] He was the starting pitcher in the final tune-up against cross-river rival St. Paul. He did well but was lifted in the sixth with a 3–1 lead. At bat he was two for two with a home run.[6]

Manager Walter Lamont chose Roger to pitch the Millers' season opening game at Milwaukee on April 28. He gave up just one earned run but lost 4–1.[7] His second start came at Kansas City six days later. He was hit often and hurt by six Millers' errors, including one of his own, in losing 13–5.[8] Following, Roger sat the bench until May 11. His complete game effort against St. Paul was lost when he blew a two-run lead in the ninth.[9]

Roger had given up 13 runs in his last seven innings pitched and was again relegated to the bench. He sat for more than a month before being released on June 15.[10]

* * *

Buffalo, also of the Western League, signed Roger at once and put him right to work. On June 18 at Columbus, he was brought in to relieve and gave up at least six runs.[11] The next day and again two days later, he played at second base, hit two singles, and fielded flawlessly.[12] On June 22 he made a pitching start. His dreadful outing ended after two innings. He allowed 10 hits and walked three which the Detroit Tigers made good for 10 runs.[13] Buffalo then joined Washington, Toledo, and Minneapolis (twice) as teams who had issued him walking papers within about 14 months. He must have wondered if any team would want him now.

* * *

Soon thereafter, the then 20-year-old found out who wanted him, and it was quite different from his major-league experience of two years before. He agreed to play for the Manistee Millionaires.

Located in Michigan's lower peninsula on Lake Michigan's shore, Manistee was a prosperous town of 14,260 that "claimed to have more millionaires per capita than any other city in the United States."[14]

Roger's play in Manistee is not widely recognized and those who do know of it are ill-informed as to how it fits into his timeline. The *Sporting News* erroneously included in Roger's 1944 obituary that he "found he could get money for playing with Manistee, Michigan, in 1895 when only 16."[15] At age 16, he was occupied playing amateur ball in Toledo and his play at Manistee beginning in 1899 is well-documented. The *Sporting News*' error stemmed from its own records.[16]

Baseball was especially popular in Manistee. Game stories were presented on the front page of the *Manistee Daily News*. The small community was home to what was classed as an amateur team[17] but all its players were salaried.[18] The Millionaires, also known as the Colts, along with Muskegon and Traverse City, were "undoubtedly the three fastest independent teams in the state."[19]

Roger did not disappoint in his initial appearance at Traverse City on Sunday, July 30, "Bresnahan had the Hustlers at his mercy." He won 15–2, striking out 10 and scoring four runs himself.[20] The next day he played center field in a win over the Columbia Giants.[21] The day after that, in his first game at Manistee, he endured a loss to the same "speedy organization of colored champions," 5–2. However, his pitching was praised, and "his work was eminently satisfactory to the fans. The young ex-leaguer has speed to burn, superb control and a good head."[22] "The next day he was back in center contributing two hits and scoring three times in another win over Traverse City."[23]

After four games in four days the die was cast—pitcher Bresnahan would be in the lineup, somewhere, when not on the mound.

And so went the season with the Millionaires generally winning as did Roger when he pitched. On August 14 the team record stood at 29–4.[24]

Roger started the season's finale at Manistee on September 17 against the Muskegon Reds. While pitching in the fourth inning and leading 7–1, misfortune suddenly struck. "When 'Speed' was in the act of delivering a fast one, his foot slipped, and his arm snapped like the crack of a whip. Bresnahan walked to the bench with the affected arm hanging limp at his side.... The arm was dislocated at the elbow and the spasmodic contraction of the arm muscles made the injury exceedingly painful."[25]

So ended Roger's 1899 season.

Roger returned to Manistee for the 1900 season. Again, he was primarily a pitcher, but his foremost secondary position was now third base. He did some catching as well and was batting .336 to lead the team in late July.[26]

He started and won his last game for Manistee on August 17 against the South Bend Greens making for a happy swansong.[27] The game was his last because of a stunning offer.

* * *

Roger Bresnahan is front and center with the Manistee, Michigan, Millionaires in 1899. He quickly earned the nickname "Speed" as a pitcher and was an everyday player primarily as a centerfielder, third baseman and catcher (courtesy the Manistee County Historical Museum).

The Chicago Orphans, now the Cubs of the National League, missed an opportunity to sign Bresnahan following his release by Washington in 1898. A club spokesman lamented, "Roger Bresnahan, Washington's recalcitrant twirler, would have been a good man to gather in and develop for future glory."[28]

The Orphans signed him on August 19.

Sporting Life reported: "Roger Bresnahan, he who pitched for Washington two years ago, has been signed by Chicago. The young man came out for practice yesterday and showed up well. Roger would not be recognized by the people who used to admire his clever box work. He has quit pitching, and is now a catcher and infielder, having played about everything in sight for Manistee during the present season. He has also changed into a large, fat thing, deep of chest, and vast of bulk. 'Tis said that he can bat a whole lot and is as good an all-round fielder as there is anywhere."[29]

His appearances were few and not productive. On August 28, he was inserted as a pinch runner during a ninth-inning rally against the Cardinals that netted two runs in a 3–2 loss, and, despite the loss, he was the headliner, "Orphans Make a Strong Finish Against St. Louis, but Lose on a Mad Dash for the Plate by Bresnahan Just as Victory is in Sight." He was thrown out at the plate to end the game. The story colorfully described the play as "a weird, wild dash for the plate, and inaugurated his second league existence by killing the last hope of victory" and said that he "took long odds, but might have made it but for perfect throws…."[30] Roger had made third base on a single by [Bill] Bradley. Another account added details and more color to what happened next, "On the first ball Bradley skipped to second, and Bresnahan tore for home, [St. Louis Catcher Lou] Criger threw down to second, the ball came back lightning fast, and Bresnahan, writhing along on his vest buttons, felt something descend on him like a brick on an extra-ripe tomato."[31]

Then on August 31, he caught the last four innings of a blowout loss to Cincinnati. He failed to hit in two tries and had two passed balls. It was said that he "showed in poor form, being nervous."[32]

The next day he was given his unconditional release. It is surprising that Chicago gave Bresnahan such a cursory examination. Four innings is hardly sufficient to make a valid verdict. The player he would become points to the lack of sound judgment on the part of the Chicago management. The *Chicago Tribune* reported that "[h]e got a cup of coffee in the league" and suggested that he "was satisfied."[33] It is unimaginable that Roger Bresnahan would have been satisfied with his performance, abbreviated trial, or his release.

His "wild dash" to home just described was seen by Cardinal third baseman John McGraw. McGraw witnessed the kind of aggressive play that he personally practiced and admired. Very soon the two would be united in a relationship, rooted in like-minded baseball.

Roger was once again let go near season's end and with no immediate prospects for the 1901 season.

Six

He Would Never Again Be Known as a Pitcher (1901)

Having his major league aspirations dashed after a short run at the end of the 1900 season, Roger Bresnahan went home. A January 20, 1901, news item reported "Roger Bresnahan…, is now a physical instructor at Auburndale, Ohio."[1] The appearance of this short bit tells that Roger—though not on a roster or reserved by a major league club—was still of interest. A week later, the *Washington Post* announced, "The former Washington pitcher, Roger Bresnahan, has been signed by McGraw. Roger—has developed into an all-round player."[2]

Despite this mention of Bresnahan's newfound versatility, many later news stories referred to him strictly as a pitcher. A subsequent announcement of the signing gave a clue of how the deal came about and confirmed that Roger was still thought of as a pitcher. "Roger P. Bresnahan—This is a youngster who was with the Chicago League club. That club, having a surplus of pitchers, let him go. He was recommended to McGraw by Clark Griffith, pitcher of the Chicago club, and is a promising man."[3] Roger, who had reached his majority the previous June, was maturing in body and was already a veteran of four professional seasons. He was listed at five feet eight inches tall and 178 pounds.[4]

The 1901 season would be McGraw's eleventh as a major league player and his second as a player-manager and he was also part owner of the new Baltimore club in the new American League.

McGraw was ambitious, aggressive, and driven to win. Biographer Don Jensen said of him, "The pugnacious McGraw's impact on the game, moreover, was even greater than his record suggests. As a player he helped develop 'inside baseball,' which put a premium on strategy and guile, and later managed like he had played, seeking out every advantage for his Giants. Known as 'Mugsy' (a nickname he detested) and 'Little Napoleon' (for his dictatorial methods), McGraw administered harsh tongue-lashings to his players and frequently fought with umpires…."[5]

As there was no baseball in Baltimore in 1900, McGraw was bound to build the 1901 edition from scratch. The opportunity came with a new major league, the American.

* * *

The timing of this 1901 expansion of major league baseball certainly worked to Roger Bresnahan's advantage. Suddenly the number of available roster spots had doubled but that may not have even mattered in his case. McGraw obviously wanted him badly as evidenced by his early signing of the youngster. Roger was among the first to report to spring camp at Baltimore and was "among the regulars at work."[6]

The club engaged in eight preseason games within the immediate area and Roger participated—sparingly in half of them—all as pitcher. The competition was not "fast company," using a term of the day, but Roger fared well giving up a single run during 15 innings pitched.[7]

* * *

The Orioles were scheduled to open at home on April 24. It rained. The next day it rained more. The season finally got underway on April 26, but Roger did not appear in that game or for the rest of the homestand. Baltimore then embarked on a road trip. The first stop was Washington, the scene of Roger's major league debut in 1897. McGraw scheduled him to start on April 30, making him number three in the season's first rotation.

It was not pretty. Roger lasted just three innings giving up six hits and eight runs and taking a 12–6 loss. In fairness, damaging errors contributed to his downfall but so did the four free passes he issued. At bat he was two for two with a double.[8]

Wilbert Robinson was the Orioles captain and front-line catcher. He did not catch Roger's debut because of illness. The backup catcher was Tacks Latimer who, like Roger, made his American League debut. "Latimer did not make a brilliant start in American League company, to say the least. Four times he tried to throw to second base—once he hit the umpire standing near the pitcher's box and the other times, he seemed to find trouble getting the ball past the pitcher."[9] It was one game and done for Latimer who was soon banished from the Oriole roster.

Still unable to play the following day, Captain Robinson was replaced behind the bat by the previous day's pitcher—Roger Bresnahan. Roger caught Joe McGinnity's 6–4 win over the same Washingtons. In its game account the *Baltimore Sun* said of him, "An unusual feature of the contest was that the catching for Baltimore was done by a pitcher—Roger Bresnahan. Robinson is still sick, and Latimer is not in good condition, so manager McGraw had no other backstop. Bresnahan did admirably, although he was a little off as to high fouls, which fact gave the Washingtons two of their four runs. But Mr. Bresnahan was sure death to base stealers, and his backstopping was perfect. He is also a clever batter and base runner." In support of the last sentence, Roger coaxed a walk, singled, stole a base and made a "pretty bunt."[10]

There are often repeated and apocryphal stories of how Roger first caught. Told in various forms they relate to the game he pitched in Washington and his frustration with Latimer's performance. The crux is that Roger challenged McGraw on the field to provide better catching for the Orioles, and that his manager's quick response was that Roger catch himself which he did—at once. An absurd version told how Roger responded to his manager's suggestion: Bresnahan glared at McGraw, flung his glove across to the dugout, strode down to the plate, stripped Latimer of his catcher's duds and donned them himself.[11]

John McGraw, the man who was in charge, simplified the story in his autobiography, "One day, when we were shy of catchers and trying to get one, he came to me and said: 'You don't have to get another catcher. I will go behind the bat myself.'"[12]

With thanks due to Tacks Latimer for the opportunity, this game marks the beginning of the shift of Roger Bresnahan's baseball-playing career from pitcher to position player. He would never again be known as a pitcher.

A May 13 announcement of Latimer's release included a proclamation of McGraw's. "When asked if he intended to sign another catcher in Latimer's place, McGraw said he did not, as he thought he already had the best young catcher in the country in the person of Bresnahan."[13]

McGraw brought Roger along slowly and played him only occasionally but in a variety of ways. All the while, he was being tutored by Wilbert "Uncle Robbie" Robinson, the Orioles' 37-year-old catcher and team captain who was destined for the Hall of Fame.

On May 15, the Orioles left Baltimore on an extended road trip of 20 games to five cities. McGraw did not take the entire roster, but Roger was included in the party.[14] This was his first lengthy road trip, and it would offer little playing time, but it included a wide range of experiences and insight into McGraw's managerial style.

Overall, the journey was not successful with five wins and nine losses, and six more games lost to foul weather. As bad as it was from a team perspective, it was packed with firsts and several eye-popping experiences for Roger. It must have been a thrilling adventure. He began the excursion to Boston and the American League's four western cities of Milwaukee, Chicago, Detroit, and Cleveland—as a rookie and a marginal, seldom-used pitcher. On return, in just three weeks, he was a catcher and a semi-regular player.

Along the way Roger faced the already legendary Cy Young and learned why he would eventually win 511 games. Roger was hitless in five trips against the veteran master. He served notice of his aggressive nature by forcing a player from a game by spiking him on a steal attempt.[15] He played in the outfield. He learned to know his teammates and what a team did during travel, off days and idle time forced by inclement weather. He saw huge crowds. He was close to, and might have been a fringe participant, in two major donnybrooks in two different cities[16] that resulted in fines and suspensions for Oriole players and their opponents and censure for McGraw.[17] He saw his team forfeit a game as a result of rowdyism.[18] And significantly he caught, albeit for a short time, regularly and began to hit major league pitching with some confidence.

The most critical and telling aspect of this trip was Roger's observations of John McGraw in action. McGraw was already becoming his mentor. Bresnahan proved to be a fast learner and soon would emulate McGraw's extremely aggressive, vitriolic, sometimes violent, and win-at-all-costs style. He watched McGraw's willingness to tangle with anyone, especially umpires, and including American League President Ban Johnson.

Johnson was pleased initially to have McGraw as a very visible member of and a top drawing card for his fledgling American League. But quickly the relationship between McGraw and Johnson soured. From Johnson's point of view, much of McGraw's behavior was counter to his aims for the style of play for the American League. Per his later stated goals he wanted to reform the National Pastime, "My determination was to pattern baseball in this new league along the lines of scholastic contests, to make ability and brains and clean, honorable play, not the swinging of clenched fists, coarse oaths, riots or assaults on the umpires, decide the issue."[19] McGraw's conduct on the field certainly did not mesh with the Johnson ideal.

* * *

When the Birds returned to their Baltimore nest for a long home stand that would last through July 2, Roger had proven himself to McGraw and was ready to assume a regular and productive role. Roger's problem, though, was that there was not a position available to him as the regular lineup was set. However, the American League edict limiting rosters to 15 players would work in his favor. Because of his versatility he was able to fill any position as needed. *The Baltimore Sun* described the Orioles as "Crippled, patched up and demoralized"[20] Especially advantageous to Roger were repeated injuries to the fingers of Robinson.

Roger caught the first three games of the home stand and *The Sun* revealed the reason: "Captain Robbie is suffering from a very sore index finger on his right hand, the nail of which was broken off recently."[21] But Roger himself was not whole, "Bresnahan caught with a very lame and painful leg...."[22] Following, Roger was moved to left field for a single game and Robbie was forced behind the plate all because of a suspension to regular left fielder Mike Donlin—"Captain Robinson is suffering with his right index finger badly swollen and dripping blood from the third inning on. Bresnahan played left field on one leg."[23] No injury to Bresnahan's leg was described nor did further reports appear in *The Sun*, but Robinson continued to catch, and Roger's play was limited for the next month.

Key injuries then prompted his return to regular play, a role that he would not relinquish going forward. On July 12 McGraw injured his knee in a collision.[24] Though he would make occasional appearances through 1907, subsequent aggravations would lead to his announced retirement as a player later that season.[25]

On July 17 Captain Robbie was injured again: "Robinson was added to the hospital list this afternoon, one of his fingers being injured so seriously in the third inning that Bresnahan had to replace him behind the bat."[26] The door had opened for Roger, and he entered—he stayed behind the bat and was there through August 20. During those 35 days he caught all the 35 games that the Orioles played including doubleheaders on August 1, 3, 5, 7, 9 and 10. He hit in 27 of those 35 games and had several big days at bat. On July 21 he had a single, triple and a home run in a win at Milwaukee. The home run was of the over-the-fence variety and the first of his major league career. He had two triples in the first game on August 3 and another three-hit game on August 10. On August 17 he drove in the winning run in a 3–2 win over Cleveland.[27]

In true McGraw style, Bresnahan emulated his manager by earning his first ejection when umpire Tommy Connolly tossed him from the August 19 home game with Detroit. "There were many tiresome protests from both sides, and Bresnahan was put out of the game and fined."[28]

We might call those days—from July 17 through August 20, 1901—Roger Bresnahan's "Arrival Month" because that is exactly what he had done. He had arrived as a full-fledged and consistently productive major league baseball player who was now an important and contributing team member.

During his "Arrival Month" Roger made a visit to his place of birth. Toledo is located on the main rail route between New York City and Chicago. The Orioles had an off day following their July 22 game in Milwaukee. The route to their next game on July 24 in Cleveland went through and stopped in Toledo. Roger got off for a short stop at home to visit his parents.[29]

Roger also spoke with reporters. Much of the discussion centered on the rivalry between the two major leagues. Roger insisted that the American was superior to the National and the proof was "[a]ll around the circuit the American is outdrawing the National almost two to one." Roger then proposed a method to settle the issue. "What I would like to see done, and which would settle the disputed point as to which of the big leagues has the strongest team, would be to have the teams in the two leagues at the close of the season meet each other in the order in which they had finished the season and let them play five or seven games to decide who were the best."[30] As we know, his proposal has been implemented, in part, as the World Series. In its entirety, the interview revealed forward thinking by the barely 22-year-old about the game that went beyond playing.

But, despite Bresnahan's successes and his "arriving" in 1901, he suffered from some shortcomings, too. Several gaffs caused Roger to be scolded by the press. On one occasion he made the third out in an attempted steal of third base in which he neglected to slide and overran the base.[31] On another his wild throw allowed two runs to score and led to a loss.[32] And, while playing left field, he stumbled and let a fly ball pass him for a triple.[33] Yet again, he was chastised for waving a runner home for an easy out at the plate when he was coaching third base. Baltimore lost by a single run. The *Sun* declared that "Bresnahan distinguished himself as the boss 'bum' coach...."[34] Some, if not all, of these events can be attributed to his inexperience and the high caliber of play in new American League where he was matched against baseball's best.

Beginning August 21, the Orioles played 39 games to complete the season. Roger and Robbie divided the catching duties. Otherwise, Roger filled in at second and third bases, left and right fields and, on one occasion, pitched in relief. With Roger clearly the front-line catcher, the Orioles finished in a rush, winning eight straight before dropping the season finale and ending with a winning record of 68–65–2.

* * *

The 1901 season had ended but there was more baseball to play. Barnstorming America was in its infancy and Roger Bresnahan was a part of it. He joined with a team of American League stars that would tour with and play against the same from the National League.[35]

But before embarking on the tour the All-Americans went to Worcester, Massachusetts, on October 1 for a game with the American League's first pennant winners—the Chicago White Sox. While catching Roger was forced to leave a losing effort against the champions early when he "burned his hand on a hot one."[36]

The tour started on October 7 in, of all places, Roger's hometown of Toledo, Ohio. Most of the National team, made up mainly of Brooklyn Superbas players, did not show because of a late-arriving train. Their roster, filled by Cleveland's Erve Beck and several Toledo Mud Hens including Bobby Gilks, got the better of the All-Americans 8–6.

But Roger had a great homecoming game. *The Toledo Bee* gushed compliments of his play under the headline: "BRESNAHAN'S FINE PLAYING: Toledo Boy Star of Yesterday's All-American-National League Game."[37] Roger had four hits, three doubles and a single, caught flawlessly and showed off his throwing arm. "Throwing to second base Bresnahan opened the eyes of the fans, and … it is doubtful if anywhere in this broad land there is another catcher who throws like Bresnahan."[38]

Family members were likely there, along with friends, former amateur mates, and other fans just wanting to see Roger and the collection of major league stars. Just two blocks from Roger's parents' home, Edward and Caroline Lidke lived. They had a 20-year-old daughter, Adeleen Marcella Lidke. We do not know if Adeleen was there or if she and Roger had a relationship, but we know that they soon would.

The tour continued from Toledo and Roger went with it catching games in Lima, Ohio, on October 6; Fort Wayne, Indiana, on October 9; Evansville, Indiana, on October 16; Greenville, Mississippi, on October 21, and New Orleans on October 27.[39]

The tour continued to Texas[40] but Roger did not. A Pittsburg newspaper announced, "Roger Bresnahan has deserted the American League barnstormers and is on his way home."[41] He travelled north with Frank Bancroft as far as Cincinnati. The Reds Business Manager had just relinquished management of the tour.[42]

Roger attended the American League's December 2–3, 1901, meetings in Chicago. He had no place in the proceedings but, he met with McGraw and signed a contract to play with Baltimore in 1902.[43] Pleased, Roger "returned to his Toledo home rejoicing."[44] McGraw told the press "that Bresnahan had received five telegrams from manager [Al] Buckenberger offering him a place on the Boston National League team."[45]

Resuming his employment as a detective for the winter months he proved he "is as good a thief catcher as he is a ball catcher."[46] Another newspaper reported on his policing success, "During the Christmas shopping season Bresnahan is reported to have caught a number of pickpockets and shoplifters."[47]

For the first time in his career Roger Bresnahan spent the winter knowing where he would be playing the next summer, but he knew only where his season would begin.

Seven

"I Signed to Catch, and That's the Only Place I'll Play" (1902)[1]

Just 23 years old, Roger Bresnahan bristled with confidence in anticipation of the 1902 season. He had agreed to a contract with the Baltimore Orioles that paid him $1,950 and was coming off a successful first full major league year during which he caught 69 games. Judging by his comment to a reporter, he considered himself the Orioles front-line catcher. He told the *Washington Post* during spring training, "they are not going to use me all around the lot this season. I signed to catch, and that's the only place I'll play."[2] Boosting his confidence was the knowledge that other teams coveted him. It was reported that Connie Mack sought to purchase him[3] and the Boston Nationals continued their courtship. Boston asked him to name his terms. Not wanting to leave Baltimore, he sent back a number so high he thought it would not be considered—$3300. But it was accepted, so Roger declined again. Boston responded by asking him "how much more he wants...."[4] On April 7 he received still another Boston offer of "a bonus of $1000 and a salary much better than he is getting from the Orioles to jump the American League." Roger "replied simply that he is done signing contracts for this year, and Manager McGraw is highly gratified at the young catcher's loyalty."[5]

The Orioles gathered in Baltimore and departed there aboard the steamship *Hudson* on March 22, bound for Savannah, Georgia, and two weeks of pre-season practice.[6]

McGraw was "determined that there would be 'no loafing' as there was last year, and that each man shall, become fit and keep himself in the condition necessary to give an adequate return for the salary he is paid."[7] His prescribed daily routine: "Report at the front door of the hotel, dressed for business, at 9:30 o'clock each morning, run to the grounds, one mile and a half, and keep at hard labor for one hour and a half, run back to the hotel and prepare for lunch; report again at 3 o'clock for another run to the grounds, where two hours net must be spent in practice. The exercise will wind up for the day with the run back to the hotel."[8]

Despite McGraw's admonition, Roger and all but six of the Orioles rented bicycles "which they will ride to and from the grounds in preference to walking."[9]

Practice began on March 27. McGraw scheduled games against local lightweights—the Catholic Library Association, for April 2 and a Savannah town team two days later. Roger caught for the librarians and then his own team in the second easy win.[10] Otherwise, games were of the intrasquad variety matching Regulars versus Yannigans.[11]

On April 10, Roger sustained an injury when he "got a severe spiking just above the knee." He was reported to be "limping badly"[12] that evening and did not play again until April 16.

* * *

The Orioles then travelled to Boston to open the American League season on Saturday, April 19. The first championship game of the of the season was played four days in advance of the other three American League openers so it could be part of the Patriots' Day celebrations in Massachusetts. Boston celebrated a win before a crowd of more than 16,000[13] but Roger did not participate.

Over the course of the following eleven days the Orioles played eight games—three exhibitions and five in the league. Roger caught in all three of the exhibitions and did not appear in the league games. Wilbert Robinson was firmly entrenched as the Orioles' catcher.

Roger saw his first league action on May 1 when Baltimore entertained Boston. He was called upon to complete McGraw's at bat after the manager was ejected for arguing. Coming to the box with a 3–2 count he lashed a single that drove in a run, but his clutch hit lost some of its luster when he was thrown out attempting to stretch it to a double.[14]

The next day, he made his first start of the season, again against Boston, but this time—in New England. He had a memorable day that started with his facing the great Cy Young. Roger ended a rare performance by the immortal one when his single drove in the Orioles sixth run of the first inning. In the bottom of the second, Oriole center fielder Joe Kelley was thrown out of the game. Despite his earlier admonition that he would catch only, Bresnahan was moved to center and Robinson replaced him as catcher. His loose lips were nothing more than bravado. McGraw needed Bresnahan in center and, undoubtedly, Bresnahan was more than pleased to go there. In the sixth, three singles loaded the bases for Roger who tripled and was, once again, out as he attempted to stretch his hit. The Orioles won 14–6.[15]

The following day he caught, and Cy Young pitched again. Young was his usual self as he shut down the Orioles on three hits in a 10–1 Boston win.[16] But for Roger, he had cracked the Orioles starting lineup.

* * *

Roger's new role as an everyday player was initiated by the absence of several key players—Jimmy Sheckard jumped back to the National League,[17] Joe Kelley suffered a charley horse on May 8[18] and was out until May 20[19] and John McGraw was suspended for five days[20] then was spiked on May 24[21] not to return until June 28.[22] Captain Robinson seemed to always be plagued by nagging injuries. In total, these absences created opportunities for Bresnahan to play center, third and catch. From May 3 through July 16, he missed only one game. On June 12 he was granted a day's leave and returned to Toledo to visit his parents "and also someone else."[23] That someone else could well have been the previously mentioned Adeleen Lidke.

Along the way Roger gave some noteworthy performances, mostly favorable but not all. Playing center against Boston on May 6 he had "two misplays."[24] He had a two-error game in center on May 10 but received high praise for his play there against Washington on May 15:

> Bresnahan was the bright, particular star of the contest. In the fourth inning dreadful Delehanty, who makes long hits just to keep his muscles in order, sent one out to centerfield, which was a triple all right, in the original package and labeled with a warning against taking something just as good. Del ran as if he were being chased by an injunction, but Bresnahan leaped down to the field like Sheckard jumping contracts and getting under the fly just about as it was to pass the time o' day with the fence he pulled it into his mitt and Del was dead. It was about the most spectacular outfield play Baltimore has made this season and Bresnahan was cheered long and loud.[25]

In another game with Washington, just two days later, the *Sun* lavished more acclaim on him: "The attack of charley horse from which 'Joe' Kelley is suffering has shown the ability of Roger Bresnahan as an outfielder. Ever since he has been in the position Roger has played great ball, letting nothing get away from him. Some of his catches have been of the genuine circus order, well worthy of Walter Brodie[26] at his best. At bat he made eight hits in the six games of the series with Washington, and some of these have been long ones, which arrived at the most opportune moments. Yesterday Bresnahan made a triple and a single and scored a run. His playing has made him popular with the rooters."[27]

More the next day: "The most important feature of the series has been the development of Roger Bresnahan as an outfielder. Kelley's lameness forced Roger to center, where nothing extra was expected of him. Instead of playing a merely acceptable game because it was not Roger's right position, he has been showing a line of star goods that has set the crowd crazy and has made him about the most conspicuous man on the team last week."[28]

Next, he would be a third baseman, filling in for McGraw. The *Sun* reported on his play at that position in a shutout win over Detroit on May 24, he "picked up hot grounders and threw to first like a $10,000 star."[29] A reversal of form was reported for the May 29 Chicago game in which he was charged with an error, "Roger Bresnahan played third in place of Oyler. He was nervous and did not manage himself well.... The hoot of derision and disappointment he received was shockingly rude."[30]

His hitting during two games on Decoration Day made headlines; "Roger Bresnahan was the star of the first game and incidentally a star of the first magnitude. He made two home runs, each time scoring another man, a double, which likewise brought a weary wanderer home, got hit and struck out. Roger's daring doings in that game made him a reputation that will last him years after he is too old to throw a ball from the box to the plate."[31]

He demonstrated speed and base running ability during a June 2 win over Cleveland: "Bresnahan got a base on balls, stole second, went to third on a wild pitch and stole home."[32]

Bresnahan and his manager, McGraw, showed baseball savvy and a will to do anything to gain a competitive edge. On June 26 in a game with Philadelphia at Baltimore Rube Waddell pitched for the Athletics: "Bresnahan was the star of a brainy play which will long live in the memory of the faithful. In the second inning he had accepted a pass, stole second and been sacrificed to third. Cronin was at bat and Bresnahan began to cut up 'monkey shines' in playing off third. He waited until he saw Waddell wound up to deliver the ball and then faked a dash for home. Waddell promptly unwound and started to catch Bresnahan at third. In a minute Bresnahan and McGraw, who was coaching to say nothing of the spectators, claimed a balk. There was absolutely nothing for [umpire] Connolly to do but allow the claim and Roger walked home…."[33]

Bresnahan had a single, double, and triple that helped the Birds beat the Athletics and Eddie Plank 2–1 on July 3. But it was his defense that made for the headline "BRESNAHAN'S GREAT CATCHES." The game story elaborated, "Bresnahan again showed that he can play third with the best in the business. Two of his running catches of fouls up against the stand were among the fielding features."[34]

Bresnahan had his first four-hit game on July 9 against Washington. The *Sun* lauded his fine day at bat but first admonished him because of his recent hitting performances: "Another little man who made several stacks of hay while the sun did shine at a temperature of 92 degrees was Bresnahan. In these later days he was not half enough. Yesterday, however, he redeemed himself. Two doubles and two singles out of four times up was his proud record."[35]

The Baltimore Base Ball Club was shaken to its very core by the July 8 announcement that its manager, part-owner and third baseman, John McGraw, had been named manager of the New York Giants.[36] Wilbert Robinson and Joe Kelley were named dual managers of the Orioles.[37] But, Robbie temporarily left the team because of the death of his mother and Roger assumed catching duties beginning July 12.

When he walked off the field following a loss to St. Louis on July 16, it marked his last game as a Baltimore Oriole.

* * *

The next game for Roger came three days later against Philadelphia. He caught Joe McGinnity for manager John McGraw. There was nothing new about this. But what was new was the league, the team, the venue, and most teammates. Roger caught that day for the New York Giants of the National League in the Polo Grounds.

How he and others got there is a story in itself. Because the scheme that caused the New York Giants to be "Baltimorized,"[38] was concocted by McGraw—likely the most influential person of Roger's development—a short summary follows.

McGraw's actions were born of his dislike for American League President Ban Johnson and were self-serving. McGraw believed that because of his ongoing feud with Johnson he would not be able to continue in the American League. He acted before Johnson did. The plan was complex and involved three teams, their owners, and players. The ploy could not have worked without the active participation of several key co-conspirators. David Fleitz included a concise summary in *The Irish in Baseball*:

> McGraw, Wilbert Robinson, Joe Kelley, and John J. Mahon all owned stock in the Baltimore team. Mahon bought up the shares held by the three players and then set to work, buying out enough of the other stockholders to give him majority ownership in the franchise. Once that task was accomplished, McGraw demanded, and received, a release from his contract. On July 8, he abruptly quit the Orioles and signed a deal to manage the New York Giants of the National League. Eight days later, Mahon shocked the baseball world when he sold the Orioles to Andrew Freedman, owner of the Giants. A National League team now owned an American League franchise outright, and destruction of the Orioles began immediately. Freedman, following McGraw's advice, released Kelley, McGann, Bresnahan, McGinnity, and other stars [Cy Seymour and, Jack Cronin] from their Baltimore contracts, making them free agents and available to sign anywhere they wished.[39]

McGraw then signed a foursome of the former Oriole Irishmen to Giant contracts—Bresnahan, Cronin, McGinnity and McGann. He had pulled off an outlandish deal that landed him in New York for life. McGraw was the highest-paid ball player or manager at $11,000 per annum for four years.[40] Bresnahan observed McGraw's ambition, drive, and ruthlessness first-hand.

* * *

Observing Bresnahan from the bench was Frank Bowerman who had been the Giants catcher to this point in the season. The rivalry for the Giant backstop position was on and, once again, Roger had a formidable competitor. Manager McGraw would spend the next weeks overhauling the Giants' roster, but this pair would remain as his catchers for some time.

Over the next three weeks the Giants played 17 games and Roger caught 11 of them. Otherwise, he played in right field, at third base, pinch hit or sat. Beginning August 9 McGraw settled the issue. For the rest of the season Bowerman was his catcher and Bresnahan his right fielder. Though an outfielder for the bulk of the time, he spelled Bowerman on three occasions and filled in at first base, shortstop and third base. Along the way he had some noteworthy games. On August 3, the Giants played a Sunday exhibition game at Bayonne, New Jersey, in which Roger did the unheard of—he caught for both teams.[41] On August 9 he earned praise from the New York press when his clutch hit helped the Giants split a doubleheader with the Chicago Cubs: "Bresnahan was most responsible for his team's victory. His home run hit into the crowd beyond the ropes in right centre scored the three runs that won the game."[42] When visiting Pittsburg on August 21, he led the Giants to an 8–1 victory over the Pirates with a single, a double, a triple, a stolen base and scored twice.[43]

Roger missed more than two weeks of playing himself because he became seriously ill. He played the final game of a series at Cincinnati on August 27 but was not present for the Giants' next game. New York's *World* explained: "A telegram received from his physician in Toledo, O stated that Roger was very ill with malaria."[44] "He was taken sick while his team was in Cincinnati, but his condition at this time is not alarming."[45] A September 4 report declared a dire prognosis: "New York is deprived of the services of Roger Bresnahan who is at home in Toledo, O. suffering from typhoid fever. He will not be seen on the diamond again this year."[46] The next day that report was contradicted by the *World* which stated, "Roger Bresnahan did not join his team as expected today, a report coming from his home instead, stating that his physician forbade his leaving for New York before the end of the week. So, Roger will not be here until about Tuesday of next week."[47]

Roger bettered that estimate and was in the lineup on Monday, September 8, but he was not happy about it. The Giants had a doubleheader that day and, because of an injury the prior day to first baseman Dan McCann, Roger "had to play against his wishes."[48] He played first base in McCann's place.

After a day off, he played another doubleheader at first base. The third doubleheader of the week followed on Thursday. He sat out the first game and filled in for McGraw at shortstop in the night cap. On Friday, the Giants were at Orange, New Jersey, for an exhibition game with Roger in left field. In its game account, the *World* commented on Roger's condition, "Bresnahan is a really sick man, and he says he will have to quit before the end of the season if many double-headers are played. He is fearful of being stricken with typhoid fever and recalls the unfortunate end of Pitcher Prentiss of the American League, who returned to the game too soon after an attack of the fever."[49]

Roger's schedule did not ease. Over the final two plus weeks of the season, he had one off day in addition to two Sundays that were not scheduled and played three more double headers, a pair of them on the season's final two days. We know of no further effects of his illness.

* * *

The 1902 season which had begun with so much promise in Baltimore ended halfway through with that promise not realized. A new promise of success in the nation's largest city replaced the first—a promise that required the remaking of the New York franchise. Roger's short-term future was secure. John McGraw had personally selected him to be one of the building blocks for the new, New York Giants—a venture that would prove to be wildly successful.

The *New York Times* on reported on August 17 that Roger had already signed for

1903: "...Bresnahan's conscientious work has been appreciated by McGraw, for the manager of the New Yorks has already signed Bresnahan for 1903, and the contract, which was left in Toledo by Roger last night, calls for $6,000 for the season."[50] Later reports in several newspapers gave Bresnahan's salary as $4,000 which is in line with the salaries of two other Giants: Christy Mathewson at $5,000 and Frank Bowerman at $4,000.[51]

* * *

The first order of business for this off-season was a little more baseball. On October 19 he was presented as catcher for the local Elks team at Toledo's Armory Park. "Roger's exhibition of backstop work, his throwing to second and his whipping to third was as pretty an exhibition of high-class baseball as anyone would care for. In addition, Bresnahan created havoc with the stick, getting three hits in as many times at bat and he stole bases [3]."[52]

Several days later, another playing opportunity was announced: "The professional ball players who make Toledo their home will invade Bowling Green [25 miles south of Toledo] Sunday and play the team of that town for fun and glory."[53] "A big crowd went out to see the game.... The Toledo players wore the uniforms they wore during the past season, representing many different clubs and a full half dozen leagues."[54] During the second inning a storm hit and prematurely ended the contest.... Nonetheless, Roger's presence was noted, "The great Bresnahan was in the catcher's box where he was the center of all eyes"[55]

* * *

Roger would be far from idle during the coming months. He acted on a plan to become involved in the business of baseball when he and a partner attempted to obtain an option to acquire the Toledo Mud Hens. A morning Toledo newspaper reported, "Charles J. Strobel has been asked for a 30-day franchise [option] on his property and is considering the matter. The prospective buyers are Roger Bresnahan and Charles Stevens. Mr. Stevens is proprietor of the Valentine cigar store.... If the deal is carried through Roger will captain and manage the team and Mr. Stevens will look after the business end."[56] A Toledo afternoon newspaper also reported the story but from Strobel's point of view which had a different twist and quoted Strobel who stated Charles Stevens, "asked me for a written option. I told him to show me the cash and I might talk to him but did not consider him in earnest."[57]

The news of the proposed deal was carried by the wire services and found its way across America. Nothing further was reported until Strobel nixed the deal after taking more than three weeks to do so. "C.J. Strobel, the Toledo mogul, put a veto as big as the lid on a wash boiler on the story that he had sold out to Roger Bresnahan saying 'I've never seen the color of any money to make that option good.'"[58]

The deal was off, but Strobel would soon sell.

With his managerial and ownership aspirations on hold, Roger turned his attention to other interests. He was reported to be forming an indoor baseball league in Toledo.[59] A week before Christmas 1902, a story surfaced linking Bresnahan to Columbia University, "Failing to get McGraw, Columbia asked Roger Bresnahan to coach its baseball squad."[60] A subsequent report stated that he had been engaged by Columbia[61] but extant records at the university are void of any mention of Bresnahan. Another announcement of Roger's involvement with indoor baseball came in January 1903, "Erve Beck and Roger Bresnahan are coaching the Toledo High School indoor baseball team."[62] The Boston Americans, once again, beseeched him to jump to them. He rejected their offer saying "I never jumped a contract and never will.... The Boston American League team has been trying to get me since I have been in New York. I have letters written me offering me a better salary than I am getting now. I did not accept, however, as I am under contract to play with the Giants. I want the money and I don't blame a ball player for getting it, but all the income I get out of baseball must be clean."[63]

Roger put this all aside because of his impending nuptials—the announcement was made that he would wed Miss Adeleen[64] Marcella Lidke on February 4.[65] The news of the wedding was carried by newspapers nationally. The *Daily Blade* told the story that evening: "Mr. Roger P. Bresnahan and Miss Adeline M. Lidke were married at 8 o'clock this morning in St. Anne's church. The bride is well known to a large circle of friends. She is an accomplished young woman. The groom is one of the most popular young men in the city. He is especially well known in baseball circles, being catcher for the New York baseball team. At 2:22 this afternoon Mr. Bresnahan and his bride left for a visit to Palm Beach, St. Augustine and Jacksonville, Fla. They will remain in that state until Mr. Bresnahan goes north to Savannah to begin training with his teammates."[66] The same story mentioned that Mrs. Bresnahan would travel with her husband during the upcoming season.

A letter from Roger, written in Savannah, was received in Toledo on February 19, stating that "they had a most delightful time" in Florida and that "he will remain at that place until he is joined by the other members of the New York Baseball club."[67]

Eight

"McGraw Has to Put Him In Somewhere" (1903)[1]

The bulk of the New York Giants pre-season roster for 1903 gathered in New York City and left for spring practice in Savannah, Georgia, on March 15. Several of their mates, Roger Bresnahan included, joined them there.[2] The first practice was called on Monday, March 16.

Dispatches from Savannah were sparse. Bresnahan, along with most of the other players, were not mentioned except in game accounts which were rare as only two were played there. McGraw had outlined his plans for the daily and morning workouts which were held at the Bolton Street Park in east Savannah, "I will devote most of the work here to limbering up the pitchers and hardening the muscles of the players by batting, running, etcetera, though we may play some exhibition games…."[3]

The two games were played against grossly overmatched opponents. Roger started both behind the bat and was relieved by Jack Warner in both cases as McGraw instituted an innovation which he explained, "Some persons do not think well of my intention to play two pitchers in each game during the season. In my opinion it will prove a very useful innovation, and I will try it for a while at any rate."[4] McGraw would not only change pitchers but catchers as well, switching batteries at mid-game.

One of those pitchers was Luther "Dummy" Taylor, a deaf mute. Because of Taylor's disability Roger, along with the rest of the Giants' roster, was required by Manager John McGraw to learn sign language.[5] Following a spring game in Dallas, the Giants were returning to their hotel and were scattered among the passengers in a streetcar. Among those passengers was a young woman who was attracted by Roger's appearance. One of Roger's mates noticed and using sign language flashed "That pretty girl is much taken with Roger." She intercepted and understood the message and "quick as a flash, signaled in like fashion, 'Yes, and he looks pretty good to me.'"[6]

The Giants left Savannah on March 26,[7] to begin playing their way north to New York City.[8] Three Southern League teams fell to McGraw's men; the Birmingham Iron Barons 7–1,[9] the Memphis Egyptians 5–2[10] and the Fishermen from Nashville 4–3.[11] They barely won against the Eclipse Club at Louisville on April 1 where Roger played first base. A local newspaper called him "one of the most valuable men on the New York team, as he can fill any position in nice style."[12] Following, two dates lost to winter-like weather in Indianapolis, the Giants headed east to Columbus, Ohio, where they bested the Senators of the American Association 5–3 on Sunday, April 5.[13] Bresnahan did not play but started the next day behind the plate—he did not last long.

With two outs in the first inning, "Bresnahan was hit by Hart's bat while working behind the plate in the first inning. He had to retire. His hand was badly swollen last night, and he will be out of the game several days."[14]

Pre-season games continued at the Polo Grounds. Fordham University opened the home season on April 9 and was beaten by the Giants 8–2. Frank Bowerman had just reported to the team. He, along with Jack Warner, who had shared catching duties with Bresnahan all spring, gave the Giants a three-man catching corp.

Bresnahan did catch a part of the Fordham University game, his and the team's first game since his hand injury three days earlier. The injury was not noted by the press at the time, but it would prove to have lingering effects and be the cause of ill feelings between Roger and his manager.

After an 11–1 win over Columbia University on April 10,[15] the Giants engaged Jersey City of the Eastern League in a home-and-home series to conclude their season's preparation. The Giants prevailed with a combined score of 19–0.[16]

The Giants appeared ready to begin championship play; so did Roger. Apart from one game in which he played first base, he caught half games per McGraw's new scheme. Overall, he played well, contributing to the offense in most every game.

* * *

McGraw's plan to use two pitchers, and batteries, each game did not materialize for the season's opener on April 17—or ever. Christy Mathewson pitched a complete game that initial day and Jack Warner was behind the plate for him all the way as Roger observed from the bench. Roger caught all of Joe McGinnity's complete game the next day contributing a pair of hits that included a home run by which he "covered himself with glory." In that same game, the Giants' Left Fielder Sam Mertes wrenched his ankle while stealing third base.[17] Mertes missed the next four games and was replaced by Roger.

Catcher had been a word often used to describe Roger Bresnahan and that usage had some history. As pointed out in Chapter Six, in 1901 John McGraw called him "the best young catcher in the country."[18] Sports Writer Frank Graham said in his 1952 history of the Giants that when McGraw brought Bresnahan to New York in 1902 he was "recognized even then as the best catcher in baseball."[19] In actuality, his playing record told a different story—at the start of the 1903 season only about half of his experience was behind the plate. To this point in his career, he had played every position on the field and logged 108 games as a catcher and 104 at all other positions. If McGraw was sincere in his rating of Roger, his signing of a third Giants' catcher, Jack Warner, was curious. Warner had been the regular Giants' catcher for

Former World's Series battery mates Joe McGinnity and Bresnahan watched the 1923 classic. The future Hall of Famers were teammates in Baltimore and New York 1901–1908. Bresnahan caught 106 of McGinnity's pitching starts, more than any catcher (courtesy the Ernie Harwell Sports Collection, Detroit Public Library).

six seasons before jumping to the Boston Americans before the 1902 season—ironic in the wake of Boston's repeated and failed attempts to lure Roger there. At any rate, McGraw enticed Warner to jump back to New York.

Bresnahan had emerged as a valuable utility player who could play well anywhere. McGraw would use him to fill gaps in his lineup in 1903. Now, Jack Warner was the team's number-one catcher and was backed up by Frank Bowerman. There was no position open for Roger. For the first month or so of the 1903 season he filled in as catcher, left fielder, pinch-runner, center fielder, pinch hitter and first baseman.

Roger had several noteworthy early season games that gained the attention of the New York press. "If the Giants had eight more Bresnahans what a slashing team this borough would have! Bresnahan is a find without a doubt. He is a great catcher, hitter and can run bases to perfection. His heart and soul are in the game, and his actions on the field inspire the rest of the team to play as hard as he does."[20]

On April 28, the Giants bested Philadelphia 12–7 at the Polo Grounds. While catching, Roger chipped in with a double, an over-the-fence grand slam home run, stole a base and scored twice. It would be 112 years before another Giants' catcher hit a grand slam and stole a base in the same game. Buster Posey duplicated Bresnahan's feat on June 19, 2015.

On April's last day the aging George Van Haltren, a fixture in the Giants' outfield for more than a decade, wrenched his back while batting and was forced to retire.[21] The next day McGraw inserted Bresnahan in Van Haltren's center field position. Roger's time in center lasted less than two games as Umpire Augie Moran tossed him for disputing calls of pitches. The ejection of Roger was the second by Moran in less than two weeks. On April 21 he was dismissed for a reason that is unfathomable today: "Bresnahan objected to Moran's calling McGann back to the bat after the big first baseman had been hit by the pitcher, as, in the umpire's opinion, the ball was not pitched swiftly, although it bounced off McGann's shoulder and struck the grandstand."[22] From this account it appeared Roger had a case although the call was one of judgment. Roger's treatment of umpires earned him a warning from his league's president Harry Pulliam, who threatened him "with suspension if he does not stop abusing umpires."[23] Apparently Pulliam's scolding was effective. Soon after, the *Washington Post* noted, "Roger Bresnahan is a subdued wild man. That warning from President Pulliam drove some sense into his head."[24]

At some point during 1903 Roger told of how he was fined because he refused to dine with an umpire. He did not name the umpire but said the incident occurred in Detroit in 1902. Research revealed the arbiter was Jack Sheridan and the date was June 13. He related that he was told to go to the bench and was levied a $5 fine for his leisurely exit pace. Roger said later, "That evening when I went into the dining room, I was escorted to a seat at a table where there were a number of other men. I did not notice who they were until I had taken my place in the chair. Then I happened to look up and right next to me was the umpire. I called to the head waiter and when he had got within hearing distance, I asked him to change my seat, remarking on the side that I did not care to eat my supper in such company as I had found at the table with me. As I arose the umpire turned to me and said: 'That will cost you another $15.' Well, I gave him the laugh as I had no idea that the fine would stick.'"[25]

McGraw told Roger that the fine would stick and so he resolved, "The remainder of the season I was as careful off the field as on it and I fought shy of giving offense to umpires."[26] That care was not long lasting.

On May 13 McGraw inserted Roger in the lineup batting him second and playing him in center field where he remained for the rest of the season. For the first time in his major league career a position was his.

The defending National League champion Pittsburg Pirates were at the Polo Grounds for the first meeting of the season between the two clubs. When play was called the Giants were tied for first place with the Chicago Cubs. The Pirates were in the third spot just a half game back. New York fans could not resist the Saturday afternoon matchup and flocked to the ballpark. "There never was such a vast assemblage of men and women present at a baseball contest as that which gathered there yesterday, the official count being 31,500 … there were fully 5,000 disappointed persons on the outside the high fence clamoring for admission."[27] The Giants pleased the largest-ever baseball crowd with a 7–3 win as Roger contributed a double and a triple and drove in three mates while covering first base for the ill Dan McGann. The *New York Sun* dubbed him a "major general of the willow" because of his hitting.[28]

Roger was injured and re-injured on Sunday, May 17, 1903, causing him to miss a single game which did not sit well with him per his personal letter that was later published:

> In the game yesterday (Sunday) with Hoboken on Cricket field, Hoboken, before 6,000 persons, Roscoe Miller pitched the Giants to victory, but the game may have cost McGraw the services of one of his stars for a week or 10 days. In the third inning, Roger Bresnahan, the idol of the fans, in skidding to the plate sprained his right shoulder and hand so seriously that he may be out of the game for a long time.
>
> In a letter to a friend in Toledo Bresnahan writes: "My right hand is so badly swollen from the injury Sunday that I can hardly hold a pen. The accident happened just as my hand was getting better from the injury I received in Columbus before the season opened. I ought to lay off for a week or more and get back in shape, but they won't let me, and every time I catch a ball or take hold of a bat the pain is awful. I am afraid the hand will bother me all summer unless I can keep out of the game for a time."
>
> In spite of the pain he suffers, Roger remains the same hard-hitting, fast fielding and base running player that has made him dear to the fans in the metropolis. A travelling man at the Boody [The Boody House, a Toledo hotel] said recently that thousands went to the game daily just to see Bresnahan play, and McGraw has to put him in somewhere to suit the enthusiasts.[29]

The Sunday injury also brought criticism from fans who were "appalled" that a star player could be lost for championship play due to injury in an exhibition contest. Because Sunday baseball was not permitted in New York City the Giants' management often booked games with nearby minor league teams. The fans expressed "that the support New York gives to a winning club is such that management cannot afford to play these 'extra money' dates." A St. Louis newspaper chimed in with, "Their howl against the playing of extra date games has been so long and loud that even the New York management may be able to hear it."[30] The management did hear—the Giants played just one more such game in 1903.

Shortly thereafter, beginning on May 23, Roger was forced out for five games because of malaria.[31]

But through all the position changes, not playing, ejections, the hand injury, sickness, and lineup-juggling he hit and was the National League's leading batter as of May 1 with a .480 average. McGraw was forced to keep Roger's bat in the lineup. And, with one exception, he batted high in the order. The exception was when he caught and was placed eighth as McGraw and many Deadball-Era managers routinely did with their backstops. His lofty batting average after the season's first month must be tempered because of his limited play but he would remain among the league's top few batters all season long. Also on May 1, the Giants were in first place in the National League.

Through June Roger continued to lead the league's batters. As announced on July 5, Roger was atop the hitters' list with a .359 average, just ahead of two Pittsburghers—Honus Wagner at .356 and Fred Clarke at .351.[32] Roger returned to his home state for a weekend series in Cincinnati mid-month. He enjoyed a noteworthy game on Saturday, June 13 as his Giants beat Cincinnati 4–0 on Christy Mathewson's one-hitter. Roger contributed the big blow off his former Toledo mate Bob Ewing, "With two on the bases Bresnahan made a home run to right centre, scoring three runs in a bunch."[33]

On July 1 at the Polo Grounds, Bresnahan participated in a defensive play against the St. Louis Cardinals that he long remembered. Playing in center field he started a triple play in which four players were "put out." The *New York Times* called it a "quadruple play" and said, "Of course the fourth 'out' was needlessly executed…." According to the *Times* game account Homer Smoot flied out to Bresnahan for the first out. Bresnahan threw home retiring the runner trying to score from third for the second out. Jack Warner, the Giants' catcher, then threw to second base to catch the runner trying to advance from first to second for the third out. The ball was then unnecessarily returned to Warner catching the runner attempting to score from second base.[34]

Other consulted accounts varied slightly. Several did not include the final play at the plate and the handler of the ball at second base was not consistent in all accounts. But the one description that varied the most was Roger's own, given the following January, which named the second baseman as being involved and altered the order of the putouts—Bresnahan to catcher to second baseman to catcher.[35]

He rated this triple killing as the most sensational play in which he had ever taken part. Roger's account differs from all others and from the record of the play as kept by the Society for American Baseball Research (SABR) which describes simply as 8–2–6 or centerfielder to catcher to shortstop.[36] Since we cannot be certain which of the accounts is completely accurate, all come into question but there is no reason to discount any one of them.

A July 3 news story cemented Roger's position in the New York outfield and contradicted earlier statements of both he and McGraw: "Manager McGraw of the New York Nationals declares that Bresnahan will never be used again behind the bat unless absolutely necessary. He has determined that Roger's forte is in the outfield. Bresnahan has had as varied an experience as any player who ever lived … and behind the plate he proved to be a great success. His ginger permeates the whole team, and his batting is of the first calibre."[37] This was an easy decision for McGraw at a time when he had two other top-flight catchers—but times would change.

* * *

July 3 was a travel day to Chicago as the Giants began a swing through the National League's western cities on Independence Day. The Giants were firmly in second place and their first foray into the west had included an eight-game win streak. Roger commented on his team's road success: "I just feel that we are going to do even better than on the last trip. I don't know what gets into the boys when we are at home. They don't seem to have the ginger that they have in the West…. We are so anxious to do well before our home crowds and to show our appreciation of its loyalty that we try to do too much and overreach ourselves. But in the West, we know that every fan is against us, and we grit our teeth and pile in."[38]

Calamity of another kind struck in the first inning of the road trip's first game and its victim was Roger Bresnahan. The *Chicago Tribune* described, "Chance sent a long fly to left center, which brought Mertes [left fielder] and Bresnahan [center fielder] into a terrific collision which caused a delay and finally retired Bresnahan from the game."[39] Mertes struck Bresnahan's rheumatic leg hurling him to the sod where he laid in agony for 10 minutes when he attempted to play but could not continue.[40] The incident received very little note in the press. Research has not revealed the preexisting condition of rheumatism. However, a later news clipping told that "Bresnahan is of the opinion that his attack of rheumatism was largely due to the fact that he had to tramp around all the afternoon in an inch or two of water in the centre field."[41] The injury proved to be serious and disabling.

Unable to play the following day, Roger settled into a grandstand seat in his street clothes to watch the game. There he saw his teammate-catcher Jack Warner split a finger and be forced to retire. Frank Bowerman, the Giants' other catcher, was absent from the team and Roger was summoned to catch. Mertes completed the inning behind the bat while Bresnahan changed. "When Bresnahan entered the game, the umpire [Hank O'Day] announced a protest on the part of Chicago, but the game was allowed to continue in order not to disappoint the big crowd of 12,000 persons. The protest was made under Rule 27, Section 1, which requires all players, who are to take part in the game, to be on the field in uniform at the beginning of the game."[42] The Giants went on to win 7–1. It seems odd that Roger himself would be considered the rule breaker, but it was announced that he was "to appear before the NL directors shortly...."[43] National League President Harry Pulliam later suspended the rule because of the "extraordinary conditions"[44] and allowed the Giants' win to stand.

Roger completed that game but was seen the next evening in Detroit headed to Mount Clemens, Michigan, to partake of the mineral baths there "in hope of driving away the rheumatism that is now lessening his value as a diamond artist."[45] In just under a week he rejoined his team in Cincinnati and "looked like a different person. His leg bothers him little, and he swatted the ball with all his former vigor."[46] He arrived on "the scene like the hero of a Bowery melodrama. Out of practice and still a bit worried with rheumatism, the Toledo wonder took up third bag yesterday, accepted four hard chances minus an error, smashed a three-bagger and made one of the four runs."[47] He played three more games at third base but could not continue and was not in the game of July 17 "being confined to his bed by rheumatism."[48] A few days later the *Detroit Free Press* added, "Roger Bresnahan is a very sick man. He did not stay in Mt. Clemens long enough and is again troubled by sciatic rheumatism."[49] He returned to the lineup 10 days later and was not disabled by rheumatism again that year.

* * *

On July 27 he assumed his centerfield defensive position and number two slot in the batting order and held both for the rest of the season. Over the last two months of the season, he battled for the National League batting championship and his team attempted to make up their 7.5 game deficit to the league-leading Pittsburg Pirates. Neither championship was accomplished but it was a fine season, nonetheless, for both Roger and the Giants.

The Giants finished second to the Pirates and just ahead of the Chicago Cubs. Their finish was a remarkable recovery, under John McGraw's leadership, from their cellar finish in 1902 and the horrible performances the two previous years. This set the stage for supremacy battles among these top three finishers going forward. The Giants were outstanding at the gate as well—second to no one in either the American or National League and drew 593,312 fans to the Polo Grounds outdistancing the Cubs by more than a quarter million spectators.[50]

Roger Bresnahan had a breakout year in 1903. He was the Giants primary centerfielder and showed his versatility by filling voids at five other positions. His offense was even better as he hit consistently throughout the season for both average and power. He finished fourth in the quest for the batting championship with an average that topped any in the American League. The order of finish in the National League was:

Honus Wagner, Pittsburg	.3555
Fred Clarke, Pittsburg	.3513
Mike Donlin, Cincinnati	.3508
Roger Bresnahan, New York	.3498

Both Roger Bresnahan and the New York Giants proved that they were winners in 1903—and they knew they would be. Roger was always confident. The Giants, during their leisure time during spring drills at Savannah, made some collective predictions for the coming season and chose the Pittsburg Pirates to win the National League pennant and named themselves as runners up.[51] They would have done well to take their bold prediction to a bookie and perhaps some did.

* * *

The Giants ended the 1903 regular season on Saturday, September 27 at Pittsburg. Immediately following, McGraw's men embarked on a barnstorming tour which ended in Buffalo on October 3. The Giants returned to New York City to continue exhibitions for more than a week while Roger went in the opposite direction to Toledo and arrived late on Saturday, October 3. He was to be feted that evening by the Elks amateur team of Toledo at a banquet given in his honor. The banquet was postponed due to his late arrival in the city, but he did play as an Elk the next day. Leaving his team amid its post-season tour may simply have been a kindness from McGraw indicative of Roger's favored status and could have included forfeiture of extra pay for the tour.

Nine

"Bresnahan Is One of the Best Ballplayers in the United States" (1903)

Roger Bresnahan turned 24 years old on June 11, 1903, his fifth season in baseball's major leagues. He was now firmly established, widely known, and respected as a utility player of the first order, as well as being a top-notch hitter.

It was his hitting, highlighted by the season-long battle with the great Honus Wagner for supremacy in the National League, that brought Roger Bresnahan front and center in the baseball world. His 1903 performance at bat would be the finest offensive season of his career. Roger Bresnahan's hitting was a topic of interest to baseball observers across the country.

One source of news about Roger's hitting was the feature story in *The Illustrated Sporting News*, a weekly magazine published in New York City. *The Secret of Batting as Told by a Master: The Man Who Leads All the Batters of the National League Explains How to Hit the Ball* appeared in the August 22, 1903, edition under the byline of Roger Bresnahan. The text was supplemented with five photographs of Roger "showing the proper way to bat a pitched ball."[1] The story was published over the next months by newspapers across America.

Roger explained his reluctance to grant interviews, "In the first place, I don't know what moment I might take a drop, and then again it puts you in bad with the team. They think your head is swelling. Wait till the season is over."[2] But for the following, the reporter persisted. Roger relented and said this about his trick for successful batting: "The trick in batting, so far as I know it, lies in stepping with the ball. Get your eyes on it as soon as it leaves the pitcher's hand. If a curve, step out; if inside, step back. Follow the ball and try to meet it square. You have six feet of box there, and you can often do the trick by stepping forward … but the best caution I know is, don't pull away."[3] Roger added a cautionary point here—to step back if the pitch is inside. This is difficult to do, and Roger's experience attests to that. During his career he was hit by pitched balls 67 times.[4]

* * *

Roger was extremely competitive, stubborn, confident, fearless, hard-nosed, and willing to do almost anything to gain an edge in order to win. The esteemed baseball scholar Bill James described him: "A short 200-pounder who was fast and strong and agile and aggressive.... Almost every paragraph written about him seemed to include the adjective 'fiery.'"[5] He brimmed with ambition as he yearned to manage and own a team at a very young age. He played everywhere on the field but wanted to catch and do so every day and probably resented that he did not do so. He often missed play because of illness and injury.

Outstanding among his personal traits was his temper and its related penchant for baiting, bashing, berating, and arguing with umpires. He was ejected by the men in blue 30 times as a player—that is more than all but five other major league players.[6] He had five ejections in 1903 alone and was personally admonished by the National League's president. He was scolded by the *Times* for his ejection on August 17, "...Bresnahan was put out of the game and off the field after giving a very careless and aimless exhibition during his time at bat. He was called out on strikes, one of which was put over by [Jack] Sutthoff while Bresnahan was arguing with Umpire [Bob] Emslie."[7] Though the league's top man did not approve of Roger's method of dealing with umpires, his own manager probably did. John McGraw was thrown out of more games than any other manager until the Braves' Bobby Cox came along. *Sporting Life* gave some simple advice when it said Roger, "...should learn to control his temper."[8] Ironically, McGraw, whose ejections far exceeded Bresnahan's, said, "Bresnahan has only one fault. He is too fond of making with the umpires."[9] This may seem contradictory, but McGraw believed that there was sometimes value in being tossed as a manager—firing up his team and future benefits from intimidating the umpire while it was detrimental to lose a player.

Ten Cents a Copy NEW YORK, AUGUST 22, 1903 Four Dollars a Year

The Illustrated Sporting News

THE SECRET OF BATTING TOLD BY A MASTER

The Man Who Leads all the Batters of the National League Explains How to Hit the Ball

By ROGER BRESNAHAN

SARATOGA: PLAYGROUND OF SPORTING AMERICA

An Interesting Article Describing the Gay Life at the Famous Resort

By FRANK W. THORP

Pictorial Features

CREW AT WORK ON RELIANCE

C. OLIVER ISELIN GIVING ORDERS

CAPT. CHARLES BARR AT THE WHEEL

INTERNATIONAL GOLF TOURNEY

TROTTING AT EMPIRE CITY

NATIONAL ROWING REGATTA

Volume I Number 15

In his first full season in New York, Roger Bresnahan was a hot commodity when "The Secret of Batting as Told by a Master" was published under his byline. Bresnahan was leading the National League in hitting at the time and finished the season batting .350 (The New York Public Library).

Roger was also a fighter and scuffling with his teammates was not off limits: "'Jack' Warner, the star catcher of the New York Nationals and Roger Bresnahan, the team's all-round fielder were the principals in a fistic engagement in the billiard room of the Southern Hotel at St. Louis Saturday morning. It is not known which received the most bruises, for both retreated by mutual consent…."[10] Following Roger's 1944 death, Leo Fischer, sports editor of the *Chicago Herald-American*, wrote, "In a day when baseball was a rough, tough game with flashing spikes and ready fists, the Rajah, was ready for a scrap at any time."[11]

Some thought him to be arrogant and egotistical: "He has been on a pedestal all season, and New York fans worshipped at his feet…. Too much success has made Bresnahan chesty, and when the swelling goes down, he will wake up to a realization that the fans are on to him. He is a great player all right but will be a still greater player when he learns to control his head."[12]

* * *

Still very much interested in club ownership and undaunted by his earlier failure to purchase the Toledo franchise, Roger made two attempts to do so during this off-season. He and Add Clark, the proprietor of Toledo's Clark Transfer Company, proposed to make an offer "that should tempt Strobel to sell." Though Bresnahan and others would be investors, Clark would "furnish the bulk of the money"[13] and Roger would be player/manager. A March 24, 1904, report put this and a later deal to rest, "Addie Joss and Roger Bresnahan wanted to buy the Toledo franchise and offered Strobel $10,000 for it. He wanted $12,000, and the difference kept the players in the American [National] League."[14]

* * *

One of the hottest baseball topics during the fall of 1903 were the trade rumors centered on Roger Bresnahan. On October 10 *Sporting Life* mentioned a possible deal, "Bresnahan was said to be on the block. McGraw cannot get along with him anymore."[15] The following day the *Cincinnati Enquirer* tied this to a swap with Cincinnati for outfielder Cy Seymour but speculated that McGraw would not let Bresnahan go for him.[16] A week later the *Chicago Tribune* added: "All season McGraw had a hard time handling Bresnahan and Roger always complained of being imposed upon. Only by coaxing could he be persuaded at times to work. McGraw's view has been that the negotiations were to trade the Giants' great batter for Seymour of the Cincinnati club or Joe Kelley [Cincinnati's player-manager]. The Reds manager says such a plan is underway, and will no doubt be closed."[17]

Just a day later the *Baltimore Sun* reported: "Roger Bresnahan has been dissatisfied with his associations on the team nearly the entire season. He has made announcements that under no circumstances will he play on the New York team next year. Recently he requested Manager Joe Kelley, of the Cincinnati Reds, to negotiate for his release, and Kelley says that a trade involving Bresnahan and Cy Seymour, who is dissatisfied with Cincinnati, is now under way."[18]

Eight days later, on October 27, Roger jumped into the fray from Toledo, "Roger Bresnahan ... emphatically denies the rumor circulated to the effect he is dissatisfied with the treatment accorded him by the officials of the club and had intended to quit the team forever. 'While I may quit my connections with the New York Club' said Bresnahan, 'no one ever heard me kick about the treatment I received from the New York Club officials.'"[19]

There is no reason to doubt that Roger was, as usual, self-promoting and looking for the best opportunity for himself and that he would not hesitate to leave New York for it. We do not know of all the talks between Roger and McGraw and others. We do know that the rumor mill continued to grind. At the same time, we see reports that Cincinnati was offering Seymour to Chicago.[20] Others said: "Chicago scribes are talking of a trade of pitcher Jack Taylor for Roger Bresnahan of the Giants."[21]

President Brush attempted to squash the speculation on November 25 when he was "said to have placed his veto on the proposed deal of Roger Bresnahan for Cy Seymour. He will try to purchase Seymour outright from the Cincinnati Club."[22] Brush confirmed his position on Bresnahan two weeks later, "Roger Bresnahan will play ball with New York next year, ... We might as well put a stop to the rumors.... I have talked with Bresnahan, I know that he wants to stay here.... Bresnahan is one of the best ballplayers in the United States, and ... he was told by Mr. McGraw that there is not the slightest chance of disposing of his services."[23]

Realizing that Bresnahan would not be joining the Cincinnati team, Cincinnati Reds outfielder Mike Donlin, a former teammate of Roger's at Baltimore, said this: "If Manager Kelley thinks the Reds' catching staff needs strengthening I would like to have seen him go after Roger Bresnahan.... Roger and I have our chewing matches on the field, but he's a corking good ball player, and from all I hear he isn't particularly stuck with McGraw's team, either. I guess Roger and his stick would not help us any, eh? Why, he can hit with any of them, and when it comes to catching he's a mighty good man: besides, he could fill utility roles for he can play either the in or outfield. I sort of got the impression that the New York club might listen to an offer for Bresnahan."[24]

When McGraw published his list of 1904 signees, Roger Bresnahan included as were all the 1903 team with the exceptions of Billy Lauder and George Van Haltren. Despite all the rumors, rancor, and rumblings, all the 1903 Giants that continued to play in the major leagues stuck with McGraw. "It is probable that a little financial salve was used in healing the sore spots of the disaffected players."[25] Seemingly all realized that the Giants were on a fast upswing and wanted to be a part of that.

Interestingly, of those prominently mentioned during the post-season rumors, Cy Seymour and Mike Donlin would be purchased later from the Reds by the Giants.

McGraw announced that players would assemble in Washington, D.C., on March 6, 1904, before proceeding to Savannah, Georgia, to begin preparations for the 1904 season.

Ten

"The Most Versatile Man in the National League" (1904)[1]

Following the 1902 season, Roger Bresnahan was thought of by many as a catcher and the Giants' catcher for the future, but John McGraw lured veteran backstop Jack Warner from the Boston Americans to his Giants. Warner was the number-one catcher in 1903 with Frank Bowerman as his primary backup. Roger wrested the center fielder's position from veteran George Van Haltren and made it his own. This—coupled with his outstanding season at bat—would seem to cement his claim as the Giants' center fielder for 1904.

It did not. Once again, McGraw made a deal that displaced Roger. He hired Outfielder Moose McCormick from Jersey City of the Eastern League. The Giants' owner and president, John Brush, explained, "If McCormick makes good in the outfield, he, Mertes and Browne will fill the outfield positions and there will not be a place for Bresnahan out there. Bresnahan is a hard hitter and a quick thinker, and there is no reason why he should not be able to play third base." He praised Bresnahan's adaptability and skills but followed with a disclaimer, "Again, there is [Art] Devlin, the Newark third baseman of last year, to fall back on if Lauder does not sign."[2] Devlin, like McCormick, had not one iota of major league experience[3] while Billy Lauder was the Giants' third baseman in 1903.

We do not know when Roger learned of the proposal to set him on third base or if he was a part of the decision. He and McGraw had opportunities to discuss the issue at contract time in late in 1903 and in January and February when he joined his manager at Hot Springs, Arkansas, to get an early start with the coming season's preparations. "Secretary Knowles [of the Giants] received a letter from McGraw, the manager saying that Roger Bresnahan was at Hot Springs with him. The outfielder thinks he can boil the sciatica out of his system at Hot Springs."[4]

Before leaving Hot Springs for Savannah, McGraw "expressed genuine confidence in the ability of his team to unfurl the league pennant at the end of the next season." He also said Roger was "…an all-around artist I class with that bulk of a Dutchman [Wagner] in Pittsburg who shouldered the prize batting average of the league last season. I think that Bresnahan may be classed with Hans Wagner in [batting] average ability, especially by reason of the fact that my man cannot only play any position in the outfield, the infield or go behind the bat, but is prepared at any moment if called upon to pitch winning ball."[5]

The players reported to Savannah on March 7 to "get into shape by systematic training rather than regular games." The team traveled to Birmingham, Alabama, the evening of March 12 to take advantage of better field conditions and the promise of better weather.[6] Earlier in the day the Giants did engage in a game taking on the Savannah Y.M.C.A. team in a 15–1 rout and with Roger on third base.[7] One report said "Bresnahan is putting up a class game at third...."[8]

The Giants remained at Birmingham through March 29, enjoying mild weather and competitive games with the Birmingham Barons of the Southern League.[9] The teams met five times with the Giants winning all and Roger playing third in each. He had eight hits that included three doubles and a triple, two steals and scored six runs. He committed one error.[10] McGraw reported, "Roger is in fine shape, and he does not expect him to be troubled by rheumatism this year as he was last."[11] The Giants and Roger appeared to be off to a good start.

McGraw and his men continued to cross bats with Southern League opponents over the next week playing two games each in Little Rock, Nashville, and Montgomery,[12] concluding their southern tour on April 5. Roger continued to rap out hits (10) and score runs (12) but had three errors. The Giants won them all.[13]

The Giants returned to New York on April 8 and had four more exhibition contests scheduled leading up to Opening Day. Roger started all at third base and filled the number-two spot in the batting order as he had for each game of the spring.

News items opined on Roger's readiness for the coming season. *Sporting Life* reported, "Bresnahan is said to be in better condition than any other Giant; better in fact, than ever before in the spring."[14] Another was worried about that rheumatic leg, "Bresnahan is shining at third in practice with the New Yorks, but he has a bad leg that may give out at any time."[15] Still another was not sure Roger was up to the task, "Umpire George Wood, who saw the Giants' work in the south, declares.... Roger Bresnahan will not make good at third base."[16] Harry Vaughn, who would be Birmingham's manager, observed Roger at Birmingham and likewise was not impressed: "Bresnahan is a great player, but he will never do for third base."[17] A short feature biography originating with the *Newspaper Enterprise Association* described Roger: "...Roger is the typical, latter-day ball player, the ideal of whom is found in McGraw. Aggressive, even to the danger point; full of fight to the last ditch, never saying 'die' until the last man is out, he combines every element that goes to make the star player. Bresnahan is of medium height, broad shouldered and sturdy. He is young, healthy, does not smoke, drink or chew. In fact, he is the ideal athlete.... He is married and owns a handsome home as a result of his healthy habits. He is one of the highest salaried men in the National League, and, barring serious injury, should be a star of the first magnitude for some years."[18]

New York's *World* provided same-day game summaries, box scores and play-by-play commentary for the city's major league teams on the front page of its 11 o'clock evening edition. Its coverage of the final preseason game with Columbia University noted that Art Devlin pinch hit for Bresnahan in the fourth inning.[19] There was no explanation for the substitution of Devlin for Bresnahan in the *World* or other consulted newspapers for this game's account and he did not appear for Opening Day in Brooklyn. The *Boston Post* explained why: "Devlin played third base in place of Bresnahan, who was injured in the game with Columbia yesterday."[20] The New York *Sun* added Bresnahan was, "temporarily on the shelf with a wrenched side."[21] The press was remarkably silent about this malady. Whatever the injury and its cause, it was significant and telling. Roger was finished as a third baseman and Art Devlin, after making his major league debut, held the job for the Giants for the next eight years.

Not only did Roger not appear in the Giants' first game but he also did not accompany his team to Brooklyn. Instead, he was among the "distinguished guests"[22] as the New York Highlanders hosted the Boston Americans in the American League opening game in Manhattan. He "was cordially greeted by the players of both teams," and "hobnobbed with Griffith's [Clark Griffith, Highlander's manager] men in the clubhouse before the game...."[23] It is difficult today to imagine a player doing this and we can only guess what Roger's motives were in abandoning his team to join with another. He did not reappear for a week.

* * *

The Giants returned to the Polo Grounds for their first home game of 1904 on April 21. Bresnahan made his season's debut starting at third base and batting second. In the fifth inning, "Wolverton bunted safely filling the bases." Bresnahan hurt himself fielding the ball and left the game, Devlin going to third. The injury sustained in the Columbia game continued to keep Roger from regular play. Over the next two-plus weeks he was limited to four pinch-hitting appearances and two innings at second base.

The Giants got off to a fast start and held first place as they began a lengthy road trip on May 2. Bresnahan's status was announced: He "went on tour with the Giants as general utility man."[24] The *Sandusky* [OH] *Star-Journal* posed a question, "Devlin looks like a fixture at third for the Giants where does Bresnahan go?"[25] Another newspaper offered an answer and confirmed Roger was still restrained by injury: "Rumor prevails around the Polo Grounds—Mac contemplates benching McCormick and placing Bresnahan in center. The move will not be made in a minute, but as soon as Bresnahan recovers from his indisposition it will be decided whether he is to return to third or not."[26] *Sporting Life* commented on the proposed shifts: "Manager McGraw is out for the pennant and his policy is apparently very plain, it being to place his men where they do the most good, whether it hurts anyone's feelings or not."[27] And from rival Pittsburg: "It's about time for Roger Bresnahan to be showing up in form. Perhaps 'Baby Rog' won't get back into the Giants regular lineup."[28]

Roger answered the call to fill in for the ill Dan McGann at first base in St.

Louis on May 10 and did so again the next day.[29] Giants' Shortstop Bill Dahlen was tossed in Cincinnati on May 12.[30] Roger finished that game for him and also covered the next three games when he was suspended.[31] During the May 15 game Left Fielder Sam Mertes was ejected in the third inning and Roger was moved from shortstop to his spot to finish the game.[32] On May 18, Roger was sent to right field for five games because regular George Browne had strained a tendon in his leg.[33] That was the fourth position Bresnahan had played in a week. The New York lineup remained healthy for about a week but then McGraw found another reason to use Bresnahan. He pulled slumping Sam Mertes after he failed in his first at bat in the game against Brooklyn on May 29 and inserted Roger in his place. Roger proved his manager's worth when he opened with a triple and added a single in a 7–3 win.[34] He stayed in Mertes' spot for four more games. Today we might refer to Roger as a super-sub. Then he was called "Handy Andy"[35] and the *Washington Post* declared "Baseball has never known a better all-around player than Roger Bresnahan."[36]

On June 3, McGraw played Roger in Moose McCormick's place in center field and left him there. Except for absences from the team that will be explained later and four games at first base, he was the Giants' center fielder for the rest of the season.

* * *

Center field was the seventh position Roger Bresnahan occupied in 1904. McGraw initially had Roger batting cleanup but moved him to the leadoff spot on June 6. He responded at once with a big day against the defending National League champion Pittsburg Pirates at the Polo Grounds. He led off the game with a home run "that electrified the crowd" and added a second circuit blow that was "the longest ever made on the grounds"[37] and was good for three runs. He later walked and singled as the Giants romped 15–2. At the end of the day the Giants were 27–12 and tied for the top spot in the National League with Cincinnati. Chicago was just one-half game back.[38] He remained at the top of the order for the duration of the season.

Beginning on June 16, the Giants ran off an astonishing 18 consecutive wins to open a 10 and one-half game margin. During the streak, Roger contributed 20 hits and scored 21 runs as his team established a commanding lead that would only increase as the season progressed. Last-place Philadelphia stopped the streak 6–5 in 10 innings on July 5, but New York won four of the next five with Roger lacing out 12 more hits. Seven of those came in a doubleheader sweep at St. Louis and included a home run, a triple, two doubles and three singles. The home run was a ninth-inning, two-run shot that provided the margin of victory.[39]

From St. Louis, the Giants moved to Cincinnati for a series beginning on July 12, but Roger did not play there because of illness—his wife Adeleen's. The *Toledo News-Bee* reported Roger had "arrived in the city yesterday [July 12] because of the illness of his wife. He left his team in Cincinnati."[40] Roger missed five games "owing to the serious illness of his wife."[41] Details of Adeleen's illness were not disclosed.

Roger's hitting continued as he garnered eight hits in three Pittsburg games. Then in the first game of a series set in Chicago, "The game was won by Bresnahan in the ninth inning by a tremendous hit to the left field fence for a home run."[42]

But then there was sad news from Toledo as Roger "…received a telegram Friday night in Chicago saying that his wife was not expected to live. He broke down completely and had the sympathy of the entire club and many friends who saw him off to Toledo."[43] Details were sparse, but the following notice published on July 30 gives some insight, "Roger Bresnahan will report for duty again next week to manager McGraw of the Giants, leaving here Sunday. Mrs. Bresnahan is still very low with typhoid fever."[44] Roger had missed six more games. He played again beginning August 3 with his wife still ailing.

Roger continued to be mindful of his future per a *Baltimore American* story: "This will probably be Roger Bresnahan's last year with the New York Nationals. The Giants' crack center fielder has received a good offer to manage the Toledo club, and he has practically agreed to accept it. He has informed McGraw of his possible intention of quitting the team after the present season, and it was due to this that McGraw secured Mike Donlin from Cincinnati. Bresnahan is not in any way dissatisfied with his present surroundings or the salary which he is receiving but believes he can do better by acting in a managerial capacity in a minor organization, with chances of taking hold of a major league team some day and attain success which has made McGraw famous."[45] Nothing further is known about the offer described above except that it did not come to fruition.

Roger continued to play every day and the Giants continued to win most days and put together another sizeable win streak, this one of 12. By September 16, their lead was 19 games. On September 22 they won their 100th game and clinched the pennant.[46]

The Boston Americans and Pittsburg Pirates, champions of American and National leagues respectively, had agreed to a playoff following the 1903 season—the first World's Series. Many assumed that the same thing would occur in 1904 but the Giants refused to take part. Owner John Brush and Manager John McGraw had long-standing animosity with American League President Ban Johnson. Brush resented that Johnson had placed a team in competition with his own in New York City and McGraw begrudged the treatment he had received from Johnson when he was in the American League. Though Brush had made it known since mid-season that the Giants would not take part, he formalized his reasons when it became clear the Giants would be National League champions: "The club that wins from the clubs that represent the cities of Boston, Brooklyn, New York, Philadelphia, Pittsburg, Cincinnati, Chicago and St. Louis, the largest and most important cities in America, in a series of 154 games is entitled to the honor of champions of the United States without being called upon to contend with or recognize clubs from minor league towns. Neither the players nor the manager of the Giants nor myself desire any greater glory than to win the pennant in the National League."[47]

"Criticism of Brush and McGraw was widespread by newspapers and fans. Some owners resented them for having ruined the game's showcase. 'The players were upset because McGraw had cost them a lot of money,' said John Thorn, baseball historian. 'It was really McGraw's decision more than Brush's. Brush was in poor health, he was wheelchair-bound. And McGraw was the real power.'"[48] Thorn is correct that McGraw was the driving force, and he was reputed to satisfy his players and, because there was no fallout from them, he likely did so in this case.

Roger was excused from his team's last 19 games, having last played on September 17, to return home earliest of all the Giants, "on account of the illness of his wife."[49] History has not told us the circumstances of how or when she recovered—but she did.

* * *

On the home front, Roger took title of a newly built home.[50] It was near his parents' house on the western edge of Toledo. His was a two-story, four-bedroom structure. It was reported that "he paid for it in spot cash."[51] Three weeks later, Roger deeded the property at 2350 Lawrence Avenue to Adeleen.[52]

Once again, Roger organized a ball game for Toledo fans. "The All-Professionals, a team captained by himself and composed of professional ball players wintering in Toledo, will play the Shamrocks, the City League champions at Armory Park Saturday afternoon."[53] Roger's Elks won 6–3 thanks in part to "his remarkable base running being altogether too fast for the league champions."[54] Some of these men continued to play into the winter in an indoor baseball venture. Teams were captained by Roger and George Mullin of the Detroit Tigers.[55]

* * *

As he had done previously, Roger attempted—this year twice—to purchase the Toledo Mud Hens. Baseball in Toledo was a losing proposition with its leadership in a state of flux and disarray, but Roger Bresnahan wanted it. He conspired with Clark Griffith to make a joint purchase. Their relationship had some history—Griffith was a short-term teammate of Roger's in Chicago in 1900 and it was with Griffith's New York Highlanders that Roger had "hobnobbed" on Opening Day that year.

Roger informed American Association President Ed Grillo of his desire to buy the Toledo franchise and secured Grillo's promise to be remembered if such an opportunity arose. Grillo passed that information to a group of several owners, who were working to secure control of the eight clubs in the American Association. George Lennon, one of that group, owned the St. Paul and one-half of the Toledo franchises. It was an easy matter for him to block the Bresnahan-Griffith bid.[56] Misled and betrayed by Grillo, Bresnahan never had a chance.

Because offers were sought in late December, Roger again went after the Toledo franchise.[57] "Bresnahan and one other party, whose name was not given, have raised a purse of $12,000, which was considered a fair price, [Michael] Kelley [representing

Lennon] having recently purchased a half interest for $6,000 or a little less. Kelley is willing to sell his half, but Bresnahan wants all or none and Strobel has not yet expressed a willingness to let go of his half."[58] Strobel did not agree, killing the deal.

Bresnahan had failed twice more in his efforts to become an owner, but he had succeeded in positioning himself to do so, because "…he is free from the New York club. His contract has expired, and there was no reserve clause in it, he says, so he does not look for any opposition from this source. He has earned good money in baseball and has saved it and is in a good position to take the team if it is for sale."[59]

Eventually, the Toledo club was sold by Messrs. Lennon and Strobel in March of 1905. Roger was not involved but Ed Grillo was. J. Ed Grillo, a former sporting editor of the *Cincinnati Tribune* and the current president of the American Association, represented himself as the buyer and was elected president of the Toledo Exhibition Company.[60] Mr. Grillo headed the newly-formed stock company for two years. Eventually it was discovered that Grillo had misrepresented himself and was not an investor at all but "was merely acting as the agent for the Cincinnati club"[61] and Owner Garry Herrmann.

* * *

It had been a good year for Roger Bresnahan and his team. The Giants won the pennant, winning a record 106 games. Roger missed some play and did not shine statistically as he did the previous season, but he was a contributor to this team's success, nonetheless. He was invaluable as a utility man, playing all positions except pitcher and catcher. He batted .284 which tied for third among the Giants and compared favorably with the league average of .249. Despite missing 45 games he led the team in slugging, on-base percentage and tied for second in runs scored.

On December 21 Giants' Secretary Fred Knowles announced that Catcher Jack Warner had been sold to the St. Louis Cardinals and that Roger Bresnahan would catch in 1905.[62]

Eleven

The Giants' First-Line Catcher and Leadoff Batter (1905)

Pre-season training for the 1905 season was scheduled in a place familiar to the Giants' veterans—Savannah, Georgia. All hands were instructed to report for work on March 6.[1] According to news reports all appeared to be in order concerning Roger Bresnahan. The *New York Times* reported his contract status: "Roger Bresnahan will play at the Polo Grounds next season and not manage the Toledo (Ohio) team, as frequently reported, is shown by the fact that he has appended his name to another contract. Furthermore, he will be transferred from the outfield to catcher, a position which he formerly occupied with much success."[2]

John McGraw explained how he had strengthened his champion team while confirming the preceding announcement, "...with Donlin in centre field every day, and Bresnahan as catcher every alternate day, the team will be improved in batting and base running."[3]

But Roger did not appear in Savannah. The *New York Times* reported on March 11 that "Manager McGraw has received word that Roger Bresnahan will join the team in Birmingham, Ala., the early part of next week."[4]

A look at Roger's hometown newspapers gave details that do not seem to have appeared elsewhere: "BRESNAHAN HOLDS OUT," Toledo Member of the New York Team Slow to Sign Under Present Conditions. Orders have been sent to all of the New York Players to report today. Roger Bresnahan is still in the city and has made no preparation to report. When seen this morning Roger said: "My contract has not been signed and I have not prepared myself to report. I am going to stay in Toledo for some time and really do not know just now what I will do." It has been known for some time that catching has been distasteful to the Toledo player and McGraw contemplates using him behind the stick this season. Perhaps this is the reason for his backwardness about signing.[5]

Obviously, this contradicts the earlier report that Roger had signed. And the bit concerning catching being distasteful for Roger flies in the face of his stance prior to the 1902 season when he said, "I signed to catch, and that's the only place I'll play."[6]

Still unsigned 11 days later, Roger decided to join his team: "Roger Bresnahan will leave this week, probably tomorrow, for Birmingham, Ala., to meet the New York team." He will get into condition with the team and make an effort to come to some understanding with the management regarding the season's work. Bresnahan has not signed his contract and probably will not unless it is changed to suit him. The salary figure is perfectly satisfactory, but the disagreement comes on the terms of the contract. The reserve clause is especially obnoxious.

When the Giants arrived in Birmingham on March 14, Roger was there to meet them. According to reporter Bozeman Bulger, Roger was in better shape than the rest of the team.[7] Two days of intrasquad games followed before the Giants took on the Birmingham Barons, the first of four Southern League opponents they would engage. The Giants beat Birmingham twice and followed with three wins over Memphis. Roger split the catching duties in each game with either Frank Bowerman or Doc Marshall.

Following the Memphis series the *New York Times* offered an early-season evaluation of Roger's play: "The catching of Bresnahan has also proved that the valuable utility man will more than hold his own as a regular wearer of the mask and wind-pad this season.[8] He is throwing beautifully, hitting in his old-time form and running bases with daring and speed."[9] The press was silent on the issues of Roger's contract and his attitude towards regular catching. The National League announced on April 28 Bresnahan's contract had been approved.[10]

Games at Little Rock and Nashville followed. All were wins and the shared catching routine continued. The Giants upgraded their competition with five games with Louisville, Indianapolis, and Columbus the American Association. These games marked the most formidable opposition they would face in the pre-season. All were Giants' wins and Roger caught every inning of every game.[11]

Following a 9–4 win at Columbus on April 5, Roger was granted leave to return home to Toledo.[12] It follows that he was in McGraw's good graces to be given such favored treatment.

* * *

As the 1905 season opened, the New York Giants loomed "as a formidable defender of the honors."[13] The team's front-line players stayed the same except that Roger Bresnahan was scheduled to replace the departed Jack Warner behind the plate.

Opening Day, April 14, at the Polo Grounds was an elaborate affair. Both teams took part in a champion's automobile parade that travelled nearly the length of Manhattan Island. As banners and flags flew on a perfect day, the National League pennant was hoisted, and a military band played a concert and the Star-Spangled Banner. Thousands were turned away but the crowd of 40,000, including many dignitaries, was rewarded with a 10–1 win over Boston behind Joe McGinnity with Roger completing the battery.[14]

True to McGraw's announced plan Frank Bowerman caught the next day as Roger sat. After five games the alternating scheme was abandoned because of the suspension of Giants' first baseman Dan McGann. Unlike recent Giants' history,

Roger was not sent to fill the void, but Frank Bowerman was—a clear sign that John McGraw regarded Roger Bresnahan as his number-one catcher.

* * *

McGann's suspension arose from his behavior in the game at Philadelphia on Saturday, April 22 when he tried to score from second base on a sharp base hit to right field. The *Philadelphia Inquirer* described the play: "Magee made a splendid throw to Abbott, and McGann was out fully 10 feet. For some inscrutable reason, McGann punched Abbott. There was not the slightest provocation for it. Abbott fired the ball at McGann, hitting him upon the fleshy part of his rear development."[15] Both players were ejected, fined, and suspended.[16]

The effects of McGann's action reached far beyond his own castigation and led to consequences for Roger and other Giants. Philadelphians were incensed:

> Thousands of the spectators, ignoring the game, left the ground in the last inning for the express purpose of laying for the Giants. When the latter got into their barouches [four-wheeled horse-drawn carriages] they found their way blocked by the crowd. For a while the mob confined itself to hooting, then to throwing peanuts, paper balls and small stones into the carriages. Finally, a half brick was thrown into one of the carriages, hitting a player. The players tried to pull down the hoods of their carriages to save themselves from the fusillade of missiles that was being hurled at them, but the angry crowd prevented them. One of the mob was hit over the head by a bat in the hands of a player, and another was locked up on the charge of rioting.
>
> The drivers of the wagons finally got their teams moving but, on their way, down Broad Street at Dauphin they were charged upon by thousands who had collected at that point. There was another volley of stones, but no one was injured. The drivers whipped up their horses, and the Giants finally reached their hotel safely.[17]

The same teams met again, two days later, and played before 17,000 spectators—the largest Monday crowd to ever witness a game in Philadelphia.[18] The game itself "passed off like a church function"[19] but as daunting as that Saturday ride to the hotel must have been, the reception the Giants, and especially Bresnahan, received following this contest was far worse:

> After the game Roger Bresnahan got into trouble, and had it not been for the police he would have been in sore straights. As it was, the policemen were forced to protect him with drawn revolvers.

A small boy precipitated the trouble, and this is the way it came about:

> As the barouches conveying the Giants turned into Broad Street on the way to the hotel, they were followed by the usual crowd of small boys and the Giants were treated to the usual hooting and jeering which invariably follows the visiting club after a game. The boys kept running after the carriages and, finally nearing Dauphin Street, the scene of the ambuscade of last Saturday, a youngster threw a handful of dirt into a barouche, striking Bresnahan squarely in the face.
>
> Bresnahan jumped out, chased the boy and gave him a hard slap. In an instant Bresnahan was surrounded by an infuriated crowd. The police, anticipating trouble, had sent an

> extra detail of 100 men to the grounds and these saved Bresnahan. The policemen were forced to draw their revolvers.
>
> But even the display of arms did not altogether subdue the crowd, for many threw vegetables, which had been in traps in front of a store where Roger had been taken for safety. One man worked himself into the store and struck at Bresnahan. The man was arrested and taken in the patrol wagon with Bresnahan to the station, where the player was released.[20]

The Giants and Phillies met the next day for the third and final game of the series with the Giants winning 8–1 for a sweep. The *Philadelphia Inquirer* reported that "the game itself was an orderly affair" and that the Giants "were permitted to retire from the scene without molestation."[21]

* * *

With Bowerman occupied at first base, Roger caught the next 12 games after which the Giants' record stood at 13–3 and they enjoyed a three-game lead.

Because of his hot bat, Roger was elevated from the number-eight position in the batting order, the usual slot for a catcher at the time, to third. His torrid pace continued. Six weeks into the season he led all National League batsmen with a .359 average which he increased to .374 by early June.[22] Following McGann's return from suspension, McGraw reverted to his plan of alternating catchers but now it was two or three days behind the bat for Roger and then a day of rest.

Around the beginning of June his hitting dropped off and he found himself in a genuine slump. From June 1 through June 16, he totaled only four base hits. The last of those came on June 16 in St. Louis. He sat out the next two days there and then we learned the reason that his hitting had declined. The Giants moved on to Cincinnati for a four-day series, but Roger was not with the team. The *Cincinnati Enquirer* explained, "Roger Bresnahan was taken quite sick in St. Louis and went direct from there to his home in Toledo."[23] The *Toledo News-Bee* detailed, "Roger led the National League in batting from the beginning of the season until about a week ago. He was taken slightly ill on the western trip and his batting suffered accordingly. His shoulders and hips have been bothering him considerably all season, and the trouble has taken a turn for the worse lately."[24]

Roger rejoined the Giants for their Saturday, June 20 game at Boston. He pinch hit in that game and caught the next two. The Giants moved to Brooklyn for four games and Roger sat out all of them for reasons unknown. Then at Philadelphia he missed the first contest, but on July 4 he started as catcher in the first game of the doubleheader but did not finish as he took a foul tip on a finger in the sixth inning and was forced to retire.[25] During the game, Roger was subjected to a cruel trick by a fan. "A foul ball was hit near the centre of the grand-stand, and, just as Bresnahan was about to gobble it up a youth in the stands drew a mirror from under his coat, and quickly getting the range of the sun, flashed a reflection in Bresnahan's eyes so that he was temporarily blinded. He missed the ball...."[26]

This was the first trip to Philadelphia since April when the Giants were twice confronted by mob action. It happened again, and again Roger Bresnahan was at the center. An attack by a gang of hoodlums was made as the Giants returned to their hotel following the second game. "Roger Bresnahan was hit on the head by a brick and was almost knocked from his seat in the carriage. A large bump on the head is evidence of the force of the blow. The carriage in which Bresnahan rode was on to the hotel."[27]

Whether the cause was the unspecified lingering illness, his shoulders, his hips, the injured finger or the bump on the head, Roger was out of action for another four games. He returned to the lineup on July 11 by entering the game late and scoring the winning run in a 10-inning 6–5 win over Chicago. The next day Chicago beat the Giants soundly 8–1. Contributing to the loss were two Bresnahan passed balls and two errors by Third Baseman Art Devlin. A war of words between the two, initiated by Roger, occurred at the Giants' bench at the end of the eighth inning. Devlin became incensed "leaped to his feet and struck his team-mate a hard blow over the eye."[28] "Bresnahan was temporarily dazed by the punch and before he could retaliate"[29] other Giants quickly diffused the confrontation, and it seems to have been quickly forgotten and was not even mentioned by several New York newspapers.

Over the next two weeks Roger caught four games and pinch hit twice. It appears that he was at full strength when McGraw reverted to the two-catcher scheme beginning on July 24. For the rest of the season Roger was a workhorse. He filled in as an outfielder on seven occasions and second base once and then settled in as the Giants' full-time catcher. On September 14 he was moved to the leadoff spot in the batting order.

* * *

Most of what we know of Roger Bresnahan's daily activities has been gleaned from the newspapers of his time. He was a newsworthy personality and those newspapers abounded with coverage of him.

An added source of personal information for some biographers is personal journals. We do not know if Roger ever kept a diary. If he had made entries during the 1905 baseball season some may have looked like this:

May 25	Bob Ewing, my former teammate at Toledo pitching for Cincinnati, beat us 5–1 with his spitball. I did not get a hit off him.[30]
May 27	We beat Brooklyn 4–1 but my bad throw to second on an attempted steal cost Matty a shutout.[31]
June 11	Today is my 26th birthday.[32]
June 29	I did not play today but we won handily at Brooklyn 11–1. Archie "Doc" Graham who has been with us all season got into his first game late but did not bat.[33]
July 3	Umpire Emslie ejected me today and I was not even in the game. He said I was shouting from the bench, but I was just cheering on my mates.[34]

July 20	Umpire Johnstone threw me out of the first game today and I was not even playing. I was coaching first, and a pop fly was hit that was an easy play for either the pitcher or the first baseman. Both pulled up when I hollered "Got it" and the ball fell safely to the ground. He tossed me and had the batter bat again.[35]
August 18	We beat the Cubs today 6–5. I had a bases-loaded single in the 10th inning to win it.[36]
August 26	Hank O'Day threw me out of the game when I reminded him that some time ago, he had called a strike on a bad pitch to me.[37]
September 13	We won in Brooklyn 5–4. I drove in the tying and go-ahead runs with a two-out double in the ninth inning.[38]
September 19	We lost the first of a doubleheader in Philadelphia 3–2 in 10 innings and it was my fault. I made a wild throw to first on a bunt allowing the runner to go to third. He scored on a long fly ball.[39]

* * *

After the games of September 19, the Giants held a seven-game lead over Pittsburg with 21 games to play. Roger was installed behind the bat for a doubleheader the next day and stayed there until the pennant was clinched on October 1 with a 5–4 win at Cincinnati.

Unlike the previous season, when the Giants also won the pennant but refused to engage in the World's Series, they were compelled to do so in 1905. Baseball's ruling body, the National Commission, had adopted a measure on February 16, 1905, that settled the issue, "The pennant winning club of the National League and the pennant winning club of the American League shall meet annually in a series of games for the Professional Base Ball Championship of the World."[40] The next day the American League champion was determined when Connie Mack's Philadelphia Athletics finalized their berth.[41] Roger expressed great respect for the Giants' adversary when he said that the Giants "are about to go against the toughest proposition they ever faced.... They will engage in the hardest battles of their career when New York tackles Mack's men in Philadelphia Monday."[42]

Like his team Roger Bresnahan enjoyed another fine season in 1905 though limited to 104 of the 154 games his team played. His .302 batting average was second among the Giants as was his on-base percentage and he ranked in the top 10 in the National League in both categories. He caught in 86 games and contributed as a limited duty utility man.

Roger proved his growing leadership by virtue of his acceptance of the catching position and his willingness to confront any teammate he thought was not doing his best. According to a Toledo newspaper he had settled his on-again, off-again love affair with catching, saying that he "has become reconciled to his catching duties, a task he abhorred in the spring."[43] A demonstration of his leadership is his dugout confrontation with Art Devlin. He took no abuse from anyone including the great Mathewson. Matty and Roger had a row prior to the World's Series. Though the reason for the confrontation is unknown "the scrappy backstop ran the big fellow out of the clubhouse."[44]

Twelve

"Bresnahan Put Up an Extraordinary Game in Every Particular" (1905)[1]

"It was the greatest of all great baseball events."[2] So wrote a newspaper scribe following the 1905 World's Series. He was right when he wrote it, and those words may well hold true today.

The Giants won the National League pennant by nine games, but the opposing Philadelphia Athletics had a harder time of it and were unable to shake off the Chicago White Sox challenge until the regular season's penultimate day. Their pennant-winning margins were not a sign of relative strength, however. The *Washington Times* suggested that the teams were "too evenly matched for anything but even wagers."[3]

The Athletics were a formidable team led by future–Hall of Fame Manager Connie Mack who Writer Tim Murnane gave high praise, "In the science of the game Mack has no equal" and called him "the ablest and most diplomatic manager in baseball."[4] His team led the American League in batting average, runs scored and slugging. Their First Baseman, Harry Davis, had a most-valuable-player-like season and led the league in doubles, home runs, runs scored and runs batted in. Its pitching staff led in strikeouts, shutouts and was a close second to Chicago in earned run average and featured a top-notch quartet—Rube Waddell with 27 wins, Eddie Plank with 24 and Andy Coakley and Chief Bender each with 18. They had a veteran smart infield and a durable savvy catcher in Ossee Schrecongost. Nobody in the American League had a better fielding outfield.

Rube Waddell enjoyed a spectacular season for the Athletics but missed most of the final month due to a controversial arm injury. "Two ineffective appearances in the last two days of the regular season"[5] proved to Manager Mack that he was out of the series. "Bettors who had been holding off to ascertain Rube's condition"[6] saw a shift in the odds that made the Giants slight favorites. Betting was heavy and included nearly $2,000 from Giants' players and $3,500 from McGraw.[7]

* * *

The 1905 World's Series is still a classic because all five games were shutouts with the great Christy Mathewson pitching three of them. With deference to Mathewson's magnificent performance, we remember here that Roger Bresnahan had a lot to do with the New York Giants becoming world champions. Francis Richter, who witnessed the games, reported in *Sporting Life*: "Next to Mathewson, catcher Bresnahan was the most important factor in New York's success, owing to his grand catching and throwing and his timely batting."[8]

The Giants appeared for the first game at Columbia Park in Philadelphia in spanking-new and distinctive all-black uniforms with white caps, belts, stockings and large "N.Y." on the chest.[9] The New Yorkers, supported by a contingent of their fans, "looked and acted like world beaters … a startling contrast to the Athletics' season-worn, worse-for-wear garb."[10]

Bresnahan sparked the offense by getting on base by four different methods in the series' first game. He was hit by Plank's first pitch of the day[11] and walked in the second inning to load the bases. He punctuated the intentional pass by leaning on his bat and smirking at Plank as he threw four wide ones. In the fifth he forced Mathewson at second but then stole second base and scored the first run of the series on Mike Donlin's single. After flying out in the seventh he drove in the game's final run with a ninth-inning single.[12]

He delivered a complete performance over the five games of the championship while playing every inning. He started each game catching and batting in the lead-off position. He remains the only catcher to bat first in the order in the history of the World's Series.[13] He led all hitters for both teams with a .313 batting average and .500 on-base percentage and fielded his position without an error while limiting Philadelphia to two stolen bases, assisting on seven put outs and picking a runner off first base.

* * *

Witnesses of Roger's play said:

- The *Washington Star:* "Bresnahan by his fine all-around work, was as near to being the star of the New York aggregation as anybody else."[14]
- Toledo Mud Hens President J. Ed Grillo: "He caught a superb game, but it was his work at the bat and on the bases that counted. He was always on those bags. He either hit safely, drew a pass or was hit. You could not keep him off and he was the bane of the Athletics. Full of ginger, he kept that team going and was just as big an instrument in the victory of New York as Mathewson."[15]
- The *Sporting News:* "Behind Mathewson was one scintillating star, Roger Bresnahan, who caught gamely and finely and with his nerve and grit jacked the other Giants up to deeds of daring."[16]
- The *Washington Post:* "Bresnahan, who outdid himself throughout the week … caught better than he ever caught before."[17]
- Garry Herrmann, owner of the Cincinnati Reds and Chairman of the National Commission: "Bresnahan put up an extraordinary game in every particular…."[18]

But he was scolded, too:

- The *Washington Times:* "So far as the conduct of the players was concerned there was only one fault to find. That was a too violent outburst by Bresnahan when Hartsel was sent to first base last Friday. That was the one exception to the perfect conduct on the field by both teams."[19]
- The *New York Times*: "Bresnahan's excellent catching display in the World's Championship Series was somewhat a revelation to 'fans' who did not think he possessed so much ability. His mark was slightly marred, however, by his constant objections to the decisions of the umpire."[20]

Many today consider the 1905 World's Series as the Christy Mathewson show, recalling his three magnificent shutouts and nothing else. The preceding reveals that many in his day considered Roger Bresnahan the principal reason that the New York Giants became champions of the world.

All the players shared in the gate receipts of the first four games and their awards were significant, perhaps a quarter or more of their season's salary for the winning Giants. The National Commission determined the amounts of $1,142 for the winning team members and $382 for those on the losing team.[21]

But few of the New York players realized their full winners' share because: "15 of the 18 Giants were so afraid to take a chance on the outcome of the World's Series that they agreed to split up with the Athletics on an even basis, no matter which team won. The three with the nerve to take a chance were Manager McGraw, Christy Mathewson, and Roger Bresnahan. These men declined to go into any splitting propositions.... As a result of their gameness the trio received nearly $1200 for his five days' work, and what is more, kept it."[22]

In addition, "Each Giants player received ... an added $500 thanks to a generous gesture made by Brush. Back in May, Brush had directed club secretary Fred Knowles to set aside for the players the receipts for the many exhibition games the team played every year, money normally kept by the club itself."[23]

"The National Commission presented beautiful and costly diamond buttons to the New York players.... The men all expressed themselves as delighted with this souvenir of the greatest event in their professional careers."[24] Roger expressed his view, "Walking up Broadway the evening after the series closed, Roger Bresnahan remarked to a friend as he viewed the button emblematic of the world's championship, 'I would rather win the honor this button represents than the money that I will get out of the series.'"[25]

Another honor that befell Roger was playing on his manager's finest team. John McGraw was a remarkably successful skipper winning 10 pennants and three World's Series in his 33 years at the helm. He later wrote of this team, "I regard the Giants of 1905 as the greatest ball club that I have managed."[26]

Although it is impossible to track Adeleen's movements, it appears that Roger's wife travelled with him. An announcement following their February 1903 wedding told "that Mrs. Bresnahan would travel with her husband during the upcoming season."[27] An indication that the practice continued is the inclusion of personal World's Series photos in the scrapbook described in the introduction. There are five of these that she may have taken, and she certainly labeled. All are dated and identified by location. One depicts Roger and Christy Mathewson on the field before game one in Philadelphia to which she added the caption, "The dandy battery of the Giants."[28]

* * *

This year's trade rumors centered on Roger being swapped to the Cincinnati Reds and sometimes included Roger doubling as manager in Porkopolis. The stories first appeared immediately following the World's Series in numerous newspapers. The following is representative: "According to certain authorities, the deal practically has been closed for some time, but it will not be made public officially until the owners of the Cincinnati and New York clubs get together at the league's annual meeting in December. Some reports have it to-day that Seymour, of the Reds, the star batter of the league, may change places in the deal."[29]

A few days later McGraw attempted to squash the rumor "when he declared that he had never even considered" a trade of "Bresnahan or any other member of this year's Giants."[30]

But the story would not die, and it again appeared in newspapers beginning on October 26. Annoyed, Roger replied: "I haven't a single complaint to make against the treatment I have received at the hands of the officials of the New York club. I would be very sorry to leave such pleasant surroundings and were I to leave the club it would be to abandon baseball entirely."[31]

Giants' Secretary Knowles, "in speaking of the reported trade, and said such a thing never for a moment was thought of by President Brush or Manager McGraw."[32]

Following, reports circulated that Roger, among others, had received an offer to join a club in the independent Tri-State league.[33] If true, Roger probably did not even consider joining what was known as an "outlaw league."

None of this "fake news" mattered. Roger Bresnahan would be a New York Giant in 1906.

Thirteen

"The Best Catcher Living" (1906)[1]

Roger Bresnahan's off-season of 1905–1906 was a quiet one. There was a report from University of Notre Dame in January stating, "It is probable that Roger Bresnahan will coach the baseball team."[2] The prediction did not come to fruition, but it did reveal that Roger was known in or connected to the South Bend institution in some way. The *Sporting News* record shows Bresnahan played for South Bend, Indiana, sometime during his career.[3] In addition, his name appears in a listing of former major leaguers who were Notre Dame students and in some other publications at Notre Dame but not in student enrollment records or in any contemporaneous student publications.[4]

The venue for the Giants' 1906 spring practice and conditioning was an unfamiliar one for the team—Memphis, Tennessee. Players were instructed to gather there on Thursday, March 1 with work to begin at Red Elm Park on Friday.[5] But, for reasons lost to us, Roger was visiting in St. Louis and did not leave there until Friday morning.[6] Consequently his Saturday arrival was not timely.

The conditioning was scheduled through March 21 and, besides the usual drills and intrasquad games, included the use of a pushball—a McGraw innovation. The pushball was an inflated ball, six feet in diameter, which was pushed across the field by two groups of opposing players. It was said to "prevent sore arms, charley horses, and similar ailments due to early exertions in the spring."[7]

Monday was the first full day of practice and Bresnahan and Dan McGann were the focus "of all eyes when they appeared on the field." Across the chest of their new uniforms appeared "World's Champions" in large letters.[8]

The Giants headed for Nashville for a scheduled three-game series set for March 22–24 with the Volunteers of the Southern League.[9] Unlike former years there was no question about where Roger would play. He was firmly established as the Giants' primary catcher—his 1905 World's Series performance having clinched the deal.

The team then returned to Memphis to wrap up their spring practice. While there, an accident befell Roger on March 27. He was hit in the mouth by a bat wielded by Henry Mathewson, Christy's younger brother who pitched briefly for the Giants. Accounts of how it occurred varied, and the extent of the injury was reported inconsistently, with either three or four teeth being broken or lost.[10]

The Giants headed north on March 30 following a now familiar path to the

Polo Grounds. Their journey stopped first at Louisville and then at Indianapolis, Columbus, and Wheeling. Roger caught on April 1, obviously not disabled by his most recent injury. The Giants' April 7 arrival in New York was followed by home and home pre-season games with the Providence Grays, defending Eastern League champions,[11] Manhattan College and Yale University at the Polo Grounds.[12] Once again the Giants accomplished a perfect pre-season record.

The McGraw Giants were on top of the baseball world having enjoyed unprecedented success during their brief history. Following McGraw's July arrival in 1902, they finished last in the National League but improved by 36 wins and vaulted to second in 1903. Seasons of 106 and 105 wins and two pennants followed. In 1906 another pennant was expected by many, including McGraw. When asked if he thought he would win the pennant again he simply replied, "I do. There was no equivocation. No ifs, ands, or buts. He had spoken directly and truthfully. He had the best team in the league; he expected it to win again; and he said so."[13]

* * *

The Giants began the defense of their championships on April 12 in Philadelphia. Roger was behind the plate and batting leadoff. The "very first ball pitched hit Roger where his mother patched his trousers...."[14] and "with a wince and a laugh he trotted down to the initial bag."[15] The Giants won the game and split the four-game series and moved to Brooklyn for a three-game set. On April 20, with a 4–3 record, they started their home season at the Polo Grounds against Brooklyn.

Roger Bresnahan was proud to be a World's Champion and his first wife, Adeleen, was proud, too. She made and added a notation to this image in 1906. The snapshot was preserved in Roger's Scrapbook (courtesy Roger M. Bresnahan).

While the Giants were playing in Brooklyn, the *Brooklyn Daily Eagle* reported a curious bit that was unconfirmed, vague, and seemingly meaningless at the time, "They say out West that the New Yorks are handicapped because Roger Bresnahan has an injured leg. Anybody notice it?"[16] This report would prove to be meaningful.

Eighteen thousand turned out to welcome their World's Champions who were sporting those very words on their chests as they had for spring games. As part of the opening ceremonies, Roger flanked the front line as the teams marched across the field and "each shouldered a blue silk flag on which were the numerals '1904, 05.' Every man of the New Yorks walked with square shoulders which bespoke the determination to complete a trinity of years, with '06 as the third."[17]

The Giants played like champions and Roger was a major part of the reason. Continuing as leadoff hitter, he singled and scored in each of the first two innings and walked, stole second and scored in the fourth.[18] With the game well in hand, McGraw rested him after five innings, perhaps because he had "stopped three foul tips with various parts of his anatomy."[19] The win launched a 10-game winning streak during which the Giants gained first place.

During that streak, "The champions lost their premier catcher, Bresnahan, early in the contest [April 25], Umpire Emslie sending him from the bat and out of the game for his violent and objectionable manner of protesting a decision on a called third strike."[20] Roger remained in exile for two additional games for his vituperation.[21]

Just six days later, when the Giants were playing at Boston, Roger was again ejected. This time he joined Manager McGraw and Captain Dan McGann in the clubhouse. The Irish trio had harassed the also Irish Umpire John Conway with abusive language and each was ejected separately.[22] *Sporting Life* called the Giants' conduct "reprehensible" and said that the Giants "bellow like bulls" and that "Bresnahan could have been heard all over the field telling the umpire to 'get out.'"[23]

Ball-player-turned-sportswriter Tim Murnane expressed that this instance of umpire baiting[24] was particularly egregious as it was premeditated, well-organized and included virtually all the Giants. He recalled that these same men "went through the great series last fall without one objectionable move and were given praise on all sides." But on this day, "the New Yorks went after the rookie umpire from the first ball pitched until the last man went out.... As each man passed the umpire would make some remark...."[25]

The three most offensive Giants, Bresnahan seemingly chief among them, were handed three-day suspensions by National League President Harry Pulliam[26] making them eligible to participate next on May 4.

But Roger did not return to the lineup until May 12. He insisted that his absence was not because of suspension but "on account of an injured leg."[27] However, many newspapers reported that he had, in fact been suspended.[28] Also factual were reports that Roger did have a malady of a leg. Recall the report of April 24 while another, on May 1 in the *New York Times*, told that he was "lame."[29] It appears that Roger's suspension was parlayed into a healing rest for his ailing leg. He was away from the game for 10 days.

Upon his return the Giants were opening a four-game series in Cincinnati, tied with the Chicago Cubs for the league's top spot. Roger got a hit and scored a run but his old friend and teammate, Bob Ewing, pitched masterfully and beat the Giants 3–2 in eleven innings.[30] The Giants rebounded and won the next three.

Roger Bresnahan at bat against the Chicago Cubs at the Polo Grounds in 1906. Partially visible on his jersey are the words WORLD'S CHAMPIONS, referring to the 1905 New York Giants. John McGraw remembered the 1905 Giants as his greatest team (National Baseball Hall of Fame and Museum).

McGraw's men moved on to Pittsburg still tied for first place but shorthanded due to Dan McGann's suspension[31] and Center Fielder Mike Donlin's leg injury.[32] The Giants were "hopelessly beaten"[33] 11–0 in the first game on May 16. In the first inning of the debacle, Second Baseman Billy Gilbert was tossed which further complicated the Giants lineup and resulted in Roger moving to center field.[34] The Giants went on to lose three of the four games in Pittsburg with Bresnahan remaining in center. The win came in the series finale, 5–1, with Roger helping with two doubles before the largest crowd in Pittsburg baseball history—20,000.[35] The Giants were two games back of the Cubs and headed for Chicago for four games.

For the second consecutive day, the Giants played before the largest crowd in their host city's history. There were 25,000 on hand Sunday May 24 to watch the Cubs blister the Giants 10–4 and move out in front by three games.[36] The Giants bore down and won the last three to pull even in the race with Roger back to catching, but it would be a long time before the New York Giants would reside in first place again.

The Giants continued to St. Louis where the press opined, "Bresnahan surely is a grand ballplayer. The best catcher living."[37] He left the final contest there after one inning his "knee being hurt."[38]

Roger was forced from the lineup again. In the ninth inning of the Decoration Day afternoon game against the Superbas at Brooklyn, "Lumley beat out a bunt. Bresnahan thought the ball was foul and was put out of the game for kicking on [Umpire Bill] Klem's decision."[39] President Pulliam came down hard on Bresnahan, banishing him "for three days for unbecoming conduct on the ball field."[40] Pulliam may have been tiring of Bresnahan's ejections—this being the third of the young season.

Roger returned to the lineup for the final game of the road trip on June 4 in Philadelphia. McGraw looked to strengthen his team by juggling his defense and again sent Roger to center field where he remained for more than a month.

The Giants returned home on June 5 to face the first-place Cubs who they trailed by a single game. These four games could be pivotal in the championship race. The crowd of 10,000 that attended the first game on Tuesday was disappointed with a 6–0 loss[41] and further disappointed the next day with another loss that dropped the Giants to third place.[42] During the latter game a fan insulted and spat upon Roger from the grandstand. Roger complained, the man was arrested and both he and Roger appeared in the Harlem Court the following day. Charged with disorderly conduct, the man was fined $10.[43] Roger may have been successful in court, but he and the Giants certainly were not on the field as they were humbled 19–0. The Giants won the final game of the series, but the Cubs left New York with a three-game lead.

The Giants won 10 of the next 14 and regained second place. During the final game of the home stand, on July 7 against Boston, Roger made it clear that he would do whatever he could to win. Trailing 4–0 entering the bottom of the ninth inning, the Giants mounted a rally that Roger kept alive by being hit by a pitch which pushed across the tying run. The Giants then scored another to win 5–4. The Bostons complained that Roger had "run up into the pitch."[44] *Sporting Life* expressed its view of the incident: "There is no doubt at all that Bresnahan deliberately allowed himself to be hit by a pitched ball and should have been denied his base."[45] There is no doubt that Roger's approach to hitting that included crowding the plate and stepping into the ball contributed to the likelihood that he would be hit by a pitch. The *Washington Post* described his method: "Bresnahan has absolutely no fear. He never thinks of being hit, but runs squarely into the ball, and when he plants his bat squarely against it a scorching line drive follows."[46]

Roger did not miss a game in center until July 14 when he returned to catching which would remain his regular position throughout the duration of the 1906 season. McGraw was able to make the move because the Giants had bought the Cincinnati Reds' fine center fielder, Cy Seymour, the league's reigning batting champion. McGraw also acquired outfielder Spike Shannon from St. Louis to help ensure that he could keep Bresnahan behind the bat.[47] Now five games behind Chicago, McGraw's nine appeared to be strengthened and poised to make a run at the Cubs.

* * *

The remade Giants set off on a 16-game trip to the National League's western cities. They won eight, but only one of four in Chicago, and fell to six behind the Cubs. Back home beginning July 26, the Giants ran off eight straight wins before Chicago came to visit for four games. In those games New York won 7–4, lost 3–1, forfeited, and lost 3–2. The forfeit occurred because of dissatisfaction with Umpire Johnstone's ejections and the resulting suspensions of Manager McGraw and Third Baseman Devlin on August 7. The New York club refused to admit the umpire to the Polo Grounds for the August 8 game. The umpire promptly declared the game forfeited to the Chicago Cubs.[48] The next day, the Giants played tough but could not prevail and were seven and a half games back.

With the Cubs out of town the Giants looked like world-beaters again. Taking on the Pirates next, they swept the five-game series to move back into second place. Roger did not play in the second and third games because of a knee injury suffered in the first when he "twisted his leg in the fourth inning and was compelled to retire from the game."[49] Apparently not at full strength, McGraw dropped him to third in the order. He responded with three hits and scored twice in the fourth game. In the fifth game he had another hit and scored twice more before retiring early.[50]

The Giants then opened a road trip at St. Louis on August 16 with three games in two days which they swept.

From there it was off to Chicago riding an eight-game win streak and facing a do-or-die four-game set. The Cubs held a seven-game lead. The Giants died—losing three of the four games to fall nine games behind. The Cubs' lead would prove to be insurmountable. Looking back over the Giants' previous 23 games, they had won 17 and lost 6. That stretch included two eight-game winning streaks with all the losses coming at the hands of the Cubs.

The Giants also lost Roger Bresnahan in Chicago. He sprained his ankle while running to first base during the third game. He was unable to take part in the final Chicago contest and had to be carried to the train when the club left Chicago for Pittsburg.[51] He was seen in Pittsburg "hobbling around on crutches."[52]

He returned to play, as catcher, on September 3 and did not miss a game until the very end when he sat out the final three for reasons unknown.

The Giants did not win the pennant in 1906 as many thought would be the case and their manager had predicted with certainty. They did finish as runners up but were a distant 20 games behind the Cubs. That disparity is a bit deceiving as they won 96 games, enough to win a pennant some years. But they could not beat the Cubs. The Giants did win seven of the 22 meetings between the pair, more than any other team. But even if the Giants had won all 22 it would not have made any difference. The reason that the Cubs won the pennant was their 116 wins—a total no team ever matched in a 154-game season.

For his part, Roger played in 124 games and hit a solid .281 (21st in a league that hit .244) and, though primarily his team's catcher, his versatility proved to be a tremendous asset. On the negative side, he lost time on several occasions because of injuries. He also lost playing time due to ejections and suspensions for unruly behavior. He was ejected six times over the season. Three of those ejections resulted in three-day suspensions. To his credit, Roger fixed that early in the year. His last day of suspension was June 2.

As the team broke up and its members headed for their homes there was already talk of the 1907 Giants. One speculated, "Bresnahan has the managerial bee in his noodle, and if he doesn't buy a club for himself, he will continue behind the bat."[53] The trade rumor mill which had been active even after Seymour and Shannon were acquired by the Giants was, for a change, quiet over the winter.

Because of photographs Adeleen had taken in New York early in the season we know she went with Roger then and, according to a neighbor, was there for the summer. That neighbor was Blanche McGraw, John's wife, who wrote in her biography of her husband that they lived in the Washington Inn at 155th Street at Amsterdam Avenue from 1903 to 1905. She related that "Roger Bresnahan and his beloved Addie also had a room there in 1905."[54] Back in their Toledo home for the winter, Roger looked after some rental property that he had bought and rested his body that had taken such a beating over the summer.[55]

Fourteen

An 8,000-Mile Road Trip with Shin Guards (1907)

The 1907 pre-season activity promised to be an adventure for the man from Toledo, Ohio. His baseball career had carried him repeatedly to the southern and eastern United States, but his western travel had been limited to St. Louis, the westernmost reach of major league baseball. That changed because their 1907 spring trip would move the Giants from the Atlantic coast to the Pacific oceanfront.

The New York Giants' spring practice base was Los Angeles. Plans called for an excursion to recently earthquake-ravaged San Francisco and a series of games through the south on the return trip. The trip covered 8,000 miles and cost the team as much as $15,000[1] was the "longest trip ever taken by a ball club in the spring."[2] This was to avoid the dreadful weather the Giants had experienced the earlier several springs. Manager McGraw, already in Los Angeles, said, "he regrets that he has not made the move before as he has never experienced such delightful conditions for training."[3]

Roger's first order of business was to agree on contract terms with the New York Giants. Several of the Giants had contract issues with the club but Roger and McGraw apparently had none. McGraw went to California weeks ahead of the bulk of the team to complete arrangements and stopped at Bresnahan's Toledo home for the contract signing on his way.

Bidding Adeleen goodbye, Roger began his journey on February 21. A Toledo newspaper commented that "Although a little over-weight, Roger is in better condition than he has been at this time for several years and it won't require much work on his part to take off the superfluous corpulence."[4]

Most of the players gathered at several points for the long trip west. Roger was the first to arrive at one such point—the Victoria Hotel, the team's Chicago headquarters.[5] He was early because:

> Bresnahan has a novel idea for protecting catchers from foul tips and came here [Chicago] early to have a local sporting goods firm make up a device for his use while behind the bat. He wants a cross between the shin guards used by football and by roller polo players. It is designed to extend from above the knee to the ankle, protecting the knee joint and shins from wicked tips which not infrequently put catchers on the hospital list. But it must be more flexible than the polo player's guard, so as to permit more freedom in bending the knees and running after fouls.

> "They may holler at me at first," said the Giant catcher "but I can stand that better than being laid up, and, if the thing works as well as I expect, all the catchers will be using them by the Fourth."[6]

This report could have alerted fans and others in the press to Roger's plans but there was a surprise on Opening Day when he appeared in his new-to-baseball equipment.

The Santa Fe Limited departed Chicago on Monday, February 25. Included in the baseball party were members of the press including Len Edgren of New York's *World*.[7] Edgren filed daily reports through the entire trip but mentioned Roger only once on the Chicago to California leg when he reported from Needles, California. "At stations along the way Indians gathered to sell curios to tourists.... Bresnahan and the Mathewson brothers have monopolized all the postal cards along the way and have sent them off to Eastern friends in batches of a hundred."[8] Arrival was February 28 at the Hotel Lankersham,[9] said to be one of the newest and finest hotels in Los Angeles.[10]

Home base for the Giants was Chutes Park and the first practice there was light and easy on March 1.[11] Locals came out to watch the former champions and were impressed with their size, "this New York bunch looks like a package of butchers for they are big and husky...."[12] The following observation reveals that the Giants' reputation for rowdyism[13] and umpire baiting had preceded them to the far west, "What they couldn't do to an umpire or a whole lot of them ... any one of them appears able to bite a bulldog."[14]

McGraw had arranged games with two opponents while at Chutes Park—the Los Angeles Angels of the Pacific Coast League and St. Vincent College. The first contest was March 3 and the Giants beat the Angels 5–3 with Roger catching.[15] Those two teams played four times during the New York team's stay with the Giants winning three.[16] In the lone loss, 6–2, on March 9, "Bresnahan was removed for his mediocre work behind the bat,"[17] but the entire team was subjected to a McGraw tongue lashing following. The collegians were completely outclassed and outscored by a composite 28–3 in the three games played.[18] Intrasquad practice and games filled the days on which there was no game scheduled. Details of these sessions are sketchy, but Edgren did tell that on March 6, "Bresnahan appeared with cricket shin protectors, and caught a bit."[19]

On Friday, March 15, the Giants left Los Angeles for San Francisco where single games were scheduled for Saturday and Sunday. The opponents were to be the San Francisco Seals, also a Pacific Coast League team. Edgren's story about the weekend games in the *World* was supplemented by a drawing of Roger wearing shin guards. This should have alerted New York readers of the impending debut of the new protective devices.

Eleven months before this trip, San Francisco was shattered by an earthquake. Among the thousands of structural casualties resulting from that horrible event was the city's ballpark. A new park was under construction but not complete. When it was announced in mid–March that the Giants were coming, efforts ramped up to ready the new Recreation Park.[20] The endeavor continued day and night. As game weekend approached all was done that could be but the final work was hampered by rain. President Cal Ewing of the Seals promised that the games would be played and he "had the diamond literally covered with bonfires to dry out the ground and put it in the best possible shape."[21]

To the men in the Giants group, "San Francisco was a shock.... But although the greater part of the city still lies in ruins the San Franciscans have not lost their old spirit of hospitality."[22] The people of San Francisco made a super-human effort to ready the facilities, both the Seals and Giants traveled there but it kept on raining. The games could not be played.

Leaving that disappointment behind, the Giants left San Francisco for Los Angeles and a final game with the Angels on Monday. Their train was seven hours late on arriving causing them to miss that game too. Net for the Giants was the expense of the trip north,[23] the forfeiture of revenue for three games and the loss of three days of conditioning and play just before they were to embark on a three-day train trip to Texas. "To make matters worse, Roger Bresnahan was lost in the shuffle."[24] Roger had missed the train in San Francisco but did catch up with the team in time to join them as they started east.[25] The reason for his tardiness is unknown to us but Joe Nealon, Pittsburg Pirates first baseman, probably knew—Roger was his guest while in "The Paris of the West."[26]

The Giant entourage arrived at San Antonio tired, dusty, and thirsty at three o'clock the morning of March 22.[27] Their accommodations at the Bexar Hotel were very different from those enjoyed in California. Players slept six to a room and the menu was limited to enchiladas and tamales.[28]

Two games were scheduled for San Antonio both with the American League's St. Louis Browns. Following a 7–2 loss, the largest crowd ever to see a baseball game in San Antonio saw the Giants bounce back 12–2. Roger caught in both.

Then it was on to New Orleans for five games scheduled with another American League opponent—the Philadelphia Athletics. The first game on March 27 went to the Giants.[29]

The next day's game did not go well. In the top of the first inning with two Giants on the bases, New York players called for a balk to be called on Philadelphia pitcher Eddie Plank. Umpire Zimmer refused to recognize a balk. "Catcher Bresnahan and 'Mike' Donlin, who were in uniform but not in the game, were the first to run to Zimmer, protesting in language that, it is said, was not at all nice. McGraw then started after Zimmer, following him about the field and abusing him for his decision." Zimmer had enough and ordered Bresnahan and McGraw from the field. Both refused to leave, and police were called to enforce Zimmer's order. Bresnahan accepted the escort, but McGraw would not budge. Instead, he ordered his team to leave the field which prompted Zimmer to direct McGraw to return his players to the game within five minutes. McGraw did not comply, and the game was forfeited to Philadelphia.[30]

The losers were the 2,000 fans that were issued rain checks. A conference was arranged for the next morning "to determine what shall be done in regard to the remaining three games."[31] The powers-to-be opted to play two games that same day.

McGraw did not appear at the grounds and delegated Roger Bresnahan, the man largely responsible for the fracas the day before, to act in his stead. Apparently refusing to play with Zimmer as umpire, Manager Bresnahan held his team from taking the field. After issuing a warning that was not heeded, this game was also forfeited to Philadelphia. Fans expecting two games and getting none were furious. After discussion and to provide a game for the large crowd Bresnahan agreed to play an "exhibition game" with another, agreed-upon umpire. The Giants lost that one as well, 7–0. Following the game, the New Orleans Baseball Park management barred the Giants from its grounds "hereafter."[32]

It is difficult to imagine how even the belligerent John McGraw would allow the response to an umpire's decision, in a game in which winning or losing was meaningless, to go from bad to worse. The series of five games with another major league club had been arranged by McGraw so that he might see his trial players performing against top-flight competition, generate game revenue and develop his team. He then allowed a charge from his bench, led by the short-fused Bresnahan, to escalate into a debacle that scuttled his own efforts. The three games not played were added to the list that was unavoidably generated by the California cancellations. Besides the "frosty feelings"[33] that resulted among the participating players and officials, the Giants were fined $1,000 by the National Commission.[34]

The Giants continued playing their way home winning in Montgomery,[35] Nashville,[36] and Louisville[37] with Roger catching and going hitless in each. The club moved to Columbus for an April 4 game that was cancelled because of a "downpour" and another for the next day in Wheeling, West Virginia, was cancelled because the same weather was expected there.[38] Instead they headed for New York City and arrived on April 5.[39]

The team went directly to the Polo Grounds for practice but without Roger and several others who had been granted leave in Louisville. Roger had gone home to Toledo, "Having a couple of off days, Roger Bresnahan cut loose from the Giants Thursday and came home Friday for a visit to his family. Roger is still heavy, although he looks to be in good condition."[40]

The Giants played and won on Saturday over Yale 8–3[41] and Newark in the New Jersey city on Sunday 8–5.[42] Roger did not take part as he was still in Toledo.[43] Games leading up to Thursday's Opening Day with Newark, Princeton and Jersey City could not be played because of winter-like weather.

* * *

On the eve of championship play most sources chose the Chicago Cubs to continue their outstanding winning record of 1906 and capture the pennant with either the Pittsburg Pirates or the Giants as runner up. But not all agreed, "Looking over the National League, one dangerous foe looms for the Cubs. This is New York."[44]

Opening Day in 1907 saw the Giants hosting the Philadelphia Phillies. Attendance was 17,000, low for a Giants' opening game, and lacked the "usual presence of many women,"[45] the latter perhaps because the weather was cold and rainy. Manager McGraw was ill at home and Roger was the acting manager.[46] The day did not have the feel of a joyous or celebratory occasion and the Giants played like it and their fans acted like it. The Giants did not hit, producing just a lone single through eight innings. Before the ninth inning could begin "at least 1,000 men and boys leaped over the fences surrounding the playing enclosure and rushed into right field ... and refused to heed the demands of [Umpire] Klem that they move back within the ropes. Klem ... awarded the game to Philadelphia as forfeited...."[47]

The Giants had started the season on a losing and sour note, but Roger made news that the *New York Times* included in its game story: "Bresnahan created quite a sensation when he appeared behind the bat for the start of play, by donning cricket leg guards. As he displayed himself, togged in mask, protector and guards he presented no vulnerable surface for a wild ball to strike. The white shields were rather picturesque in spite of their clumsiness, and the spectators rather fancied the innovation. They howled with delight when a foul tip in the fifth inning rapped the protectors sharply. But Bresnahan, recollecting the many cracks on the shins he suffered last year, had slightly the better of the situation."[48]

The *New York Daily Tribune* reported that "Bresnahan, the Giants catcher, caused considerable amusement by wearing long shin guards similar to those worn by cricket players."[49] From today's perspective, the introduction of a piece of equipment that quickly became an essential part of every baseball game played would be a newsworthy event. It was not so in New York in 1907. It was strictly a local story and not all New York City newspapers carried it. Out-of-town newspapers, even in Philadelphia which sent staff to the game, did not report the event. Perhaps the bizarre game ending overshadowed the equipment story.

In the days that followed it became clear that some liked the idea while others did not. *Sporting Life* had alerted its readers a week before Roger's unveiling of the new equipment that Bresnahan "has invented a shin guard" and pointed out that Jack Warner, a former Giant catcher then with Washington, was interested in using them as well.[50] Then, just after Roger's formal introduction of the guards, *Sporting Life* called them "clumsy" and pointed out that strapping them on would result in "delaying the game" and suggested that "It is doubtful that the fad will become popular."[51]

Roger's boss, John McGraw, took some convincing before giving his approval. Bresnahan told one reporter, "McGraw thought they would interfere with my running, and looked askance at them at the beginning of the year, but he has changed his mind.... Last year my legs were bruised from the knees down, and part of the time it was all that I could do to walk after a game. That interfered with my running more than shin guards can possibly interfere."[52]

Some sources then, some later and even current sources speculate that Roger

Roger Bresnahan demonstrated his agility at New York's Polo Grounds. In 1907, Bresnahan was the first to wear leg guards openly. He was ridiculed, but soon all catchers adopted his innovation as standard equipment (courtesy Roger M. Bresnahan).

was the inventor of shin guards and the first to wear them in a baseball game, but Bresnahan never claimed to be the inventor or the first to use guards. "I didn't invent anything," Roger said in a 1926 interview. "I simply got a pair of shin guards, such as cricket players wore, and I strapped them outside my stockings. I was sick and tired of wild pitches, foul balls, thrown bats, and flying spikes bruising my legs."[53] Roger knew that at least one other major league catcher wore shin guards before he did and there are numerous claims of earlier-than-Roger amateurs, professionals, catchers, infielders and even pitchers employing guards for their lower legs.[54]

He may have resolved to pursue wearing shin guards himself because of an incident with another major league catcher who used them before he did. The following is based on comments made by Philadelphia Phillies catcher Red Dooin:

> ... Dooin always maintained that Bresnahan got the idea from him.... "We were playing the Giants in Philadelphia, and I blocked the Rajah as he came flying into the plate," said Dooin. "In the collision he went down and came in contact with my legs." "Say, what have you got under your stockings?" the astonished Bresnahan asked. "In the clubhouse after the game I showed the guards to Roger. Afterwards he went down to a Philadelphia sporting goods house, where I had mine made, and purchased a pair for himself. But because of his bulk and the fact that any additional weight would slow him up if he wore the guards like I did, Bresnahan had to put aside the idea of leg protection. He continued to experiment, however, and the white cricket shin guards resulted."[55]

Dooin's story coupled with the account of Roger's ordering shin guards in Chicago may be how it happened that Roger appeared on April 11, 1907, outfitted in plainly visible shin guards. The shin guards were nothing new and known to Roger. No question that Roger was not their inventor, but the exactness of his custom order reveals that he certainly was an innovator.

There are two major differences in Roger's shin guards when compared to others said to be used in baseball previously—they were designed for baseball and substantial which meant that they could not be hidden under clothing. Because of their design they proved to be successful and because they were first worn by Roger, they soon became universal because he paved the way by absorbing the initial mockery, hazing, and taunting which he had predicted. As those claims surfaced, predating what Roger had done, he left no doubt as to who was first as he stood, armored, for the world to see.

What Roger Bresnahan did on Opening Day in 1907 had a permanent effect on the game and saved countless injuries and missed play. Roger said amid all the objections and ridicule directed at him, "I ought to have a Red Cross or Carnegie medal for introducing something that will keep catchers out of the hospital."[56]

Fifteen

"He Was the Best Ball Player in America" (1907)[1]

The 1907 Opening Day forfeit was followed by two days of rain on the Polo Grounds and a Sabbath without baseball. After a 6–5 win on Monday the Giants took to the road.[2] Just across the East River in Brooklyn, Roger hit a triple and scored in a 4–1 win. The *Brooklyn Daily Eagle* had little to say about his shin guards but suggested they were not without fault—"Bresnahan's guards were not high enough to save him from a foul off Jordan's bat, and he let out a wail when he was reminded of the fact."[3] The following day the same newspaper reported, "If Roger Bresnahan expects to make those shin guards popular he will be sadly disappointed. They not only delay the game but make it look altogether like cricket."[4]

The fans in Boston were next to see Roger and his leg protection. Following the Giants' first game there, Roger was featured, without comment, in a cartoon drawing sporting his shin guards.[5] The following day he played a "Grand Game," picking two runners off first base and scoring the only run of the game in the ninth inning. The *Boston Herald* included a favorable comment in its game account saying Roger, "...has the good sense to provide himself with a set of shin-pads." Further, its opinion was other catchers would be wearing such protection within a short time.[6]

Three games in Philadelphia passed without mention of shin guards. Following, the Giants stopped in Brooklyn for a single game which they won 2–1 on Roger's ninth-inning two-run single. The Giants then returned to the Polo Grounds with a 10–3 record, a modest three-game winning streak and found themselves one game behind the first-place Chicago Cubs.

The first six games of the homestand were against the same eastern teams—Philadelphia and Boston. The Giants won all of them extending their win streak to nine. Roger helped in one game when he "hammered out a four-bagger over the fence elevation in right field."[7] In another he scored in Christy Mathewson's two-hit, 1–0 victory. The Giants manufactured a run, typifying the times, when Roger drew a walk, was bunted to second, bunted again to third and scored on a single.[8] On Sunday, May 5, Roger got a rest of sorts when the Giants travelled to Albany for an exhibition game—instead of catching he pitched.[9]

The season's first invasion of the western clubs followed, beginning with the Pittsburg Pirates, on May 8. The Giants won both games of the weather-shortened series, but Pittsburg protested the loss of the second game because of Bresnahan's shin guards. Player-Manager Fred Clarke claimed that "…in trying to steal home his spikes struck Bresnahan's guards and kept him from reaching the plate."[10] He said further "that Roger, when equipped with his shin guards does not fear spikes and covers the plate so that no one can slide into it."[11] National League President Harry Pulliam rejected the Pittsburg protest on the basis "…that there is nothing in the rules or precedents to warrant prohibition of the offensive guards." Pittsburg President Barney Dreyfuss accepted the decision and interestingly said that he would provide shin guards for his catchers but predicted "they are going to cause trouble."[12]

Cincinnati was next to visit the Polo Grounds and McGraw rested Roger. St. Louis followed. After sweeping a doubleheader from the Cardinals,[13] Roger led the way for yet another Giants' win—their seventeenth straight. He scored three times, and his three hits included a double and a home run.[14] The streak ended the next day as the Cards prevailed 6–4, leaving the Giants in first place with a 24–4 record. But Chicago was just a single game behind. The Cubs, sporting a 23–5 record, were next on the schedule.[15]

Going into the showdown games with the Cubs, *Sporting Life* commented on Roger's play and value: "Roger Bresnahan's work continues to be a marked feature of every game in which the armored backstop appears. The brilliant catcher's throwing to the bases is accurate and deadly in its effect on the opposing base runners." The story continued, "The team is playing with clock-like precision and continues to avoid clashes with the umpire."[16]

The first game of the series was on May 21 and featured the combatants' aces—"Three-Fingered" Brown of the Cubs and Mathewson. Two glaring errors by Bresnahan—a dropped throw on a play at the plate and a wild throw to second base[17]—allowed two runs to score and were "mainly responsible for his team's 3–2 downfall."[18]

Many of the disappointed crowd of about 22,000 found fault with umpires Emslie and O'Day, rushing the field in pursuit of them at the conclusion of the game. Roger not only contributed to his team's loss but also had a hand in the ensuing riot. His ninth-inning actions were described in a rare *New York Times* page-one story on sports: "Bresnahan, who had reached first base [walked], was touched out on the line to second by Evers on McGann's hit, and a double play completed. But when Umpire Emslie announced the decision, Bresnahan, who had really lost the game for the Giants by his errors, raised an outcry, which was instantly taken up all over the stands. He continued his vehement protests, inflaming the crowd the longer he kept it up, so that the roughs were ripe for the outbreak that followed when, an instant later, Dahlen flew out and the Giants were beaten."[19]

At the end of the day the Giants and Cubs shared first place and it had not been Roger Bresnahan's finest hour. The Giants won the next day without Roger in the lineup. The Cubs won the third and final game of the series with Roger behind the bat.

Roger was not in the lineup the day after the Cubs left town because: "The defeats inflicted by Chicago seem to have upset McGraw and his men. There is dissention on the team, too, for to everyone's surprise it develops that Roger Bresnahan has been suspended for insubordination by McGraw ... it is understood that Bresnahan refused to follow orders...."[20]

Roger Bresnahan at the Polo Grounds circa 1907 (courtesy Roger M. Bresnahan).

Sporting Life confirmed the root of the problem causing Roger's suspension was indeed the first game with the Cubs. "Just what the cause of the trouble was McGraw and Bresnahan refused to state."[21]

Roger did not play in the next two games against Boston. The next day he pinch hit against Philadelphia, singled and scored as part of a game-tying, eighth-inning rally. Apparently, McGraw tailored the suspension to fit the team's needs. He completed his three-game suspension on the following day.[22]

* * *

Following the Cubs' departure, the Giants wrapped up their homestand by winning just three of eight games against the league's second-tier teams. Now it was the Giants' turn to make the long road trip and they headed west to their first encounter—with Chicago.

Once again, the Giants were no match for the Cubs in losing all three, the last two by a single run. Roger's shin guards, called "Mr. R. Bresnahan's top boots" by one Chicago scribe, received attention including a satirical cartoon.[23] Frank Bowerman who caught the second game, "continues to use the Bresnahan shin guards while catching and says he finds them a great help."[24]

The Giants soothed their wounds at last-place St. Louis winning three straight. Roger played sparingly against the Cardinals, but he did go to bat wearing his shin guards and "caused much amusement among the fans."[25] He silenced the laughter with a single, moved up on Dan McGann's single and then led a double steal, though he over-slid third base to end the inning.[26] Another report confirmed that Roger was wearing his shin guards when he stole third base.[27]

The next stop was Pittsburg where the Pirates had already seen Roger's shin guards, but their fans had not. Roger "was hooted when he took his place behind the bat in the first inning, and each time he appeared after that the crowd enjoyed a hearty laugh." The story also pointed out how Roger's guards delayed the game "Once yesterday he was on base when the third man was retired. He hustled in to don his armor but was so long about it that McGraw sent Fitzgerald out to catch Mathewson until Roger was ready."[28]

The Giants won the June 17 opener in Cincinnati 9–1. Roger aided the win by drawing a walk, knocking out three singles and scoring twice. "He wore his guards to bat the last half of the game and made a couple of hits…."[29] "It was the first time the Cincinnati fans have had a chance to see Roger Bresnahan and his shinpads, and while the bunch decried the idea and yelled all sorts of things at him, it was the consensus of opinion, after the game, that the innovation was one of the best that has been introduced into the game of baseball since the advent of the mask and the big mitt. Bresnahan has been consulting with the catchers along the road and is convinced that all of them will take to the pads before the opening of the next season."[30]

* * *

The next day's game was described in Chapter One.

Press statements of Bresnahan's condition originated that night varied greatly and most were premature, and some were extreme.

"For two hours Bresnahan improved steadily, and the doctors telephoned to McGraw at the grounds that he would be able to return to the game to-morrow."[31] McGraw told the *New York Times* at 6 p.m. that the "injury was not serious, and that the reports from the grounds were exaggerated. Bresnahan had been sent to the Seton Hospital, so that he would be kept quiet. McGraw said he thought Bresnahan would be around as usual after a few hours rest at the hospital."[32]

But a dispatch to New York reported that Bresnahan had died.[33]

Under the front-page headline "Bresnahan Dying from Blow by Ball," the *New York American* reported:

> But shortly before 6 o'clock the catcher began to sink again. Late to-night he was still sinking, and the physicians then said there was not one chance in a hundred that he would ever don a mask again.
>
> Told that his great catcher would probably die, John McGraw, captain of the New Yorks, burst into tears. "He was the best ball player in America," the manager sobbed. "He could play anywhere; he always played honestly, and he put more heart into the team when luck went bad than any man I ever knew. Bresnahan could no more be replaced upon the New York team than you could replace a victorious general in an army. I'm not much on praying, but to-night I pray with all my heart that he gets well."[34]

An early medical report appeared without attribution in the June 19 *Cincinnati Enquirer*: "Last night there was a lump on his head the size of a hen's egg. The danger now is that the extreme force of the blow may cause a blood clot to form on the brain, in which case an operation will be necessary that will prevent him from playing for the balance of the season. If he escapes this he will still have to stay in bed at the hospital for several days, possibly a week until his system recovers from the shock."[35]

Adeleen Bresnahan arrived in Cincinnati from Toledo along with Roger's sister, Margaret Henige, the evening of June 19. The ladies assisted with nursing and planned to escort Roger home to Toledo upon his release from the hospital.[36]

Select press reports:

> June 18, Tuesday: "'I will keep him in bed for three or four days, and he will not be able to leave Cincinnati with his team,' said Dr. Arndt… 'I do not fear the formation of a blood clot on the brain, considered a possibility at first, and believe that he will be all right after a few days' rest.'"[37]
>
> June 19, Wednesday: "Dr. Pirrung, who is a warm friend of the catcher, said last night that Roger might possibly be able to accompany the Giants to Pittsburg this evening. 'He is of such powerful physique and in such perfect physical condition,' said the doctor, 'that he has rallied much faster than was to be expected after such a severe shock. A weaker man would have surely been seriously injured. I do not think there will be any complications and I believe he will be entirely himself in a few days.'"[38]
>
> June 20, Thursday: "The Giants left last night for the East, but Roger Bresnahan was not able to take the trip. His wife is here, however, and is constantly at his bedside. The physicians reported last night that he would probably be able to be out by tomorrow and that there will be no bad effects from his knock on the head."[39]
>
> June 21, Friday: "Roger Bresnahan is still confined in the Seton Hospital, and as yet there is no immediate likelihood of his getting out … judging from the reports from the hospital, it will probably be two weeks before he will be able to take his regular turn behind the batter."[40]
>
> June 24, Monday: "Roger Bresnahan, the Toledo lad who was badly hurt by a pitched ball at Cincinnati last week, is rapidly recovering and will soon be able to be moved to his home in this city. Roger sat up in bed for the first time yesterday but will not be able to leave the hospital before the latter part of the week. He won't join the Giants for several weeks."[41]

After spending nine nights in Seton Hospital, Roger was released by Dr. Arndt with strict orders for a further recovery period at his Toledo home. He was accompanied there by his wife and sister on Thursday, June 27. Just before leaving the Queen City, he spoke with a *Cincinnati Post* reporter:

> "It's all right to lay in bed when one is injured, but when a fellow is up and around and then cannot get back into the game it hurts," he said.
>
> Besides playing ball for the money that I receive, I love the game for itself, and hate to be idle. Of course, I will not take any chances, and will rest until I feel in the best of shape again—but it's awful.
>
> When that ball hit me, I thought it was all over with me. I thought I was a goner. I cannot remember it all, but I know I called for a priest, and was prepared to go.
>
> I have been hit on the shoulder and body a thousand times, at least, since I have been in the game, but that seemed to be my finisher.
>
> I hold no feeling against Andy Coakley for hitting me. Coakley is one of the finest gentlemen the game has ever had, and through *The Post* I want to thank him for the kindly interest he has taken in me since I have been in the hospital. Not one day went by but what I received fruit or flowers from Andy or a telephone message inquiring about my condition.[42]

The *Cincinnati Enquirer* reported his arrival at Toledo:

> Minus several pounds of flesh and looking weak Roger Bresnahan, New York's great backstop, has arrived at his home here. Although Roger has recovered to a great extent from the effects of the terrible blow, he is far from himself. He still has pains which shoot from one place to another in his head, his legs are in bad condition, his back is injured and altogether he is in bad shape. His physician here agrees with Dr. Arndt that he must not again put on his baseball togs for at least a month, or he will suffer an attack of vertigo, and the consequences might prove fatal. The physicians lay the condition of Roger's legs to the blow he received on the head and that they will soon regain their strength when the effects of the blow leave.
>
> "Had I been moving as I usually do when at bat the ball should never have hit me," Roger said to *The Enquirer* correspondent. "That day, however, I was standing still at the plate. I believe that was the fastest ball Andy Coakley ever turned loose. I saw it coming, saw it was going to hit me. I remember turning my face from the ball and that is the last I knew until I found myself in the clubhouse with eight physicians working over me. I expect to be out before 30 days if possible."[43]

Update from Toledo, on July 8: "Roger Bresnahan will join the Giants in New York today … but he is still far from playing condition. Only the fighting spirit that has made the Toledo boy the great ball player that he is takes him back to New York. He will work into the game gradually."[44]

* * *

Roger returned to the Giants lineup on July 12. It was of his own volition and foolhardy. "Roger Bresnahan joined the Giants last week in spite of the doctor's orders to take a further rest for a few weeks."[45] He was specifically ordered not to leave home.[46]

He planned to don protective headgear to shield himself from recurrence of his horrific injury. The plan was well publicized and caused much anticipation. Earlier in the year he had become the first catcher to wear shin guards openly and regularly. Fans seemed eager to see another Bresnahan innovation. On the day he returned, the *New York Journal* featured a prominent photograph of Bresnahan on page one above the fold wearing his ear guard.[47] Despite the ballyhoo, Roger appeared "without even the semblance of his much-touted headgear."[48] Research for this work has not shown that Roger ever wore head protection in a game.

Ball player turned sportswriter Sam Crane described the Giants game of July 12, 1907:

> Roger Bresnahan played his first game yesterday since he was nearly killed in Cincinnati on the Giants last trip there, and the popular player gave an exhibition of brilliant work both at bat and in the field that proved conclusively that he has entirely recovered from the injury.
>
> In fact, it was Roger's two timely singles that, as much if not more than anything else, enabled the Giants to win the game by the close score of 3–2. It can thus be seen how much he figured in the victory. Roger played centerfield in Seymour's place.
>
> It was a strange coincidence, too, that Pitcher Coakley, who nearly ended Bresnahan's earthly career, was the Reds' pitcher in yesterday's game.…

> There were many who were fearful that Roger would show loss of nerve when he first faced a pitcher and particularly so when Coakley was in the box, but Roger never turned a hair. He was just as plucky and nervy as he ever was, and he swung his bat with the snappy aggressiveness that made him famous.
>
> When Roger stepped up to the plate for his first time at bat, he was given an ovation. But after that there was a silence that could be felt. Every spectator and the players, too, were on the anxious seat to see how Roger would perform....
>
> But the game player did not cause long worriment. He clouted the very first ball on a dead line to centre and everyone drew a long breath of relief....
>
> And how the crowd did cheer. The hit sent in Browne from third.
>
> On his next time up Roger flied to left and did the same on his fourth, but on his third, with Devlin on first he stung the ball so hard to right that Devlin could get no farther than second. Both Devlin and Bresnahan scored by reason of Hannifin's neat sacrifice and Bowerman's timely swat to deep left.
>
> In the field Roger was all there also. He collared two difficult flies and made a line throw that everyone on the grounds, but Umpire Emslie thought had pinched a Red runner.
>
> There was a pretty little incident in connection with Bresnahan's reappearance that made a big hit with the crowd and showed baseball and baseball players at their best.
>
> As Bresnahan walked in from centre field after the Reds had taken their first turn at bat, he passed near the pitcher's box, where Coakley had taken his position to warm up.... Roger proved himself a gentleman, for without any hesitation, he strode toward Coakley and offered his hand. Coakley grasped it with avidity, and they shook hands like old friends. Coakley seemed much relieved that there was no animosity.[49]

Never has the author noted in contemporary literature even a hint that Coakley's striking of both Bresnahan and McGann was anything but an accident. *The Times-Star* said the day following the beaning that "[n]o one is worried more about Bresnahan's condition than Andy Coakley, who was really not to blame for the accident."[50] "Another newspaper noted that following the Bresnahan incident Coakley was completely unnerved for the moment, and when the next batter faced him, he was visibly affected."[51]

Despite medical advice to the contrary, Bresnahan continued to play, though he eased back into his usual duties. He was in center again the next day. Following, the Giants enjoyed an off day and then Bresnahan sat but pinch hit in the ninth inning. Beginning July 16, he played all the Giants' games for a week at first base. Not only was playing at first less physically demanding than his usual position behind the bat, but there was also a void there as Dan McGann still had not returned to the lineup following his encounter with Coakley.

* * *

Bresnahan resumed his responsibility as the Giants' regular catcher, on July 23, though handicapped by chronic right leg sciatica.[52] With the exception of a single game in which he pinched hit, he caught every contest through mid–September including an eight-day stretch that included a 13-inning game and five doubleheaders.

When Roger returned to the lineup the Giants were still in second place but had fallen nine games behind the Cubs. That deficit increased to 16.5 games when Roger next had a day off on September 12. The race was all but over, and the Giants played like it, winning just seven of the remaining 25 games. Losing the last seven caused the Giants to finish in fourth place, a long fall from their outstanding start to the season.

A short late September news item concerning a little-used National League catcher capped the 1907 saga of the introduction of the shin guard into baseball, "Catcher Harry Smith, of Pittsburg, has adopted the Bresnahan shin guards. Looks as if the protectors would be in general use next year."[53]

* * *

Roger began his vacation from baseball by pursuing what became a life-long interest—hunting. He was reported to be duck hunting with fellow Toledo ball players Addie Joss and Fred Merkle, "taking a month's hunting trip through Southern Illinois in a Wayne touring car."[54]

Roger Bresnahan was a lifelong outdoorsman and especially fond of hunting with his dogs. Besides having dogs for hunting companions, he owned, trained, and showed countless others (courtesy Roger M. Bresnahan).

The Giants' poor finish fueled the always present rumor mill and, as usual, Roger was a subject. This year McGraw was included as well. Some accused McGraw of "lack of interest in baseball and his team" and suggested that he be replaced by Bresnahan.[55] When the Giants passed over Roger and appointed newly-resigned Mike Donlin captain for 1908,[56] some thought that was a signal that Roger would be traded—as there is "a feeling that on a certain basis Bresnahan may be traded to the Reds."[57] Fred Knowles, the Giants' secretary, attempted to quell all of that by saying, "the club has no intention of letting him go to become manager of the Cincinnati Reds." He "also expressed the opinion that Bresnahan had no desire to leave the team despite some differences … with McGraw last season."[58] A report out of New York on December 21 detailed a three-team, five-player deal that would send Roger to Cincinnati as player-manager.[59] A week later, another report offered that Roger himself initiated a direct appeal to Garry Herrmann, president of the Cincinnati club, "to make a deal with the New York National League club, by which Bresnahan can become manager of the Reds...."[60]

McGraw and Bresnahan met in Chicago on January 5. McGraw left that meeting with a signed contract for 1908. According to J. Ed Grillo: "Roger Bresnahan, who has for months been telling us that he would never again don a mitt for John J. McGraw, has dipped his pen and put his John Hancock to a New York National League contract, a club that McGraw will manage. So long as Bresnahan thought there was a chance of his getting the Cincinnati management he tried hard to create the impression that he could not play for McGraw in the hope that the latter would accept any sort of a proposition from the Cincinnati club for Bresnahan's release. But McGraw was not successful, and Bresnahan came out of his hole and got in line."[61]

Roger said of the signing, "I am feeling fine ... and am glad everything has been fixed up for next season. We are going to have a great team in New York, and we will give the Cubs a good fight from the very start for the 1908 pennant."[62]

Sixteen

"It Is the Big Catcher's Natural Way to Fight for a Game" (1908)[1]

Roger Bresnahan's optimism for 1908 was due in large part to a trade between his team and the Boston Doves. The swap was agreed to December 13, 1907, the final day of the National League meetings in New York. The Giants sent half of their infield, Shortstop Bill Dahlen and First Baseman Dan McGann, and received their Boston counterparts, Al Bridwell and Fred Tenney, in return. Outfielder George Browne and Pitcher Cecil Ferguson also moved to Boston in the five-for-three-player deal.

The final piece of the trade involved backup catchers Frank Bowerman of the Giants and Tom Needham of Boston. Bowerman had been poison since any doubt of who the Giants' primary catcher was had been removed by Roger's outstanding performance in the 1905 World's Series. Bowerman "firmly believed that he should be starting, and so made first-string catcher Bresnahan's life miserable,"[2] which may have been a factor in Roger's occasionally-expressed desire to leave the Giants. Roger signed after Bowerman had been traded.

The result of the trade for the Giants was a greatly improved infield and the removal of the disruption of the "friction between the two receivers."[3] Another benefit was the Giants' starting lineup, which had only Bresnahan and Devlin batting from the right side, had "a number of men now who can hit left-handers as easily as they can right-handers."[4] Another addition was Mike Donlin who returned after an absence of nearly two seasons.

* * *

Manager McGraw spoke about his catcher missing the opportunity to manage the Cincinnati Reds and how he figured into the Giants' plans for 1908: "Roger Bresnahan, like any other good ball player, is ambitious, but even though he will not get a chance to manage Cincinnati I have no fear his work will slump. He's a great player and I bank largely on him in the reconstruction of the Giants. In the talk of a trade with Cincinnati involving Bresnahan he was offered to the Reds not because he was a disturbing factor on the local team, but for the simple reason we did not care to stand in the way of any man's advancement."[5]

Roger prepared for the upcoming season and did a bit of coaching as well:

"Roger Bresnahan has started a school for 'Giants,' having Fred Merkle and Roy Beecher, two New York recruits, under his care. Roger is getting the youngsters in condition with basketball and handball and is teaching them the art of batting. He is also tipping them off on many scientific points of the game and will have them fit for the fray when the squad leaves for the training trip"[6]

Roger and his charges left Toledo on February 16 for St. Louis.[7] There were joined by four other recruits and Giants' second baseman, Larry Doyle and continued to the Giants' spring base of operations at Marlin Springs, Texas.[8] Roger's group arrived on February 20 and found at least four more Giants' players there. With Bresnahan acting as manager, practice began that day.[9] Roger ran two more days of practice that were "hard work," a "whirlwind"[10] and "busy" which left "the youngsters weary."[11] A run back to their hotel preceded a "mineral water shower bath followed by a good rub."[12]

John McGraw and more ball players arrived on Washington's Birthday after a three-day trip from Los Angeles.[13] McGraw continued practices of conditioning and drills until beginning a series of intrasquad games on February 29.[14] Initially the squads were headed by McGraw and Bresnahan with new Captain Mike Donlin taking over for Roger upon his arrival in camp.[15] By March 3 all the regulars were in camp, and the total players numbered 29.[16]

McGraw split his roster, with the regulars generally kept together, to play against outside competition. On March 7 the regulars beat the Dallas Giants 2–0 and the Colts beat the Fort Worth Panthers 8–3.[17] With the exception of two games against Austin College these two teams were the exclusive adversaries of the Giants until they left Texas on April 3.[18] Roger did most of the catching for the regulars but also helped in right field and pitched on one occasion.[19]

From Texas the Giants contingent started the journey to New York, stopping first at McAlester, Oklahoma, the hometown of Giants pitcher Joe McGinnity. Weekend games between the Giants and their Colts were scheduled but the Saturday game was rained out. Since the Colts were scheduled to play the Mud Hens the following Tuesday and Wednesday, Manager McGraw allowed Roger to leave for Toledo. After the Sunday game at McAlester, Captain Mike Donlin also set out for Toledo with the Colts while the regulars headed out for games at Little Rock, Arkansas, and Columbus, Ohio.

Roger's homecoming was a festive event with Mayor Brand Whitlock presiding at the pre-game ceremonies. "Both Toledo boys were well received. Merkle was presented with a floral offering. Bresnahan also got a bunch of flowers and a beautiful Elk's head watch charm, set off with a glittering diamond."[20]

Roger's Colts team featured several Giants veterans. Hooks Wiltse pitched a complete game as the Giants topped Toledo 7–1. Roger impressed the hometown folks as he "certainly looked good behind the plate. The Toledo boy has one of the best whips in captivity and the way he heaved the ball to the bases was a revelation."[21]

The next day's game was cancelled because of wet grounds which was especially disappointing to the Toledo fans as Christy Mathewson had arrived in Toledo to pitch against the Mud Hens at Armory Park.[22] The Giants were reunited in New York and played final exhibitions at the Polo Grounds on Saturday and Monday.[23]

* * *

The New York Giants were primed to unseat the Chicago Cubs as National League Champions. The team had been strengthened by the huge trade and the addition of one of its former stars. They were in top shape and brimming with confidence. No one expressed their confidence more often and more emphatically than the team leader—Roger Bresnahan. Despite not being named captain, Bresnahan was the true leader. There were questions regarding Captain Donlin's commitment and perseverance and: "…by selecting Donlin as captain the management doubtless calculated that with this added responsibility Donlin will take more interest in his work, while on the other hand Bresnahan is always in the game for all it is worth no matter how matters stand. It is the big catcher's natural way to fight for a game in any event."[24]

An obvious sign of his leadership was McGraw's giving Roger charge of the team when he was absent. As for confidence, Roger's was unmatched. Though he sometimes failed, he was willing to try anything on the field—not fearful of failing. He demonstrated his confidence in his 1908 Giants by putting his money where his mouth was before he left Toledo for spring practice when he "took occasion to notify his friends that if they found anybody offering odds against the Giants as pennant winners to cover the money quickly and to notify him if cash was needed."[25] He also said, "The only team we have to beat is the Cubs…."[26]

* * *

More books have been written about the 1908 baseball season than any other—and for good reason. Never have there been two races so closely contested. Baseball's most controversial game ever was a factor in one of them. With two days remaining on the schedule three teams were in contention in each league and both contests were decided on the final day.

The storied season began for the Giants in Philadelphia on Tuesday, April 14. They started on a winning note but lost their next game before winning five straight, the last being the season's first home game. With their 6–1 record the Giants found themselves sharing the top spot in the National League with, of course, the Cubs. Roger started all seven games behind the plate and batted fifth but did not hit well in the early going.

Fast forward to May 20 and find the Giants in St. Louis for the first of a four-game series which they lost 1–0. Following the contest, the Giants' record was 13–13 and they trailed the Cubs by four-and-a-half games. This is not what the Giants had in mind for their season, and they not only trailed Chicago but also Pittsburg,

Philadelphia, and Cincinnati. To make matters worse, they went on to lose three of the four games to the lowly Cardinals and had their nemesis Cubs next on the schedule.

Roger did not play the first game against the Cards but returned the next day. We are not certain of the reason for his absence, but we know that he was visiting Toledo on Tuesday, May 19 which was a scheduled off day, and it is likely that he had simply been given a days' rest as he had started every Giants' game to this point in the season. While in Toledo Roger told a hometown newspaper that his team was "not in very good shape ... and is now away off edge." But added, "I firmly believe that we are going to cop the bunting."[27]

Even though Roger was confident, and the season was young, the four-game series in Chicago was an important one—the Giants came to the Windy City five and a half games behind the Cubs and in fifth place.

In the first game on Sunday, May 24, the Giants prevailed 6–4 with Roger scoring twice and contributing a home run when "he poled out a smite that went far down the lea, and Roger made four bases by terrific sprinting."[28] The next day, New York suffered a tough loss 8–7 in 10 innings. It was tough because they had come back from a 5–1 deficit after just two innings and tougher still because they lost Roger Bresnahan. During the second inning, a foul ball off the bat of Frank Schulte "nearly broke Bresnahan's bare wrist."[29] The Giants won the next two games and the series three games to one. It was the first time that the Giants had taken a series from the Cubs in two years.

As it turned out, Roger's injury was to a finger on his throwing hand and "it was found the bone was splintered and that an abscess had formed." He returned to Toledo for treatment and to convalesce.[30] He left Toledo on June 4 to rejoin the Giants in New York[31] and was back in the lineup on June 8—much sooner than expected.

As he had when he was out of action with a head injury the previous year, he sought a means to prevent recurrence of his injury. He spent a part of his healing time "working on a design for a right-handed glove which will not interfere with his throwing. He has already had made a hard leather protector for the back of his hand, with finger guards long enough to protect the ends of his digits, but it did not work well...."[32] Though he was remarkably successful with his shin guard innovation he was most often ridiculed and maligned by the press for his continuing efforts to protect himself. Following his finger injury, the *World* published a satirical story about Roger's latest invention, an "accident-proof catching glove" which was accompanied by a half-dozen cartoon drawings and dubbed Roger "The Edison of Ballplayers."[33]

Roger also introduced, probably at some point during this season, a simple but very beneficial innovation that is basic today when he "attached leather-bound rolls of padding to the wire rim of his catcher's mask to cushion the shock of foul balls."[34]

Roger's first day back was a win against the Cardinals and the Giants hoped that it would be a precursor of the results in their next series. Rival Pittsburg with the great Honus Wagner was the next team to visit the Polo Grounds. The third-place Pirates were a notch ahead of the Giants in the tightly-packed standings. They won the first, 8–2, but lost 1–0 the next day with Roger getting two of his team's six hits. Mathewson was beaten the next day and the Giants were shut out again in the finale, evening their record at 23–23 and leaving them six-and-a-half games behind the first-place Cubs.

Furthermore, after just five games back from injury, Bresnahan was lost again because of an accident. After singling in the second inning, he was out and hurt on a play at the plate compelling him to retire. There was no lost love between the Pirates and Giants and their supporters and, judging from how this injury was reported, that bias extended to the press as well.

New York's *World* reported: "On an attempted steal Bresnahan was out at the plate.... Bresnahan twisted his ankle in the slide for home and had to be carried off the field by the players and the club physician."[35]

The *Pittsburg Press* gave this account: "...Roger Bresnahan, of the Giants, is always spectacular. When he sprained his ankle yesterday, he stretched out in front of the home plate for five minutes, with both teams around him, and the spectators wondering how long he would live. After a long delay he decided that he had to be carried to the club house, a distance of about 800 feet. Roger is not a featherweight, and the man who carried him was in worse shape at the end of the journey than his patient. The Pirates were sorry to see Bresnahan hurt, as they hoped he would be in the Cincinnati and Chicago series at the Polo Grounds."[36]

Despite making light of Roger's injury and suggesting he sought sympathy, the writer apparently appreciated Roger's value to his team and was sorry to see it weakened because next on the Giants' schedule were those ahead of the Pirates in the standings. It did appear that Roger would miss those games because he "may not be able to play for a long time."[37]

William Kirk, writing in New York's *American*, expressed a like thought on Roger's value, "The accident to Bresnahan is a calamity indeed. Needham [Giants' backup] is a good, steady catcher but he cannot infuse ginger into the local lads with anything like the skill shown by Bresnahan, and if there's anything we need now it is ginger."[38]

The Giants won all three against the Reds without Roger, but, as always, he returned ahead of schedule as always, and in time to greet the Cubs. New York dropped the first of the four-game series but swept the last three to win a second straight series from the league leaders. Mathewson won the third with a masterful shutout. Roger helped his pitcher control his pace when he left his position "to stoop down and pick up a little gravel, or stall in some other equally genteel way so's Matty wouldn't be so fast."[39] "Mr. Bresnahan was all there, lame leg or no lame leg. His throwing was beautiful and his batting timely."[40]

As the Cubs left town, the Giants remained in fourth place but only three-and-a half games out of first.

* * *

News that Roger was planning to retire from baseball at the end of the season came from his Toledo hometown early in August by an announcement made by Chris F. Wall, secretary and treasurer of Toledo's Boody House Hotel. "When Roger was here two weeks ago ... he and I talked the matter over, and he stated his intention of quitting baseball for good at the end of the season. If he does quit, it will be to come here and take a position at the Boody House. He owns stock in the hotel and would make a good man here."[41] The story as run by many newspapers across the country added, Roger "desires to devote his entire time to his commercial enterprises here."[42] We can only guess Roger's true intentions for his future at the time. Perhaps he was planting the seed of a bargaining chip to be used in his future contract negotiations as he did when he said he would no longer play in New York and later agreed to do so.

* * *

With the start of summer, the Giants began a push for first place, a task that took until the dog days of summer had passed to accomplish. At the close of business on August 20 the Giants and the Pittsburg Pirates were in a virtual tie for first place with the Chicago Cubs three-and-a-half games behind. For the summer push of June 23 through August 20 the Giants won 36 and lost 19 and Roger Bresnahan had plenty to do with this success. Following are some of his contributions to the Giants' climb to first place and notes of some Bresnahan antics:

- Despite beginning this series of games with a sprained ankle he started 54 of the 55 games at catcher, including eight doubleheaders.
- He reached base in 48 of the 55 games, increased his batting average from .246 to .275. McGraw moved him up to third in the batting order.
- He was not ejected.
- On June 25, "Harry Smith, the Boston catcher, got hit on the arm yesterday and a boy brought him a glass of water, and Roger Bresnahan, the batter, took the glass and drank it, the jolly old cutup."[43]
- On July 4 he caught Hook Wiltse's 1–0, 10-inning no-hitter.
- On July 15 he had an RBI triple and three sacrifice hits in an 11–0 rout at Chicago.[44]
- On August 4 he drove in the winning run with a twelfth-inning single.[45]
- On August 10 Roger's double was the only hit in a three-run first inning helping the Giants beat the Cubs 3–2.[46]
- On August 15 he "stole" a base against the Cardinals when he "...drew a base on balls, and then was picked off base. He just quietly walked to second base, claiming a balk, and Mr. Johnstone [the umpire] approved of it."[47]

- On August 20, the "Giants Reach the Top at Last" by winning 2–0 at Cincinnati. Roger figured in both runs by walking to keep a scoring-inning alive and later walking again and eventually scoring the second run.[48]

The win on August 20 enabled the Giants to tie the Pirates. Their records stood at 64–42 with the Cubs not far behind at 61–46. Three days later, Roger and his mates, with a modest four-game winning streak, were headed for Pittsburg and following to Chicago.

The table was set for an unprecedented battle to the finish.

Seventeen

"The Most Popular Player That Has Ever Stepped Inside the Polo Grounds" (1908)[1]

The Giants rolled into Pittsburg for a four-game series beginning with a doubleheader on Monday, August 24. The two teams were just a half game apart at the top of the standings. Chicago, lurking close behind, hoped that the pair would beat each other so that they could gain ground on both.

The Giants seized the moment. Behind Wiltse and Mathewson, they swept the twin bill 4–1 and 5–1. Trailing 1–0, the Giants struck in the eighth when Bresnahan smashed a two-run triple, followed by Mike Donlin's home run to end the game. Sam Crane described Roger's key hit: "Bresnahan was on pins and needles. Dear old Roger had his teeth set and his head up. He lined a beauty over second that [Center Fielder Roy] Thomas tried to make a circus catch of and pitched forward onto his face in a vain attempt to clutch the sphere. Roy plowed up the ground for yards with his nose, but the ball scooted under him and netted Roger three bases."[2]

New York won the final two games of the series giving them a three-and-a-half game lead over the Pirates and Cubs.

The next day J.W. McConaughy wrote in the *Evening Journal* his opinion of the value of Roger Bresnahan to the New York Giants: "Bresnahan knows baseball as few men know it, and he has the build and force to put his knowledge into action ... he is a composite of ginger and bad language. In his clumsy shin guards and wind-pad, his head in a wire cage, through which at intervals comes a stream of reproof and comment as he fusses around the plate.... Bresnahan does not have a delightful personality. He isn't there to be loved.... In the batting box he is almost as valuable as behind. He is a game, vicious hitter and when it takes one to bring in needed runs fans would as soon see Roger at the plate as some men who are ahead of him in percentage."[3]

Standings of the National League's top teams, with games behind the leader:

August 26	
New York	
Chicago	3.5
Pittsburg	3.5

The Giants moved on to Chicago with their winning streak at eight and an opportunity to put their nemesis Cubs in danger of falling out of the race. But the trip to Chicago did nothing except tighten the standings. Chicago won all three, the last two by one run.

August 30	
New York	
Chicago	.5
Pittsburg	1

The road trip ended with four games in Boston and a like number in Philadelphia. The Giants won seven of the eight.

September 7	
New York	
Pittsburg	.5
Chicago	2

Back in New York on September 8 the Giants battled Brooklyn and St. Louis, the league's bottom two teams. The Giants won them all.

The season was winding down; the Giants had a three-game lead, a hot hand having won their last nine and 16 of their last 17. The Pirates and Cubs were next to visit New York.

September 17	
New York	
Pittsburg	3
Chicago	3

The Giants hosted the Pirates for two games on September 18 and won them both but they each had a different feel—the first was a shutout by Matty, 7–0, while the Giants piled up 12 runs in the second. Despite leaving both games early, Roger helped the offense in several ways—a pair of sacrifices, a base on balls, three hits including two doubles, two runs scored and five driven in. The *New York Times* called the attendance of "at least 35,000 the largest crowd that ever attended a game in the history of the National sport."[4]

September 18	
New York	
Chicago	4.5
Pittsburg	5

The reason Roger left both games in the eighth inning is John McGraw wished to rest his key player as much as possible. Roger was on pace to catch more games than anyone ever had. He had caught every Giants' game, save one, since June 18. Catching coupled with his aggressive style of play invited injury and fatigue, increasing the odds of a hurtful accident. When a game seemed to be decided, McGraw would pull Roger in favor of Tom Needham seven more times before the season ended.

The euphoria was tempered a bit when the Pirates won the last two games of their visit, and even more when the Cubs won the first two of their scheduled four-game series. All four of those games were close and hard-fought but losses, nonetheless.

September 22	
New York	
Chicago	
Pittsburg	1.5

The third game with Chicago was a 1–1 tie. Drawn games in the Deadball Era were not uncommon. Most often tied games were caused by darkness and replayed later. The game between the Chicago Cubs and New York Giants on September 23 was declared a tie for the stated reason of darkness but the true reasons were more complex. That decision has made the game "the most celebrated, most widely discussed, most controversial contest in the history of American sports."[5]

The Merkle game has been researched and written about ever since. Accounts vary now as they did then, and no new evidence of the game's events will be forthcoming. The study of this game could be a work of itself and is not the purpose here. One interpretation that gives the basics of the story follows:

> The incident occurred ... at the Polo Grounds under the most dramatic of circumstances. It was the last half of the ninth inning in a 1–1 game between the Giants and Chicago Cubs. As the two teams were tied for first place, the winner would take the lead in the National League. New York had two outs, with Moose McCormick on third and Merkle on first. Al Bridwell singled to centerfield, and McCormick crossed the plate with what appeared to be the winning run. The play, however, would not be complete until Merkle touched second base ahead of the ball. If Merkle did not touch second, he could still be retired by a force at the base—since, when there are two outs, no run can score until a possible force play has been completed. Although there were claims to the contrary on the part of Merkle and others.... Merkle apparently veered right toward the clubhouse in center field before touching second. He presumed the game was over when McCormick crossed the plate, causing him to stop short of the bag. At this point, Cubs second baseman Johnny Evers signaled for the center fielder to throw him the ball so he could tag second. Jubilant with their apparent victory, fans and Giant players rushed onto the field, creating mass confusion. Before Evers could retrieve the ball and record the out at second base, a spectator grabbed the ball and threw it into the stands. The Giants pushed Merkle back to the base, as the ball, recovered by a Chicago fan, was tossed back to Evers. But all this took place after the umpires had left the field. Even though the New York papers credited the Giants with the win, it was decided by National League President Harry C. Pulliam that the game be recorded as a tie. The drawn game was replayed.[6]

This basic version of the story contains "facts" that are not consistent with some others that say Giants' pitcher Joe McGinnity threw the ball into the stands. Some point out that the ball returned to Evers was *a* ball but not *the* ball. Further this version presumes to know what Merkle was thinking. But this should not be a surprise because all that is known about this game comes from those who witnessed the events, and their accounts differ greatly.

We are certain that the game was—because of presidential decree—a tie. We also know that, by rule, Merkle needed to make second base for the run to count. We also know that, if Merkle did not touch second and headed to clubhouse instead, he did something that had been done many, many times before. Though it was the rule it was not the custom of the times.

Our protagonist took part in this game and helped secure the tie by way of his sixth-inning sacrifice bunt that led to the Giants' run. It is surprising that he was not mentioned in any of the accounts of the game-ending events I consulted. It was not his nature to avoid controversy. Perhaps he made it safely to the Giants' clubhouse thinking that his team had won.

Roger Bresnahan knew and understood the rules and had been involved in a situation identical to Merkle's. Fred Tenney, in whose place Fred Merkle was playing on the fateful day, was previously player-manager of the Boston Nationals. He related the story of that September 6, 1904, game to the *Boston Herald* in 1907: "We had a game with New York and one run was needed to win the game. New York had men on third and first and two out. Bresnahan was on first. The batsman hit a ball to centre for a base and the man on third ambled home, but Bresnahan, as I noticed, did not run down to second. I ran down to second and yelled for Cannell to throw the ball to me. This made Bresnahan take notice and he made for the bag. Had Cannell thrown the ball accurately I would have had my man, but he threw a trifle wide. All that Bresnahan said was, 'I believe the ball belongs to us, Fred,' and I handed it to him."[7]

Roger never forgot what had happened or did not happen. He, "nearly four decades after the game, quipped that 'Johnny Evers hasn't completed the force out of Merkle yet.'"[8]

The Giants beat the Cubs the next day 5–4 to regain first place. Roger had two singles, a stolen base and scored a run to aid the cause. A look at the standings at the end of day on September 24 revealed that the first-place Giants held a one-game lead over both Chicago and Pittsburg.

However, the Giants had 15 games to play while the Pirates had 10 and the Cubs only nine. Thirteen days to go with doubleheaders scheduled on four of them meant the Giants' already-thin pitching staff would be stretched. To make matters worse, the Giants were a battered lot. "The Giants were in poor shape to play those games. As the *Sporting News* put it, 'Tenney, Donlin, Seymour, and Bresnahan ought to be in the hospital with Larry Doyle.' … Bresnahan suffered from a sciatic nerve problem…."[9]

September 24	
New York	
Chicago	1
Pittsburg	1

A pair of those doubleheaders was played the next two days with Cincinnati. The Reds won both the first day and the Giants did the same the next. In the fifth inning of the first game, "in making a fine stop that saved another run the catcher's finger was badly hurt."[10] Roger left the game as a result but returned for the final three games with the Reds and knocked out five hits.[11]

September 26	
Chicago	
New York	.5
Pittsburg	1

The Giants were then slated to play the Philadelphia Phillies in eight straight games—the first four at the Polo Grounds followed by a series at Philadelphia. Each city would host a doubleheader. The Giants won the first 7–6—Roger had two singles, a double, drew two walks and scored three runs, the last of which followed his leadoff hit in the bottom of the ninth inning to tie the score.[12]

The following day, the Polo Grounds twin bill was played. The first game was won by the Giants 6–2, sparked to a fast start by Roger when he doubled in a first-inning run and later scored himself. In the fifth inning his triple plated two more runs. Then, with two outs, Roger broke for the plate on a ground ball to the shortstop, knowing not if the batter would be retired—which he was. Roger crashed into Phillies' Catcher Red Dooin. Both were injured, Roger twisting his ankle, and both retired from the game.[13] Both started the second game. Dooin completed it, Roger did not. Gym Bagley of the New York *Evening News* explained:

> Now here's the problem: If Bresnahan had caught the second game, would the Giants have lost ... if he could have stood up behind the bat on that bum gamp for nine innings, [could he] have pulled his team through?
>
> There was one way for him to stay in, not to hit the ball and in consequence be compelled to run the bases. He could have intentionally struck out each time up. Even if he was of no use at the bat, *he would still have been the directing hand and mind.*
>
> But the first time up he singled. That hit was his undoing. He had to hopscotch to first. He could only put down one leg. Now it stands to reason that a guy getting to first on one leg would have to hit far away. But Bresnahan didn't. It was an infield hit which he beat out—on one foot.
>
> Both [Shortstop] Shean and [Second Baseman] Knabe went after the ball. They committed no error on the hit. And Roger was on the bag before the ball was returned.
>
> I'm no mind reader, but if the truth were told, I'd gamble a bag of Harry Stevens' gubers that when Shean and Knabe saw Bresnahan hobbling so painfully down the line they came to the conclusion that it would be a shame to throw out so game a player.
>
> Roger had to give in for a pinch-runner, and of course that put him out of the game.[14]

Indications were Roger "might have to give up for the rest of the season.."[15] The *Philadelphia Inquirer* opined that Roger's loss would diminish the Giants' pennant hopes because, "Bresnahan is the backbone of the outfit."[16]

September 29	
Chicago	
New York	.5
Pittsburg	.5

Following the games of October 1, the three teams were within a half game. The Giants had five games to play, the Cubs three, and the Pirates four, so any one of the three could still win. Roger had missed three games and despite an October 2 admonition; "it begins to look as if Bresnahan will not be able to play for many days,"[17] he played that very day. Sportswriter Bozeman Bulger of New York's *World* was with Roger the evening of October 1. He described what he saw for his readers, "Last night I looked at the injured ankle while the doctor was treating it, and it is truly a fright. About two inches above the ankle bone the leg is puffed out until it is almost as large as his knee. At that, he wants to put on a uniform and do what he can to help win the pennant."[18]

He played the complete game on October 2, a 7–2 win. He "was his old brilliant self behind the bat, and not a single Quaker ventured a dash for second base."[19] He caught nine innings the next day, but the Giants dropped a close one to Harry Coveleski and the Phillies 3–2. Coveleski, a 22-year-old rookie and late-season addition to the Philadelphia roster, had beaten the Giants three times in five days and was instantly dubbed "The Giant Killer."[20] To show their gratitude, the Cubs took a collection to reward the youngster.[21]

October 3	
Pittsburg	
Chicago	.5
New York	1.5

On Sunday October 4, 1908, the Cubs hosted the Pirates in the final scheduled game of the season for both. If Pittsburg won, the pennant was theirs. If the Cubs won, they would have a half game lead over Pittsburg (the Giants and Cubs were slated for a season shortened by one game because of their September 23 tie) and a one-and-a-half game lead over the Giants. The Giants had three games remaining, all with Boston at the Polo Grounds. The Giants still had a chance—if the Cubs beat the Pirates and the Giants beat Boston all three games, the Giants and Cubs would be tied.

Naturally, the interest of many New York fans was focused on Chicago that Sunday. More than 5,000 of them witnessed the game at the Polo Grounds via the

Compton electric bulletin system. Among the crowd were Roger Bresnahan, several other Giants and some of the Boston team that would be playing there the next day.[22] It was a happy time at the Polo Grounds as the Cubs prevailed leaving the door cracked open for the Giants.

Needing three wins to tie the Cubs, the Giants did just that and they did it convincingly outscoring the Boston Doves 19–4 for the series. And they did it without using Christy Mathewson and were able to allow Roger an early exit twice.

The National League Board of Directors met during the series to consider appeals and rule on the September 23 game between the Cubs and Giants. They announced on October 6 that the game, judged a 1–1 tie by the umpires and upheld by National League President Pulliam, was indeed a tie game and ordered a replay in New York on October 8.[23] Replaying of tie games was routine business during the Deadball Era. Not that this game was routine. It would, in fact, decide the National League pennant but it was not a playoff game.

"Despite rumors to the contrary, the decision was not accepted in good grace by the local club. Bresnahan was perhaps the most outspoken in his criticism and his remarks indicated that the players were inclined to balk when it came to playing that extra game with Chicago."[24] McGraw was so incensed over the board's decision that he considered not playing: "McGraw was furious at the board's decision; the players, like himself, believed they had won the pennant and should not have to play another game for it. But when McGraw let them decide whether to play, they voted to send a delegation to Brush [Giants owner] and ask his opinion [Bresnahan was included].[25] I am going to leave it to you," Brush said. "...But I shouldn't think you would stop now after making all this fight." "The players huddled briefly and told Brush they would play."[26]

* * *

"Never before have two teams been tied at the end of a season. Never has the race been so close. Never has it been necessary to play off the tie of six months' baseball in a single gigantic battle."[27] Never before had the outcome of a sporting event had such an impact—the stakes and gambling interests were extremely high.

Not only was the game as major a sporting event as there ever was but so was the press coverage. Newspapers everywhere carried the stories, many on the front page. Newspapers that generally included line scores at best featured exhaustive detail.

The short story was Chicago 4, New York 2. The short reason was Mordecai "Three Fingered" Brown. Jack Pfiester started the game for Chicago by hitting the first batter and walking the next. Bresnahan had an opportunity to give his team an early lead but struck out and the runner was picked off at first base. A double scored a run and was followed by another walk. Chicago Manager Frank Chance was quick to act and brought in Brown who finished the game allowing just a single run. The Giants were left to wonder what the inning might have been had Roger hit safely and the double play had not occurred. Roger helped mount a mild threat when he singled in the third giving the Giants two on with one out, but they could not capitalize. Mathewson surrendered four runs in the third but otherwise, with help from Hooks Wiltse, held the Cubs in check. Brown had no such lapse, but even so, Roger was heard to say late in the game and in vain, "Never mind fellows, we'll get 'em yet."[28]

The loss of this game and the National League pennant was a huge disappointment, and many held Fred Merkle personally and solely responsible. Merkle was maligned by the press and fans—for years—and labeled "Bonehead." He suffered immensely but John McGraw did not blame him nor did his teammates. In the author's opinion his treatment was grossly unfair. The charge that his base-running gaffe cost the Giants the 1908 National League pennant is baseless as the team lost 52 other games in 1908 (which they could not replay) any one of which had the same effect. For those who wish to identify a single point cause for the Giants' failure to capture the flag, it could be the *team's* inability to beat the upstart Harry Coveleski three times.

* * *

Bill Klem and Jimmy Johnstone had umpired the last Boston-New York game on October 7 and were scheduled to work the Cubs-Giants tie-game replay the next day. Following the October 7 game, Dr. Joseph Creamer, the Giants' team physician, approached Klem and offered him $2,500 if the Giants won the next day. Creamer renewed the offer with cash in hand as Klem was going to work the next day. Johnstone was also approached on two occasions by different men. Both umpires reported the bribe attempts to the league office on the morning of the game. There were no controversial calls during the game and there was no mention of the incidents until National League President Harry Pulliam informed the owners at their annual meeting in December. The owners were appalled and struggled with how to best manage the news. The source of the bribery funds was never determined by the league's investigation but most of the owners believed that gambling interests were behind the attempt to buy the umpires. Creamer was banned from baseball parks for life. Baseball people were not found to be implicated in any way, but the story is mentioned here because of hearsay reported by one of the owners—Garry Herrmann of Cincinnati who had heard "the men behind Creamer were John McGraw, Roger Bresnahan and Christy Mathewson." Author Maury Klein has opined that the owners did not believe the story but has suggested confirmation of what Herrmann heard: "The story circulating through the baseball world also included 'the positive assertion that the $2,500 … belonged to three members of the New York Giants who wanted to make it a sure thing that the Giants would get into the World Series … and thereby secure a part of the large gate receipts.'"[29]

The upshot of the story was that the bribe attempt failed because of the honesty of Messrs. Klem and Johnstone.

* * *

The 1908 National League season is still noted for its season-long and evenly-contested battle among three teams. Not only did New York, Chicago and Pittsburg finish the season within a single game of each other but also they played each other evenly. The Giants played both the Cubs and Pirates, 11–11–1, while the Pirates took their season series with the Cubs, 12–10. Since the teams played each other 22 times and rosters were far more stable than today the players knew those on opposing teams well and engaged in hard-fought competition with them. Rivalries were intense and words like *hate* were sometimes used to describe rival teams. Conversely, the players held their passion for the game in common and on occasion talked freely about it. It is hard to imagine Cubs and Giants discussing the finer points of the game, such as how to outwit their sometimes-common adversary—the umpire—but they were known to do just that.

Cubs Second Baseman Johnny Evers told of meeting with Bresnahan and other players one 1908 evening at the Polo Grounds. They all agreed that it was impossible for an umpire, working alone, to see everything and suggested: "when either a bunt or hit-and-run was attempted, the umpire always ran down into the diamond, in front of the play in order to see a play either at first or second base, and that the catcher could, therefore, stop, trip or interfere with the batter without the slightest danger of being seen.... The following day, early in the game, Chicago had a runner on first base and the batter tried to sacrifice. Bresnahan cut ahead of the runner, bumped him off his feet, and after the other runner had been forced at second the luckless batter was doubled at first base. Two innings later Kling [Chicago's catcher] did the same thing to a New York batter."[30]

The next day two umpires worked the game.[31]

Roger engaged in another instance of the player/rival bond during the 1905 World's Series—"...Powers, the Philadelphia catcher, hurt his ungloved hand so that he stopped play and walked around shaking it for a moment. Bresnahan ... was at bat at the time. He saw Power's difficulty and knowing from experience what it meant to get a swift ball from a pitcher in the wrong spot, he laid Power's hand across his knee and rubbed it till the Philadelphian felt able to get back to work."[32]

* * *

"The Real Champions, 1908" was inscribed on medals Giants' Owner John Brush had struck for his players.[33] He, his players and Giants' fans believed that the pennant had been taken from them by the umpires, the league president, and the board of directors. Brush showed that he believed with his money as well by giving the proceeds from the replay of the drawn game—$10,000 to his players. The fans showed them that they believed by giving them the earnings from a benefit performance by "the stars of the theatrical world"—$3,500. Congressman William Sulzer presented each player with a "watch fob of solid gold, studded with genuine diamonds" also from the fans. Mr. Sulzer invited Roger Bresnahan forward for the first presentation and addressed him as "the greatest living catcher."[34] When all the cash was gathered and divided; the regular players received $700 and the substitutes $300.

* * *

Roger Bresnahan's contributions to the New York Giants' success in 1908 were immense. He was unquestionably the leader of the team on the field, and he was on the field. He caught more games than any other catcher ever had (139).[35] It was also the first time during his career that he played only one defensive position. His presence, play, confidence, and grit—his willingness to disregard pain and play despite injury—helped his team to achieve more than expected as most money was on the Cubs to repeat as champions.

Roger's season does not seem eye-popping offensively, but it was very good. He batted .283 which ranked eighth in the National League that hit .239. His on-base percentage of .401 stood third and was aided by a league-leading 83 bases on balls.

Roger's real worth to his team was realized and proved by the fans. With just a few days remaining in the season New York's *World* asked, "what member of the Giants is doing the most to win the pennant for New York?"[36] Readers were asked to vote for their choice. One could suggest that Christy Mathewson might be that player. He had won the triple crown of pitching with 37 wins, a 1.43 earned run average and 259 strikeouts besides five saves and 11 shutouts while amassing 390.2 innings. The tally was not even close as Mathewson's 23,120 votes paled in comparison to Roger's 91,333. Roger was awarded a diamond-studded medal by the newspaper.[37]

* * *

Even before Roger left New York for his Toledo home, the now annual rumors of his imminent trade were circulating. On October 13, the *News-Bee* headline "BRESNAHAN FOR ST. LOUIS: Old Rumor Is Again Revived" speculated that Roger would be named manager of the Cardinals for 1909. The story stated in part, "Bresnahan, it is said, has written a close personal friend in St. Louis to the effect that he has been tendered the position and will accept under certain conditions."[38] Roger arrived in Toledo on Saturday, October 25, and immediately denied, "any prospects of his leaving the Giants for the managerial role with the St. Louis Cardinals."[39]

The next day Roger played a game for the home folks at Armory Park in downtown Toledo. The teams of Toledoans playing professionally were led by Roger and Addie Joss. Fred Merkle was nowhere to be seen.

On October 28, the St. Louis Cardinals announced that Manager John McCloskey's resignation had been accepted.[40]

On November 1, John McGraw firmly stated his intention to keep Roger with the Giants: "I don't want to stand in the way of Bresnahan's advancement in the profession, but if called on I will have to say 'Nay, nay' to any proposition looking toward a change in the residence of the Toledo sleuth. Last year I came mighty near making a mistake and allowing Bresnahan to depart for pastures new.... Bresnahan undoubtedly has the ability to manage a team, but I don't see how I can spare him, and he apparently is well satisfied with his berth with the Giants."[41]

Late in November the waters were muddied even more when Cincinnati Reds Owner Garry Herrmann again made overtures regarding Bresnahan.[42]

Yet another wrinkle was introduced on December 8. According to Toledo's *News Bee*, "The belief is prevalent here [New York] that [Stanley] Robison [St. Louis' Cardinals' owner] has traded a slice of stock in his team to Brush for Bresnahan." The story went on to state that in addition to the stock, some St. Louis players would go to New York and that "terms for the trade were agreed upon six weeks ago." The story originated in New York and called Roger Bresnahan "the most popular player that has ever stepped inside the Polo Grounds."[43] A related *Sporting Life* story reported that Brush's investment was to be substantial, and he would send Bresnahan to St. Louis to look after his interests there.[44]

* * *

On Saturday, December 12, Robison ended the several months of rumors, speculation and posturing when he announced that a deal had been struck that morning. Roger was traded to St. Louis for the Cardinals' best pitcher, Bugs Raymond; their best position player, John Murray; and Catcher Admiral Schlei who would be Roger's replacement for the Giants. The Cardinals had acquired Schlei for two pitchers from Cincinnati for the purpose of completing the New York-St. Louis deal.[45]

Stanley Robison returned to his home in Cleveland and invited Roger to visit. An announcement followed their meeting—the parties had executed a contract making Roger Bresnahan the manager and catcher of the St. Louis Cardinals for the next three years for $25,000 for the term.[46]

Following the announcement Robison revealed "that he and Bresnahan had practically agreed on terms some time ago," confirming that the months of rumor had basis. For whatever reasons, the principals (Bresnahan, McGraw, Robison, Brush and possibly Herrmann) saw fit to keep the deal under wraps until after the December league meetings.

Hal Lanigan, writing later for the *St. Louis Times*, suggested that Roger initiated the trade scenario on July 5 when he proposed coming to St. Louis as player/manager to Robison who "fell for it quickly."[47]

Further affirmation of Robison's agreement with Roger for "some time" can be found in Fred Lieb's 1944 history of the Cardinals. He told that McGraw offered Bresnahan to Robison "for a price" during the Giants' last 1908 trip to St. Louis, August 15–17. He suggested that Robison explore the idea with Bresnahan first. McGraw and Bresnahan concocted a plan to keep their scheme from the press. McGraw instructed Robison to take a room at the Marquette Hotel and register as John Doakes. Roger then inquired from the clerk for Doakes' room number which was on the third floor. To be even more elusive Roger took the elevator to the fourth floor, walked down to the third and entered Robison's room without knocking. Roger accepted the management job and Robison promised to meet his demands of salary, new players and free rein.[48] Robison and Bresnahan had secured what they wanted, and McGraw set about extracting his price.

At age 29, Roger Bresnahan had realized his ambition to manage a major league baseball team. He said of his new deal: "I am very thankful to Brush and McGraw for allowing me to get away and go to St. Louis. It has always been my ambition since I became a baseball player to someday become a manager, and the height of my ambition has been realized. My relations with the New York club and Manager McGraw have always been the friendliest and it is with regret and only pleasant memories that I leave New York."[49]

All was going Roger's way but the task before him was daunting; the Cardinals had finished dead last in the National League in 1908 with a 49–105 won-lost record.

Eighteen

"Something Besides Last Place Seems Certain to Ensue" (1909)[1]

Reaction to Roger Bresnahan's acquisition was positive and hopeful in St. Louis. Local sportswriter James Crusinberry opined, "It was a step that has set fans to thinking that a new era is about to dawn on the Cardinals in St. Louis, and it was a step that will put new life and confidence in the players themselves."[2] Another writer dubbed Bresnahan "Moses" suggesting he would lead the Cardinals out of the wilderness. The ever-confident Roger's own prediction was more temperate as he expected "to finish better than last place"[3] and suggested "It's some other team's turn for that cellar."[4]

Reaction to Roger Bresnahan's trade from other fronts varied. President and Owner M. Stanley Robison was criticized for breaking up his team and giving up "between $50,000 and $60,000 in players for his manager, probably the greatest amount ever paid for one player."[5] Robison argued, "You cannot push a team down lower than last place...."[6] Connie Mack, the Philadelphia manager, criticized the other principal: "McGraw can't afford to let Bresnahan go. He is the Giants' only catcher, best run getter, most exasperating base runner, and hardest worker and pluckiest performer."[7] Joe Tinker, the Cubs' Hall of Fame shortstop, was pleased with the trade because he felt that it eliminated the rival Giants as a pennant contender. Tinker paid tribute to Roger: "New York lost half of its fighting strength when Bresnahan was let go, and he can't be replaced. I want to say that Bresnahan is one of the greatest ball players that ever lived.... I claim Bresnahan was half of the Giants' strength."[8] Tinker further praised his opponent, "We always dreaded to see him at bat, and it was almost impossible to steal bases on him unless the pitcher gave us a long lead."[9]

Many others leveled criticism at McGraw and later blamed the Giants' failure to win the National League pennant in 1909, at least in significant part, on Roger's absence. Blanche McGraw wrote in her biography of her husband, "John never stood in the way of any player who had a chance to manage. He could hardly spare a catcher of Bresnahan's caliber in 1909, but no one was more deserving of the opportunity than the Duke."[10]

* * *

The new Cardinals would not need to be world-beaters to be successful—showing improvement could define their success. Knowing that the Cardinals could not be remade overnight, Crusinberry wrote about how the new manager's spirit could compensate for the subpar talent—"Roger Bresnahan is the sort of man who never gives up in a contest, and always sees that he gets everything coming to him. This kind of spirit is a splendid thing on which to build a ball club. It's probably just as good as having nine star players with no spirit."[11]

Knowing he had much to do before Opening Day, Roger quickly dove into his managerial career. His task was far more than managing the Cardinals on the field and being their primary catcher. Given free rein by Owner Robison, he was also charged with rebuilding a roster that had not performed well for years and had lost four of its better players in exchange for himself. He had experience observing the Cardinals—who had lost 400 games during the previous four seasons—to know that to be successful he must change the organization's culture. If he could induce his players to perform with the same enthusiasm, vigor, and never-quit attitude that he himself always had, the fans—who had turned out in smaller numbers than those of any other National League city during the previous two seasons—would be lured to the Cardinals.

Early in his reign, Roger opted to discontinue the annual pre-season series with the St. Louis Browns. His stated purpose was to devote more time to the younger Cardinals rather than grooming the veterans for the rivalry games. Even though it meant a loss of revenue, the owner agreed with his manager's call.[12] Roger also sent pitcher Art Fromme to Cincinnati to complete the three-team trade for himself.[13]

Upon his hiring, the Cardinals were the only major league club that had not secured a training camp for spring. Wishing to have Roger exercise "entire control," Robison left the matter to him.[14] Though suffering with a cold, Roger arrived in St. Louis on Monday, December 21, met with Robison and departed that evening for Little Rock, Arkansas, to inspect training grounds.[15] Roger returned to St. Louis and had breakfast with Robison at the Marquette Hotel on December 23. He reported to the owner that he had booked the Little Rock grounds and planned to depart for Arkansas about March 1 with approximately 35 men. Roger left St. Louis for Toledo that evening with plans to return following the holidays.

Roger's holidays in Toledo were not pleasant. His cold turned to pneumonia. He was so sick he was unable to sit up until December 31.[16] He remained "blanketed in bed" through the National Commission's annual meeting that began in Cincinnati on January 4. The quiet time gave him an opportunity to consider his manpower needs. Chief among them were a shortstop, outfielders, and pitchers.[17] He considered only three on the present roster as sure to stay—First Baseman Ed Konetchy, Outfielder Joe Delahanty and Second Baseman Billy Gilbert whom he would make his assistant. He intended to obtain young material, forgoing veteran players.[18]

Roger was well enough to leave Toledo on January 14 to visit John McGraw in New York in hopes of obtaining player help.[19] He returned with an option on the

Giants' Steve Evans who became a fixture in right field for the Cardinals.[20] While in New York Roger suggested a young catcher to his former manager—his 19-year-old brother Phil. Mac agreed to take him south for a trial[21] and quipped, "Got to have a Bresnahan on the Club."[22]

Another trade opportunity was the meeting to approve both the American and National league schedules beginning February 16 in Chicago.[23] While there, Roger received congratulations from many managers and owners seeing him for the first time since his appointment.[24] Despite tireless effort, Roger came away empty-handed.

Roger Bresnahan was acquired by Stanley Robison (right) in 1908 as the player-manager for his 1909 St. Louis Cardinals. Bresnahan, a veteran player but rookie manager, was given free rein and reversed the financial losses of the Cardinals. Harold Lanigan wrote in *Sporting News* in 1940 that Roger "always dressed well, favored rubies and owned, and always wore, several valuable ruby rings, a smart ruby watch fob and an equally smart ruby scarf pin" (courtesy Steve Steinberg).

Roger made his first significant player acquisition when he claimed Reds' outfielder Rube Ellis off waivers,[25] bringing the ire of Clark Griffith, his old friend and now the Cincinnati manager, upon himself. Griffith had intended to use Ellis in a trade but since Roger claimed him the proposed deal was killed. Griffith felt Bresnahan had violated baseball courtesy and said, "Someday he may need something this club would be in a position to give him, but all he will get will be the cold shoulder."[26] In spite of this admonition the Reds sold Rudy Hulswitt to the Cardinals three months later. Ellis became a fixture in Bresnahan's outfield for the next four seasons while Hulswitt helped at shortstop for two seasons.

The six weeks following the Chicago meeting saw Roger beating the bushes for players. Numerous newspaper reports revealed that he was extremely active in putting together a group of about 25 players, some of whom gathered in St. Louis on Monday, March 1, and departed for an overnight ride to Little Rock.[27] Bresnahan's Cardinals attracted an early following—"several hundred fans gathered at the station to cheer the club on its way."[28]

* * *

The train arrived at Little Rock late, so the players did not reach their accommodation at the new Capital Hotel until 9 o'clock on Tuesday morning. Uniforms were distributed before noon and the players were ordered to be ready to leave for practice at 2 o'clock. The field was at West End Park[29] which was more than two miles from the hotel but on the streetcar line. Roger expected his players to jog back to the hotel as they rounded into shape.[30]

Players were curious about the practice routine and wondered "just how Roger would do it." One remarked, "He showed us all before fifteen minutes had passed. It took him just that long to establish himself as a true leader." After that first practice Crusinberry wrote, "Roger rules with an iron hand. It took but one afternoon for the St. Louis Cardinals to realize that they have a manager at last who is boss in every sense of the word."[31]

Roger Bresnahan was a graduate of the McGraw school and brought those teachings to the Cardinals. Roger knew that the New York Giants worked harder and longer during spring practice than any other club. He also knew that "New York fans always saw the Giants in shape to play ball at top speed from the very first day of the season. They did it by hard work…." He professed demanding work in spring practice because "A victory in the early spring counts just as much as one in August"[32] and reasoned his team might win an early game or two it might not later in the season.

Roger held two practices each day. This encouraged his men to retire early, to rise early and to eat breakfast before going to work at nine o'clock. Roger felt the two-a-day practices and regular habits were keys to being ready to start the season. Morning practice was devoted to conditioning and fundamentals while the afternoons were devoted to game play pitting the regulars against the Yannigans for whom Roger played.

Total practice time encompassed about eight hours each day except Sunday and had a distinct "military strictness."[33] Rules prohibited smoking and drinking.[34] Roger included extensive use of medicine balls, "soccer football" and extra work for the "fat squad" in which Roger participated as he did in all the team's activities.[35] Fundamental drills emphasized bunting and hit-and-run practice but excluded the squeeze play which Roger disdained.[36] Practice was hard, regulation was strict, and, according to a player who was a Cardinal in 1908, there was "a whole lot of difference in the discipline of the club, this year," adding, "So far as I know, there are no soreheads on the team … the fellows all know that he [Bresnahan] does it for the team's good."[37]

The club engaged with another club for the first time on March 25 and defeated the Little Rock Travelers of the Southern League, 13–5.[38] The next day the same two teams squared off with Roger behind the bat. He was "rusty," but the Cards prevailed again, 11–6.[39] The Cardinals next played March 29 and lost to the Travelers 4–3. Roger expressed his disappointment in losing to a minor league team to his players.[40]

Cardinals' Owner Robison came to Little Rock on March 28[41] and was followed by John McGraw and the New York Giants who were to play the Little Rock team.

Robison, Bresnahan and McGraw met in hopes of the Cardinals obtaining players from the Giants. According to *Sporting Life*, "It is stated on good authority that most of McGraw's excess players will be offered to Roger Bresnahan.... It is believed that this arrangement is a sequel to the deal"[42] that brought Roger to St. Louis. Two players were offered but Roger was not interested.[43] Even though this pair of Giants might have helped the Cardinals in 1909 they did not fit Roger's stated criteria of young players he could develop into mainstays of a championship caliber club over the three years of his contract.[44]

The final game in Little Rock was played March 31 and the Cardinals rebounded 5–0.[45] The team then headed for Memphis to begin playing their way north for their Opening Day date in Chicago with their manager's admonition to "play every exhibition game as though it were to count in the race for the pennant."[46]

The Cardinals took care of business in Memphis by beating the Southern League's Turtles 5–0 on April 1 and 4–3 the following day.[47]

At Paducah, Kentucky, the Cardinals won twice in two days over the outmanned Indians of the Kitty League.[48] Moving on, the Cardinals beat the River Rats of the Central League 18–6 at Evansville, Indiana, on April 5.[49] Another win came at the expense of another Central League team the next day as the Terre Haute Stags fell 5–1.[50] Taking on the Columbus, Ohio Senators, the Cards netted another win in a game played in a "chilling gale" on April 7.[51] Dayton was victimized the next day. The Central League Veterans lost10–2.[52]

The tour's remaining games were with member teams (as Columbus was) of the near-major American Association.[53] At Louisville, the Colonels were twice beaten by identical 6–2 scores on April 10 and 11.[54]

Roger was looking forward to the Cardinals' next stop—Toledo, his hometown. Two games were on tap there with the Mud Hens on April 12 and 13.

The *Toledo Daily Blade's* account of the first game spoke to the contrast in spirit of the two clubs opining that it was "painful" for the local fans to witness the contest as the mettle of Roger's boys far outclassed that of the Mud Hens. The native son was given credit, "Roger is the big magnet that draws all the enthusiasm out." The Cardinals won handily 8–1.[55] The *Blade* pointed out that Roger was far more than the magnificent player they had watched as he was a man of many hats because, besides playing, "He was selected as manager for a tail end team of 1908, its ranks riddled, and its fighting spirit gone. He had to dig in, get players, infuse life and direct operations."[56] The local writer understood the breadth and scope of Roger's undertaking.

The second game at Toledo was cancelled because of wet grounds,[57] giving the Cardinals a day of rest before opening the National League season against the Cubs on April 14.

The Cardinals finished their exhibition tour with a wonderful but meaningless record—losing only one game to teams of lesser rank. But they did win them and showed positive signs and some promise but as *St. Louis Post-Dispatch* Sporting Editor, John E. "Ed" Wray, wrote: "...nothing but the actual test [championship games] can tell about the club. On paper the team has lost strength from last year. But the improvement in tone of the members, enhanced by the inspiration of Bresnahan, to say nothing of his intrinsic baseball ability, promises results. Roger has every man on his club with him and, with the proper spirit and the McGraw tactics of hustle and work with which Roger is saturated, something besides last place seems certain to ensue."[58]

Nineteen

"Roger Bresnahan Is the Most Popular Man in St. Louis" (1909)[1]

The St. Louis Cardinals of 1909 were in excellent physical shape and infused with a fresh fighting spirit but short on talent and experience. Major concerns were a weakness at shortstop, a need for another front-line pitcher and a capable outfielder as well as overall team hitting. Strengths included just two first-rate players—Catcher Roger Bresnahan and First Baseman Ed Konetchy. Bresnahan was a major plus but was untested as a manager. The hope was that the team's rigorous spring practice and conditioning would give the Cardinals an early advantage and result in a fast start which would allow the young team to develop over the course of the long season.

The National League schedule, however, was not designed to give St. Louis a fast start. The Cardinals opened with a four-game series at Chicago on April 14 against the three-time National League pennant-winning and two-time defending World's Series champion Cubs.

The Cardinals team that was presented for the opening game included seven starters who were holdovers from the 1908 Cardinals. The other two were himself and Right Fielder Steve Evans who Roger had obtained. Roger had the experience of 10 major league seasons while the remaining eight members of the first-day lineup had a combined 18.

Nonetheless, the Cardinals proved to be a "worthy opponent for the world beaters" but managed only three hits and fell 3–1. Johnny Lush pitched well but was outdone by the veteran Cub Oral Overall. Roger caught and batted third. He had a bunt single while Joe Delahanty had the Cardinals' other two hits and scored their only run. Chicago's *Inter Ocean* commented, "The opening round showed that the Cardinals were ready to give battle," and "The McGraw spirit was evident from the start of yesterday's game until the last man was out."[2]

The Cubs prevailed again the next day when, after the Cardinals had assumed a 4–3 lead, they knocked the Cardinals' Fred Beebe out of the box in the seventh inning and went on to a 10–4 win. St. Louis managed just six hits. According to Sportswriter I.E. "Cy" Sanborn of the *Chicago Tribune*, the turning point in the contest came when Bresnahan was wrongfully ejected by Umpire Steve Kane. In the bottom of the sixth inning Kane called Artie Hofman, who was trying to return to first base, safe on a play that should have ended the inning. Sanborn called it "a long distance call which will have to be awarded the world's record," and noted that "Bresnahan rushed at Kane with so much language in a bunch that the umpire ordered him from the field of battle.... The fans who knew Hofman couldn't be safe unless he wore fingers as long as his legs, sided with Roger and roasted Kane to the finish." Sanborn went on to say that following the loss of his manager *and* his catcher, "Beebe lost his grip."[3] Even though correct, Roger's action was costly to his team, and he would repeat it 10 more times over the course of the season as "He battled the umpires even more furiously on his own than when he was McGraw's fighting lieutenant in New York."[4]

The Cardinals' good play returned, and their fortunes changed for the next two games at Chicago which they won 3–1 and 4–1 thanks to some good pitching by Slim Sallee and Charlie Rhodes.[5] The *St. Louis Post-Dispatch* reported, "The Cubs played faultless ball, but they were simply out hustled."[6] The upstart Cardinals headed for Cincinnati having broken even with the World's Champions.

The first contest at Cincinnati was played on Sunday, April 18 before the largest crowd ever to attend a baseball game in the Queen City—19,187. Even though "Bresnahan's men put up a tempestuous battle" the Reds prevailed 5–3.[7] The Reds won again the next day 3–2.[8] Following a rainout the Cardinals won 9–6.[9] That win snapped a Cincinnati five-game win streak and sent the Cardinals on their way home with a 3–4 record.

Despite gloomy and raw weather, spirits of 10,000[10] or more were high for the Cardinals season home inaugural. League Park had been refurbished and seating capacity increased but the condition of the field itself suffered because of recent rains. But the festive day went on—a band played, Mayor Kreissman pitched to Bresnahan, and floral horseshoes abounded. Roger was welcomed and presented with a silver loving cup engraved, "Presented by the Sons of Erin of St. Louis to Roger P. Bresnahan, St. Louis Cardinals at Opening Game, April 22, 1909, Caed Mille Falthe [translated from Gaelic: A Hundred Thousand Welcomes]." The game itself brought joy to the players and fans—for a time. The Cardinals held a 3–2 lead after seven innings but a Cubs' five-run rally in the next frame ended the fun and gave the Cubs a 7–3 win.[11]

The Cardinals turned the tables the next day 6–3 but lost two more to the Cubs before welcoming the Pittsburg Pirates on Monday, April 26. The Cardinals threw everything they had at the Pirates who prevailed 4–3 in a "clean, snappy game"[12] that took 12 innings and featured "one of the most exciting finishes ever seen"[13] in St. Louis' League Park. The Cardinals tied the game by scoring with two out in the bottom of the ninth. In the bottom of the 10th, Roger crashed into Pittsburg catcher George Gibson when sliding into home while attempting to score the winning run. "Two decidedly close decisions" at the plate followed—one in the bottom of the 11th denied the Cardinals a run and the win. The other in the top of the 12th allowed the winning margin to the Pirates.[14]

St. Louis lost more than the game. Roger was injured during his collision with Gibson and was advised by Dr. Max Starkloff "not to play for at least a week."[15] He suffered an internal injury and a spike wound to his foot.[16] He was compelled to finish the game as the Cardinals' bench had been depleted of position players. He sat out the next seven contests.

Limping and still in pain, Bresnahan donned his uniform two days later to manage.[17] On Sunday, May 2 the Cardinals split a doubleheader with Cincinnati before 16,000 and he felt well enough to get ejected for arguing with Umpire Bill Klem.[18]

While fans kept an eye on him, Manager Bresnahan intently watched the action from the Cardinals' dugout in 1911. With his bat in hand, he looked ready to fulfill his role as player (Bain News Service, Publisher. Roger Bresnahan, St. Louis, NL baseball, 1911. Photograph. https://www.loc.gov/item/2014690047/).

On May 5 Bresnahan's Kids began a three-week 22-game road trip that included stops in all seven other National League cities. The St. Louis record stood at 7–11 with the Cardinals in last place by percentage points but only three-and-a-half out of first place—a good showing considering all their games had been against teams that would finish the season in the league's first division. The schedule did not ease a bit with the first stops in Pittsburg and Chicago. The Cardinals won two of those five and Roger returned to the lineup. The tour progressed to Brooklyn where Roger—despite his team's May 12, 10–0 shellacking of the Superbas—protested Umpire Bill Klem's calling of balls and strikes. He used unbecoming language that was overheard by some of the spectators. Complaints were lodged with Brooklyn's President Charles Ebbets who relayed them to acting National League President John Heydler who suspended Bresnahan for three days.[19]

On the heels of a four-game sweep in Brooklyn, the Cardinals met the Giants at the Polo Grounds. Roger was honored in pre-game ceremonies and gifted with a nearly three-foot tall silver loving cup that was encased in a floral replica of itself that was taller than Bresnahan and engraved "To our pal, Roger Bresnahan, from his New York admirers, Polo Grounds, May 24, 1909."[20] He was also presented with a "resolution containing a list of names that looked like a superlatively edited list of 'Who's Who' in New York politics, theatrics and sport."[21] The 10,000 fans in attendance "let no chance slip by to voice their friendship for the visiting manager."[22]

In the game itself, the Cardinals faced the great Christy Mathewson and came out on top 3–1 due to two costly Giants' errors and the fine pitching of St. Louis' Johnny Lush.[23] The "applause he [Roger] received the first time he went to bat lasted five minutes. Hand clapping also came from the press box...."[24] It was a shocker for Mathewson who had beaten St. Louis in 24 straight games.[25] Unbelievably, the Cardinals rested in sixth place with a 15–18 record and percentage points ahead of New York.[26]

Further honors were heaped on Roger that evening during a formal banquet given for him at Kennelly's restaurant on Broadway.[27] He was presented with a large silver punch bowl and cups with the inscription "Presented to Roger Bresnahan as a Token of Esteem of a Few Friends" along with the names of 33 of those friends.[28]

Roger had a chance to extend the storybook tale of his New York return when he came to bat in the eighth inning of the second game with his team losing 1–0, the bases full and two outs. With a 3–1 count, he took a pitch, threw down his bat had headed to first base. Umpire Jim Johnstone called the pitch a strike and called Roger back to the plate where he, after fouling off a pitch, took another for a called strike. The Cardinals lost 1–0.[29]

The Giants prevailed again the next day before the Cardinals headed for home, by way of Cincinnati and Pittsburg. The final game in Cincinnati was a laugher for the Cardinals as they piled up eleven first-inning runs and cruised to a 12–2 win. The victim of the outburst was Roger's long-time friend, Bob Ewing, who started but did not retire a batter. Roger did not play but was in the coaching box doing anything he could to prolong his team's big inning. He was penalized for his words, but the *Cincinnati Enquirer* took exception to the umpire's doing so and approved of Roger's actions: "Umpire [Cy] Rigler was pretty strict in enforcing the coaching rules. He put Roger off the lines in the first inning for doing nothing but call Bob Ewing's attention to the fact that a few pitchers were being sent to warm up. Bres was putting a lot of life into the game, and that is what the fans like to see. It is a question if the umpires do not go too far in demanding serene quiet on the field."[30] Roger was not ejected but restricted to the dugout.

The final game of the long road trip was scheduled for June 1 in Pittsburg but was rained out. Roger left immediately after the postponement was announced for Toledo to consult with a surgeon that night because of his lameness.[31] The *St. Louis Post-Dispatch* added details suggesting Roger "...is not a well man by any means. He has not been himself for over six weeks as he met with a serious accident about that time that has been bothering him ever since...."[32] Six weeks prior to this revelation is about the time of Roger's home-plate collision with George Gibson that reportedly caused internal injury and a spike wound to the foot. No mention of lingering effects of that injury had been mentioned until this but *Sporting Life* added Roger

May 24, 1909, was Roger Bresnahan's first appearance at the Polo Grounds after being traded. Roger (center with arms folded) received a silver loving cup from Monte Ward (hat in hand), former Giant player and manager. The cup was inscribed, "To our Pal, Roger Bresnahan, from his New York admirers..." (1909. Photograph. https://www.loc.gov/item/2001704417/).

was "rather lame, owing to an injury sustained in New York."[33] Roger rejoined the Cardinals in St. Louis in time to begin a homestand against the Giants on June 4.

* * *

After their first 40 games the Cardinals' record stood at 17–23, a slight two-game improvement over 1908 and found them in seventh place, one position better. The latter caused a St. Louis headline proclaiming the team's style of play had "rescued the Cardinals from last place." Crusinberry supported and had written favorably from the time of Roger's appointment, and now was a believer in his methods and gave him "credit for detecting early where the strength of his team lay." He wrote that Roger took advantage of his team's overall speed and ability to hit by making frequent use of the hit and run play which has "caused terror to every pitcher in the National League" and pointed out that the defense was improved by the purchase of Shortstop Rudy Hulswitt from Cincinnati. He further suggested more starting pitching was a continuing need but difficult to remedy.[34]

Owner Stanley Robison was delighted with Bresnahan's performance and with the results and called him "the most progressive leader, not to say the most aggressive player, in the major leagues to-day." He noted that attendance was increased eighty percent as compared to the first four weeks of 1908 and predicted that he would "make a fortune this year."[35] Part of his optimism was because Roger "was one of the best drawing cards on the road."[36] The St. Louis club sought to protect against the loss of his services by insuring his life for $50,000. The policy's five-year term exceeded the length of Bresnahan's contract by two years.[37]

Sporting Life also noted the rejuvenated Cardinals and said despite being forced to meet the topliners from the very beginning of the season, had "fought such teams as Chicago, World's Series champions, and Pittsburg, near champions, off their feet." The same publication featured a front-page photograph and short biography of Roger and commented he "has made good and has his team now fighting to the last ditch for every game."[38]

Roger was making baseball news in New York as well. Typical of numerous reports were: When the Giants let Bresnahan go they "threw away a fortune … and are not the same"[39] without him and "the loss the Giants sustained when they lost Bresnahan is becoming more evident."[40] The *New York Sun* opined, "With Bresnahan in a New York uniform McGraw's men would have been higher up than they are in the race…."[41] New York fans began to realize that "Roger Bresnahan was a part of the Giants' backbone and stamina in years gone by."[42]

Roger may have been pleased with his team's progress but was wisely a realist when he said I "will have a first-class team within two years."[43]

* * *

The homestand started with the New York Giants on June 5. Despite his various injuries, Roger was in the lineup and made a pair of hits helping the Cardinals to an early three-run lead which they could not hold, disappointing the enthusiastic homecoming crowd of more than 10,000.[44] Two days later Roger "flew into a fury" over the calling of balls and strikes by Umpire Harry Truby in the ninth inning of a 2–0 loss to Brooklyn.[45] The outburst resulted in his second three-game suspension of the season.[46]

Roger was not idle during his suspension. He often used both scheduled and added days he was forced to be away from the field for team building. With only three pitchers he could count on—Johnny Lush, Slim Sallee and Fred Beebe—he was desperate for mound help. He lamented that other National League clubs were reluctant to release their excess players to him either through trade or outright purchase. He cited the owners' "stinginess and short-sighted business policy for the fact that his team is not making a better showing than it is…." He noted that the most successful clubs—Chicago, New York, and Pittsburg—were talent-rich but their refusal to deal caused the league's disparity. Perhaps the possibility of success and competition by Roger's Cardinals outweighed the benefits of a National League strengthened from top to bottom in the minds of the other owners. And it was not just Bresnahan who was affected in this way. His former mate, Frank Bowerman, now manager of the Boston club, was being shunned similarly.[47] Left little choice, Roger looked elsewhere for players who could help—the minor leagues.

During his suspension Bresnahan and Owner Robison visited Decatur, Illinois, and took in a Three-I League[48] game. They liked what they saw and purchased three of the local players on the spot for $2,500.[49] Only Pitcher Grover Lowdermilk ever played for Roger, but he did so immediately, and he lasted in the majors for nine years. A week later Roger bought Pitcher Steve Melter, who also provided immediate help, from Sioux City of the Western League for $3,000.[50] Two more pitchers were brought into the Cardinals fold during Roger's mid–June buying spree—Bob Harmon from Shreveport of the Texas League[51] and Les Backman from the Ohio League's Portsmouth team.[52] Both made early-summer debuts for St. Louis.

Roger returned from his suspension and played regularly during the rest of the home stand, which ended with a disappointing 8–14 mark. A 3–2 win, with Roger catching, at Chicago on Sunday, July 4 began a road trip. The next day's game at Chicago was postponed and, without warning, Roger left his team for his Toledo home. The *St. Louis Post Dispatch* reported his leaving and told the reason was a "mystery" and that he would probably be awaiting the team when it arrived in Boston following the Chicago series. The *Chicago Tribune* suggested Roger's mission was "to scout around Ohio for ballplayers."[53] Other reports clouded the reason for Roger's absence suggesting that he was serving yet another suspension.[54] The reasons for Roger's absence of more than a week and his whereabouts are unclear and confusing because of conflicting and vague reports. A summary of National League 1909 suspensions published in 1910 confirms that this absence was likely his third suspension of the season but does not identify the cause or length of the penalty.[55]

With Roger away, the Cardinals lost three of the four games. His return righted the ship—St. Louis won three of five games in Philadelphia but lost Roger as a player. During the final game of the series on July 15 he injured his right shoulder when he "tried to make a snap throw to second base."[56] Doctors diagnosed a torn ligament and suggested Roger's playing career was threatened. Roger "expressed his fear that he was permanently out of the game."[57] He received treatment from the celebrated non-physician John D. "Bonesetter" Reese,[58] and returned to regular play on August 24 but his injured limb troubled him for the rest of the season.

The Cardinals and Roger followed with three wins in five tries at New York. Slim Sallee won two and young Bob Harmon beat Bugs Raymond in a 16-inning marathon with both going the distance.[59] "Roger Bresnahan was bent on doing his best to accomplish the undoing of the New Yorks for his team played high-class ball from start to finish, and ... played with aggressiveness and vigor worthy of a championship team."[60]

Returning home, the Cardinals won six of ten from Chicago, Boston and Philadelphia and pushed their record to 40–51 and fifth place on August 6—a nine-game improvement over 1908.

The next team into St. Louis was the Giants which avenged the embarrassment laid upon them just three weeks before by humiliating the Cardinals in five straight games, the last by a score of 19–3. Roger was ejected and suspended, once again during the lopsided defeat.[61] The losses started the Cardinals on a losing spiral that finally culminated with a 15-game losing streak that ended on September 23 with a doubleheader loss to the same Giants.

* * *

Having only three dependable pitchers was not enough in 1909 or in any era since. The big three were Johnny Lush, Slim Sallee and Fred Beebe. On the season, the trio accounted for more than half the Cardinals' innings and recorded two-thirds of their wins. Of the remaining eleven pitchers on staff, nine were rookies.

Complicating the pitching woes was the curious case of Sallee who found himself in serious trouble with his no-nonsense manager because of unauthorized and prolonged absences from the team. On August 9, during the five-game series with the Giants, Roger acted by suspending his pitcher and fining him $100. Sallee had been particularly effective against those Giants so his loss could not have happened at a worse time, but Roger had no choice—Slim was not there. This was a repeat performance. Roger had levied a $50 fine earlier in the season for a similar offense.[62] Sallee returned to the lineup on August 12 and pitched the entire 12 innings of a 6–6 tie with Brooklyn. It was the hottest day of the summer, but Roger left him in the game "determined to make the boy pay for running away"[63] Sallee then blew late-inning leads in his next three starts and was suspended, again, on September 1, for failure to stay in condition—the root cause of his issues being "boozing."[64] The term of this leave was 30 days.[65] Sallee did not pitch again in 1909.

Bresnahan's own play and absence from the field contributed to the Cardinals' late season swoon. He was never the same following the July 15 injury to his throwing shoulder and made only 25 appearances the rest of the way with just 11 of those as catcher. He was sorely missed behind the bat by his young and inexperienced pitchers. His 72 games played, and .244 batting average were the lowest of his career.

Being lost as a player because of injury was unavoidable but Roger was absent from the field a great deal because of an avoidable reason—his ungovernable temper. With Roger always intense and focused on winning, his temper got the best of him more than it ever had or would during the 1909 season. He was ejected eleven times and suspended four times which caused him to be away from his club for as many as fourteen days.[66] While he was away his team "floundered around like a bunch of lost sheep."[67] He was rightfully and roundly scolded by the press. One writer pointed out "His presence is so valuable on the field that he should never put himself, as he does frequently, in position to be banished by the umpire."[68]

Roger was very busy during August, continuing to sign minor league players and, despite the reluctance of most teams to deal with the Cardinals, managing a pair of trades. He "changed the makeup of the team entirely, not with the idea of bettering it for the present time, but of procuring material that would develop the future."[69] He traded Chappy Charles to the Reds for Mike Mowrey who proved to be a valuable addition.[70] In a deal that soured, he obtained Jap Barbeau and Alan Storke from the Pirates for Bobby Byrne.[71] Neither Barbeau or Storke contributed to the Cardinals' cause or any other major league team after 1909, but Byrne played eight more major league seasons.

"Overwrought Cardinals in Need of a Rest" and "Strain of Hard Work Under Bresnahan Is Telling on the Willing Youngsters"[72] were *St. Louis Post-Dispatch* headlines the day following the 19–3 debacle against the Giants. The story suggested that the young Cardinals were exhausted following their climb to fifth place.

Roger designed lineups during the latter part of the 1909 season for player auditions, development, healing, and rest. He chose to bench the injured Mowery, Hulswitt and himself in favor of the new men.

The way was extremely long and rough—the Cardinals won just seven of their next 47 games and fell to seventh place by September 23. They won 7 of their last 15 games and finished with five more wins than in 1908, missing sixth place by a half game.

* * *

The Cardinals' fast start and brief attainment of fifth place on two occasions prompted high praise for Roger Bresnahan. He was acclaimed "the most popular man in St. Louis."[73] Other descriptors included "New York fans think Roger has made good,"[74] "the equal of any baseball general in the country"[75] and "Bresnahan is a great leader."[76]

By season's end, some negativity began to creep in. A St. Louis writer proclaimed Roger "in hot water."[77] *Sporting Life* reported on a McGraw interview in which the Giant skipper said, "That's a bad team Bresnahan has in the field right now," adding that front-line players not in the lineup are "missed."[78] An *American News* story went so far as to suggest Bresnahan did not "have a friend in St. Louis."[79]

For the two men most connected to the Cardinals organization, Owner Robison and Manager Bresnahan, the season was a success. The immediate and most notable accomplishment was St. Louis did *not* finish last in the National League as was nearly universally predicted.

Robison was happy with the upturn of his business—Cardinals' attendance increased by nearly fifty percent and the club turned a profit of about $75,000.[80] St. Louis Browns Manager Jimmy McAleer noticed in early July what was going on at Sportsman's Park, "the Cardinals on Sundays used to get our overflow, now we get theirs, Bresnahan having made a National League city of St. Louis."[81] Even though the Cardinals faded after McAleer's observation, "the fans kept up their trips to the League Park grounds to see what Bresnahan was doing with his new players."[82]

Bresnahan was "fairly well satisfied with his first season as a major league manager."[83]

Especially during the second half of the season and after seeing his first team perform, he sacrificed winning now for the future. Unable to secure veteran players via trade he sought out and acquired promising young players he hoped to develop. He felt that the foundation had been laid for a bright future.

Sporting Life was sometimes critical but offered overall approval: "Bresnahan, in his efforts at team management, scored a decided success, as he infused aggressiveness and ambition and kept his team keyed up nearly all season … the results produced were, if not particularly brilliant, at least encouraging for the future."[84]

Twenty

"Bresnahan Shows Himself to Be a Great Baseball General" (1910)[1]

Roger Bresnahan's off seasons were no longer his to spend as he pleased. Winter months were free of the regular season's daily grind and much of his time could be spent at home, but his managerial role continued. His major focus was improvement of the St. Louis Cardinals by upgrading its talent. He was given a free hand. The owner "bade him to go out and secure whatever players he chose ... and anything he suggested was sanctioned by Mr. Robison."[2] He learned that other clubs generally "were not given to helping one another through trades."[3] He constantly had an eye out for promising youngsters playing in the minor leagues who he could purchase or other major league teams' castoffs he could claim from waivers.

John McGraw was busy too. He was rebuilding his New York Giants and wanted Roger's Ed Konetchy to play first base. It was rumored in November that he offered Fred Merkle and Buck Herzog for him. Roger's response was definite—"never even dreamed in letting the Greek champion go to New York."[4] In a separate move, McGraw wanted to send Bill O'Hara, his 1909 centerfielder, to the minors but Roger "was the only National League manager who refused to waive claim and O'Hara became the property of the Cardinals."[5]

Roger and Robison attended the National League annual meeting in New York in mid–December hoping to deal. No trades materialized though McGraw again made a pitch for Konetchy, upping his offer to four or five players. Roger held firm.[6]

Following Christmas, Roger attended the American Association annual meeting in Chicago. There he frankly commented on the state of his Cardinals, "I've got a rotten club, but I have some good players." He explained that he needed "a few others of major league caliber to make up a good team."[7]

Roger's New Year's resolution for 1910 was to catch all Cardinals' games during the season because he felt he could "get better results out of the players by working behind the bat every day."[8] His goal was lofty but worthy considering the poor play of his team during his many absences in 1909. He started training by early January to lose "superfluous weight."[9]

Roger continued his quest for players through the winter. After several meetings with Manager Clark Griffith of Cincinnati, his persistence paid off with a major trade. Fred Beebe, his most valuable pitcher, went to the Reds along with Infielder

Alan Storke in exchange for Second Baseman Miller Huggins, Pitcher Frank Corridon, and Outfielder Rebel Oakes.[10] Huggins and Corridon each had six years as major league starters while Oakes was the Reds regular center fielder in 1908 and a promising young player. Some questioned letting Beebe go but Roger answered by buying the contract of right-hander Vic Willis from the Pittsburg Pirates.[11] Willis was a veteran of 12 major-league seasons during which he had won 240 games including 22 in 1908. In total, the two deals netted the Cardinals a starting second baseman, a starting center fielder and two veteran pitchers for one player given up. Also added to the pitching staff, for the purchase price of $4,500, was Rube Geyer who won 20 games for Columbus of the American Association in 1909.[12]

Roger declined to predict the Cardinals' finish for the upcoming season but said: "I do believe we'll win more games than last year and play a whole lot better baseball."[13]

Spring practice was scheduled for nearly a month at Little Rock, Arkansas, followed by a series of exhibition games with American Association teams at St. Louis.[14]

Passing through St. Louis on the way to his training camp, John McGraw "expressed satisfaction at knowing Roger Bresnahan, his former lieutenant, will go into the National League race with the Cardinals a much-improved team over that of last season."[15]

Bresnahan had about 44 players (half of them pitchers) reserved for 1910 and ordered them to report to St. Louis by March 6 or directly to the Little Rock training site the following day.[16] Several players arrived a day or two early and took in a view of their League Park home that was being refurbished by the replacement of bleachers which increased capacity to 24,000.

The playing surface was upgraded by moving the diamond.

* * *

The Bresnahanigans[17] were given a hearty send-off from St. Louis and were greeted by "quite a gathering at the station" on their arrival for a second straight year at Little Rock.[18]

Practices were twice daily with intrateam games in the afternoon. Morning sessions included the usual baseball drills, running and the medicine ball with Roger taking part with his men every step of the way and keeping his eye on the youngsters. Roger later added "soccer football" to the routine.[19] There was no mention of the shoulder injury that was so bothersome the previous season. One correspondent wrote, "Bresnahan insists on keeping up the same earnestness in practice as in championship battles."[20] Another reported, "he swears a blue streak" and "while he is severe in his handling of the kids at bat and in the field, he is kindly and generous to them at all times in general."[21]

Roger announced a modified spring schedule on March 19. Following games with the Cleveland Naps at Little Rock on March 23, 24 and 25, the team would immediately return to St. Louis and play team practice games there Easter Saturday and Sunday (March 26 and 27).[22] The team would then practice at home and then entertain Milwaukee, Louisville and St. Paul beginning April 1.[23] The National League opening game was scheduled for April 14, also in St. Louis.

The American League Cleveland second team plus Cy Young arrived as scheduled and provided Roger's team with outside competition for the first time. The Naps administered a taste of reality to the Cardinals winning all three games 3–2, 4–3 and 8–0.[24]

Home at League Park the next day, the Regulars beat the Yannigans before 7,500[25] fans and did so again on Easter with about 9,000[26] looking on. The Milwaukee Brewers, whose Manager John McCloskey was Roger's predecessor as Cardinals' boss, came in for two games the following weekend. Both were rained out further delaying the Cardinals' development.[27]

The St. Paul Saints arrived for three games in three days beginning Friday, April 8. The first game drew 3,500 fans and was lost 3–2.[28] With one out in the bottom of the ninth inning slugger Ed Konetchy momentarily thrilled the crowd but was thrown out at the plate attempting to score a home run.[29] The Cardinals won the next day 5–2[30] but managed only two hits in losing the series finale 2–0.[31]

The team announced roster cuts on Saturday, April 9, trimming their roster to 24 players.[32] Surprisingly, Roger kept only eight pitchers. Three of those making the cut were not with the team. Third Baseman Mike Mowery and Catcher Jack Bliss were recovering from injuries but were expected to report when ready.[33] The other, Harry "Slim" Sallee, was a much-needed pitcher and was again in trouble with his manager. He reported late to spring practice but was forgiven and then "turned an ankle when working with the team." He then reportedly was injured again "when his foot slipped in another manner" and, a week later, was still away from the team. Roger, frustrated with his talented left-hander, fined him a whopping $500 for "breaking club rules."

Two exhibition games remained. The first, on April 11, was rained out.[34] The next day the Cardinals beat Louisville 6–4.[35] With two days left before the games that counted began the Cardinals were not as ready as their manager had hoped they would be. Though conditioning was adequate, missed days robbed time needed to hone pitching and hitting skills. Roger's guidance may have been inadequate for some players simply because the manager was spread thin because of the large number in camp.

Ready or not, the regular season was upon them.

* * *

The 1910 edition of the St. Louis Cardinals was created by Roger Bresnahan adding acquired players to carryovers from 1909. Just six players who were with the Cardinals when Roger arrived remained with the team. Comparing Opening Day lineups reveals a significant improvement in experience—total years of major league experience, not including Roger, increased from 18 to 34.

As in Roger's rookie managerial year, his Opening Day opponent was the World's Champions. This time it was the Pittsburg Pirates. The *Pittsburg Press* announced the opening of the campaign, "With fair weather conditions prevailing, with the Pittsburg World's Champions, the greatest aggregation of diamond stars on earth as the opponents of Roger Bresnahan's revivified Cardinals crew, and with interest among fandom at white heat, the National League baseball season will be opened at League Park...."[36]

The Cardinals out hit the Pirates 8–7 but were outscored by the visitors 5–1 before nearly 20,000 spectators. The *St. Louis Star* called the Cardinals' play "creditable."[37] St. Louis won the next day 6–5[38] and, following a postponement, St. Louis lost the series finale, 4–2.

The Chicago Cubs were next into St. Louis for three games, the first two of which were not played due to unfavorable weather giving Roger an opportunity to tend to club business. One such item was the continuing saga of Harry Sallee who had presented at a hospital "unconscious and raving."[39] Roger had seen him "soused" and it was reported that he had the "DTs."[40] Now recovering and "again on his good behavior" he was taken back by Roger.

This Charles Condon photograph was taken at the Polo Grounds during Bresnahan's tenure as St. Louis' manager and player, 1909–1912. Both Hall of Famers, Umpire Hank O'Day and Roger Bresnahan were together for all of Roger's 16 seasons (1902–1915) in the National League. Umpire O'Day tossed Roger on six occasions (courtesy Roger M. Bresnahan).

The last game of the homestand had a bizarre ending. Both teams had six o'clock trains to catch and agreed to stop play at five o'clock. In the bottom of the seventh inning St. Louis had scored twice to close the score to 5–4 and had the bases loaded when Umpire Hank O'Day saved the Cubs and dashed the Cardinals' hope by announcing that it was five o'clock.[41]

* * *

The Cardinals began their first road trip of the season on April 21 at Pittsburg where they were humbled three times. While there, Third Baseman Mike Mowery, recovered from knee surgery, reported.[42] He was in the lineup two days later. Roger laid off catching for the first two games, scuttling his goal of catching every game of the season.

St. Louis won three of seven of

the remaining road games in Chicago and Cincinnati. Roger was surprised before the final game at Cincinnati on May 2 when he met Jim McGinnis, the lone umpire who was not a regular league official. Roger was presented with a telegram from the recently elected National League President Thomas J. Lynch[43] naming McGinnis as umpire for this game because the league *forgot* to send regular umpires. McGinnis had been secured by the Reds at the request of Lynch. Roger told Cincinnati Manager Griffith he smelled liquor on McGinnis' breath and thought he was drunk and suggested that they each name a player to umpire or do it themselves. Griffith refused both offers wanting to comply with Lynch's directive.[44]

The game proceeded with McGinnis stationed behind the pitcher. Bob Bescher singled but was caught napping off first. He dashed for second base and was called safe on a close play. Bresnahan protested. Following a walk, Dick Hoblitzell hit a ground ball to Shortstop Arnold Hauser who threw to third. Bescher was again ruled safe. Bresnahan and other Cardinals protested. After one inning the Reds led 5–1.

Roger was scolded by some of the press of both Cincinnati and St. Louis for his actions following the first inning saying he made a "silly farce" and a "joke"[45] of the game by using position players as pitchers. The strategy worked rather well—his pitchers gave up seven runs in three innings while his position players surrendered two runs in five innings. The *Cincinnati Enquirer* admitted the "decision on Bescher at second base might have been wrong."[46]

Roger protested the game to Lynch "alleging that Umpire McGinnis was incompetent."[47] He proposed a remedy of "no contest,"[48] a replay. President Herrmann of the Reds also protested saying Bresnahan's actions made the game a "ridiculous exhibition."[49] Lynch responded to Bresnahan, "McGinnis had full authority to umpire this game by my orders … therefore, your protest cannot be considered, and the game stands as played." He added, "I would not hesitate to inflict on you the severest penalty the law allows [but for] …the failure to have regular umpires on hand was due to a mistake pure and simple by this office." Further, he lectured Roger on how he should behave, twice mentioning his "good salary." Particularly grating to Roger was Lynch's directing him how to redeem himself—"get in the game and catch every day, and by your actions and deportment on the field help put the St. Louis club where it belongs"[50]

Roger responded to Lynch: "…Your advice about my getting into the game is a charge of bad faith on my part and a remark unworthy of a gentleman holding the high office you do.… I want you to understand that I am for St. Louis and the St. Louis club first, last and all the time. I shall continue to fight for the rights we are entitled to until such time as the owner of the club finds it advisable to dispense with my services."[51]

Roger's behavior marked a milestone event in his development as a manager—he controlled his temper. He played out an "already lost" game saving his pitchers for another day and filed a protest. He avoided an ejection and possible suspension.

The Cardinals ended their trip with a 4–10 record, tied for seventh place in the eight-team National League.

* * *

Playing at home on May 4 to start a three-week stay, the Cardinals topped the Reds 12–3 amassing 12 runs in the first three innings. The teams were honored by the presence of President William Howard Taft.[52] Before the game Harry Sallee worked out with the team and appeared to be himself following a week-long hospital stay. Roger reinstated him and lifted the $500 fine.[53]

After losing the next two games to the Reds, the Cardinals took two of three from Boston and then welcomed John McGraw and the New York Giants whom they had not defeated in St. Louis since 1908. There was no team that Roger would rather beat. Beat them he did and in convincing style—handing Christy Mathewson his first defeat of the season by driving him from the box with eight runs in the second inning.[54] Harry Sallee made his first appearance of the season in game two and rewarded his manager's support with a 9–3 win.[55] Game three of the series was on a Sunday and 15,500 turned out to watch a third straight win over the Giants.[56]

The win was a costly one as Roger was lost, once again, to injury when he received two wounds on his right hand from the sharp spikes of a sliding Cy Seymour. "The blood spurted from Bresnahan's hand a moment after he was spiked by Seymour. The out was the third of the inning and Roger ran to the bench and poured water on the wound. Then he chased to the clubhouse and called for a doctor from the stand. McGraw, walking from the coaching line to the Giants' bench, picked up the ball at the plate. It was covered with blood."[57] "The back of the hand was sewed up, but Roger declined to permit any stitches being taken in the palm for fear of permanent soreness." It was thought that Roger would be out of the lineup for three weeks, but he was back for game four with the Giants managing from the bench in street clothes.[58]

After that game Roger exclaimed, "I was happy Sunday night, after making it three straight but I'm ten times happier tonight."[59] The four-game sweep of the Giants was followed by three more wins against Philadelphia that pushed the Cardinals winning streak to eight, their record to 14–13, and fifth place. Two weeks later they crashed through the second division ceiling and enjoyed a two-day stay in fourth place—the first Cardinals team to be in the first division, after the season's Opening Days, since the 1901 team finished fourth.

National League President Lynch had been in St. Louis for several days and gave an interview during which he spoke highly of Bresnahan, "He is a grand ball player, clever manager and an honest gentleman. He has my best wishes for his success … and says the new leader of the Cards deserves great credit for the showing he has made with the local National Leaguers." High praise indeed but he added the warning, "Bresnahan, however, must respect the umpires and obey their rulings."[60]

* * *

The Cardinals were the talk of St. Louis, had captured the attention of the National League and appeared poised to continue their winning ways, because the lineup was set, catching was set with Roger and Ed Phelps sharing the duties and the revamped pitching staff appeared to be coming around following a slow start.

Over the two months following the eight-game win skein, the Cardinals won at slightly less than a .500 pace despite a flurry of ninth inning pitching collapses. Between July 4 and July 14, they lost five games in which they led going into the ninth inning. They stood in sixth place entering the dog days of summer.

Pitching woes continued as the bane of Roger. Several of his corps showed proficiency on occasion but none was consistent. Youngsters Harmon and Backman were inexperienced while veterans Willis, Corridon and Lush were not contributing as expected. Lush was predicted to have a "breakout year" but was not. Geyer, a promising acquisition, had arm trouble. Roger sent him home "with no pay until he gets into condition."[61] And the Harry Sallee story continued. The day following Geyer's departure, Roger suspended him, once again, for breaking training rules—he did not report to the park for several days. Roger told the press, "I'm through with Sallee."[62]

Roger Bresnahan turned 31 on June 11, 1910, and was in his twelfth major league season and second as a manager. His annual salary was $8,333. During the decade 1910–1919 the average worker's salary was about $750 a year.[63] Roger, with his grade-school education, is an example of why a man capable of doing so gravitated to baseball for his livelihood.

Roger landed an outstanding talent in 18-year-old catcher, Ivey Wingo from the Greenville, South Carolina Spinners.[64] He did not provide immediate help but joined the Cardinals in 1911 and went on to a 17-year major league career. Another addition was holdover Catcher Jack Bliss who reported late because of a wintertime broken leg.[65] Rube Geyer returned to the team following but was of no use.[66]

Harry Sallee was reinstated and started against the Giants at St. Louis on July 21. Harry stunned all by tossing a six-hit shutout at the Giants, giving credence to his manager's belief that Sallee was the best left-handed pitcher in baseball when he was right. The *Post-Dispatch* quipped, "Slim Sal has joined the 'Never Again' Brigade for the steenth [*sic*] time."[67] Three days later, he faced the Giants again but lost 4–1. McGraw left town without Sallee but still wanted him.[68] A week following his loss to the Giants, the Cardinals began a road trip leaving Sallee behind. He was suspended again and did not pitch again in 1910.

Roger recovered from his hand injury and returned to catching on June 13. A week and a day later he was ejected by Umpire Jim Johnstone for disputing a call on a play at the plate at St. Louis. It was his first ejection of the season. Roger asserted that he had tagged Bobby Byrne of the Pirates who was trying to score. According to a later news report, Roger made no fuss after being ordered from the game and refrained from swearing. The *St. Louis Post-Dispatch* supported him saying that he "clearly had him out."[69] There was so little notice paid to the incident that it was not mentioned in the game reports of two St. Louis and two Pittsburg newspapers.[70] Roger felt that the ejection was a sham because "Johnstone, earlier in the day, had told Phelps that he (Phelps) would be doing the Cardinals catching before long. An indication that Roger was to be banished."[71] The league office acted quickly, and the three-day suspension was announced in the next day's newspapers.[72] Roger had made his bed with Tom Lynch and the president had the last word on the Cincinnati "joke" game. Roger was ejected thrice more during the season but otherwise he was the best-behaved of his career. The effort to control his temper was noted by at least one writer who expressed he "is suppressing himself with marvelous success."[73]

Though Roger's play was limited for assorted reasons since he had been in St. Louis, he was playing very well. His batting average reached a season high of .315 on June 30 and he finished at a respectable .280. Sportswriter Bryce Hoskins expounded on Roger's performance in a game against his former New York Giants: "The forcefulness of Bresnahan's aggressive nature, the wonderful power of this great human dynamo, was exemplified to the great delight of a great crowd in a truly convincing manner. McGraw who tutored Roger for years, must have experienced a thrill of pride in the work of his erstwhile understudy, as he saw the game slipping away from his own team, because Manager John detects and appreciates the finer points of the game,perhaps more readily than any other man in baseball."[74]

* * *

The Cardinals' record stood at 39–47 and they were in sixth place after the games of July 27, five games behind the Reds who occupied the final spot in the first division. The Cardinals had just beaten the league-leading Chicago Cubs in the first of a six-game series but then their season turned—a thirteen-game losing streak followed, dropping the team to seventh place.

The shortcomings of the Cardinals' pitching staff and a collective hitting slump by the outfielders were brutally exposed as the season progressed. "Bresnahan's pitching staff was a bigger failure than was ever anticipated.... The failure of Ellis, Oakes and Evans [the outfielders] to hit up to their 1909 marks has surprised even more than the cracking of the pitching staff."[75] Pitching became so thin that Roger was forced to change from catching to pitching in the same game in order to finish one contest.[76] He sent out an amateur on another occasion.[77]

The loss streak shifted Roger's focus ahead to 1911 and he was relentless in his search for pitching help. He signed several minor league players who would report to the Cardinals when their shorter season was completed. His intention was that they "will be shoved into the game and given a chance to show what they are made of."[78] He did just that with pitchers Bill Steele, Cy Alberts, Roy Golden, and Bunny Hearn who were a combined 8–12 for their short major league seasons. Steele and Golden would-be Cardinals' contributors in 1911.

On the season's final day, the Cardinals needed to defeat the World's Series-bound Cubs in Chicago to finish sixth. Because of a 4–1 loss the Cardinals finished exactly as in 1909—one half game behind Brooklyn. St. Louis writer Ed Wray saw beyond the lowly finish, the losing streak and the pitching woes and told his readers,

"...although the standing of the club has not risen materially, the quality of the team has greatly improved as to reach the point where pitchers only are needed to make it great."[79] A comparison of basic performance data for Roger's two seasons and the year prior to his taking the reins validates Wray's assertion of progress:

Year	*Wins*	*Runs*	*Attendance*
1910	63	639	355,668
1909	54	583	299,982
1908	49	372	205,129

Remembering the 1908 team was gutted makes the above even more impressive and the improvement at the gate made the 1910 season "a most successful one in a business way...,"[80] the club clearing $90,000.[81]

The local consensus was "that Bresnahan should have the banner year of his career as a big-league manager next season."[82]

Twenty-One

Bresnahan's Wrecking Crew (1911)

Following the 1910 World's Series Roger Bresnahan exclaimed he had "forgotten about baseball since the season closed and will not let the pastime worry him until the National League meeting in December."[1]

Roger had no chance of adhering to his own admonition as he had earned the confidence of his boss and was the "real as well as the nominal director of affairs"[2] for the Cardinals. He attended the National Association of Minor Leagues meetings in Chicago[3] and journeyed to Cincinnati to visit Reds' owner, Garry Herrmann,[4] and manager, Clark Griffith,[5] but made no player deals. He announced plans for spring practice at a resort in West Baden, Indiana, for light workouts for 10 days before serious training at League Park in St. Louis.[6] He also divulged resumption of the spring city championship series with the St. Louis Browns to begin on March 25.[7]

Roger left his Toledo home for the December 13 National League meetings in New York and was joined in Cleveland by Stanley Robison.[8] Roger acquired no new players at the meetings but unloaded plenty—selling Catcher Eddie Phelps and Pitchers Johnny Lush and Lester Backman to Toronto.[9] In another deal he shipped Pitcher Frank Corridon to Buffalo.[10] A few days later he sent Pitcher Vic Willis to Baltimore.[11] Roger's wisdom was questioned for letting Phelps, his fine backup backstop, go as well as four pitchers from his already thin staff but this aligned with his philosophy of looking to the future with young players he could develop. It also reflected the faith he placed in the several young pitchers he had signed along with his youthful catcher, Ivey Wingo, and his belief that Harry Sallee had mended his ways.

Though Roger did not acquire players while in New York, but he did not return home empty-handed. He was accompanied by a dog.[12] He had long been and would continue to be a dog fancier, owning many over the years. He owned various breeds of setters, bulldogs, and terriers.[13] Some dogs he trained for hunting while his latest, a Japanese Spaniel, was likely to be a pet.[14]

Later that winter Roger reportedly received a bird dog in exchange for a pitcher. As incredible as that sounds, there is some basis in fact—Dick Kinsella, owner of the Springfield, Illinois, team, had obtained Pitcher Bill Hopper from the Cardinals.[15] Roger related that Kinsella came to him looking for a pitcher. He told Kinsella Hopper was about to be released and he was welcome to sign him. Kinsella told

Roger that if Hopper developed, he would give the Cardinals the first opportunity to purchase his release and added he wanted to do something for Roger, and so, delivered a bird dog to him. Roger later said that calling the deal a trade was an "absolute falsehood."[16] *But* Springfield got Hopper and Roger got the dog. Hopper eventually made it to the major leagues and knowledge of the deal preceded him as fans welcomed him with "a chorus of imitation barks."[17] Memory of the "trade" is perpetuated in present day baseball biographical sketches which give "Bird Dog" as Hopper's nickname.

Owner Robison departed for Panama in January to "get away from cold"[18] and "in search of health."[19] His health began to fail in 1905 and by 1907 he was noticeably impaired.[20] He left Bresnahan in full charge.[21]

The Cardinals were ordered to report at St. Louis with uniforms, gloves, and shoes for a March 6 departure for West Baden, Indiana, where an innovative spring practice commenced—innovative because the bulk of the training took place on the club's home field and not in a southern locale.[22] Light workouts, hill climbing and sipping of mineral water were planned. The weather was good enough that the regimen was expanded to include throwing, batting, pitching, soccer, football, medicine ball and long runs—all designed to take off weight. Roger needed to shed 12 pounds himself.[23]

The team returned to St. Louis for what Roger called the real practice of baseball drills and intrasquad games at League Park. There were three sessions each day—two in uniform and one a run of several miles. Players were up before dawn and rigorous work was imposed.[24] A weekend series at Kansas City against the Blues of the American Association was scheduled in addition to the games with the Browns.[25]

The veterans beat the second teamers in the first two practice games and Roger must have been pleased to strike out twice against a sharp Harry Sallee.[26] The weekend series at Kansas City began March 18 and the Blues proved no match for the Cards, 9–1 and 17–1.[27]

Back at League Park on March 20, a week of practice remained before the first Browns game on Saturday. Prophetically, the *St. Louis Post-Dispatch* declared, "There is no doubt as to Bresnahan being the real and only boss of the local National League ball club."[28]

On Friday, March 24 that was confirmed when Martin Stanford Robison died at the family home in Bratenahl near Cleveland.

* * *

Robison had returned from his sojourn to the tropics on March 3.[29] Soon after, the 54-year-old bachelor checked in to Chicago's Presbyterian Hospital where he was treated for locomotor ataxia.[30] From Chicago he went to St. Louis and then to Cleveland on March 18. Despite his long illness, his sudden death—attributed to blood poisoning[31] and resulting heart issues[32]—was unexpected. Roger was moved to tears and "was greatly shocked and depressed." He and the owner "greatly admired each other and their relations had always been most friendly."[33]

The day following Robison's death, the business of baseball continued with the start of the City Championship series between the Cardinals and Browns. All the players wore a black article in memory of the Cardinals' owner. A full 20,000 watched a 10–2 Cardinals' win at League Park. Newcomer Bill Steele pitched a complete game with Roger catching. A Sunday game scheduled for the Browns' Sportsman's Park, just two blocks from the Cardinals' home field, was postponed because of wet field conditions. Roger left that evening for the Robison funeral in Cleveland, leaving Miller Huggins in charge of the team.[34]

Roger acted as a pallbearer and remained in Cleveland to advise the family on Cardinals' baseball operations.[35] Robison's will was probated the next day and specified that everything he owned be left to his niece, Helene Hathaway Robison Britton, the daughter of his deceased brother Frank De Hass Robison (75 per cent), and her mother, Sarah Carver Hathaway Robison (25 per cent). First among the assets was all but one share of the stock of the American Baseball and Athletic Company of St. Louis, operator the Cardinals. Additionally, Helene's inheritance was to be free from any control by her present or any future husband.[36]

Mrs. Britton was a 32-year-old mother of two and no stranger to baseball and its management. Her father and her Uncle Stanley had owned teams since she was a girl and exposed her to the game and its workings. She knew baseball and was suddenly in the unprecedented position of female owner of a major league baseball team.

Most doubted that a woman could hold ownership or be actively involved in its management. She was unsure herself and wary of her acceptance by the other owners.[37] A leading voice doubting the viability of a female owner, National Commission Chairman Garry Herrmann, suggested there would be a change of ownership. Charles Weeghman of Chicago was rumored to be a potential buyer.[38] Another thought was that a syndicate would purchase the club for Roger Bresnahan.[39] Rumors placed Schuyler Britton,[40] her husband, or Fred Abercrombie, a former Cardinals' treasurer and friend of Stanley Robison, as president of the club.[41] Through all the speculation, Mrs. Britton firmly denied any intention of selling her stock.[42]

Roger returned to St. Louis on Wednesday, March 29 and commented on his meetings in Cleveland. He said the Cardinals would not be sold, the playing policy would be unchanged, and he did not know who the president would be, but Stanley Robison's successor would be named within a week. As a minority voice he had no objection to a woman owner saying, "It is her club and I fail to see where she can be prevented from holding it."[43]

He rejoined his team with his new owner's "utmost confidence in his ability."[44] The Cardinals won twice more over the Browns the weekend of April 1 and 2.[45] Roger directed but did not play as he was hampered by a cold.[46] With Roger in his sick bed and Miller Huggins acting as manager, the Cardinals prevailed again on Thursday.[47]

Helene Britton arrived in St. Louis on Wednesday, April 5 to attend the Cardinals' directors' meeting which was scheduled at her behest. She was accompanied by her husband, attorney Schuyler Britton, and Abercrombie, the named executor of Stanley's will.[48]

St. Louis contractor Edward A. Steininger was elected president on Thursday. Mrs. Britton was named vice-president. The election results were in keeping with Robison's directive that the president be a man.[49] The election announcement, under the headline "Cardinals New Owner to Keep Off; Roger Is Real Baseball Boss" told that Steininger would represent the club at National League sessions.[50]

Helene Hathaway Robison Britton became the first woman owner of a major league baseball team when she inherited the St. Louis Cardinals in March 1911 from her uncle, Stanley Robison. She publicly praised the management of Bresnahan and rewarded him with a rich five-year contract. However, concerned by his complete control and influenced by others, she summarily dismissed him with four years left on their contract (ca. 1911. Dec. 28. Photograph. https://www.loc.gov/item/2003689092/).

We know Mrs. Britton expected gender prejudice and her immediate actions sought to eliminate or reduce opposition to her involvement in team management. Her realization that woman-owner prejudice was real prompted her to deal with it by controlling her interests through Steininger and Bresnahan. That she had prior knowledge of her inheritance seems likely as she named her lieutenants so quickly and during a time when she was engulfed by grief and had not "given a moment's thought to baseball."[51] It was later revealed that she had told Steininger she wished he would be club president the day following Stanley's death.[52] It was also revealed that Roger Bresnahan insisted that Steininger be named.[53]

Roger had Mrs. Britton's ear and she had great respect for him and his opinion. She said of him, "My great aim will be not to interfere with, but rather further the system Mr. Bresnahan already has in effect.... We adore his system."

On Friday, Mrs. Britton saw her first Cardinals game as the club owner and was treated to a thrilling win over the Browns at League Park. With ailing Roger not in the lineup, the Cardinals scored five times in the ninth inning to win 7–6.[54] Roger returned for the final two games of the St. Louis City Championship series on Saturday and Sunday. The Cardinals won both to sweep the seven-game series with Mrs. Britton in attendance.[55] She departed Sunday evening for Cleveland. She promised to return for the Cardinals' home opening game on April 20 and was reportedly "elated over victory."[56]

The Cardinals left for Chicago to take on the defending league champion Chicago Cubs on the season's Opening Day. Four games were scheduled for Chicago and the same following in Cincinnati before opening at home. As for all teams and all times, hopes were high but there seemed to be good reason for this Cardinal team. Roger offered, on the eve of championship play, "The success of my club depends on what my young pitchers do."[57] The opinion that the Cardinals were an improved lot was nearly universal.

* * *

The Cardinals team presented in Chicago was well conditioned, prepared and rested and called by some the "Ladybugs"[58] because of its woman owner. Harry "Slim" Sallee, apparently salvaged by Roger, drew the Opening Day assignment and was masterful in an 11-inning, 3–3 tie played before 18,000 Wednesday-foul-weather-braving fans. The game was halted by darkness. The next day's game was postponed due to rain.[59] Following, Roger won Friday's game but lost a close friend. The Cardinals won 2–1 behind Bob Harmon but earlier that day, the great Cleveland Naps pitcher, Addie Joss, died in his Toledo home.[60]

The first game's score and outcome were duplicated on Saturday, this time in 10 innings with Roy Golden going the distance.[61] Most importantly, Roger's young pitchers showed very well.

The following set of games in Cincinnati was shortened to three because of rain. There was a loss, win and an extra-inning tie.[62] During the hard-fought deadlock Roger's usual "practice of kidding and insulting every batter who comes up to the plate"[63] got the best of one Red—Bob Bescher "without warning swung on Bresnahan's nose."[64] After the game, he initiated a battle on the way to the clubhouse. Others stopped the melee and Roger spent the next morning in a dentist's chair.[65]

The Opening Day game in St. Louis was on Thursday, April 20 and was hard-fought with the Cardinals battling back from an early deficit but losing 9–5. The Cubs went on to sweep the four-game set. A contributor to the losses was a rash of injuries. Four starters were out at one point. Roger played through a knee injury caused by a foul tip[66] and a charley horse incurred running the bases.[67]

The regular starting lineup was not restored until May 5. The recovery was aided by a forced six-day rest that included two scheduled off days and the postponement of an entire series with the Cincinnati Reds due to St. Louis rains.

The St. Louis team continued to be referred to as the "Ladybugs" by some, but Mrs. Britton and the Cardinals' management were largely silent. She did travel to St. Louis from her Cleveland home and saw the five season-opening home games.[68] Understanding the effect of the injuries she was confident, "as soon as Mr. Bresnahan gets his men back again and has them in good shape, we will do much better."[69]

She was correct.

The Cardinals embarked on their first trip to the National League's eastern cities—Brooklyn, New York, Boston, and Philadelphia—but stopped at Pittsburg for five games and squeezed in a Sunday game at Chicago on the way. They lost all the games to the Pirates but won the single Chicago game. Mrs. Britton came from Cleveland to Pittsburg and watched the first two losses and granted an interview. When asked if she took an active part in managing her team, she laughed and replied, "Oh, dear no. I have a president and he does all that sort of thing. I am content merely to have a nominal control, for I think that the men know more about the real work of managing than I do."[70]

Moving east to Brooklyn the Cardinals won three of four games. The next stop was New York City for four games with the Giants. Though good and respectful friends, Roger Bresnahan and John McGraw liked nothing better than beating each other. Each put his best pitcher forth for their first game—Christy Mathewson for New York and Harry Sallee for St. Louis. Mathewson retired the side in the first inning, but Sallee gave up hits to the first four Giants he faced. Roger wasted no time and changed pitchers, but it was too late. The Giants went on to score 13 in the inning.[71] Both managers realized the outcome was decided. McGraw pulled Mathewson to save him for another day and Bresnahan took himself out during the first inning debacle. The Giants won the next day too. Roger was confined to his hotel room due to a severe cold—the first game he had not caught in 1911.[72] The Cards turned the tide in game three. Sallee, with Roger again catching, came back to win the fourth gaining a series split.

St. Louis then swept the Boston Rustlers and won the first two games at Philadelphia running their winning streak to eight and evening their seasons' record at 15–15.

The second division-leading Cardinals returned to League Park and lost to the Cubs in 11 innings on May 27. Following a rainout, they hosted the Cincinnati Reds for a scheduled four-day, seven-game series beginning on Decoration Day which was seemingly designed to tax Roger's four-man pitching rotation. To add to the difficulties, it was announced that Roger had suffered an attack of pleurisy and was nursing a charley horse but hoped to catch one of the holiday games.[73] Bob Harmon won the first game and St. Louis staged a four-run comeback to gain a tie in the second. The rally avoided a loss, but the replay added yet another game to the already demanding schedule. The teams split the next day and St. Louis swept the Reds on May 31 thanks to what Roger called "the most sensational rally I have ever seen during my baseball career."[74] Roger did not play in it and may not have even seen it. The Cardinals had fallen behind the Reds 7–0 when he "threw up his arms in disgust and quit the game for the clubhouse."[75] The Cardinals scored 10 runs in the seventh inning and went on to win 15–8. The Cardinals and Reds split their fourth doubleheader in as many days due to another miracle finish in game one when St. Louis scored all its runs in the bottom of the ninth inning to win 6–5. In his account of the miracle comeback, Ray Webster, writing in the *St. Louis Star*, dubbed the Cardinals the "Wrecking Crew."[76]

Webster was the first to use the term to describe a baseball team and his paper then used this vivid descriptor nearly daily. The Cardinals' success even inspired musical compositions—Pete Cavallo arranged a melody titled *Bresnahan's Wrecking Crew.*

Despite his ailments, Roger caught in all eight games of the marathon series missing just five innings.[77] By taking the Cincinnati series 5–2, the Cardinals had won 16 of their last 22 games and were in fifth place and just five games out of first place. Roger's team-building efforts were beginning to pay dividends. All members of the St. Louis roster—except for First Baseman Ed Konetchy, Catcher Jack Bliss, Pitcher Harry Sallee and himself—were his acquisitions. He was behind the bat in all but one of the team's first 40 games steadying his young pitchers and batting .298 to boot.

Columnist Ed Wray expounded on the leadership skills of Bresnahan and his ability to get the most from his men, calling him "A Moses of the diamond, [who] can wave his magic wand to a baseball desert and cause results to spring."[78] In another column Wray praised Roger as a *teacher* writing, "Every player on the present club … will tell you enthusiastically of all he owes to the 'Duke'" and "All the team owes something to Roger, if only fighting spirit."[79] He was also an effective communicator and held game-day team meetings at 10 o'clock in the morning to discuss strategy for that day's game. The meetings were mandatory, closed to outsiders and generally lasted two hours.[80]

Roger Bresnahan may have had more than managing the Cardinals in mind—ownership was a possibility according to one story that suggested that if Mrs. Britton decided to sell the team, Roger and his associates (John McGraw was said to be one) had "been offered first chance at the club."[81] *Sporting Life* also reported on possible Bresnahan ownership on the front page of its July 1 issue: "It is said that Roger can get local backing enough to buy the controlling interest in the club, and that he has progressed so far that he has secured an option on enough shares to control the organization. It is a worthy ambition for Roger to want to become a big-league club owner, but by being so would not the game lose one of its best catchers? That would indeed be a catastrophe, for, while the game could go on just the same without Roger in active service, still his throwing would be a sad loss to the sport. A catcher-president would be a rare article to see on the diamond, but it is not an impossibility."[82]

* * *

During the ensuing weeks of late spring and early summer the Cardinals' winning pace slowed slightly with the club at a .628 clip through July 10. Despite the lingering charley horse and "two stone bruises on his left hand"[83] Roger knocked in the winning run in the bottom of the ninth to beat Philadelphia 9–8 on June 10[84] and again drove in the game-winner with a triple three days later.[85] On June 11, the Cardinals spotted the Phillies a 4–0 lead in the first inning but came back to win 6–5 handing Roger a one-day stay in the first division as a 32nd birthday gift.

The Cardinals opened a four-game home series with the New York Giants on

June 15. It was a long day for Roger. He and his wife were awakened at four o'clock in the morning by a crank call to their Buckingham Hotel residence. His business at the ballpark was likely distressing as well. He levied $100 fines on two of his players because they "imbibed too freely of the foaming amber"[86] and followed with a 3–0 loss to his former team and boss. Roger and Adeleen arrived at the hotel at about one o'clock the next morning when Roger "registered a protest against practical jokers being allowed to call him on the telephone" with Night Clerk Joseph Wheatley. According to a police report, Wheatley "talked back" and Roger "tried to mop up the floor" with him. Both men were arrested and taken to the police station where they shook hands and Wheatley declined to prosecute. Both were released and Bresnahan later added, "I only regret that I did not hurt him more than I did."[87]

On June 23 at Cincinnati the "Wrecking Crew" fell just short of another miracle comeback. Trailing 7–0 after six innings the Cardinals scored twice in the seventh, once in the eighth and four times in the ninth and, due to a bizarre ending, lost 8–7. Roger had inserted himself as a pinch hitter, doubled and replaced himself with a pinch runner in the ninth and was on the bench as the inning continued. Mike Mowery was at bat with two outs while Steve Evans rested on third base after tripling in two runs. Cincinnati brought in Keefe who "pitched two strikes to Mowery, when Bresnahan protested that the second was a balk. While Bresnahan was protesting Keefe put over a third strike ending the game.... Bresnahan made an enraged rush at [Umpire Bill] Klem, who met him with a straight right to the face."[88] Others, including Umpire Bill Brennan, quickly separated the pair who went their separate ways without further incident.[89] Bresnahan protested the game and Klem reported the incident to his boss, National League President James Lynch.[90]

Still in Cincinnati, the pair was at it again on Sunday, June 25 when Klem banished Bresnahan for "protesting a decision."[91]

Lynch convened a hearing in St. Louis on June 27 which the *St. Louis Post-Dispatch* called the "Klem Trial" and named Klem the defendant. On his way, Lynch stopped in Pittsburg to talk with members of the Reds about the incident.[92] Following closed meetings of about 45 minutes each with Bresnahan and Klem, Lynch issued a statement which focused, for the most part, on Bresnahan. Klem was fined $50 while Bresnahan was censured.[93]

Lynch wrote, since "Roger was not playing in the game ... [he] had no business rushing the umpire to enter a protest.... I have been easy on Manager Bresnahan for the reason that his general conduct this season has been first class." Of Klem he opined: "Klem forgot the most essential part of an umpire's duties, that of keeping his temper...."[94]

Roger called Lynch's decision "...about the biggest joke I ever heard."[95] "On the other hand, some in Cincinnati reveled in the decision. Ten men there raised $50 to cover Klem's fine and arranged for a dinner to be given him on his return to Cincinnati."[96]

Prologue—Pitcher Keefe "smilingly admitted he had balked, and he didn't know how Klem had come to miss it."[97]

Despite the distractions, the Cardinals continued to roll at home beating the Cubs in two of three games and finally getting the best of the Pittsburg Pirates by beating them in three of four and moved into fourth place in what was now a five-team race for the pennant.

Roger had a big day at bat in the 7–1 win over the Cubs on June 28 with three hits and four RBIs,[98] played the next day against the Pirates but on the following day then gave way to Jack Bliss, saying, "my hand is healed but as long as Bliss is catching nice ball and the team is winning, I will not break up the combination."[99] This was a telling statement from Roger and reveled his recognition that playing was no longer his primary focus. As a full-time player he did all he could to get into a game. In this case, though capable of playing, he chose to manage instead.

The Cardinals completed their home stand on July 2 with three consecutive wins over their nemesis Pittsburg Pirates. In their first game, Honus Wagner was safe on a close play at third base making a triple. Disagreeing fans responded to the call with a shower of pop bottles onto the field. Roger himself helped in the cleanup which avoided a forfeit. The *Pittsburg Daily Post* did not condone the throwing of pop bottles at the umpire but commented "the loyalty shown the home team is something worthwhile thinking about. They are with Bresnahan down there, heart and soul."[100]

The club then left for their second invasion of the National League's eastern cities—Philadelphia, Boston, Brooklyn, and New York stopping in Pittsburg on the way. Roger began catching again in Philadelphia and his team won three of four against the Phillies. The second game featured the now almost usual rally, a six-run outburst in the ninth inning that sealed a 9–4 win. Following a 4–2 loss to rookie Grover Cleveland Alexander in the series finale, the Wrecking Crew left Philadelphia for an overnight journey to Boston.

Twenty-Two

"The Player, Man and Hero" (1911)[1]

The Cardinals boarded the Federal Express at Philadelphia the evening of July 10, 1911, bound for Boston. The team faced an overnight train ride followed by an afternoon game against the Boston Rustlers.

The Federal Express ran from Washington, D.C., to Boston and was a Pennsylvania Railroad operation for the first leg of the trip—from Washington, D.C., to the Bronx. The New York, New Haven & Hartford Railroad assumed control of the train there for the remainder of the route.

The train consisted of nine cars—a car carrying live fish, a baggage car, a day coach and six Pullman sleepers.[2] The Cardinals occupied two of the sleepers which were located near the front of the train.

The railroad's route past the Hudson River and on to New England was by barge around Manhattan Island. The train entered the docks at Jersey City, New Jersey, where, with passengers remaining in the cars, the train was separated, loaded on barges, and hauled across New York Harbor and up the East River to Port Morris in the Bronx. The train was reassembled at the Mott Haven Yard but now the cars were in a different order—the Cardinals occupied the last two cars, the eighth and the ninth. A New York, New Haven & Hartford Railroad crew came aboard, and engine No. 813 was attached.

The train left the Bronx at 1:52 a.m. on July 11 and was 57 minutes behind schedule, a deficit Engineer Arthur Curtis and Fireman Walter Ryan tried to erase.[3]

Cardinals' players on the train were Otto McIvor, Lee Magee, Ivey Wingo, Wally Smith, brothers Lou and Grover Lowdermik, Rube Geyer, Miller Huggins, Arnold Hauser, Mike Mowery, Ed Konetchy, Harry Sallee, Bob Harmon, Bill Steele, Roy Golden, Jack Bliss, Rube Ellis, Steve Evans, Rebel Oakes, and Jack McAdams who had just joined the team the previous day. Others in the party included Trainer Kirby Samuels, Player-Manager Roger Bresnahan, Treasurer Herman Seekamp and two St. Louis newspapermen, Dick Collins of the *St. Louis Republican* sports staff and William J. O'Connor, the *St. Louis Post-Dispatch* baseball editor.[4]

The train was scheduled to change tracks as it approached Bridgeport, Connecticut, by passing through a crossover switch which was located on a viaduct. Speed for switching was limited to 15 miles-per-hour by railroad safety regulations.[5] At 3:30 a.m.[6] the Federal Express entered the switch at 60 miles per hour.[7]

When the heavily vestibuled train of nine cars struck the switch at full speed the locomotive leaped, rocked and swayed over the ties for nearly 150 yards and finally plunged to the street below, dragging six cars down the bank. The coupling broke between the sixth and seventh cars, leaving three sleepers upright on the embankment, two of them still on the rails [the Cardinals' cars].[8]

The first three cars were flung on their sides on the street below. The fourth, the day coach, was ripped open. The left side of the car caught on the ironwork of the viaduct crossing over Fairfield Avenue, and the entire side was torn off like so much tissue paper. Then the day coach lurched forward on the right side ... winding up its aerial plunge 50 feet away from the stone wall of the viaduct. Piling on top of it came the two sleepers....

The train was filled with people. The five [six] sleepers were filled to capacity, the day coach as usual crowded....

In the crash over the viaduct the train swept into telephone, telegraph and electric light wires, and trolley wires. There were dozens of short circuits and a brilliant electrical display flashing through the gray dawn added to the terror of the wreck.

Shrieks and groans, sputtering of wires and the hiss of escaping steam, following the successive crashes as the engine, tender and cars came tumbling off the viaduct awoke persons living within several blocks.[9]

Fatalities were 14 and more than 40 were injured. There were about 150 passengers in the berths and day coach.[10] "The greater number of fatalities were in the day coach."[11] It was entirely crushed.[12]

Steve Evans related his experience: "At the first shock some of us were thrown out of our berths, but we have been thrown before in that manner when traveling at night and we didn't think much about it. However, it didn't take us long to find out what had happened, for our ears were almost immediately pierced by the screams of the women and children. Then we heard Bresnahan's voice ordering us to throw on some clothes and get out of the car. He told us there was plenty of work for us to do."[13]

Bresnahan was not awakened by the crash—he was having a smoke when it occurred.[14] Lee Magee told of his manager's actions: "If ever a man lived who possessed a cooler head, I have not heard of him. We were barely picking ourselves up off the floor. He seemed to be the first who recognized an accident had occurred and our assistance might be needed. He was the first man to leave our coach and we all followed."[15]

Evans continued:

> Some of us went out just as we were, in our night clothes, but most of us put on our trousers and shoes. When we first left our car, we couldn't see a thing. It was pitch dark.
>
> Then in a minute or two the baggage car caught fire and then the whole scene was lighted up and a horrible scene it was. Women were running about frantically. Some of them had lost their babies and seemed to have been driven insane.
>
> We got axes from our car and the next one and started clearing away the wreckage so that we could get at the bodies of the dead and dying. It was hard work, for the flames from the baggage car were soon extinguished and we were left in the darkness once more.

> ... We struggled on until the sun was shining brightly. I don't know how much good we did, but I do know that I saw enough horrors to last me all through my life.[16]

Rebel Oakes described the carnage: "Men, women and children were sticking out of the debris. Some had arms cut off. Others were minus legs. In some instances, the tops of heads had been crushed."[17]

The Cardinals instantly became first responders. The players pitched in and helped extricate victims from the rubble. Wally Smith retrieved two infants from under the wreckage. Bresnahan and Ivey Wingo saved a woman's life when they pulled her from under debris where a fire had started.[18]

When policemen and firemen arrived on the scene, the ballplayers continued rescue efforts by working alongside them. It took four of the athletes pushing and two policemen pulling to remove a woman weighing nearly 300 pounds from one of the sleepers through a hole that had been chopped through the roof. Another woman was pinned beneath splintered timbers and a huge granite block which had been dislodged from the viaduct. Doctors tended her and gave her stimulants for an hour and a half until police and ball players by "[u]niting their strength they dislodged the rock sufficiently to get the timbers loose." She was finally dragged out, laid on a section of broken picket fence that had been placed in one of the physician's automobiles, and taken to a hospital.[19]

The Cardinals "worked unceasingly until dripping with perspiration, begrimed with soot and dyed with the blood of victims they finished the rescue work nearly three hours later."

"Men schooled to scenes of carnage and suffering were sickened by the anguishing incidents of the worst wreck in the history of the New Haven road in these parts."[20] Roger said, "I can stand a lot. But the groans and screams of those mothers and babies was too much for me."[21]

* * *

None of the Cardinals were reported hurt either in the crash or while performing rescue and recovery work but it could have been much different. Recall that the train was reassembled in the Bronx. The day coach and one of the sleepers displaced the Cardinals' cars that were near the front of the train and moved them to its end. All the consulted contemporary sources agree on this point. However, they do not agree on the reason for the reordering.

Most newspapers saw nothing unusual in the process of reassembly and suggested that the different order was a mistake or done for convenience.[22] The *New York Times* account of the accident a day later and gave a different reason—the assembly was done on the demand of Bresnahan. According to its report, Bresnahan complained that his men could not sleep because of engine noise and the changes were made to appease him.[23] *Sporting Life*'s account echoed the *Times* in naming Bresnahan as the reason the order of cars was changed.[24]

Top: "Members of the St. Louis National League baseball team did heroic work in rescuing men, women, and children from the debris caused by the wreck of the Federal Express at Bridgeport...," Connecticut, on July 11, 1911, quote from the *Boston Globe*. Some of the Cardinals involved are shown. Sitting: Arnold Hauser, Rube Ellis, Lee Magee, Steve Evans, Roger Bresnahan. Standing: Treasurer Herman Seekamp (not verified), Wally Smith, Ivey Wingo, Jack Bliss, Grover Lowdermilk, Bob Harmon, Ed Konetchy, Rebel Oakes. Receiving a laying on of hands is Ellis with a facial injury. *Bottom:* Team members had been on the train but escaped serious injury. Despite the efforts of the players and others, 14 people died and more than 40 were injured in the horrific mass of twisted wreckage (both photographs courtesy the Bridgeport History Center, Bridgeport Public Library).

Whatever the reason for the changes, they dramatically altered the outcome. The day coach, the center of destruction and death "was crushed and splintered as no other car. It could not possibly be recognized after the wreck as having once been a railway coach or anything else having form or purpose."[25] "Most of the dead and severely injured were in the day coach … now at the bottom of the wreckage, and these were the ghastly images the Cardinals' players saw as the sun came up on the pile of rubble that, had they not changed positions, would have been their car." Roger recognized this when he told a reporter, "Our car, would ordinarily been near the engine. If that were so, the St. Louis team would be wiped off the map."[26]

Then there was "the strongly held belief that if members of a baseball team were on board, a train would never get in a wreck. A 1911 survey of traveling men stated that when they were to ride on a train bearing a ball club, they did *not* take out accident polices on the trip."[27] And, "…never in the history of professional baseball has a player been killed in a railroad accident."[28]

Two months later the Interstate Commerce Commission report found the accident was caused by the train changing tracks at too high a rate of speed and placed blame on Engineer Curtis. The investigators found Curtis to be competent and familiar with the rules, tracks and signals at the accident site but refused to attempt explanation for his actions.[29] Curtis could not aid in the inquiry because he perished in the crash along with Fireman Ryan, eleven passengers and another railroad employee.[30]

The work the Cardinals "did at the Bridgeport wreck has raised them forever above the mere plane of celebrity in the sporting world to a secure eminence in the memory of a grateful country."[31] Newspapers across America declared them heroes. The railroad rewarded the players with $25.00 checks and paid their individual losses.[32]

A special train arrived at about six o'clock in the morning to transport survivors on to Boston. The players returned to their coaches, dressed, and posed for a photograph. Roger promised his men of "a few cases of Budweiser."[33] Members of the Boston team were on hand to greet their rivals when the train arrived at noon at Boston. Most of the players hurried to the Copley Square Hotel in want of sleep. Roger requested and was granted a postponement of the day's game.[34]

Their ordeal behind them, the players prepared to return their focus to playing baseball. Some expressed concern that the day's events might have some lasting negative effects on team performance. Roger recognized the possibility: "It was horrible, horrible. What effect it will have upon the nerve of my men can only be told from their future performance on the diamond."[35]

* * *

The Cardinals returned to the field for two games at Boston's South End Grounds the next day and "the player, man and hero" was given a great reception by the Boston Rustlers' fans. When Bresnahan stepped to the plate for the first time,

"Everyone there seemed to be pulling for the fighting manager, and he received a tribute that will long live in his memory. The 5,000 fans rose en masse and cheered vociferously. The cheers continued with every step and his face was flushed when he reached the plate.... It was one of the most remarkable demonstrations in the history of the famous park."[36]

The Cardinals won the first game 13–6. The second was a 10-inning 6–6 tie. The next day Roger contributed a home run and threw out four runners at second base in a win that pulled St. Louis to two games from first place. Pennant fever gripped St. Louis and the baseball world took notice with many marveling at how Bresnahan, with the same team as the previous year, brought the Cardinals to such a position.

In their mid-season review the *Post-Dispatch* pointed out Bresnahan, Ellis and Konetchy were hitting over .300 and the team average was a league best .268. Pitching was a different story as the team had only three reliable starters and was "on the verge of wobbling."[37]

After splitting the final two games Boston, the Cardinals moved to Brooklyn where they won three of four. The Giants awaited next, and John McGraw was anxious to slow the rushing Cardinals and had his ace Christy Mathewson ready. The Wrecking Crew knocked Matty from the box in the second inning on the way to winning and—though they lost the next two to the Giants—finished their run through the east with a 9–5 record. St. Louis picked up another win at Cincinnati on their way home but lost Roger when he was hit on the fingers by a foul tip.[38] He missed the next eight games.

During the three-week homestand Roger hoped to fix some bothersome issues—sickness, injuries, the lingering effects of the Bridgeport wreck and a short-handed pitching staff. But not much was fixed. Some players may have gotten over their sniffles and slept better in their own beds and Roger did return to the lineup on July 31—but was lost again on August 7 when struck on the right foot twice by foul tips.[39] Pitching fortunes worsened when Roger suspended early-season mainstay Roy Golden for "failure to keep in condition."[40] Slim Sallee did not pitch for the last 10 days of the homestand amid rumors of drinking once again. Roger stuck by his pitcher, saying he was being saved for the first game of the road trip against the Cubs.[41] A team hitting slump added to team woes. After three straight losses to the Giants, two by shutout, Roger ordered the first morning practice in several weeks.[42] After faring so well on the road against the four eastern teams, the homestand with the same opponents ended with a disappointing 7–8 mark. Still very much in the race, the Cardinals fell from fourth place to fifth.

* * *

Before the Cardinals embarked on a long road trip, Roger predicted the team which beat the Cubs would be the team to win the National League pennant.[43] That opportunity was at hand as Chicago was the first stop on the tour. Despite his foot injury Roger departed with his team. X-rays revealed no broken bones, but he was in extreme pain and lame. He went directly to his hotel and remained there for the first game[44] leaving Miller Huggins to manage.[45] Despite his "rest" Sallee lasted only four innings and took the loss and the Cubs moved to first place. The next day's game was rained out.[46] Roger returned the day after that to manage another loss from the bench in "citizen's clothes."[47] Sallee pitched a masterful one-run complete game in the Chicago finale, but it was wasted as the Cardinals did not score.

Roger returned to the lineup in Pittsburgh[48] on August 14 and "seemed to aid the Cardinals materially in putting starch in their spinal columns"[49] in a 3–1 win. The Cardinals moved to Philadelphia to launch their third and final season's tour of the four eastern cities. It was a pivotal time for the 57–47 Cardinals who stood in fifth place, seven and one-half games behind first-place Chicago with Pittsburgh, New York, and Philadelphia in between. Their fans were hopeful that pitching would hold up and even be enhanced by contributions from formerly little-used members of the staff and hitting would rebound. With Roger back on the field they were expecting the Cardinals could gain on and even pass some of the teams ahead of them in the standings before returning home.

Hope quickly faded in the first inning of the first game in Philadelphia on August 16. The Cardinals were dealt a severe blow. With two outs the Phillies had Hans Lobert on third base and Sherwood Magee on second. Magee was picked off and broke for third. Lobert followed suit and headed for home. Cards' Second Baseman Miller Huggins threw to Bresnahan at the plate in plenty of time to get Lobert whose "ample feet jostled the ball out of Bresnahan's hands and at the same time spiked the manager in the arm."[50] Bresnahan, holding his bleeding arm, flew into a rage and shouted at Umpire Hank O'Day, who had allowed the run, that the spiking was intentional. Magee picked his way through the crowd of Cardinals who gathered around their wounded leader and scored. O'Day ejected both Huggins and Bresnahan because of their protests.

Lobert had elevated himself "two feet from the ground" as he approached Bresnahan, causing some to declare the spiking deliberate. There was also some speculation that it might have been retaliatory as the Phillies' catcher-manager Red Dooin had suffered a broken leg in a home plate collision with the Cardinals' Rebel Oakes on July 26 putting him out for the rest of the season.[51] But most accounts suggested the spiking was accidental. Secretary Seekamp lamented that a run of Cardinals' bad luck began the month before when the Cardinals left Philadelphia on their ill-fated trip to Boston and now continued with this "accident to Roger."[52] Roger, days later, remarked that he and Lobert had always been friends and he thought the spiking was "purely accidental."[53]

Various prognoses appeared in the nation's sports pages, but none were correct because Roger's playing proved to be essentially over for the season.

The Cardinals went on to split the four games in Philadelphia. Then Sallee won the opener at Brooklyn and earned his team a one-day stay in the first division—one day because they lost the next two there. Sallee was assigned to pitch the opening game at Boston on August 24 but was knocked out of the box by the league's tailenders. For unexplained reasons, Roger was not at the game and the *Star* noted, "It was clearly evident that with Bresnahan out of the fray, they are weakened greatly and robbed of half their scrappy disposition."[54] The loss had far-reaching effects on Cardinals' fortunes because it appears to have been the final straw in the latest Harry Sallee saga.

After losing two of three games to lowly Boston, the Cardinals moved on to New York City to take on the first-place Giants in a four-game series. Roger always wanted to make a good showing in New York and opportunities to gain on the first-division clubs were running out. He had saved Sallee to pitch two of those important games.

In New York, but before play commenced, Roger delivered stunning news—"he had indefinitely suspended Harry Sallee … for failure to keep in condition" and fined his pitcher $200. The *Post-Dispatch* suggested "Sallee fell from the water wagon after his defeat in Boston."[55] In all probability Sallee had likely renewed his relationship with alcohol several weeks before as evidenced by his recently reduced appearances.

Sallee had beaten the Giants and Christy Mathewson on July 28 in St. Louis. Several St. Louis newspapers reported that Sallee had been lured to drink by Larry Doyle of the New York Giants on the eve of the Giants and Cardinals game of July 31 in which Sallee was scheduled to face the Giants again. The ruse apparently worked and Sallee was knocked from the box after four innings and took the loss. He was so disheartened that he did not join his team for their next game on August 2.[56] Roger reportedly searched for him to get him back into the fold and had apparently been working with his pitcher since the alleged Doyle incident but his falling out following the Boston game was too much for Roger to bear. Roger was so disgusted with his pitcher that ordered him to St. Louis to get himself in condition.[57] Sallee did not pitch again in 1911.

So, without Sallee and Bresnahan available, the Cardinals lost the first two of the scheduled four-game series. Losing was halted by rain which caused postponement of the final pair. Mrs. Britton arrived in New York City on August 29—the owner was pursuing Roger whom she was endeavoring to sign to a new contract as his current deal was to expire at the end of the season.[58]

Following the games in New York, the Cardinals headed for home, stopping for two games in Pittsburgh and six in Chicago on the way, winning just three of the eight games. Arriving home with a record of 64–60, they rested in fifth place but just two-and-a-half games behind Philadelphia and the first division.

* * *

Roger announced a reset team goal before the season's final homestand on September 7—finishing in fourth place. He intended to play his regulars for a week or two and if the goal proved to be unattainable, he would give trials to his recruits. Thirty games remained with all but the final three at home.

The Pirates, with slim pennant hopes alive, were the first to visit St. Louis and the teams split four games. The first Cardinals' win was claimed by Gene Woodburn and was his only victory of 1911. The rookie allowed only one hit, a scratch single in the ninth inning, and was aided by his veteran catcher—Bresnahan.[59] It was the first game Roger had caught since being spiked on August 16 and he declared his "right hand as good as ever."[60] It was also the last game he caught that season as he gave way for the development of another rookie, Ivey Wingo. Following, the Cardinals won three without a loss over Cincinnati and took two of three from lowly Boston giving them a 7–4 record on the homestand, but they had lost another game in the standings to Philadelphia.

Mrs. Britton, becoming known as Lady Bee,[61] came to St. Louis to attend board meetings. She and the board were well-pleased with Roger's performance which fostered a season so successful that the club turned a profit and retired old debts.[62] Accordingly, a new contract was proposed, signed by Roger, and announced by the *Post-Dispatch* on September 13. The agreement was for five years with other terms not made public.[63] The annual salary was later revealed to be $10,000[64] per year—the same as his previous three-year contract.[65] In addition, he signed a "civil contract whereby he was to receive 10 per cent of any profits." The new deal had the potential of making him the highest paid man in the game. Had the same contracts been in force for 1911 when the Cardinals cleared $165,000[66] Roger would have taken home $26,500 and been baseball's top earner. John McGraw was reportedly the highest paid man in the game in 1911 with $25,000 in salary and profit sharing.[67]

At this point Roger declared, "Our campaign for honors this season is effectively through."[68] He turned his attention to 1912 and began wholesale substitution of "juvenile" players into the lineup to judge their capabilities under game conditions saying, "If we lose, it is all right, and if we win it is better."[69]

The rampaging and pennant-bound New York Giants followed the Reds into St. Louis and beat the Cardinals four times in five tries sending them into a tailspin that saw them win just four of the season's last 15 games. The Wrecking Crew needed to win two of the last three games at Cincinnati to finish with a winning record. They did so.

The Cardinals accomplished their first winning season since 1901 finishing with 75 wins and 74 losses. Attendance was nearly two-and-a-half times more than the year before Roger's arrival. The turnstile count at the newly renamed Robison Field of 447,768 was by far the franchise record which stood until 1921.[70]

Their season neatly fell into three sections—a slow start lasting just into May, a hot streak that carried into July and saw the team contending for first place and a season-ending slump terminating in a fifth-place finish. What the fans saw, not only in St. Louis but in all the National League cities and remembered was how the Wrecking Crew played during the middle section.

The end of the regular season was not the end of play for the Cardinals. They had a date to defend their St. Louis City Championship with their neighbors the

Browns. A seven-game series was planned to begin on Wednesday, October 11 at Sportsman's Park. The Series was to continue through the following Wednesday, alternating with Robison Park. The players received half of the combined receipts of the two teams for all seven games with 60 per cent of that going to the winning team.[71]

Rain caused the scheduling of two doubleheaders. The first game was a 0–0 tie. The Cardinals won the second 3–2 but did not triumph again until the finale losing the series 2–4–1 to the American League cellar dwellers. Although embarrassed, the Cardinals did better than their winning counterparts financially because the Cardinals' management turned over their entire share to the players and Roger kicked in his portion as he did not play.[72]

In 1911, the Wrecking Crew was never as good as it was from June 1 through July 8 when it won 23 of 36 games but many believed it could reach that level again by simply strengthening pitching.

The club "had money for new players and looked forward to a bright future,"[73] thanks to Roger Bresnahan.

* * *

THE ST. LOUIS STAR

ST. LOUIS, TUESDAY, JULY 11, 1911.

CARDINAL LEADER'S WIFE HELPS WOUNDED AND DYING IN WRECK

MRS. ROGER BRESNAHAN

Mrs. Roger Bresnahan, who was occupying the next to the last coach when the train wreck happened today, retained her self possession and directed a party of rescuers who were frantically trying to give aid to women and babies in the wreck. She remained calm throughout the height of the excitement.

This is the only known image of Adeleen Lidke Bresnahan, Roger Bresnahan's first wife. This report in the *St. Louis Star* is incorrect as she was not near the mentioned train wreck (*St. Louis Star*, July 11, 1911).

Note on 1911 Newspaper Research

News of the Bridgeport train wreck was of national interest. News services transmitted much of the same information nationally. Newspaper people rushed to the scene and published extensive same-day accounts and photographs. Perhaps because of haste, reported facts and details varied greatly. For this reason, the author relied heavily on the local *Bridgeport Evening Farmer*, the *St. Louis Post-Dispatch* which had a reporter on the train and the *New York Times* that delayed its story a day.

One colossal error, however, resulted in a great find. The *St. Louis Star* ran a same-day short story with a large photograph under the headline "CARDINAL LEADER'S WIFE

HELPS WOUNDED AND DYING IN WRECK" on the front page of its second section.[74] But Mrs. Bresnahan was not there. Perhaps she was observed by the *Star* leaving St. Louis with her husband about the time the Cardinals embarked on their eastern tour. However, according to the *St. Louis Post-Dispatch*, she traveled only as far as her Toledo home and Roger continued and joined his team in Pittsburg.[75] The happy result is the discovery of the only known extant photograph of Adeleen Lidke Bresnahan.

Twenty-Three

And Now He's the "Duke of Tralee" (1912)[1]

Prospects for a successful 1912 St. Louis Cardinals' season were bright indeed. Roger Bresnahan had taught his players how to win and convinced them they were capable of doing so. The previous season the team delivered—albeit inconsistently. Most who followed and those who wrote about the team suggested that strengthening pitching and adding a hard-hitting outfielder would improve the consistency of winning and propel the team to new heights.

Bresnahan aimed to fix these shortcomings late in the 1911 season by giving trials to several minor league players. None proved capable of providing immediate help which left the manager with only one option—acquiring veteran players.[2] He was on record as being willing to trade anyone, except for Ed Konetchy, if it would strengthen the team. Outright purchase was not likely, but Roger was "empowered with the full authority from the owner of the Cardinals to spend whatever amount is necessary in purchasing the players he seeks."[3]

The winter of 1911–1912 was a busy one for Roger as he strove to secure the experienced players he needed and to dispose of as many as one-third of his reserved 36 players before spring practice.[4] He reasoned; I do not wish to "waste any time with any man whom I know will not be able to add strength to the team."[5] He made countless contacts, entered into discussions with other clubs and attended three major gatherings of baseball people endeavoring to meet his goals.

With an eye to the future Roger remade his scouting staff. He let Jack Houston and Charlie France go.[6] He replaced them with veteran baseball men who had proven records as judges of talent—Dick Kinsella and Bill Armour.[7] Kinsella was a former player, an owner and scout for the New York Giants. Armour, also a former player, had extensive managing experience and had been president of the Toledo Mud Hens.

* * *

As we have already learned Roger certainly fostered and likely originated his erroneous middle name of Patrick and birthplace of Tralee, Ireland. Clarence F.

Lloyd of the *St. Louis Post-Dispatch* likely created the moniker that has stuck to this day. He dubbed Roger the "Duke of Tralee" in his column on December 29, 1911.[8] A month later the following limerick appeared:

> There was a young man from Tralee,
> Who tried to set Ireland free.
> He fired a torpedo.
> Then skipped to Toledo.
> And now he's the Duke of Tralee.[9]

* * *

Roger was active during the National League meetings held December 13–15 at the Waldorf-Astoria in New York where he tried, unsuccessfully, to put through several trades. Owner Mrs. Britton and President Steininger were also there. Lady Bee took "no part in the proceedings, leaving that to Steininger" and added "I always leave everything about the players to the judgment of Mr. Bresnahan.... I have unbounded faith in him."[10]

In 1912 Bresnahan was one of 25 players featured on "Helmar Silks" which were player images on satin. They could be obtained by mail in exchange for 20 gift-slips which were packed with Helmar Turkish Trophy Cigarettes. The silks measure seven by nine inches and are exceedingly rare (1911. Photograph. https://www.loc.gov/item/2007685658/).

On the final day of the meetings, Roger was engaged in some extracurricular activity with Owner Charles Murphy of the Chicago Cubs. Murphy was enraged that Roger had blocked a trade he had made by claiming one of the players off waivers. The two nearly came to blows in the hotel café after Murphy publicly called Bresnahan a liar. Roger was restrained by bystanders but later vowed to bring the matter to the league directors.[11]

Writing on club stationery from his Toledo home the following Monday, Roger made his complaint—not to the National League but to baseball's ruling body, the National Commission. The commission was composed of Garry Herrmann, Cincinnati Reds owner and president, and the league presidents, Ban Johnson of the American and Thomas Lynch of the National.

In his letter to Chairman Herrmann, Bresnahan told that Murphy had said to him, "You are a liar, I know the whole thing and I've got something on you and will have you put out of the National League." Murphy was likely referring to his assertion that Bresnahan's team had intentionally not played its best against his former team. He went on to tell Herrmann, "I don't need the protection of the National Commission, but base ball does … in order to protect the good name of the cleanest and most wholesome of all outdoor sports." He demanded that Murphy be cited before the National Commission and suggested, "If what Murphy says is true, I ought to be kicked out of the National League; if it isn't true, then Murphy ought to be kicked out of baseball."[12] While waiting for a response, Roger continually demanded a public apology through the press.

Murphy called the whole affair a "kidding match."[13]

The commission did not rule on the complaint and bounced it to the National League for resolution. Following the annual league scheduling meeting attended by Bresnahan and Steininger in February, it was learned that the league directors took no official action on the matter and "intimated that the trouble would be settled amicably outside the meeting."[14] Steininger "had nothing to say about the rather abrupt ending to the Bresnahan-Murphy row. 'Roger is satisfied' is all the Cardinal executive would say."[15]

Not only did Roger come away from the February league meetings without the satisfaction of a public apology from Murphy, but he also failed, yet again, to improve his roster. He did sign two free-agent veterans—Harry Steinfelt, the former Cubs' third baseman and his old friend Bob Ewing who he hoped could bolster pitching.[16] Steinfelt was a hedge against regular Third Baseman Mike Mowery who was holding out. Otherwise, Bresnahan was resigned to go to spring practice with the same players who were his regulars in 1911.[17]

* * *

Roger planned the same schedule of preparations for the season as he had employed successfully in 1911—a week's stay at West Baden, Indiana, followed by a return to St. Louis for the remainder of spring practice.… It did not work out that way.

The Cardinals' manager deemed that only players with signed contracts were welcome to participate in spring practice.

Roger mustered his charges in the lobby of the West Baden Springs Hotel at five o'clock in the morning on Saturday, March 2 and began the 1912 season with a two-hour hike. Events that same afternoon set the tone for the week—Roger led the team on a six-mile hike in a "blinding snowstorm."[18] Sunday they recovered from the trek and Monday's scheduled walk was called off due to four inches of snow on the ground.[19] Confinement to the hotel continued until the Cardinals departed West Baden, on schedule, on Saturday, March 9 for St. Louis.[20]

The weather was no better in St. Louis, so Roger hastily arranged to move the

Cardinals to Jackson, Tennessee. He sent Groundskeeper Dick Shaner ahead and followed with the team on Sunday.[21] Shaner and more rain greeted the team in Tennessee, so Roger quickly moved on to another Jackson—this one in Mississippi.[22]

The Cardinals were welcomed in the Mississippi capital early Tuesday morning and found that the rain had stopped after falling for a week.[23] The city provided a field which was home to the Jackson Senators and first-class accommodations at The Edwards Hotel.[24] Shaner set about getting the field in order by utilizing a "force of 20 Negroes, several tons of hay and one hundred gallons of gasoline."[25]

Roger was extremely busy not only as manager but also as the team's secretary, treasurer, and the official guide—who purchased railroad tickets, paid hotel bills, corralled the players, looked after baggage, and procured training quarters.[26] He stated he would never again gamble on St. Louis weather for spring practice.

The sun shined on the Cardinals for the first time on Wednesday, March 13 and only 10 days remained before the series with the Browns was scheduled to begin.[27] A two-hour morning practice ended with a soccer skirmish and a six-inning game between the veterans and Yannigans followed.[28] Short practice games on Thursday and Friday were followed by a full nine-inning affair on Saturday.[29]

Pleasant weather followed the week of March 17 and allowed the established two-a-day practice schedule to continue without a hitch. Players reported at 8:45 a.m. for a two- and one-half-hour practice and again at 2:15 p.m. for a session of four hours or more. Games were played in the afternoon and Roger's system kept the men working all the time they were not engaged in actual play. According to scribe W.J. O'Connor, who was travelling with the team, Roger's "strenuous training methods whipped his squad into shape in three days."[30] Roger was having a hard time of it, spent some time on the sick list with a severe cold and was told by a doctor he had pneumonia.[31]

As planned, the Cardinals left Jackson Thursday for St. Louis and the start of the series with the Browns on Saturday, March 23. Just before departure, Roger learned that the Saturday game had been postponed until March 30 because of wintry weather in St. Louis.[32] Although he preferred to remain in Mississippi he proceeded anyway because the tickets had been purchased and the baggage was already at the station when he learned of the delay.[33]

The Cardinals left Jackson with the same 30 players and Mike Mowrey remained a holdout. Roger praised the host city and Mayor Crowder and suggested that the Cardinals might return in 1913, "I have been trailing around the training camps of the South for the past sixteen years ... and I can say frankly that never before have I been treated with more generous hospitality than here in Jackson."[34]

The team arrived home Friday and Roger promised to continue twice-a-day practices at Robison Field despite the cold.[35] Ahead lay the finalization of the roster which meant cuts and resolution of the Mowery issue before the start of National League play on April 11.

Practice plans were quickly dashed by the condition of Robison Field—it was covered with a foot of snow[36] and would, obviously, be unplayable for some time. Scrambling to find alternatives, Roger arranged to send six pitchers and two catchers under the direction of newly appointed Assistant Manager Harry Sallee to Hot Springs, Arkansas, to continue training in warmth. The veteran Sallee had been in and out of hot water with Bresnahan the previous two years but looked "in the best of condition," was "determined to have a great season"[37] and had been a "model of deportment" in 1912.[38] Those remaining in St. Louis would practice indoors at the First Regiment Armory where work was limited to running, basketball, indoor baseball, and the ever-present medicine ball.[39]

* * *

Roger was also dealing with several contract issues. He had sent his players contracts just after the first of the year. Most, if not all, included a raise in salary and were signed and returned.[40]

Veteran holdout Mike Mowery returned his unsigned because he expected more money than was offered. He wrote that if the club did not see fit to increase the amount, he would sign the original anyway. For whatever reason, Mike heard nothing from Roger, and he was labeled a holdout. The stalemate was broken on March 25 when Roger received a letter from Mowery expressing his wish to play for the Cardinals. Roger welcomed the news and asked him to report. Mowery arrived in St. Louis on March 31 and signed the next day.[41] It seems there must be more to the story as Mowery waited for a response for two months or more and did nothing despite news reports he was a holdout and Roger prepared to begin the season without his proven third baseman and made attempts to trade him. Though both may have been stubborn, Roger could have helped himself and his club by facilitating a smoother negotiation.

Despite Roger's admonition that players who had not signed contracts would be forbidden from participating in spring practice, at least three did anyway. Two key pitchers, Bob Harmon and Bill Steele, failed to report for the March 25 afternoon workout at the Armory. Roger announced the pair was holding out for more money.[42] Both came to terms within a week.[43] A day later speedy outfielder/infielder Lee Magee tried his hand at holding out. He, too, rejoined the fold in short order.[44] In these cases, Roger did not display his usual firm hand and displayed favoritism. His failure to enforce his order banning non-signers from spring practice was known to all Cardinals and their followers.

Another contract-signing tale concerned the team's first baseman, biggest star and Bresnahan favorite. The story purportedly occurred in February 1912[45] but the earliest account of it found by the author was not published until 1944. Fred Lieb told it in his *The St. Louis Cardinals: The Story of a Great Baseball Club:*

> Eddie Konetchy, the La Crosse Chocolate Dropper, had enjoyed a fine season and wanted a substantial raise for 1912. Bresnahan invited him to St. Louis to talk over terms. About 9 a.m., Roger telephoned Sid Keener, then a young baseball writer on the *St. Louis Times,* that if he came over to the *Planters' Hotel* Bresnahan would have a story for him.

> "I found Roger and Koney seated in one of the side booths," said Sid. "It was early in the day, but they already had a number of beer bottles in front of them." Roger had nothing to announce, but said, "stick around a bit." I did for several hours; a lot of beer was consumed, but nothing happened. I went to the office and came back around noon. They were still beering up, but still there was no story. Again, I returned to the office, and was back at the Planters' at 5 o'clock. By that time, you couldn't see the table for the empties. "Well, Sid," Roger said, "Ed was a little stubborn; he needed lots of convincing, but he has just signed a new contract."
>
> A manager then needed not only to outsmart and outtalk his players but outdrink them.[46]

Both Lieb and Keener are respected journalists, but the story raises a question. Konetchy was already under contract and in the final year of a three-year deal in 1912.[47] However, we have just seen that Roger did not handle all player contracts uniformly and may have been responding to a Konetchy request to revisit the salary clause.

* * *

Ready or not, the delayed start of the best-of-seven game City Championship series with the St. Louis Browns was upon the Cardinals—beginning on Saturday, March 30. Neither team was ready for competitive play, but it appeared that the Cardinals lagged the Browns in this respect. Because of their extended search for good weather the Browns labeled the Cards "tourists" and suggested they were "sightseers and not a ball club."[48] The Cardinals had not faced another club; no pitcher was

The Cardinals beat Manager Bobby Wallace's St. Louis Browns to win the 1912 pre-season city championship. The Cardinals played like the Wrecking Crew of the previous season and raised hopes for the 1912 campaign (*St. Louis Globe-Democrat*, April 8, 1912).

ready to go nine innings and the team's hitters had not had a bat in hand for nine days. Except for the troupe of pitchers sent to Hot Springs, the Cardinals had no baseball activity outdoors since their return to St. Louis.[49]

Game day was glorious as Sportsman's Park was bathed in sunshine and warmth and filled with at least 18,000 spectators—the largest crowd there in at least a year saw the underdog Cardinals top the Browns 6–4.[50] The Browns came back to win the next two games.[51] Then the Cardinals rekindled their Wrecking Crew image by scoring four times in the ninth inning to win game four, 7–6. Roger stepped to the plate in the bottom of the ninth inning of game five with the score tied at four, two outs, the count full and the bases loaded and lined a bases-clearing double.[52] By plating five in the ninth inning the Cardinals prevailed 7–4.[53] Enthralled with Roger's performance, the *St. Louis Star* proclaimed him "the biggest individual factor in baseball today for any team."[54]

The Cardinals' fourth win, 9–7, in game six on Saturday, gave them the City Championship. Roger expressed that he was "the happiest man in town."[55]The Cardinals had exceeded expectations though the strength of the Browns would not prove to be great. Nonetheless, the Cardinals had, by far, their best preparation experience for the National League championship games that would begin in four days.

Twenty-Four

Bresnahan versus Britton (1912)

The Cardinals' promise-filled 1912 season began on Thursday, April 11 at St. Louis' Robison Field. Bookmakers were not as optimistic as the Cardinals fans, realizing the club had not been strengthened, especially in pitching. The bookies tabbed the club to finish fifth in the National League.[1] The opening-day lineup confirmed that thinking as it was the same as the previous season with one exception—Jack Bliss caught because Bresnahan was not fit to play. Eight of the starters were under 30 and seven of them had been acquired by Roger.

Roger, respecting the Giants and Phillies, did not pick his team to win the National League pennant but suggested the Cardinals "should be up there fighting" and perhaps finish in the first division. He did, however, make a rare prediction—to deliver a pennant to St. Louis before the end of his five-year contract.[2]

The season's first opponent was always-contending Pittsburgh led by the "dean of shortstops,"[3] the best player the game had seen—Captain John Peter Wagner. Honus had two hits, half of his team's total, as Bob Harmon humbled the Pirates 7–0. It rained the next day, but the Cardinals won again the following day, 6–5 in 10 innings.

Another pennant threat, Chicago followed and lost two of three to the Cardinals with the home team amassing 20 runs in the last game. The Cardinals left for Pittsburgh, Cincinnati, and Chicago with a 4–1 record and tied for first place. The short trip was a disaster as the Cardinals lost seven of the eight games and returned home in seventh place. The home confines did not help. The Cardinals lost four straight to Cincinnati followed by another sweep at the hands of the Giants. The Cardinals had lost nine straight and 15 of 16 and rested in the National League cellar. The Wrecking Crew of 1911 was dubbed the "Ex-Wreckers."[4]

The major problem was pitching. Roger's three-man rotation of Bob Harmon, Bill Steele and Harry Sallee was not effective. The pitching issues were exacerbated by the absence of Roger in the lineup. His appearances during the first month of the season had been limited to pinch hitting twice. The St. Louis sporting press recognized Roger's value on the field commenting, "The Cards without Bresnahan in the game are lost"[5] and "Cardinals lack spirit when Bresnahan is out."[6]

Roger had multiple health issues. He had been diagnosed with pneumonia during the team's stay in Mississippi[7] but delivered a robust performance in the pre-season series with the Browns. His aggressive play in those games left him "lame in leg and arm"[8] with his arm "so sore he could hardly use it."[9] He developed an attack of tonsillitis so severe he could not take to the coaching lines let alone play.[10] His condition worsened, and he was admitted to St. Luke's Hospital in St. Louis on May 2. Dr. Louis P. Butler reported "Mr. Bresnahan has had a series of colds and an attack of tonsillitis and now has developed a slight attack of bronchitis. There's nothing serious in his condition, but he is not fit to play and he's badly in need of a rest."[11] Pneumonia was later added to his maladies.[12] Roger was released from the hospital the morning of May 8 and was on the Cardinals bench that afternoon. Dr. Butler advised Roger was improved but would not be able to play for two weeks.[13]

The state of the team Roger returned to was aptly described by the headline "Injuries Bench Five Cardinals; Team Shattered."[14]

* * *

Though absent from the field, Roger continued dealing in players. During the season's first week Roger trimmed five from his roster including veteran Harry Steinfeldt.[15] Speedy outfielder Frank Gilhooley was optioned subject to recall. Roger recognized potential in the young Toledoan that did materialize. Gilhooley enjoyed a 20-year professional career.

Owner Britton also made her presence known. She introduced "Ladies Day" at Robison Field on April 15 allowing free admittance to "fanettes" accompanied by a male escort.[16] She was subject of a *St. Louis Post-Dispatch* feature celebrating her first anniversary as Cardinals' owner. During her interview she called Roger Bresnahan "the best manager anywhere."[17]

A report of April 21 suggested Lady Bee was tightening the reins on Roger and his control of the Cardinals' operations was no longer complete—"she wants to know the full details of every trade that is proposed by Roger Bresnahan before negotiations are concluded, and that expenditures for uniforms and other equipment must be submitted to her scrutiny before they are finally OK'd."[18]

Mrs. Britton was embroiled in a continuing court struggle for control of the Cardinals' administration. Edward Steininger was president of the club and administrator of Stanley Robison's estate. Britton feared Steininger would attempt to vote shares of Cardinals stock under his control as administrator[19] and secure complete charge of the company.[20] She sued to have the stock turned over to her.

During the trial she was asked if she knew the value of her stock. She replied, "I simply can say that Roger Bresnahan offered me $500,000 for the club franchise and park."[21] Her testimony confirmed a year-old rumor. Roger was asked by W.J. O'Connor of the *St. Louis Post-Dispatch* for his side of the $500,000 story. His reply concerning the events of the previous year:

> When Stanley Robison died in the spring of 1911, I was called to Cleveland by Mrs. Britton. She at that time was very unprepared to take charge of the club. A meeting was held the day after Mr. Robison's funeral. We met at the Hollenden Hotel. Mrs. Britton, her

attorney, Mr. Ginn, Fred Abercrombie, Mrs. Britton's mother, and Mrs. Bresnahan, my wife, were present. Mrs. Britton told me then that her uncle, the late Mr. Robison, had told her to rely on me and she intended to leave the club in my care. Then she asked me whether it would be advisable for her to sell the club.

...My answer was most emphatically NO. I pointed out that the club had earned $40,000 in 1909, my first year here, and it had earned $60,000 in 1910 and stood an excellent chance of making more the coming year, 1911. I knew the club figured to improve and, incidentally, to earn more profits. I then left Cleveland for St. Louis to play in the spring series.

When I arrived in St. Louis, I was called over the long-distance phone by Harry Frazee. He then was on his way to Boston to buy the National League team of that place. When he read that Stanley Robison had died, he changed his plans and decided to make an offer for the Cardinals. He ... told me to make an offer for him. I was looking out for the interest of Mrs. Britton. I told Frazee that the club was worth $500,000. He laughed and said it was—less $150,000. He thought $350,000 was a fat price, but I held out.... I intended to recommend that she sell for no less than $500,000.

A few days later I made the offer. She declined to sell, although I thought the offer was an elaborate one. I had been promised an interest in the club if I swung the deal.... Understand, I made just one offer, that in the early part of April 1911.[22]

Harry Frazee, a friend of Roger's, later owner of the Boston Red Sox and remembered as the man who sold Babe Ruth to the Yankees, "promised to give the Cardinal leader one-third of the club's holdings if he [Frazee] gained control of the club."[23]

Hearing the story, some thought Roger's offer was a personal and recent one causing one publication to suggest the Cardinals' current losing woes were an effort by Roger to diminish the value of the Cardinals.[24] Another charge against Roger claimed he was "trying to lose games that he might get the club away from 'a poor defenseless woman.'"[25] Yet another "intimated he might not have been ill during the time he was in St. Luke's Hospital."[26]

* * *

Roger's return to the field had a near-immediate positive effect. After two losses to the Giants, the Cardinals won six straight games. They were blessed to have their manager back and blessed to have the league's two worst teams, Boston and Brooklyn, in town. The more formidable Reds and Phillies followed into St. Louis and the Cardinals won five of those nine games.

As always Roger was busy with roster work. To reach the league-mandated 25-player limit he released Bob Ewing, whose release was later reversed, and two with intriguing names "Wheezer" Dell and Ten Million.[27] A news report suggested Mrs. Britton was "interfering with [the] playing end."[28]

On their way to their first tour of the National League's four eastern cities, the Cardinals stopped in Pittsburgh for a five-game series beginning on May 27. Confidence among the Cardinals was high, Ed Konetchy said the team would return home in second place.[29]

Roger Bresnahan made his first appearance behind the bat in the series' opening game, caught flawlessly and made his first hit of the season—a two-run triple—to help his team win 6–3. He started as catcher the next day, had a perfect day at bat and exited in the sixth inning with the game in hand.[30]

From Pittsburgh it was on to the Polo Grounds, for a May 31 date with the Giants. The New Yorkers were formidable with their 28–7 record and seven and one-half game lead over second place Cincinnati.

The Friday afternoon matchup featured two lefthanders, Joe Willis, a spot starter, for Bresnahan and Hooks Wiltse for the Giants who were riding a nine-game winning streak. Willis was magnificent in stopping the Giants 5–1. But, according to Sam Crane, he was not the headliner: "...it was Roger Bresnahan who was more directly responsible than anyone else for his team's brilliant victory and the magnificent game they put up. Roger was behind the bat with all the fire, pepper and gingery enthusiasm that distinguished him while a Giant."[31]

The Giants' bats boomed in the final three games exposing the Cardinals' weakness, but the Cardinals bounced back by winning two of three games at Philadelphia.

From Philadelphia the Cardinals repeated their fateful train trip to Boston eleven months earlier. With Brooklyn following Boston on the schedule the team had an opportunity to resume winning. The Braves altered that thinking with an 11–3 thumping of the Cards in their first match on June 11. Roger went in to catch the next day and lost 2–1 in 10 innings. The Braves went on to win three of the four games. Pitching was faltering again. Roger planned to bench himself in favor of Ivey Wingo complaining still of the injury to his right hand caused by the Hans Lobert spiking the previous season.[32] A week later the hand "was swollen to twice its normal size."[33] O'Connor opined, "Wingo is working brilliantly behind the bat" ... and "is being groomed for next year and years to come."[34] Wingo would prove to be a durable major league catcher. He added, "Something seems radically wrong, but it is difficult to detect just what that something is."[35]

The Cardinals proved O'Connor's observation by losing all four games at Brooklyn and another at Pittsburgh and limped home losers of six straight and 12 of 15.

* * *

During the Cardinals' eastern swing there was more going on within the Cardinals' organization other than losing games.

Roger held trade discussions in both Boston and Brooklyn to no avail.[36] He released excess catcher Mike Murphy[37] and signed a college player.[38] He shook up his lineup and sought treatment for his injured hand. He signed another catcher, found by Scout Dick Kinsella in Flint, Michigan.[39] Frank "Pancho" Snyder became a National League mainstay for 16 seasons. The Snyder signing was one of the first dividends provided by Roger's hiring of veteran baseball men as scouts. All this activity caused O'Connor to suggest that "[a] playing manager is burdened with too much work"[40] and Mrs. Britton to say, "I consider Mr. Bresnahan the hardest and most conscientious worker in baseball."[41]

Mrs. Britton prevailed in the courts and Cardinals' stock held by Ed Steininger as executor of Stanley Robinson's estate was turned over to her as intended by Robison. She now had complete charge of the club and secured Steininger's resignation as president.[42] At the stockholders' meeting on Tuesday, June 4, Cardinals' officers were elected at her pleasure. St. Louis attorney James Coulter Jones was made president and Lady Bee vice-president. Herman Seekamp was kept as treasurer and acting secretary.[43] Soon after, W.G. Schofield was named secretary and Seekamp had the title of business manager added.[44] The stockholders also announced that "Roger Bresnahan, manager, would have absolute control of the team on the field and off."[45]

* * *

Returning home beginning on June 20, the Cardinals continued their losing ways, winning just four of their next 13 games while compiling a June record of 7–20 and falling to seventh place.

Writing in the *St. Louis Star*, Ray Webster lamented Roger's non-participation as a player weakened the club. He stated that Bresnahan "is not in condition to play and has not been in condition at any time this season." He noted, as others had, that Roger was overweight by "thirty or thirty-five pounds."[46] Billy Murphy, also writing in the *Star*, broke news when he pointed out on June 21 the Cardinals' woes were because Roger was handicapped because he did not have "the authority to get players of class."[47]

* * *

While in Cincinnati, Roger met with Garry Herrmann who, on June 29, proposed a deal in a letter sent to Bresnahan's Cincinnati hotel. He offered Dick Hoblitzell along with pitchers Art Fromme and Bobby Keefe in exchange for the Cardinals' Ed Konetchy and Rube Geyer.[48] The proposed trade was not made public until July 20 when the *St. Louis Star* reported, "a big Cincinnati deal had been called off."[49]

Mrs. Britton confirmed Murphy's June 21 breaking news by promptly replying "no" when asked by a representative of the *St. Louis Post-Dispatch* on July 18 if Roger's name had been sent to the National Commission as one authorized to make trades for the Cardinals. She added, "Mr. Bresnahan is privileged to arrange any trades he desires to make and then submit them to club officers, who will pass final judgment before the deal becomes a valid transaction."[50] In practice the procedure was for Roger to arrange the deal and take it to President Jones for approval.

When asked if Jones had made or prevented any Cardinals trades, Mrs. Britton responded, "Mr. Bresnahan is running the playing end of this club.... However, recent rulings of the National Commission contradict[ed] this statement." The *Post-Dispatch* cited one case in which the National Commission ruled the sale of Pitcher George Zackert to Montreal, submitted by Bresnahan, null and void because he was not authorized to represent the Cardinals. The *Post-Dispatch* went on to say similar cases since the season had opened, averaging about one a week, were ruled against the Cardinals. When asked about this Mrs. Britton responded, "There's something queer about that. However, I think things will right themselves soon. We shall investigate all these cases."[51] But to be clear, Mrs. Britton knew full well that Bresnahan had not been authorized to make trades for some time because, just days before on July 15, she had written the Commission, "...the release of players shall be under the hand of the President of the Company, as heretofore."[52]

Roger had been doing business as he had in the Stanley Robison days and his name had been replaced by another as representative of the Cardinals. The current person was Jones. It is apparent, at least initially, that Roger was not aware his name had been removed and that the National Commission may have wrongly accepted his submissions as previously authorized.

Nonetheless Roger responded to Herrmann on July 24 stating the offer did not "balance the scale" but countered asking for Hoblitzell, Mitchell and either McDonald or Art Phelan.[53] Herrmann was agreeable and replied on July 28: "Your letter of July 24th just received. Ascertain at once whether your people will consider the deal as outlined in your communication, that is to say we take your first baseman for Hoblitzell, Mitchell, and McDonald. I will take the same proposal up with my people and let us keep it absolutely confidential."[54]

Herrmann revealed that he was aware that Roger is no longer the final word on Cardinals' trades.

As Bresnahan and Herrmann were exchanging letters, St. Louis' *Daily Globe-Democrat* announced a trade was pending and called it "one of the biggest deals in baseball history," reported eight players would be involved and advised that Miller Huggins was included to serve the Reds in a dual capacity—player-manager.[55]

Garry Herrmann continued pursuit of the deal and arranged to have Max Fleischmann, a part-owner of the Reds, meet with Bresnahan in New York on August 10. Roger wanted to have Art Phelon instead of McDonald causing Fleischmann to call off the deal. Roger then suggested another swap—Huggins and George Ellis for McDonald and Mitchell.[56]

Fleischmann reported to Herrmann by Fleischmann Company Private Telegram on August 12:

> ... Bresnahan and I closed on this proposition.... Then Mrs. Britton [also in New York] this morning steps in and blocks same.... I have been working with her all morning and have another engagement with her at one o'clock, ...Bresnahan is sore as a boil. I told Mrs. Britton that before I went as far as I did with Roger I asked him if she had empowered him to talk trade with Cincinnati or with Cincinnati's representative and he had assured me that he had the power, and I having the same, I considered that the matter had been closed and it was a breach of faith not to confirm it. She thereupon tried to use the loophole that he had power to deal for the first baseman [Konetchy], not for Huggins and Ellis. I did not try to get rough this morning with my handling of her, but if she doesn't give a favorable answer when I see her at one o'clock, I am going to. I am going to tell her that one way I can let myself and Bresnahan out in this matter is to give it to the newspapers that she has violated an agreement, and if necessary, I might take it up with

> the National Commission; in fact, try to throw a scare into her. In addition, I can tell her that when Huggins finds out that she is the one blocking his chance for betterment, it stands to reason that he will be rather sore at her, and the effect is bound to be felt. I am not going to try any other deal at present.[57]

Herrmann replied by telegram at once and advised Fleischmann to "not get rough with Mrs. Britton." Using plain words rather than names for security he went on—"You might be able to talk her into the matter. If you cannot get the men you want [Huggins and Ellis] renew your proposition for the first baseman [Konetchy]."[58] The one o'clock meeting was held as scheduled and a summary of both the morning and afternoon meetings was sent by private wire to Herrmann.

The missive included Bresnahan's reaction to Mrs. Britton's trade repudiation. Roger "told her very flatly that she had put him in charge of the team with authority to build it up and now that he had gotten it to making money she went back on the agreement, and she would have to find someone to take his place."[59]

In the afternoon meeting Fleischmann did mention this was "the first time that any member of the league had ever reneged on an agreement" and that Herrmann had "expressed surprise at her action." Mrs. Britton "weakened quite some" and agreed to "think things over" regarding the Mitchell and McDonald for Huggins and Ellis proposal. The pair agreed to meet the next day and Fleischmann was to bring a draft agreement in case an understanding was reached, and the deal could be implemented immediately.[60]

Herrmann was confident the deal would be closed on Wednesday, August 14 and was hopeful that both clubs could have their new acquisitions in place on Thursday when both teams began home stands.[61]

Following the meeting Fleischmann wired Herrmann—"Saw Britton woman. She called the Huggins deal off. Said she would consider K. [Konetchy] deal a few days ... but there is no chance of it going through."[62] He followed with a letter containing details: "When I tried to get an answer on the Huggins proposition, she said 'I have another proposition to make you. How would you like to get Bresnahan?' She went on to tell me that she and Bresnahan were not on very good terms and his contract had four years to run at $10,000 per year. 'I laughed at her and told her I thought she was in rather a bad way.' ...I told her we did not want Bresnahan and 'she has a loadstone around her neck and that she would have to carry it.'"

Fleischmann made a final attempt to deal for Konetchy, but Mrs. Britton demurred saying, unbelievably, she would have to see Bresnahan. Fleischmann ended by telling Herrmann "there appears to be nothing doing with any trade with St. Louis."[63]

Bresnahan, who had returned with the team to St. Louis, sent Herrmann a telegram that evening, "Just received wire. Party in New York has advised against pending proposal. I am very sorry."[64]

* * *

After returning to St. Louis, Roger requested a meeting with Mrs. Britton. She referred him to President Jones who passed him on to Mrs. Britton's attorney, Lon Hocker. Bresnahan asked Hocker why he had not been given the right to trade players and was told he "might trade away the club."[65] Roger was so angered he asked Hocker "if he could have his unconditional release and what it would cost." Hocker said he would need to call a meeting to find out. The meeting was held but the release was not to be forthcoming.[66] Roger then told the press, "I have decided it is useless to make any more such arrangements with any of the owners, and from this [moment] on I will devote all my time and energy to running the team on the playing field."[67]

Mrs. Britton said, "if Huggins is good enough for Cincinnati as a manager, he surely is good enough for St. Louis as a player." She added, "I presume that Mr. Bresnahan will continue as manager. I have never given anyone else consideration."[68]

In response to the statements of Britton and Bresnahan the *St. Louis Daily Globe-Democrat* proclaimed "open warfare" in the Cardinals organization and declared, "Woman Owner of Cardinals Has Practically Become Manager."[69] Mrs. Britton had every right to protect the assets of her enterprise and would have been foolhardy if she had not. However, Bresnahan, the only person within the Cardinals' front office with significant baseball experience, had complete control of the team's operations for three years and been extremely financially successful. The club was a losing operation when he arrived but beginning in 1909 earned profits of $40,000, $60,000, and $127,000.[70] Despite Mrs. Britton's constant public praise for him, she failed to utilize his skills and knowledge to her advantage. Rather, and for whatever reason, she excluded him, and he resented it.

* * *

July was a much better month for the Cardinals, due at least in part to Roger being more active. He caught in 11 games and pinch hit six times as the Cardinals moved up a notch to sixth place in the standings by posting a winning record—14–13. He was still acting as a complete manager despite knowing he was no longer the final say in dealing players. During July—evidently with approval—he signed two players, released a pair, and engaged in trade talks with the Boston Braves.[71]

The Cardinals continued the July pace through August and finished the month 12–14 still in sixth place. Roger did not catch a game during the month, giving way to Wingo once again. By the end of the month, the signed minor leaguers had completed their seasons and joined the Cardinals. Roger planned to see what his youngsters could do during September.

* * *

Mrs. Britton returned to St. Louis on August 23.[72] The press was anxious to speak with her as they had not done so since the trade blocking issue was made public. Her responses to questions were generally not enlightening and even uncooperative. She replied, "I have nothing to say"[73] or "I do not know"[74] several times. She did say that she knew nothing of trouble in the club's affairs.[75] She confirmed that she had blocked Roger's most recent trade proposal and that both she and Mr. Jones were empowered to stop or approve of trades. When asked if she intended to replace Bresnahan with Huggins as manager, she replied, "I have never even considered such a proposition."[76]

Three-part rumors abounded in the nation's newspapers over the next few days. Roger was to be traded to the Brooklyn Trolley Dodgers for Zach Wheat and Nap Rucker and would manage there. Miller Huggins would replace him as boss of the Cardinals. Mrs. Britton would not deny the story, saying, "I have nothing to say at all."[77] About the same time another story broke—Roger going to Cincinnati. Attorney Lon Hocker visited Garry Herrmann in Cincinnati to sell him Bresnahan's contract. Herrmann rejected the idea because he was unwilling to assume the 10 percent profit sharing provision that would be due to Roger.[78] Herrmann confirmed in a private letter that the Cardinals' efforts to move Bresnahan to both Cincinnati and Brooklyn and said, "I would not have Bresnahan as Manager of our team if we could secure him for nothing."[79]

Mrs. Britton met with St. Louis sportswriters on Thursday, September 5, and announced she would answer all questions. Asked if Mr. Bresnahan would be retained as manager she responded: "Of course, he will.... I never have considered disposing of Mr. Bresnahan's contract. The thought never was ever entertained by me, and I can truthfully say I believe it never will. My business dealings with Mr. Bresnahan always have been pleasant. I regard him as a great baseball man—who should eventually give St. Louis a winner. [After confirming she blocked the trade of Huggins she said] there has been no ill-feeling caused by that transaction.... Mr. Bresnahan is a hard worker and I know it."[80]

Mrs. Britton was convincing as evidenced by a headline the next day—"*Roger Positively Will Be Leader of Cards in 1913.*"[81]

* * *

Through all this Roger appeared to be undisturbed and was "going along as though all was serene in the business office and in the face of such disquieting rumors his conduct is commendable."[82] Following Lady Bee's September 5 news conference, rumors of dissension in the Cardinals' management ranks and of Roger's demise dwindled.

Roger began September playing his recruits and sometimes catching his new pitchers to judge their abilities firsthand. Through the season's last month, he caught in 10 games, pinch hit eight times and showed the youngsters how to hit by posting a .436 batting average. On September 20 at Philadelphia, he tutored young pitcher Phil Redding to his first major league win from behind the plate and had a perfect day at bat that included a three-run home run.

When in New York for four games, he inserted his regular lineup and top pitchers against the Giants denying the Cubs' Charles Murphy another opportunity to charge him with favoritism. On October 1 he sent his recruits home signaling he was out to win the season's final two games against Murphy's team and the post-season City Championship series against the Browns.

The Cardinals lost those final games in Chicago 3–2 and 4–3 even with the Cardinals' regular lineup and two top pitchers. Slim Sallee started game one and was relieved by Bob Harmon. In the second, Harmon started and Sallee relieved him. St. Louis' season ended with a disappointing 63–89 record left the team resting in sixth place. Roger himself had played in the fewest games of his National League career but batted .333 in 48 games.

There was still more baseball to play as the best-of-seven game series against the Browns opened on October 9. The Cardinals prevailed 7–6 in 10 innings and went on to build a 3–1 series lead. The Browns then won a doubleheader. Bill Steele gained his second win of the series in the deciding game 6–1 on October 16. Roger caught in four of the games as his team successfully defended their City Championship title.[83] Following the game, Roger went to Mrs. Britton's box where she reached out to shake his hand and congratulate him.[84]

Roger and Mrs. Britton remained in St. Louis to wrap up the season's business. The press speculated that since Roger's contract called for 10 percent of the clubs' profits he was waiting for a settlement.[85] Both Britton and Bresnahan were still in town on Wednesday, October 22 when the following page-one headline of the *St. Louis Post-Dispatch* shocked St. Louis and the baseball world:

> "BRESNAHAN FIRED
> BY MRS. BRITTON
> BUT HE WON'T QUIT
>
> Cardinal Manager, Asked to Quit,
> Cites Contract, Settlement Is Offered.
>
> COURT FIGHT EXPECTED
>
> Catcher Called to President
> Jones' Office—Huggins Wanted
> As His Successor"[86]

A fight was on.

Twenty-Five

"I Never Quit on the Ball Field, and I Won't Quit Now" (1912–1913)[1]

The firing of Roger Bresnahan, manager of the St. Louis Cardinals, came as a surprise to most. Though many signs of discord between him and Owner Helen Hathaway Robison Britton had surfaced since early spring, they did not appear to be of the magnitude to warrant dismissal and were offset by Mrs. Britton's frequent public statements lauding the performance of her manager.

The news of the dismissal, attributed to "a man close to those in control of the team" or "a friend of Bresnahan,"[2] appeared in the nation's evening newspapers on Tuesday, October 22, 1912—often on page one. Earlier in the day, Bresnahan would not discuss the situation or admit the owner had acted. Also contacted on Tuesday, Mrs. Britton was dismayed that the story had broken. Speaking by telephone with a *St. Louis Post-Dispatch* reporter who had asked for a statement, she said: "I don't want anything printed about that.... It is terrible this has got out." Mrs. Britton's voice quavered as if she were on the verge of weeping. She pleaded that nothing had been made public, but when asked if she wished to make a direct denial she said: "No, I will not deny it. But I can't see how it got out. I understood that none of us were to say anything about it."[3] Later that night Cardinals President Jones enumerated Bresnahan's shortcomings:

> "Roger is a regular bull in a china shop," said Jones. "Things have gone from bad to worse under his administration. The club had a most unsatisfactory season financially this year. Bresnahan has been at loggerheads all season with Mrs. Britton, principal owner of the club; also at cross-purposes most of the time with his players. The ball players complain that he has been driving them too hard. The team fell behind in its 1911 record in club standing and percentage.
>
> Roger has had a strong desire to get rid of Huggins, and has complained that Mrs. Britton was interfering with his prerogative as manager when she refused to sanction several deals involving the transfer of Huggins."[4]

Eight of the Cardinals' players who were gathered at the home of Ed Konetchy in Wisconsin were "completely surprised" by the announcement and expressed "sympathy with Bresnahan and praised his work as manager." That same evening Roger related the events of the previous several days and was described as "never so disturbed" and "boiling over with rage":[5]

"Saturday afternoon I went to the office and then learned that I was no longer wanted as manager of the team. Mrs. Britton told me then that she was dissatisfied. I asked her what I had done and why, if she was not satisfied with my work, she had not come to me and spoken about the matter. She then asked why I had never come to her. I replied that I had no occasion to come to her, which remark led her to say that she did not think the coolness that existed could ever be patched up.

That was about all that was said Saturday, but I was informed that a meeting of the directors would be held Monday at the office of President Jones in the Third National Bank Building. I attended this meeting, and besides myself there was present Mrs. Britton, President Jones, Lacy Crawford and Treasurer Schofield. The purpose of the meeting was to go over the books, but principally what I would take in the way of a compromise on my contract. I informed all present that I would not accept a cent until I was paid every nickel that was coming to me on my contract, including the 10 per cent of the club's earnings. No answer was made to my request for a complete settlement Monday, but another meeting was called for Tuesday afternoon.

Tuesday I again visited the offices of President Jones. I again made my demand to the club's officials for the money I had earned. I was told that the money would be paid provided I would compromise on my contract, which has four years to run. This I refused to do, telling them that I thought I was being 'railroaded.' They then asked me to step outside for a moment. When I was called back into the office, I was told that I was dismissed."[6]

It later was related by Roger that the compromise offered by Jones included a threat—"We can and will break your contract, if necessary, but we are willing to give you your unconditional release and $2,500 in cash, if you surrender the contract." After Roger inquired about his 10 percent share of the profits, Jones reported the amount to be $1,500 which would be paid only if Roger agreed to the proposed settlement.[7]

Roger vowed "not to accept their proposition under any circumstances" and suggested he would "spend every nickel" he had to compel the club to honor its contract in the courts.[8] He further pledged, "I never quit on the ball field, and I won't quit now."[9]

* * *

Roger made the next move—he retained attorney and former judge George T. Priest.[10] Two contracts, both five-year terms, were in question. The first was a standard player contract which could be terminated by the club with 10 days' notice. The second contract was a civil document and concerned the managerial agreement. It specified a salary of $10,000 per year and an annual payment of 10 per cent of the club's profits. Roger demanded all this was due to him.

Recourse in such a dispute would normally be sought through the courts but baseball had its own rules. If Roger went to the courts, bypassing the baseball system, he could suffer banishment from the game by being blacklisted.[11] It was decided, then, for Roger to seek remedy through the National League. If he failed to be satisfied, he could appeal to baseball's ruling body, the National Commission. The courts would be the last step.

It was not until October 30 that the club provided Roger with official notice of his outright release which caused him to be put on waivers—subject to be claimed by all other National League teams.[12] The Cubs, Pirates and Dodgers claimed him during the signing period, but none finalized a deal, making Roger a free agent on November 8 and enabling him to sign with any team.[13]

The next weeks revealed that Roger's services—both as a player and as a manager—were in demand, but he let it be known that he would not make an agreement with anyone until his dispute with the Cardinals was settled. The Pirates were in hot pursuit of Roger and Fred Clarke, their manager, scheduled a meeting with him in Toledo. Roger was three hours late for their meeting because of an automobile accident—a narrow escape for him as a gasoline tank explosion destroyed his car.[14] The Dodgers, St. Louis Browns, Cincinnati, and New York Yankees also expressed interest.[15] Roger explored ownership of the Philadelphia Phillies and, once again, the Toledo Mud Hens.[16]

Concurrently, changes were being made within the Cardinals' organization. The front office confirmed rumors by naming Miller Huggins as manager on November 4.[17] Scout Dick Kinsella was asked by Mrs. Britton to attend the upcoming minor league meetings to dispose of excess players. She sought and received his recommendation of which players should be sold but overruled him based on the opinions of others in the Cardinals' office. Kinsella resigned in a huff, writing, "I refuse to let lawyers, amusement promoters, stenographers and accountants advise me in matters of baseball." Shortly thereafter Bill Armour, the other Cardinals scout, resigned.[18]

On November 5, Roger sent his contract to the Board of Directors of the National League and requested their "consideration ... before appealing to the courts."[19] He asked if the board "had jurisdiction in the matter." This was construed as a complaint, and so, a hearing before the board was granted for December 9, the day before the regular National League meeting.[20]

Bresnahan and his team of defenders knew he had supporters on the board. "Representatives of Bresnahan visited the various National League owners and got their views on the matter, some weeks ago, and it was known then that four delegates had committed themselves to Bresnahan's cause"[21]

David Fultz, "Players' Union" president, expressed Roger's contract "cannot be thrust aside" because it was "all but iron-clad." He went as far as to suggest the "St. Louis National Club's franchise could be forfeited for failure of the club to fulfill its contracts." Though such an outcome was unlikely, "for once the player, not the magnate, has a chance to win a case, before a biased body of baseball men, in a controversy over a contract."[22]

Many others also sided with Roger. The *St. Louis Star* sponsored a letter-writing contest, inviting readers to support Britton or Bresnahan. Of the "hundreds of letters" submitted, Roger prevailed by a four-to-one margin.[23] New York's *World* said "Nine-tenths of baseball people appear to side with Roger" ... and if Roger's "contract is not upheld it is believed that in the future a contract will not be worth the paper it is printed on."[24]

President Jones wrote National League President Lynch on December 4 on letterhead which had Bresnahan's name as manager crossed out and Miller Huggins' name written in pencil. He pointed out that Bresnahan had requested information only of the directors and that Bresnahan was rightfully terminated because of his conduct.[25]

Roger chimed in that he "'was going through with it,' not only for himself but also for the benefit of other players."[26]

* * *

The Board of Directors convened behind closed doors on Monday, December 9, specifically regarding the Bresnahan matter. Five board members were present: Charles Ebbets, Brooklyn; Charles Murphy, Chicago; Cornelius Sullivan, New York; Barney Dreyfuss, Pittsburgh, and Garry Herrmann of Cincinnati. They did not "adjudicate the case at issue," rather; they discussed "the jurisdiction of the directors in the case." The board finally agreed that they did have the authority but "did not desire to exercise that authority."[27] This created a quandary because support of Bresnahan would be a verdict against themselves as owners, because "...Bresnahan has so many friends in the baseball world and the opposition to feminine connection with the councils of the sport is so strong that in the present case the clubs are aligned against the St. Louis club head."[28]

Following the presentation of evidence, "it was apparent that Bresnahan had stumped the organized baseball machine." Both Herrmann and Ebbets commented, "Bresnahan had an iron-clad contract." The board was "anxious to sidestep the case" and so instead of ruling, called in the attorneys for each side and instructed them to arbitrate. Bresnahan's attorneys were Priest and Arthur W. Sager, the author of Bresnahan's contract, while James C. Jones, president of the Cardinals, represented Mrs. Britton who did not attend.[29]

The attorneys withdrew and came to an agreement. The directors gave tentative approval to the plan which called for the arbitration to be held in Missouri and instructed the attorneys to finalize the plan and present it for final approval.[30]

Settling on an arbitrator became hopeless when the person suggested by the club was withdrawn after being accepted by Bresnahan, leaving the issue as it stood.[31] Herrmann then proposed a resolution that was approved by the board: "Resolved, that a copy of Mr. Bresnahan's complaint be furnished to the St. Louis Club officially by the secretary of the league, and that the St. Louis Club be required to submit an answer thereto within twenty days, so that this matter can be taken up as a special order two or three days before our meeting in February, and that both sides be required to be ready for trial at that time."[32]

All this meant a delay for any settlement to come Roger's way and for those pursuing his services. Fred Clarke was on hand hoping to sign Roger as a Pirate. When Garry Herrmann heard this, he promised to outbid any other club for Bresnahan's services.[33] Philadelphia and Chicago joined in pursuit predicting a pennant if he joined them.[34] Manager Charles Dooin said Roger would benefit his Phillies in three ways—strengthen his own team and keep him from aiding contenders Pittsburgh and Cincinnati.[35]

Roger had agreed in writing to give the Pirates first call for his services in 1913.[36]

Bresnahan visited Herrmann in Cincinnati on December 20 to discuss a contract but, reiterated he would not complete any deal until his differences with the Cardinals were settled.[37] Herrmann suggested he could help effect a settlement with the Cardinals provided Roger signed with the Reds. He offered Roger a three-year deal for $40,000 with $17,500 to $20,000 to be paid in cash and the balance over three years.[38]

Charles Murphy, of Chicago, made what he called his "final offer" on December 26 when he phoned Roger at his Toledo home. His proposal was for three years "at a figure that he nor no other ball player could possibly afford to decline." Upon completion of the call, Murphy "was satisfied" Roger would sign.[39] But Roger denied even speaking with Murphy.[40]

The league announced that their trial would be held in St. Louis about February 12.[41] Meanwhile there was a hint that a deal was being pursued. Arthur Sager, one of his attorneys, and Lon Hocker, the Cardinals' legal adviser, were both in New York on December 20.[42] No reports of their business were forthcoming; however, the city was home of the National League's offices and that body considered settlement of the dispute vital. It could be that a deal was encouraged or even facilitated there. The January 1 20-day deadline for the club to respond to Roger's complaint came and went without response. With Roger already in St. Louis,[43] Mrs. Britton arrived there on Saturday, January 4.[44]

The very day Mrs. Britton arrived in St. Louis the speculation of a possible settlement proved true. Sunday's edition of the *St. Louis Post-Dispatch* reported:

> Roger Bresnahan's claim against the Cardinal club has been compromised.
>
> At a conference held yesterday afternoon, the warring factions reached an agreement whereby tomorrow, Bresnahan will, upon receiving a stipulated cash consideration, destroy his unexpired contract and sign a quit claim to his lien on 10 per cent of the club's profits for the next four years.
>
> No details of the settlement were made known, both sides agreeing to keep secret what happened at the conference....
>
> Because he has opportunities of getting a salary of $10,000 from other clubs in the National League, Roger had little chance to collect from the local club on his straight salary contract. However, he had a claim on 10 per cent of the club's net profits for the next four years, and it was this clause which the club officials really satisfied.[45]

Roger's award was later revealed to be $9,000 and detailed—10 percent share of the clubs' 1912 profits, $1,500, expense of claim $2,500 and contract surrender $5,000.[46]

"After balking for considerable time, the local club finally swung into line and paid the penalty ... the compromise is generally construed as a victory for the disposed leader."[47]

The unquestioned winner in the settlement was the National League. The compromise avoided airing the case in the courts saving further embarrassment to the league and baseball in general. More importantly it avoided setting a precedent which could have caused untold future damage.

It cannot be known what would have been the fortunes of the St. Louis Cardinals and Roger Bresnahan had Stanley Robison lived or if Mrs. Britton had managed as he had. Harold Lanigan of the *Sporting News* wrote at the time: "The Cardinals' future, also the Duke's, was ruined when Roger's bosses wouldn't permit him to swap Huggins back to Cincinnati … if Mr. Robison had not been called out by the Great Umpire the Cardinals would be a first-division team today and a candidate for championship honors in 1913."[48]

Roger remained in St. Louis and on Monday afternoon collected his proceeds from the Cardinals. He then called Charles Murphy in Chicago and confirmed their tentative deal. The next day, he departed for his Toledo home to receive his new contract.[49]

Suddenly Roger Bresnahan was a Chicago Cub.

Twenty-Six

"A $12,000 Coach, Murphy's Mistake or a White Elephant" (1913)[1]

Roger Bresnahan, an experienced manager and still one of the premier catchers in the game, was a free agent available to all 16 major league teams. He chose the Chicago Cubs—a seemingly unlikely choice. The Cubs had already placed a new manager for 1913, had an outstanding catcher and Roger and the Cubs' owner had been at odds for some time. But the club offered two things Roger cared about—winning and money.

Since Roger had entered the National League in 1902, all the league's pennants had been won by either Pittsburgh, New York, or Chicago and the Cubs had the most wins of all during these years. The club was especially productive during Murphy's reign beginning with his first full season of 1906. Roger had witnessed all this and predicted another championship season in 1913 for the Cubs.[2]

Definitive compensation data is not known but Roger said, "Mr. Murphy made me a much better proposition after I had received the final offers of others."[3] "He made me an offer I couldn't refuse."[4] Considering the issues with Chicago and the appeal of playing for Herrmann with whom he was friendly and in his home state, a package of more than $40,000, as offered by the Reds, seems logical.

It was suggested that Murphy's real purpose in making Roger a Cub was twofold—to have him on hand to replace his long-time second baseman and now manager Johnny Evers at a moment's notice and to weaken incumbent catcher Jimmy Archer's salary demands.

* * *

Roger's signed contract arrived in Chicago on January 14 with the advice to Murphy that he wanted to catch at least 100 games in 1913.[5] A feature article in the *Chicago Tribune* introducing Roger to Chicago's fans defined his role with the Cubs as "reserve catcher and pinch hitter."[6] Obviously, he had some convincing to do. He reported to the Cubs training camp in Tampa, Florida, at playing weight and "in the best condition of any man in the squad."[7] He was of a mindset to unseat Archer who was not in camp as he was holding out for more money. Roger did the catching for the regulars until he had a fingernail torn loose by a foul tip on March 15.[8]

The Cubs broke camp on March 18 with a full slate of games on the schedule which was wrecked by the weather.[9] Roger did not play again until March 30 at Louisville.[10] The team was scheduled daily through April 8 at Jacksonville, Chattanooga, Memphis, Nashville, Louisville, Kansas City and Chicago. The Cubs concluded their practice games on April 8 and rested a day before their Opening Day game against the St. Louis Cardinals in Chicago on April 10.

Archer and Murphy agreed to a four-year contract with a salary of $7,000 for 1913.[11] The extreme strength of the Cubs' catching staff, which also included Tom Needham, was well known. Most in the press gave Archer the nod as the number-one man. Archer was younger and stronger physically and threw exceptionally well. Roger, regarded as the brainiest of players, was not far behind physically, was the better hitter, was more experienced, and was an excellent teacher of the game. Roger possessed insider knowledge of the Opening Day opponent Cardinals—Sanborn wrote in the *Chicago Tribune*, "Roger knows the men he used to manage better than they do themselves."[12]

Because of rainy weather the opening game was delayed until April 12. In a cold drizzle, with Roger catching and Archer playing first, the Cubs lost to the Cardinals 5–3. On his first plate appearance as a Cub, Roger drove a long fly to center scoring his boss Johnny Evers.[13]

After entertaining Pittsburgh, the Cubs travelled to St. Louis. The first game there was "Bresnahan Day." Prior to the game, Roger was presented with a diamond watch fob by St. Louis Mayor Henry Kiel. The gift was a token of appreciation from Roger's St. Louis fans.[14] The pre-game ceremonies would have been approved by the Cardinals' management but comments on the outpouring of affection for the team's former manager were not recorded. Roger joined in the celebration by driving in the game's first run with a solid single as the Cubs cruised to a 7–1 win. The next day Roger took a foul tip and "dented the bum finger" he had gotten in Florida and went to the bench to recover.[15] It would be nearly two months before Roger would again catch regularly.

During those two months he caught in eight games and pinch hit on three occasions. His primary function now was overseeing the pitchers: "When he came to the Cubs Evers turned the pitchers over to him recognizing the wise head under Roger's cap. It took time to make winners out of the material the Harp [nickname bestowed by Chicago's *Day Book*] had to work with, but he stuck to the job and results show for themselves. If he never caught a game all year Bresnahan would be worth his salary for the miracles he worked with that porous pitching staff."[16]

Roger got back into the fray on June 13 when Archer was hit on the throwing hand by a foul and dislocated his middle finger.[17] He caught 14 straight games, some of which took place in extremely hot weather. A Chicago scribe described the effect of the heat in one, "Roger Bresnahan created a mud puddle back of the plate because of his exertions. He soaked two hits [one], got two bases on balls, scored three runs, and stole a base, coasting to second on his belt buckle.... Between innings Roger waved a fan in his own face."[18]

Earning a rest following his yeoman's duty, some who had formerly referred to Roger as a "$12,000 coach, Murphy's Mistake or a white elephant," now gave him his due and raved about his pitcher handling and said, "he is going too well to be kept on the bench."[19]

Archer returned on June 29 and shared the position with Bresnahan but not for long. Archer was hit on the same wound on July 8 and was projected to be lost for two weeks.[20] Roger assumed the position again but a week later was benched in favor of Tom Needham. Evers denied published reports that he had taken the action because of "not catching according to orders and for indifferent work" on Roger's part but rather to see if a change would stem the team's recent losing ways as he had tried everything else. Whatever the reason, there seemed to be growing friction between Evers and Bresnahan. Some other Cubs enjoyed and even promoted seeing their manager disconcerted. A former Cub participated in efforts to get Evers' goat. Joe Tinker, then Cincinnati's manager, once greeted Evers, "Well Johnny, what pitcher has Bresnahan picked for you today?"[21]

Roger was reinstated following a long-distance telephone call from Murphy to Evers while the Cubs were in Philadelphia. Not understanding how anyone could "select Needham over Bresnahan" Murphy "commanded Evers to supplant Needham with Bresnahan."[22] Roger held the job longer than expected because Archer injured his troublesome digit a third time on July 28.[23] Following Archer's return on August 6, Bresnahan's appearances were sparse for the remainder of the 1913 season. He did catch two games in St. Louis in early September and was reportedly "sad at the discomfiture of his former crew."[24] The Cubs swept the Cardinals who were mired in the National League's cellar and destined to finish a distant last under Miller Huggins.

Roger caught the season's final game, a 5–1 win over the Pittsburgh Pirates. The season had to be a disappointment for him. His hopes of catching 100 games and the Cubs winning the pennant did not come to fruition. The Cubs were respectable, finishing third in the National League with 88 wins—the same as second-place Pittsburgh. The New York Giants were the class of the league with 101 wins. Roger, not including his contributions as pitching coach, was not very respectable, catching in just 58 games, pinch hitting in 11 and batting a career-low .228.

The Cubs had more baseball to play—the best-of-seven game Chicago City Series with the White Sox. The Sox prevailed 4–3.[25] Roger was on hand for all the games but saw no action. Most of the team then embarked on a barnstorming tour but Roger left the team.[26]

* * *

Virtually nothing was heard from Roger during his 1913–1914 winter hiatus from baseball. He returned to work as a private detective in Toledo, visited St. Louis, made a hunting trip to the South in January, and added 20 pounds.[27]

While nothing was heard *from* Roger a lot was heard *about* him from the ever-present rumor mill. And most of what was heard concerned where he would be in 1914.

The renegade Federal League proclaimed itself a major league in 1914 and was desperate for personnel. Roger was suggested as an owner for a Toledo franchise or as manager of the St. Louis Terriers.[28] Many newspapers speculated that Roger was headed to Brooklyn, but Wilbert Robinson got the managerial job instead.[29]

Unbelievably, the *St. Louis Star* reported Mrs. Britton wanted to reinstate Roger as manager of her Cardinals.[30] This story was squashed days later when Mrs. Britton said she was satisfied with Miller Huggins and wanted to give him another chance.[31] The release of Joe Tinker as manager of Cincinnati gave new life to the tale that Roger was headed to Porkopolis.[32] This story made sense as Roger was considered expensive and excess baggage by some in Chicago. Cincinnati needed both a manager and a catcher—both roles could be filled by Roger.

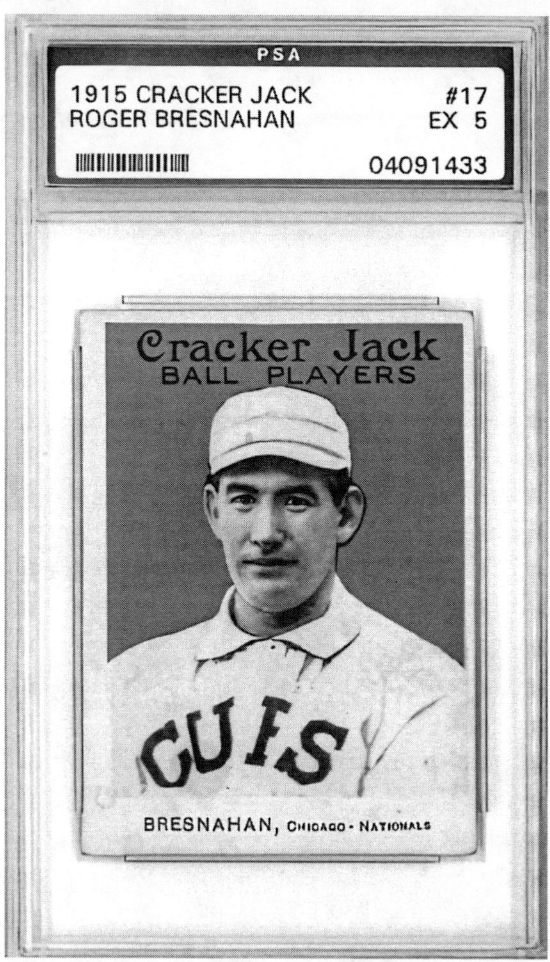

In 1913, following his firing in St. Louis, Roger signed a three-year deal with the Chicago Cubs. In addition to playing and tutoring pitchers for three seasons, he managed the club during his final year there. He left after the 1915 season to become principal owner of the Toledo, Ohio, club (courtesy Joel Tschantz).

Charles Murphy shocked the baseball world, just days before 1914 spring practice began, by what he did and what he did not do. For the second time in little more than a year he unexpectedly fired his manager.[33] What he did not do is name Roger Bresnahan as Johnny Evers' replacement.

Concurrent with Evers' dismissal, Murphy announced Hank O'Day would be his replacement. O'Day, a Chicagoan, was a former player and veteran umpire with premier status—and a former manager who had led Cincinnati in 1912. He was well known to Murphy, but his appointment came as a complete surprise.

That Roger Bresnahan was passed over for the position was indeed a puzzle since he had been hired, at significant cost, with this exact situation in mind—to succeed Evers at any time he fell down. This was reinforced following the 1913 season when Murphy invited Bresnahan to his office and told him directly, "I want you to manage my ball club next year [1914]." Roger "neither accepted nor refused but went to his Toledo home to await developments."[34] He must have been absolutely stunned when he heard of these developments.

When all was said and done, Roger Bresnahan remained as a Chicago Cub player.

Twenty-Seven

"Bresnahan Is Boss" (1914)[1]

Roger Bresnahan arrived at the Chicago Cubs' Tampa, Florida, training facility on Friday, February 20, 1914—two days following the start of camp.[2]

The reason for Roger's tardy arrival was related to yet another attempt to buy the Toledo Mud Hens. Charles Somers, principal owner of both the Toledo and Cleveland franchises, announced following a meeting of stockholders in Toledo on February 16 that he was moving the Toledo team to Cleveland.[3] His purpose was to provide continuous baseball in Cleveland to make his city less attractive to the outlaw Federal League. Roger headed a Toledo syndicate that had failed to make a deal to purchase the franchise. In reporting the story, Cleveland's *Plain Dealer* stated Bresnahan had hoped to obtain his release from the Cubs and manage at Toledo because he "has little love for the Cubs" since they had not made him their manager.[4]

How Roger and his new manager, Hank O'Day, reacted when they met as teammates for the first time is not recorded but there was no sign of discord. Chicago's *Day Book* opined 10 days later, "Bresnahan and O'Day seem to be getting along in perfect harmony, and Roger is being consulted by the manager on many questions...."[5]

Roger was robust at "1/10 of a ton"—more accurately 218 pounds.[6] He set about fixing that by running a mile wearing a rubber shirt after the morning session. In the afternoon he hit ground balls to infielders and resumed his role as pitching coach.[7]

* * *

O'Day was still looking for Bill Sweeney to report. Sweeney had been obtained when Charles Murphy traded Johnny Evers to the Boston Braves to replace Evers at second base.

John Tener, the sitting governor of Pennsylvania, was elected president of the National League by the body's board of directors (the eight team presidents) on December 9, 1913.[8] Tener faced an early-presidency issue of importance and summoned the board to Cincinnati for a February 21 meeting for resolution.[9]

"The way Evers was 'bounced' [traded to the Boston Braves] stirred up an unprecedented flood of criticism..." towards Charles Murphy and his "double-crossing tactics." The incident brought to a head the long-brewing sentiment to rid baseball of Murphy which was prevalent among the owners and included

American League President Ban Johnson, who exchanged vitriolic statements with Murphy.[10]

The purpose of the meeting was ambiguously stated—"to decide on what measures to take to protect themselves from 'internal strife.'"[11] But all the attendees understood the "purpose of the session was to straighten out the Evers tangle" and do something about Murphy.[12] Murphy was too ill to attend.[13]

The meeting did not come off. Instead, Tener met with Cubs stockholders, Charles Taft and Harry Ackerman, National League attorney, John Toole, and Murphy via telephone. The group reached an agreement—Taft bought Murphy's stock and Murphy resigned as Cubs' president.[14] Just like that Murphy was out of baseball and the game had, once again, resolved an issue of interest to the public internally and quietly.

Murphy was pleased with the arrangement. Details of the deal were not revealed but he enjoyed a very handsome return on his investment. His eight-year venture as Cubs owner was remarkably successful in terms of team performance and financial gain. His teams won four pennants and two World's Series and made him a rich man.[15]

After just a week in camp, an intrasquad game was scheduled with the Regulars beating the Yannigans, 3–1. Roger captained and played second base for the losers.[16] Three days later the Cubs began a five-game series with the St. Louis Browns at Tampa, followed by a visit by the Philadelphia Phillies for two contests. Roger shared the catching and was "ailing most of the time" but he never missed the morning practice.[17]

The Cubs left their Tampa camp on March 15 and arrived in Jacksonville to begin playing their way to the National League's Opening Day—at Cincinnati on April 14. Meanwhile the Cubs and the Braves settled their quarrel over the Evers trade giving him a $25,000 signing bonus while the Cubs signed Sweeney to a three-year deal. At the same time, Taft was trying to sell the Cubs, revealing he was party to a deal that quietly removed Murphy. Taft made Charles Herman Thomas, a Cubs' stockholder, president.[18]

At Jacksonville, the Cubs were defeated three times in as many days by the Phillies with Roger catching two. Leaving there on March 18 the team continued its northward journey playing at Savannah, Memphis, Nashville, Louisville and then to the Indiana cities of Evansville, Terre Haute and Indianapolis. Roger left the team in Evansville to visit with his sick parents in Toledo and returned to the team three days later at Indianapolis.[19] The final leg of their trek to Ohio was, except for one game at Cleveland, washed out by prolonged rain.

* * *

The Chicago Cubs were a team of unknowns when they opened the 1914 season on April 14 at Cincinnati. There was a new owner, a new general manager, and a new manager. The game's best second baseman, Johnny Evers, had been traded away.

Their glory years were behind them—they were four years removed from their last pennant which was their fourth in five seasons—and now they faced competition at the gate from two teams—the White Sox and the outlaw Federal League Whales. The magnitude of the Whales threat was unknown, but the team was said to "look like leaders" and was managed by former popular Cub, Joe Tinker. The *Chicago Tribune* suggested the Cubs were a "good but not great ball club."[20]

Unchanged going into the season was the Cub's primary catcher. Jimmy Archer kept his position while four others were listed as reserves: Bubbles Hargrave, Earl Tyree, Tom Needham, and Roger Bresnahan.[21]

Roger did not appear in the season-opening games in Cincinnati but did in the following series at St. Louis. As a pinch hitter he drove in a run with a fly and caught a game to spell Archer. The *St. Louis Post-Dispatch* noted he was in the best condition he had been in since 1911.[22] While in St. Louis he was entertained by Ed Steininger, former Cardinals' president and then president of the St. Louis Terriers of the Federal League.[23] That meeting and another with James Gilmore, president of the Federal League, fueled rumors of Roger jumping to the upstart organization, perhaps as manager in St. Louis.[24] These rumors persisted but never materialized.

Roger got a start behind the bat on April 30 due to Archer's "slight sickness" that stretched into a five-game absence.[25] Archer was back in the lineup for just four days when struck on a finger by a foul tip giving Roger an opportunity to catch regularly.[26] He caught every Cubs game until May 28 when he was hit by a foul tip and forced to retire, giving way to Archer whose finger was still swollen.[27] The regular work had benefited Roger. His always-present rheumatism had been "gradually working out" and he had raised his batting average from .125 to .333.[28]

On June 6, Archer was felled by yet another injury when he lunged for a loose ball and landed on his right arm and sustained a "double fracture of the elbow."[29] Needham finished catching the game.

Bresnahan returned for the Cubs on June 8 despite his still swollen and sore right thumb and injured toe.[30] The next day he was cracked on the same toe by a foul tip and forced to retire.[31] But after that and despite injuries to hand and foot and aches and pains he started the next eleven games before giving way to Needham for a week of healing. That week included an exhibition game with the World's Champion Philadelphia Athletics at Roger's hometown of Toledo on June 23. Roger did not play but was on hand to receive a 32-piece silverware set presented by the Old Sod Club because he was born in Ireland.[32] Some in attendance, Adeleen among them, knew better. From Toledo, the Cubs continued their schedule at Cincinnati where Roger complained of stomach pains and was diagnosed with ptomaine poisoning and sent to bed.[33]

With Needham and Hargrave catching, the Cubs won the four games Bresnahan missed. Roger returned on June 26 and the winning continued—from June 19 through July 25 the Cubs won 25 of 32 games including the last nine straight and vaulted from sixth place to second, just two-and-a-half games behind the New York Giants.

Aside from those first four games and the last two, Roger caught them all playing through his rash of injuries and drawing rave reviews. Chicago's *Eagle* declared "Roger Bresnahan is catching the best ball of his career right now."[34] The *Day Book* added, "...Roger's active brain and baseball generalship have a lot to do with getting the Cubs up where they are."[35] A comparison of Archer and Bresnahan called Archer a "cracking good catcher" who lacked "the contagious fighting spirit" of Bresnahan.[36]

Roger's injured thumb continued to bother him and made it difficult to grasp his bat firmly causing his batting average to drop during the 32-game hot streak.[37] On July 14 he took a foul tip on the knee and was so lame he could not run down a wild pitch fast enough to prevent a runner's scoring from second base and was forced to retire.[38] In spite of the new injury, he was back behind the bat the next day though he "limped perceptibly."[39]

Yet another injury occurred to Roger on July 21 when he was struck by a foul tip which cut and dislocated a finger causing a swelling "as big as a house."[40] After a four-day rest Roger returned at Boston on July 27. The Cubs' ended their winning streak of nine games that day and went on to complete their visits to the east with a horrible 3–12 record. They never recovered their winning ways.

Archer did the bulk of the catching for the remainder of the trip. Back in Chicago, Roger was reinstalled as the regular catcher on August 17 and the *Day Book* exclaimed "the Cubs finally won a game" adding that Bresnahan "makes the Cubs about 30 per cent stronger when he is in the game." Roger was still hopeful "for a slice of the World's Series coin."[41]

Bill Sweeney incurred a charley horse during the game of August 26. Roger assumed his second base position and Archer supplanted Roger behind the plate.[42] Roger played at second base until Sweeney returned a week later. Archer remained as catcher for the rest of the season. Roger was limited to spelling Archer occasionally and pinch hitting for the year's last month. He showed well when he did play—in one game he had three sacrifice hits and twice he had perfect batting days. The *Chicago Tribune* was prompted to comment, "For some reason he [Bresnahan] has been used infrequently in recent games. He is more valuable than Archer."[43]

* * *

Despite a myriad of nagging injuries and illnesses, Roger Bresnahan played in and caught more games than he had since 1908. His season's batting average of .278 was second among the Cubs and exceeded the league average of .251. Thanks to his keen batting eye he drew sufficient bases on balls to register an on base percentage of .401, not far behind league-leader Casey Stengel's .404.

His body of work during the 1914 season was recognized by sportswriters from the league's cities who determined the winner of the Chalmers Award—the Most Valuable Player Award of the time. He ranked eleventh. Had there been a comeback player award, Roger would have contended.

* * *

The popular post-season Chicago City Series began on October 7 at the White Sox's Comiskey Park. Roger was a mainstay in this best-of-seven game series that went to the limit. He caught every inning of the first six games. The Cubs took a three-games-to-one lead. In the fourth contest, the Cubs won thanks to two rallies. In the ninth inning the Cubs scored twice to tie the score at 2–2. The Sox scored a single run in the 10th. In the Cubs' half, with a runner on second, Bresnahan doubled to tie the score. Another double followed, scoring Roger, and securing the win. "Bresnahan was seized by ardent admirers and borne off the field."[44]

Following two White Sox wins, the deciding game entered the ninth inning with the south-siders leading 3–2. After two were out Bresnahan went in to pinch hit with runners on second and third. He worked the count full but then flied out to short left field—the final out of the season for Chicago baseball.[45]

* * *

On the heels of the 1914 season's conclusion, Roger was faced with decisions concerning his future. He had been courted by the St. Louis Terriers of the Federal League in April. In July, Ed Steininger, Terrier's president, came to Chicago to again offer Roger the managing post of his club.[46] Roger refused because Archer was hurt, and the Cubs were fighting for the pennant but was open to considering the job later.[47]

It was now later, and on October 22 Roger was in Brooklyn talking with the management of the Federal League Tip Tops about managing.[48] Three days later a *Chicago Tribune* headline read "Roger Signs as Manager of Tip Tops." The story specified a three-year term and a $10,000 signing bonus and was called "iron clad."[49] Papers across the nation carried the story but none of it was true.

It was revealed in December that one of the opportunities "open to Roger was the position of manager of the New York Americans as successor to Frank Chance." Apparently, that was the opportunity that was the most alluring to Roger, who saw the immense possibilities should he be successful in making a winner of the Yankees.[50]

Negotiations continued between Roger and George Ward of Brooklyn *and* President Thomas of the Cubs. After a series of meetings with both in Chicago, Roger indicated he would "take three days in which to think over the various propositions."[51]

In January 1915 Roger exposed the terms of the two offers he had refused in an affidavit filed in a trust suit brought by the independent Federal League against organized baseball. The St. Louis offer was "close to setting a record for baseball salaries" and included a $12,000 salary, $25,000 worth of stock and a $5,000 signing bonus. The Brooklyn package was $50,000 for three years with a $5,000 a signing bonus.[52] Roger had asked for $60,000 from Brooklyn thinking it would be his last baseball contract and perhaps he would not be welcomed back in organized baseball after having jumped to the independents.[53] These were huge offers—the average American man earned $687 per year in 1915.[54]

Roger was also pursuing another option which would have precluded his managing any team other than his own. He joined with his former St. Louis Cardinals Scout William Armour to purchase the Cleveland American Association franchise with the aim of returning it to Toledo.[55] Armour revealed to Noah Swayne that the pair hoped John Willys, Toledo automobile industrialist, would finance their venture.[56]

The path that Roger chose and the offer he did accept began to crystallize when Charles Murphy returned from meeting with the Cubs' principal owner, Charles Taft, on November 18—yes, Charles Murphy the former owner and president of the Cubs who was thought to be completely out of baseball. The *Day Book* suggested that he was the "real boss" of the Cubs. Shortly after Murphy arrived in Chicago President Thomas headed for Cincinnati with Roger in tow.[57]

Taft, Thomas and Bresnahan met in Cincinnati. Following their talks Thomas called Chicago with the news that Roger Bresnahan had been engaged as Cubs manager for three years[58] Compensation was later disclosed by the *Chicago Eagle* quoting a "trustworthy source" as "$6,000 as a player and $12,000 as a manager or $18,000 a year" and included the provision that Bresnahan could not be "dethroned without his consent."[59]

"Bresnahan is to have free rein in the management of the Cubs, for three years, according to his own and the statement of President Thomas." Roger no doubt secured the understanding and acceptance of this point to avoid a repeat of events that led to his departure from St. Louis.[60] The *Day Book* firmly stated "Bresnahan is boss, and he will be in fact as well as name, or there will be considerable muss stirred up."[61]

Roger began routine shuttling between Toledo and Chicago that continued through the winter. His priority was the Cubs' roster—the issue of a second baseman and the number of players reserved that needed to be reduced to 21 by May 1, 1915.[62] He set about his task in his usual style of working behind the scenes and not sharing progress with the press. Rather, he preferred to complete the task or culminate the deal before making it public, which sometimes gave an impression of inactivity.

He and President Thomas attended the regular National League meetings in December[63] and the body's February scheduling meeting prepared with trade proposals and blank checks.[64] Efforts were made but no deals were finalized. The pair gave the impression "that they were planning to tear the Chicago team to pieces and rebuild it with new material." Roger and John McGraw of the Giants engaged in protracted talks.[65] Roger made at least two trips to Cincinnati to talk trade with Garry Herrmann.[66]

Failing to complete a trade, Roger made a purchase of a second baseman securing Polly McLarry from Louisville.[67] He began roster reductions by giving four players their release. Among them were the previous year's second baseman Bill Sweeney and Tommy Leach, the team's popular but aging center fielder.[68]

Twenty-Eight

"Bresnahan Has Held the Cubs in the Race" (1915)[1]

On Saturday, February 27, 1915, Roger Bresnahan left Chicago for his 17th major league season and fourth season as a player-manager. About a third of the Cubs' 35-man roster, President Thomas, Secretary Cooke, and Physical Director Hart accompanied him. The remaining players traveled directly to Tampa where practice was scheduled to begin on Tuesday, March 1. Due the next day was Charles Murphy. The Cubs' former owner was described as having "a strangle hold on a majority of the stock" and as the "phantom owner."[2]

Formerly the Cubs left Florida early and scheduled games nearly every day on their way north. Many of those games were played with American Association teams in cities where the weather was no better than Chicago's. Some of these games—the revenue they generated and training benefits—were lost to foul weather. "Bresnahan altered this when he wiped out the majority of the exhibition games on the northern trip and arranged for the squad to be in Tampa for a full month."[3]

Roger—admitting to the habit himself—issued a season-long edict banning cigarette smoking for all, calling it "the insidious enemy of athletes."[4] As always, Roger's emphasis was on physical hardening and included soccer. The first intrasquad match was played on March 5 with the regulars defeating the Goofs 2–0. Bresnahan caught for the regulars and Archer for the Goofs.[5] Intersquad games began at St. Petersburg, the spring home of the Philadelphia Phillies. Roger sent his first team—managed by Jimmy Archer—while he stayed in Tampa with the aspiring Cubs. Roger had appointed Archer as his chief assistant.[6]

The routine of morning drills and afternoon games continued through March except on Sundays when baseball was forbidden by Florida blue laws. Either afternoon intrasquad games or full nine-inning affairs were held with the Philadelphia teams training nearby—the Phillies and the Athletics—as well as the Louisville American Association club and a visiting Cuban team.

The Cubs broke camp in Florida on the last day of March.[7] The stay in Florida for the month paid dividends as the Cubs did not miss a day's work outdoors and most of the team, including Roger was in "bully condition."[8] The good luck with the weather continued for the Cubs during their travels through Georgia, Alabama, and Tennessee, but there was a disabling injury—Catcher Jimmy Archer injured a finger on his throwing hand keeping him out for more than a week.[9] Despite of "a slight injury" of his own, Roger caught daily ensuring he would be ready for regular games if needed.[10] He looked ready to play making "a home run inside the lot" in one game and picking two runners off second base in another.[11]

* * *

The Cubs were ready physically and Roger addressed issues concerning the players' mental approach to their work. He stressed the importance of eliminating dissension because it interfered with "real teamwork."[12] He laid down rules that emphasized maximum effort at all times and promised offenders that they would be fined.[13] Overall he had instilled "some fire and determination in the troop and each fellow is starting the season with a determination to do his level best."[14]

Opening Day for the 1915 Chicago Cubs was April 14 versus the St. Louis Cardinals at Chicago's West Side Grounds. The Cubs' roster—limited to 21 players on May 1—contained 24 names.[15] In mid-March Bresnahan had already identified his 21 men.[16] Only two new men were included—pitchers Karl Adams and Alfred Standridge.[17]

In Sanborn's roster review and season prognostication, the writer presented a biography of Roger which revealed a truth: he was *not* born in Ireland but rather in Toledo, Ohio.[18] This admission by Roger reversed his long-standing contention that he was born in Tralee, County Kerry. His disclosure apparently received little notice and the legend of his fantasy birthplace continued.

The veteran team with new leadership was considered a pennant contender by critics.[19] Cubs' President Thomas unequivocally predicted his team would win the National League pennant.[20] Sportswriter Bozeman Bulger visited 14 of the 16 spring camps and polled more than 200 players for their championship team picks and his straw vote placed the Cubs third behind the Giants and the Braves. His opinion was the Cubs were in the best physical condition of any team he saw, and he expected them to get off to a fast start.[21] Grantland Rice, writing in the *New-York Tribune,* picked the Cubs for third place.[22] So it was with promise and some respect that the Cubs began championship play.

* * *

From the preliminary festivities through the end of the game, the National League's Opening Day was a huge success.

Stepping off in the afternoon, a motorcade with hundreds of automobiles left Grant Park, wound its way through the Loop and on to the West Side Grounds. The players in spanking new uniforms were at the forefront of the procession. At the ballpark, band concerts and cabaret stunts entertained.[23]

The game itself was a one-sided affair. The Cubs' Jim "Hippo" Vaughn completely outshined the Cardinals' lefty ace and former Bresnahan project, Slim Sallee. The hits were even with eight for each team but six stolen bases by the Cubs and nine

Cardinals' errors contributed to a 7–2 Chicago victory. Second Baseman-Manager Miller Huggins uncharacteristically had four of his team's misplays. Roger did not play but deferred to Jimmy Archer because, "Archer's popularity entitles Jim to the first show before the home populace."[24]

The Cubs and Cardinals split the season's initial series, each won twice. By May 10, the Cubs' record had progressed to 13 wins and eight losses, and they rested in second place, a half-game behind Philadelphia and a half-game ahead of third-place Boston. At this early-season juncture, the race was on, and the Cubs had already made two lineup changes.

Roger quickly recognized that Polly McLarry was not the answer to the team's second base issues. The hard-hitting third baseman, Heinie Zimmerman, was moved to replace him and Art Phelan took over at third. Both remained for the duration of the season.

The other change concerned Roger himself. Roger intended Jimmy Archer to be the Cubs' primary catcher backed up by himself and Bubbles Hargrave. But Archer was unable to play beginning April 18 and remained out of service for more than three weeks. During his absence Roger caught every inning of every Cubs game. The *Day Book* welcomed the change: "Archer is as good a mechanical catcher as could be desired, but the manager is out in front alone when it comes to steering heavers. He holds them up and helps with control."[25] Following Archer's return he and Roger caught on alternate days.

Roger Bresnahan was a student and teacher of all aspects of the game and besides managing he showed how to play the game of the Dead Ball Era. He especially shined in a two-game series at Cincinnati. In game one, he had "three hits of assorted sizes" including a long double and a short bunt. Following a single he scored on a hit-and-run play. His bunt, which he beat out for a hit, scored the runner from second base and he promptly stole second base.[26] In game two, he drew three walks, stole two bases, and scored a run.[27]

Archer's return coincided with the Cubs' first invasion of the National League's eastern cities. They gained a split in the first series at Brooklyn by amassing 19 runs in the finale. A few days later against the Giants at the Polo Grounds they won by the minimum score when Frank Schulte scored the only run by stealing home in the first inning.[28] Then, during a four-game sweep of the defending World's Champion Boston Braves, the Cubs moved into first place.

* * *

After playing 27 of the season's first 39 games on the road, the first-place Cubs began an extended home stand against the New York Giants on Saturday, June 5 before 11,000 spectators. They lost 3–0 but still held a slim one-game lead over Philadelphia. Uncharacteristically, the Giants stood last in the league standings but only five games behind the Cubs—making the race as tight as a "closed up accordion."[29] The homestand included a six-game winning streak that allowed the Cubs to build a four-and-a-half-game lead. The first win was a 19-inning game on June 17 and came on the strength of a still-record pitching performance by Zip Zabel who pitched 18.1 innings in relief.

By posting a modest 16–13 record for the homestand, which was interrupted by a five-game trip to Cincinnati, the Cubs' lead over Philadelphia had shrunk to two games.

The trip to Cincinnati included a violation of Roger's primary tenet of play—"to keep on hustling and fighting, running out every play to the last inch, no matter how far ahead or behind the team may be"[30]—by one of his better players. Heinie Zimmerman hit a tough grounder to shortstop and Roger related that he "failed to do his best to beat Herzog's [Cincinnati manager and shortstop] throw to first in the sixth and I called him for it."[31] "Zim responded in terms of a rather harsh nature." Roger reacted quickly, fined his second baseman $100 and removed him from the game.[32] Following a lengthy meeting the next day Roger rescinded the fine. "This was the first fine Bresnahan had pulled on any of his players, as he does not believe in taking an athlete's money if there is any other way to convince said player that he is working for the ball club instead of for himself and the players' union."[33]

A week later Roger was subjected to banishment because of a bizarre stunt he pulled against the Reds. He attempted to rattle Pitcher Rube Benton by moving about the batter's box. With three balls already called and Benton just beginning his windup, he "jogged across the plate, tossed his bat away, and ran down to first base." Umpire Ernie Quigley called him out. Roger was furious. He charged Quigley, "pulled up short under the umpire's chin and stamped his spikes on the umpire's feet." Quigley responded with an attack of his own but was promptly restrained by players before he could land a blow.[34] The next morning Roger apologized to Quigley and explained the "spiking" had been unintentional. The umpire accepted the explanation ending the issue as simply an ejection.[35]

Quigley's was Roger's only ejection as a player during the 1915 season, but he was told to leave on five occasions in his capacity as manager. Roger's quick temper had been an issue throughout his career though some of his ejections, especially as a manager, may have been by design—motivation for his team or intimidation of an umpire for future benefit. In all Roger was ejected 61 times during his career ranking him 19th among all major league players and managers and his 33 as a player rank him sixth.[36]

* * *

The Cubs stopped at Pittsburgh for a single game on the way to their second 1915 eastern trip. After a win over the Pirates and a day off, the Bresnahans opened a four-game series at Brooklyn with a three-game lead in the pennant race. They lost all four and moved on to Manhattan for five games against the Giants. They lost two more, running their losing streak to six and dropping to second place after the games on July 14. Except for two days, they had held the top spot since May 21.

Chicago's *Tribune* beat writer covered spring practice and all games home and away. Sanborn had filled the role for the Cubs through July 4. Beginning the next day, he switched teams with James Crusinberry who had been following the White Sox. Crusinberry was well acquainted with Bresnahan from his days writing for the *St. Louis Post-Dispatch* from 1908 to 1910.

Crusinberry added humor when describing the first game of the July 14 double-header in which the Cubs earned a split and ended their losing streak. Roger caught the first game, a 6–5 loss, of which Crusinberry wrote, "Roger Loses Some Weight": "It was a sweltering hot day and one of the features of the entertainment was the perspiring of Roger Bresnahan. He caught the opening game and the sun at that time was so high that the shadows of the grandstand did him no good. Roger looked as if he had been dipped in something before the fourth inning was over. In the fifth he started a vigorous attack by slamming a single to right field and then stealing second base, but when he hit the dirt at the middle bag, he jarred his breakfast loose from the linings of his stomach and had to have time called while he recovered."[37]

In contrast Heywood Broun wrote simply in the *New-York Tribune*, Bresnahan "was so clearly overcome he was forced to ask for a time out."[38]

The following day Roger called a team meeting and "explained in words of one syllable that he was going to have a ball team that tried all the time, whether it won or not."[39] The team responded that afternoon with a 5–2 win.

The Cubs lost the finale in New York and headed to first-place Philadelphia for four games—still in second place just one game behind the Phillies. Pitching the opener for the home team was the great Pete Alexander whose record stood at 17–3. Thanks to Larry Cheney's pitching and hitting, the Cubs pulled into a virtual tie for the league lead by winning 4–0 before 18,000 onlookers. With Bresnahan behind the bat, Cheney was magnificent in recording the shutout and figured prominently in the Cubs' scoring. At the end of the day Brooklyn was in third place just one game back, while New York, St. Louis and Pittsburgh were tied for fourth place, four games back. Also, at the end of the day, the White Sox and Whales joined the Cubs as all three of Chicago's major league teams resided in first place—a circumstance that has not been repeated.[40]

The Cubs played an excellent game in all regards in beating baseball's best pitcher in what was their most crucial game of the year. They had won three of four games to climb back to the top of the league standings. With the season at its halfway point, the big win served to restore team confidence.

* * *

Bad luck, sickness, injuries, and a decline of competitive spirit on the part of some players all surfaced at the same time and rudely squashed the joy the Cubs felt after their big win over Alexander the Great. Roger, President Thomas, and most of the team enjoyed Sunday on the beach and boardwalk of Atlantic City before Monday's engagement with the Phillies, when troubles began to mount[41]:

- July 19—A freak home run was the margin of defeat. An opening in the fence that provided access to the scoreboard was left open, allowing what would have been a single to roll through for a home run.[42]
- July 20—First Baseman Vic Saier injured an ankle sliding into home. Out until August 12.[43]
- July 20—Pitcher Zip Zabel was suspended, sent back to Chicago "to get in condition" and fined $100.
- July 23—Third Baseman Art Phelan confined to bed with severe tonsillitis.[44] Out until August 5.
- July 23—Bubbles Hargrave, backup catcher, confined to bed with severe tonsillitis.[45] Out until August 8.
- July 23—Roger was injured while playing in Boston. The Braves' Sherry Magee turned himself completely around while swinging and stepped on Roger's toe.[46] The Cubs' manager sustained a fracture. Out until August 18.[47]

Five of the allowed 21 roster players were on the shelf. Forced to reorder his lineup, Roger moved Zimmerman to third base for Phelan and filled his position with Pete Knisely, the Cubs' reserve outfielder, who had not played the infield in two years. Polly McLarry filled in at first base for Saier while Archer went behind the bat. He had no backup.[48]

Despite the short roster, the Cubs played competitive baseball but could not win. The trip through the east produced a 3–14 record with eleven losses by a single run. The Cubs limped home with a 43–43 record. Though they did not win much, the Cubs earned a lot of money for the stockholders by drawing big crowds in every city. The club took in more money than any other Cub team on an eastern tour since 1908.[49]

* * *

The start of the homestand was delayed by three days of postponements—healing time for players. The Cubs and Giants did not square off, off until July 30. By then the Cubs had fallen to fifth place.

Roger let it be known that the upcoming homestand was critical and if the team did poorly "drastic measures will be adopted." He also noted that he had lost faith in "a lot of his players" saying "he had only three or four men on the team who were really trying."[50] He was especially dismayed with some of his veterans: "You can't teach an old dog new tricks, and I guess you can't teach an old ball player to play the game any differently than he has been accustomed to playing it. It looks to me like the proper way to get a winning team is to begin with live and enthusiastic youngsters."[51]

When the series began, Roger was "wearing citizen's clothes and a cane" managing from the bench.[52] The teams split their four games. Five straight wins from the Phillies and the World's Champion Braves followed. The last win over Boston featured a three-run ninth-inning rally that propelled the Cubs into second place 1.5 games behind Philadelphia. Brooklyn came to Chicago for five games that closed the homestand. The Robins won four of five.

The homestand was a mixed bag and ended with an 8–6 record. Except for Bresnahan, all the sick, injured, and suspended players had returned to active duty. There were two July acquisitions. Red Murray was claimed off waivers from the Giants and provided good-hitting outfield help. During the catching crisis, Bob O'Farrell, an 18-year-old catcher out of Waukegan, Illinois, who had been on Roger's radar all season, became a Cub. O'Farrell did not supply immediate help but was quite a find—he went on to catch for 21 seasons in the National League. He later recalled his just-out-of-high school experience with the Cubs: "Mr. Bresnahan helped me a great deal. He … showed me the ropes and how to catch.… Except for Bresnahan nobody paid any attention to me.… They didn't want a rookie to come in and take one of their buddies' jobs. But they weren't too bad. They just more or less ignored me."[53]

* * *

The Cubs' quest for the pennant continued with the launch of a month-long road trip. Such a lengthy trip was a daunting task but may have favored the Cubs as it meant 24 of their last 26 games were to be played at home. The trip included stops in all the National League's cities except Cincinnati. It began at St. Louis on August 12 and made stops in 10 cities (two of them twice) over 28 days with play on 24 of them. There were seven doubleheaders and five exhibition games in the mix.

The Cubs compiled a 10–17–1 record in championship games which crushed their pennant hopes. By the time they reached home they were in fifth place 11 games behind first place and the eventual winner, Philadelphia.

One of the exhibitions was in Toledo, Ohio, on August 16 against the semi-professional Toledo Railway and Electric Company's Rail-Lights and was Roger's first action since breaking his toe on July 23. He was not the only Bresnahan in the game—Martin Bresnahan, the Rail-Lights third baseman, was a veteran of seven minor league seasons. In the sixth inning of the Cubs' 6–1-win, Roger tried to go from first to third on an infield hit and "crashed" into his nephew who made the putout.[54]

Chicago's *Day Book* assessed the Cubs' state of affairs—"With the material at hand Bresnahan has held the Cubs in the race about as long as possible. They have made their bid, withered, and will not threaten the top again … all efforts must be concentrated toward finishing in the first division."[55]

Certainly, Bresnahan would have preferred finishing in the first division, but his focus turned to preparing for the 1916 season. He set about that task in earnest while on this trip. At Toledo he played several amateur and semi-professional players to observe them in action. Among them was Charlie Pechaus, a Chicago amateur infielder, who was accompanying the Cubs as a winner in a *Tribune* competition.[56] He soon after signed with the Cubs. Roger traded veteran pitcher and the Cubs' mainstay Larry Cheney to Brooklyn for Joe Schultz, a young infielder he had tabbed as his future shortstop. The *Tribune* called the trade "the first step by Bresnahan in a campaign to get rid of the Cub veterans and build up a new ball club of youngsters for next season."[57]

* * *

The Cubs began their homestand on September 11 in fifth place—two weeks later they rested at the bottom of the league standings. In a scenario unimaginable just a few years earlier, the Cubs and the Giants had been waging a battle for last place. But following a one-day stay in the cellar, the Cubs won five straight over Cincinnati in three days to move up to fourth. Roger had been playing prospects but, needing a win against St. Louis on the season's final day to finish in the first division, he played his regulars including himself and his pitching ace Jim Vaughn. Thanks to a seven-run second inning the Cubs prevailed 7–2.

The Cubs win meant something as it extended their first division finishes streak to 10 seasons. Just 2,800 fans were in the stands for one of three season-ending games played in Chicago that day. The south-side White Sox drew 3,500 for a game that meant nothing to the American League's third-place team. The big event was the north side's doubleheader played Federal League's Chicago Whales who squeezed 34,000 fans into Weeghman Park (now Wrigley Field). The Whales' second game win provided the narrow margin needed to secure a pennant.[58]

The National League standings from top to bottom were the tightest before or since of any major league organized as a single division.[59]

* * *

The regular season was over, but the annual Chicago City Series remained to be played beginning Wednesday, October 6, and Roger was serious about it. He ordered all hands to report the two mornings before the series start for "long sessions of batting drill."[60]

The formant was the best-of-seven games and the Sox got off to a fast start 9–5 in game one at Comiskey Park.[61] Not only did the Cubs lose the game but also their catcher when "Ray Schalk [Sox catcher] took a big piece out of the big toe on Bresnahan's left foot when he slid into the plate safely in the seventh inning...."[62] Roger finished the game but did not return for the remaining games.

The Sox won the next three games to easily earn the championship. Roger was coaching at third base when the last out was made and though extremely disappointed, "He dashed to the Sox bench, grabbed Rowland [Sox manager] and said 'Congratulations, Clarence. You had the better team. And from what I have seen of you in this series I am ready to believe all the good things they have been saying about you all year.'" His display of sportsmanship was recognized by Rowland and the Chicago press.[63]

Rather than returning to his Toledo home, Roger stayed in Chicago for a time to discuss his plans for revamping the team with President Thomas and to begin implementing them. He convinced Thomas, and the owners in turn, that drastic action was necessary to improve the club.[64] The problem lay in the so-called ironclad contracts that 17 of his 21 players had in force. The remaining term of those contracts was one, two or more years—meaning they would be paid for the duration of their contract no matter how they performed. Further, if the Cubs disposed of such a player to the minors or another team who paid them less, they would be on the hook for the difference.[65] Roger felt he needed to remove four or five players from the roster and procure three deluxe pitchers and a prominent hitter to go along with several younger players he already had.[66] He indicated that the owners were willing to pay a fabulous sum to have a half-dozen or more players to accomplish Roger's planned make over.[67]

Following the city series Roger was involved in an accident and charged with driving an automobile while intoxicated and assaulting R.P. Smiddy and his wife with his vehicle. He was alleged to have collided with Smiddy's buggy.[68] Roger appeared in Speeders' Court where the assault charge was dismissed because Smiddy did not appear. Regarding the intoxication charge, the arresting officer told the judge Roger had driven him to the police station following the arrest and "he thought he detected the odor of liquor, but admitted the Cub manager did not appear to be intoxicated and was booked on that charge merely to hold him." The officer was admonished and that charge against Roger was also dropped. The *Chicago Tribune* opined, "Needless to add, the arrest took place on the south side at Michigan Avenue and Thirty-Fourth Street."[69] The author notes the proximity of the accident site to Comiskey Park and surmises the Cubs-White Sox rivalry was already established.

Twenty-Nine

Roger's Long-Time Dream Realized (1916–1919)

President Thomas and Manager Bresnahan departed Chicago on December 10, 1915, for New York City to attend the National League meetings. The pair stopped in Cincinnati to confer with principal Cubs' owner Charles Taft to review Roger's plans for strengthening the team. Roger intended to "submit various trade proposals to the other National League managers" but realized the other fellow had to consent for a deal to happen.[1] He came away empty-handed.

What Roger did during the meetings depended on which issue of the *Chicago Tribune* was read. On December 15 "no one was busier," but three days later the same newspaper reported, "Roger Bresnahan hasn't mentioned a trade to another manager since he came here. He has seen all the shows in town and met all his friends and is wondering why he should have his expenses paid for doing that."[2]

However, the lack of trades made no difference to the futures of the Cubs and Messrs. Thomas and Bresnahan because of other over-shadowing events concurrently at work:

- A peace pact between Organized Baseball and the Federal League was being negotiated.
- The Chicago Cubs were about to be sold.
- Charles Somers was losing his Cleveland American League and American Association franchises.

The independent Federal League had challenged Organized Baseball's monopoly for two seasons by placing teams in some of the establishment's cities and signing their players. Charles Weeghman of the Chicago Whales was one of the Federal's leaders who sought peace between the warring organizations and was in New York promoting the cause.[3] Serious talks took place, but it was not until a meeting in Cincinnati on December 23 that an agreement was reached, and the Federal League ceased to exist. A key provision allowed defecting players back into Organized Baseball.[4]

Of great interest to our protagonist, the peace agreement provided that Weeghman could purchase the Chicago Cubs. The deal had been prearranged and Weeghman announced that he would combine the Cubs and Whales into one National

League club and play on Chicago's north side.[5] "He stated positively that Joe Tinker would be manager and offered no solution of the problem of disposing of Roger Bresnahan and his ironclad contract which has two more years to run."[6]

Meanwhile, Charles Somers was being forced to dispose of his Cleveland teams because of financial difficulties. One of the terms of the tentative peace agreement—likely included because of Weeghman's influence—specified "Roger Bresnahan who has a two-year contract with the Chicago Nationals is to be paid in full and assisted to purchase the Cleveland American Association club and to take it back to Toledo, his hometown."[7]

Rumors concerning potential financial partners for Roger abounded during the following weeks. Bresnahan's desire to own the Toledo club had long been known and he appeared to be the universal choice to head Cleveland Spider club.

Weeghman was the key to sealing the deal because of his contract with Bresnahan. He supported Roger throughout the process but, of course, remained mindful of his own interests.

Roger's contract was an issue because it bound him to the Cubs and his release was necessary before he could pursue the Toledo franchise.[8] Eventually, an agreement gave Roger a $10,000 payment and his release.[9]

The American Association needed Toledo to maintain an eight-team circuit and was anxious to aid Roger. Two of the league's owners—Mike Cantillon of Minneapolis and Al Timme of Milwaukee—agreed to buy the Spiders on a temporary basis and pass the franchise on to Roger after he was released from the Cubs. Roger organized and incorporated the Toledo Base Ball Company along with partners Charles F. Northrup, George W. Ritter, John B. McMahon and W.M. Richards, making the enterprise wholly Toledo-owned.[10] He finalized the deal on April 15 when he paid Cantillon and Timm $30,000 due on the full purchase price of $40,000.[11] The deal included the franchise, equipment, players and a lease with an option to buy Swayne Field.

The *Chicago Tribune* sent Roger on his way with these words: "For years Bresnahan has wanted to control the Toledo club. This is his hometown, where there are not many more men more popular than the famous catcher, who has been known in the big show as the Duke of Toledo. The Toledo ball park is probably the best minor league enclosure in the country. With a civic hero in charge of the team and home capital behind it there is little doubt that the town will support a club of A.A. [American Association] caliber. In his long experience in the major leagues Roger has gained the friendship of all big managers and owners, which will be useful in landing material for his team."[12]

Roger Bresnahan had fulfilled an aspiration to head his hometown baseball team that had been known at least since 1903.[13]

* * *

Manager Bresnahan had a great deal of team building to do as Opening Day loomed on April 18. He began acquiring players immediately following league approval of the transfer on March 7.[14] American Association rules limited rosters to 16 which included Roger. Pressed for time, he quickly signed five Federal League refugees including George Stovall, a former manager and likely headliner.[15] Stovall was made his assistant and team captain.[16]

Ten players were included with the purchase of the club but only two—Second Baseman Earle Gardner and Outfielder Roy Wood—made the team.[17] Roger continued to acquire experienced major league players but said he would "catch every game if injuries don't stop him."[18]

President Bresnahan announced from the Mud Hens' spring camp in Dawson Springs, Kentucky, that he had made Lloyd Rickert the business manager. Rickert was a formerly a St. Louis Browns' official and a senior executive of the Federal League.[19] He also revealed the Toledo team would forgo tradition, drop the Mud Hens' cognomen, and be known as the Iron Men. Bresna-Hens had been used sparingly for both Roger's Toledo and St. Louis teams.[20]

The short spring practice in Dawson Springs began on March 20, included two games with the Columbus Senators, and ended when the club broke camp on April 7.[21] The Iron Men moved to Springfield, Ohio, for exhibitions with the Reapers then headed for Toledo.

The Iron Men arrived in Toledo the morning of Wednesday, April 12 and boarded at Toledo's posh Boody House. They participated in two-a-day practices at Swayne Field leading up to Opening Day the following Tuesday.[22] Toledo's *Daily Blade* joyfully proclaimed Roger's returning of baseball to the city with the headline: "So Long Sorrow, Howdy Joy, Soak 'Em Roger, 'Atta Boy'."[23]

The day before the season's start was a busy one for the Iron Men. The players were securing their living quarters—their responsibility when the season began. In the evening they were feted at a "Fan Night" celebration at the packed Toledo Coliseum. "No greater reception was ever tendered in Toledo than that which Roger Bresnahan received … tears rolled down his cheeks."[24]

Sizing up the 1916 American Association pennant chase, Dick Meade, sporting editor of the *Toledo-News Bee* and a Toledo baseball authority, quoted the predictions of circuit experts: the Minneapolis Millers and St. Paul Saints to fight it out for the championship with the Kansas City Blues, the Indianapolis Indians and the Louisville Colonels contending. The Milwaukee Brewers and the Columbus Senators were tabbed to fight it out for last place. Unknown and untested Toledo was picked to finish anyplace from third to sixth.[25]

Game day festivities began when a 60-car automobile parade escorted Bresnahan and his team from downtown Armory Park to Swayne Field.[26] The game was preceded by band and choral music and with presentations by President John Tener of the National League, President Thomas Chivington of the American Association, Toledo baseball supporter Noah Swayne and the Mayor of Toledo Charles Milroy.[27]

The contest with the Milwaukee Brewers did not disappoint the crowd of 16,467—the largest to ever attend a game at Swayne Field. Roger scored the first run and Hugh Bedient pitched a complete game 4–2 win.[28] All Toledo players had major-league experience and the lineup proved to be remarkably stable throughout the season. Bresnahan did not make good on his promise to catch every game. He caught just 12 and was unavailable while recovering from a fractured ankle.[29]

The prognosticators proved to be correct as the Iron Men finished sixth in the standings. Their record of 76–86 and season's attendance of 124,363 were not exemplary.[30] *Sporting Life* later reported that Roger admitted to losing $10,000 for the season.[31]

Dick Meade offered his differing opinion: "All things considered, the Duke did very well. He brought back the game to Toledo, had a very successful season financially, and got fair baseball out of his athletes. Bresnahan had a very short time in which to secure a club last spring, and under the circumstances, his showing was exceedingly good."[32]

Roger Bresnahan returned to his native Toledo, Ohio, where he was the principal owner of the team from 1916 through 1923. He also was president, manager, coach, and player (courtesy the Toledo Mud Hens/National Baseball Hall of Fame and Museum).

* * *

The 1917 Toledo Iron Men were barely recognizable when compared to the previous year's edition. Only two, Catcher Ed Sweeney and Outfielder Steve Evans, were regular players for both seasons. Roger's major rebuild was fueled by his long-held desire to have a team of young, hungry, and up-and-coming players who he could teach to play his way. He collected 33 players and gathered the hopefuls at Dawson Springs for spring practice beginning March 12.[33]

Roger's usual two-a-day practices were hard and were supplemented by games against outside competition. The first, against Cincinnati, featured a reunion for Roger and Red's manager Christy Mathewson.[34]

The team broke camp on April 4 and headed for a pair of games in Cincinnati.[35] Meade declared, "Toledo looms up as a dangerous contender" to challenge Kansas City and Louisville for the American Association championship.[36] The games in Cincinnati

Roger Bresnahan's 1917 Toledo Iron Men and others at spring training in Dawson Springs, Kentucky. Front row: Steve Evans, Abe Bowman, Roger Bresnahan with dog, Colonel Hamby, John Fluhrer, Bunny Fabrique, Charles Donnelly. Second row: Al Schultz, Lute Boone, Charlie Mullen, Hugh Bedient, Dazzy Vance, Neal Brady. Third row: Mayor Ed Sweeney, Russ Ford, Roy Hartzell, *Toledo News-Bee* Reporter Mitch Woodbury, Chamber of Commerce President. Back row: Angel Aragon, Bill Bailey, Harold Wise, Ray Keating, *Toledo Times* Reporter Harold McNaughton. Bresnahan called his team Iron Men for three seasons before reverting to the traditional Mud Hens (courtesy the *Toledo Blade*).

were cancelled because of bad weather and the Iron Men moved on to Toledo, arriving on Friday, April 6.[37]

As they stepped off the train, the Iron Men entered a changed country. The United States of America had declared war on Germany. War, which had been raging in Europe, had come to America that day. The specter of war would encompass all Americans, and, before season's end, 10 Iron Men would be enlisted in military service.[38]

Roger had scheduled four games at Swayne Field with three major league teams leading up to the start of the regular season on April 11. The final, a 12–1 whipping by the Cleveland Indians, on April 10,[39] was followed by a trip to Indianapolis for the start of championship play.[40]

The Iron Men lost three games at Indianapolis and three more at Louisville before returning home. The team was feted at the second annual "Fan Night" celebration on the evening of April 17 but lost the first two home games before winning.[41] The club never recovered from their 0–8 start and finished a distant last in the American Association with a 57–95 record.[42]

The most gripping baseball played by the Toledo Iron Men may have been the two pre-season games with the World's Champion Boston Red Sox. Despite wintry weather, Toledo won both before about 7,000 fans—significant attendance when compared to the total of 98,921 that attended the regular season games at Swayne Field.[43]

The first game featured the compelling matchup of Ty Cobb facing Pitcher Babe Ruth.

The story of how that came to be began in Dallas, Texas. During an exhibition game between the New York Giants and the Detroit Tigers on March 31, Cobb slammed hard into the Giants' Buck Herzog at second base. A fight ensued and Cobb, but not Herzog, was thrown out of the game. Cobb was enraged and refused to play the rest of the series against the Giants and went to Cincinnati to work out with the Reds instead.[44] Cobb also found the Toledo club in Cincinnati and accepted Bresnahan's invitation to join them. Cobb continued to Toledo and played in an Iron Man uniform against Boston the weekend of April 7 and 8. Toledo beat Ruth 6–0 with Cobb contributing a single and a walk on Saturday. On Sunday, Toledo again beat Boston 6–1 with Cobb getting another single.[45] Cobb rejoined his team on Monday and the Tigers beat Toledo 8–5.[46]

* * *

Roger Bresnahan suffered the first of a series of 1918 losses, difficulties, and disappointments when his father, Michael Cornelius Bresnahan, died on January 4 in his Toledo home.[47] Looming was the Great War that threatened baseball and the beginnings of the Spanish influenza outbreak that would eventually involve the entire world. In consideration of the war effort some minor leagues cancelled their seasons.[48] The American Association shortened its schedule to 140 games and delayed the season's start until May 1.[49] Roger opted to hold spring practice in Toledo to save travel and began the "avoirdupois melting premier" on April 1.[50]

Roger—like all in similar positions—had trouble assembling his 1918 team because of the scarcity of players and the loss of some of those under contract to the military. He scoured the ranks of the recently retired and signed former Cleveland Player-Manager Joe Birmingham but his offer to the great Honus Wagner was rejected.[51] The team he put together was hampered by poor weather and suffered from a lack of competitive play. Several exhibitions with Toledo's semi-professional Rail-Lights were played but only one with a team from Organized Baseball.

Dick Meade pegged Toledo as one of the second division clubs which he called "not impressive crews."[52] Toledo was not even that good. The Iron Men lost their first five games before finally winning and went on to post a 23–54 record—a distant last place—for the season which was further shortened and ended July 21.[53] The end of play was welcomed by Roger because of his season-long struggles in securing players and "getting fans to attend games in paying numbers."[54]

Because of injuries to his ankles the previous two years, Roger did not expect to contribute on the field.[55] He appeared in 19 games—13 in center field and just three behind the bat.[56] Two of his games catching came on the season's final day at Louisville when he loaned his catcher to the Colonels and slammed the last home run of his career.[57]

The roster for 1918 was always in flux and by season's end the Toledo club had sent another 10 into service.[58] Bresnahan had sent more players into the National Army than any other team in baseball.[59] He commented, "the army needs the men more than baseball does."[60]

Uncle Sam's edict that baseball was a non-essential occupation compelled players to work or fight. Roger, at 39 and married, was exempt from the federal decree but, "wanting to do his share of work toward putting the Kaiser out of business," signed on as purchasing agent at the United States Government Nitrate Plant in Toledo.[61]

* * *

The Great War had ended—though many ball players remained in France—and the Spanish Influenza pandemic was waning as Roger began preparing for the 1919 season. He attended the National and American Leagues' January meetings in New York and the American Association meeting in Chicago.[62] He left the latter early in a huff over the proposed league schedule which included only one holiday—Memorial Day—for Toledo and had his team's first 28 games scheduled at home. The long early-season homestand caused a hectic late season on the road and increased the season's rail travel from 7,800 miles to 11,000 adding expense he did not wish to bear.[63] He later voted against approving the schedule but lost the battle though he was awarded two holidays—July 4 and Labor Day.[64]

News from the Swayne Field offices was sparse through the winter but the "dead silence of several weeks" was broken on March 11 with the announcement that Roger had sold two players.[65] A week later it was revealed that—due to the later than usual April 23 beginning of the season—spring training would be held, once again, at Toledo's Swayne Field.[66] Roger then sold another pair of players and traded mainstay catcher, Ed Sweeney, to Pittsburgh.[67] He followed with the promise of more players from the New York Yankees who were anxious to have their younger players developed by Roger whom they "looked upon as one of the wisest generals in the game." The deal with the Yankees was slow to develop and spring training did not begin in Toledo both for the same reason—put bluntly by Dick Meade, Roger was "broke."[68] A report following the aborted 1918 season stated that for his first three seasons at Toledo he had lost "about $65,000."[69]

Several schemes for raising money and reorganization were investigated and the survival of baseball in Toledo was in question. On April 10 Meade reported in the *Toledo News-Bee* that 10 men, among 63 stockholders, had backed a note giving Roger the necessary cash to obtain promised players and start training.[70]

Roger began the process of gathering players including Rollie Zeider, an infielder recently of the Chicago Cubs. On April 16, President Bresnahan's retirement from the field and his appointment of Zeider as manager were announced.[71] Roger Philip Bresnahan promoted his brother Philip Roger to assist him as the club's business manager.[72]

The first practice was held by Zeider on April 17 just six days before Opening Day and with only 10 players in the fold.[73] Players continued to file into Swayne Field but, for the most part, were not in condition to play and had little time to develop as a team—they barely knew each other.

Opening Day was delayed three days and no practices were held because of poor weather. The circumstances had not allowed anything close to proper preparation for the season and that became painfully obvious when the weather finally allowed play the weekend of April 26 and 27. Toledo gave up 27 runs in losing two games to Kansas City though more than 10,000 watched.[74]

Roger continued to beat the bushes for players and did have some success but the team, quietly redubbed "Mud Hens, kept losing."[75] They did not win a game until May 6 and by June 9 had a record of 6–27.[76] Roger, who was not traveling with the team, quipped "it is hard to hear about the Mud Hens taking a lacing, but it is not quite as painful as seeing them take it."[77] The press noted the team's penchant for "bunching errors and passes."[78] Playing Manager Zeider's legs were ailing while the losses continued to mount (21–48) resulting in his resignation on July 15. Roger immediately stepped into his shoes.[79]

Under Bresnahan, the Mud Hens compiled a 38–43 record for the remainder of the season and passed Milwaukee to finish in seventh place and avoided a third straight cellar finish.[80] Just 89,712 fans attended games at Swayne Field.[81] Fans stayed away from the usually well-attended morning and afternoon games played on July 4 for two reasons—Toledo hosted its biggest one-day event ever—the world heavyweight championship fight between reigning champion Jess Willard and challenger Jack Dempsey, and the temperature rose to 95 degrees.[82]

Despite the paltry attendance, "the club made money" though not "very much."[83] The bottom line was helped by excellent attendance on the road and proceeds from exhibition games.[84] In the last of these, the Mud Hens hosted and whipped Roger's long-time friend, John McGraw, and his New York Giants in their home finale 12–2.[85]

At 40 years of age, Roger did not appear as a player for the first time since he was a teenager.

At their September 15 meeting, the Mud Hens' stockholders voted to increase capital by placing $25,000 worth of preferred stock which had been held in escrow for Roger Bresnahan on the market to "give the Duke an opportunity to get the players he seeks to place the Mud Hens on a winning basis in 1920."[86] Roger had survived efforts to oust him as president and was able to reorganize the Toledo Baseball Company during the remainder of 1919.[87]

Another difficulty was handed Roger at Swayne Field during the September 4 game with Milwaukee when he was served with divorce papers. Roger said only that he expected it.[88] Adeleen Bresnahan's complaint charged Roger with "gross neglect and extreme cruelty" and stated he had consorted with other women for five years, struck and threatened to shoot her, and had ceased to support her.[89] In his formal response Roger stated that he had left home "a year ago" and said "that his wife had accused him of consorting with other women, but that she lived with him after the accusation, 'thus condoning any such alleged misconduct.'"[90] Adeleen would eventually prevail but the issue would not be settled until January 25, 1921.[91]

THIRTY

Bresnahan "Rather Enjoyed Presidenting the Team" (1920–1923)[1]

The Spanish flu and the Great War were left behind and "the financial difficulties that handicapped the club last season and the year before had passed." *Toledo News-Bee* Sporting Editor Dick Meade suggested "the baseball outlook is more satisfying than at any time since Roger Bresnahan took over the franchise."[2]

Armed with cash, Roger was an active player-purchaser during the early weeks of 1920. One of the first acquisitions was Pitcher Jean Dubuc of the Giants whom Roger would make his assistant.[3] He followed by buying a pair from Brooklyn, three from the Boston Red Sox, one from the New York Yankees and yet another from Louisville.[4] In addition, the Yankees released three of their players and the Giants two of theirs to Bresnahan.[5]

The Yankees and Mud Hens had developed a special relationship likely stemming from the longtime relationship of Bresnahan and Yankees' manager, Miller Huggins. Besides turning players over to Toledo for development, the Yankees supported Bresnahan financially.[6] The Giants were also close to Toledo because of the exceptional friendship of Bresnahan and John McGraw.

Meade reported that Roger had spent $18,000 for players since the close of the 1919 season and was prepared to spend more—Bresnahan "is not going to let anything remain in his way of constructing a real team for this city this year."[7]

Abandoning Toledo as his spring practice venue for the previous two seasons, Roger set up camp in Paducah, Kentucky. He assembled his players, cast off some and began to mold a new team. Despite poor weather that allowed just three exhibition games, he made considerable progress during a month's stay. Plans to present the new Mud Hens for pre-season games at home were scuttled, again because of rainy and cold forecasts. Roger moved the team directly from camp to Indianapolis for the season's first regular season game on April 14 where the Mud Hens prevailed over the Indians behind newcomer Jim Middleton, 1–0.[8]

The Mud Hens continued on the road compiling a 5–3 record before their first game at home on April 27. The game itself was a 10-inning thriller with Toledo coming out on top 5–4, but the day's highlight was the crowd of 15,009.[9]

A community-wide effort enabled Toledo to win the loving cup awarded to the American Association city with the largest Opening Day attendance.[10] The community-wide endeavor enabled Bresnahan's city to win.[11] The cup survives and was a gift from Roger Michael Bresnahan, Roger Philip Bresnahan's grandnephew, to the Toledo Mud Hens and the people of the City of Toledo.

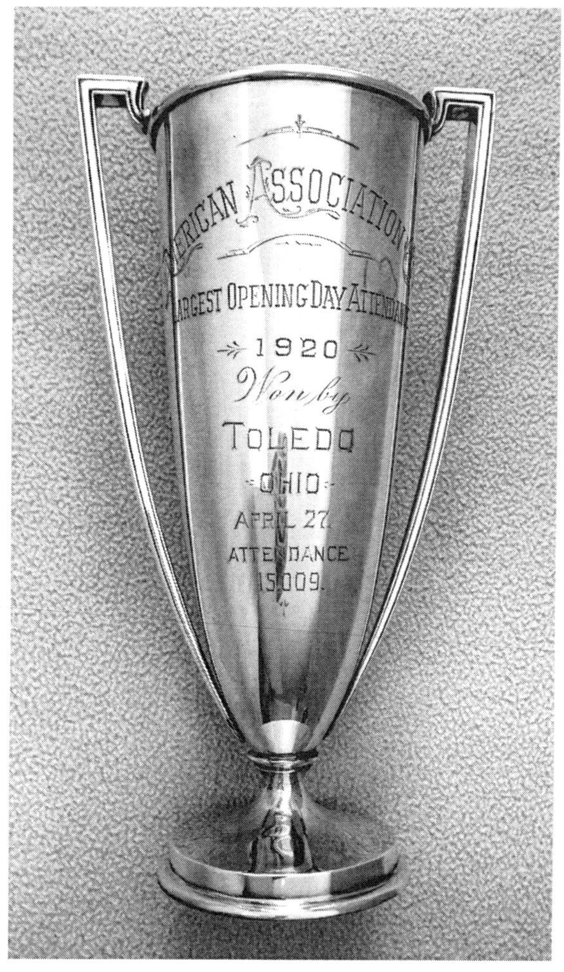

The 1920 American Association honored the Toledo community which had supported Roger's team with the largest Opening Day attendance. The cup survives and was a gift from Roger Michael Bresnahan, his grandnephew, to the Toledo Mud Hens and the people of the City of Toledo, Ohio (author's collection).

The Mud Hens continued their winning ways over the course of the 10-game homestand, 7–3, and maintained their second place standing. The team did not maintain the pace and slipped to a 50–50 record by the end of July when team captain, Joe Kelly, resigned. Roger appointed Jean Dubuc to replace him and made the veteran his assistant manager. Widely circulated reports that Dubuc was named manager were refuted by Roger who stated, "I am still manager of the club."[12] "Roger never really retired as manager of the team, but placed Dubuc in there as temporary head of the Mud Hens."[13] Play improved and the Mud Hens finished with an 87–79 record, good for second place in the American Association.[14] The season's home attendance was 241,718, the highest in the league and the most ever for Toledo.[15] Roger reportedly earned $75,000—"the greatest financial season in Toledo's history."[16] The club's income stream was aided by good attendance on the road and exhibition games. The most notable of such games was a visit by the New York Yankees on September 15 which drew 12,000 fans on a Wednesday afternoon. Toledo won 8–7 despite two home runs by Babe Ruth.[17]

The remainder of 1920 included some distressing events for Roger Bresnahan—one was the saga of Jean Dubuc.

Dubuc came to the Mud Hens from the New York Giants and following a nine-year major-league pitching career. Despite Roger's words to the contrary,

Dubuc was viewed by many as Toledo's manager and thought to be planned for that role in 1921. Dubuc fell from Roger's favor when he was implicated in baseball gambling and the fixing of the 1919 World's Series.[18] Additionally, John McGraw accused him of attempting to help Milwaukee win its September 19 game with Toledo.[19]

Roger was among the baseball notables who gathered in Chicago on the periphery of the Cook County Grand Jury investigation of the World's Series fix.[20] While there, Roger learned that Dubuc's testimony was that he had been aware of the fix before it occurred.[21]

Bresnahan appeared to be stunned when he learned the extent of the scandal: "'Eight men on one team," said Bresnahan. "I can't believe it. I can understand one crook, anywhere, but eight on one ball club. Good Lord, there aren't that many crooks in one jail who would do a thing like this. Selling out for $5,000. Why I simply can't get it thru my head."[22]

Roger conducted his own investigation of Dubuc's alleged offenses and said that both were unsubstantiated. Despite his public stance of no wrongdoing, he gave Dubuc his unconditional release.[23]

The focus on gambling and tampering with players caused by the happenings in Chicago gave rise to additional charges revived by a former owner of the Philadelphia Phillies, Horace Fogel. Fogel alleged two separate charges involving two New York Giants teams of which Roger Bresnahan was a member. Further, Fogel said, both charges were known to club owners and the National League's executive staff who suppressed the evidence of crookedness and allowed those involved to go unpunished.

The first charge centered on the 1905 World's Series and Philadelphia star Pitcher Rube Waddell who, according to Fogel, confessed to accepting a $17,000 bribe to not pitch in the series against the Giants. He said that Waddell faked an arm injury and did not participate in the series.

Fogel's second accusation was leveled at "a former New York player, now a magnate in a Western town in a minor league"—obviously, Roger Bresnahan. Roger's alleged offense was attempting to bribe Phillies players prior to the Giants' eight late-season games with the Phillies in 1908.[24] Red Dooin, Philadelphia's catcher at the time, corroborated Fogel's story in 1924. He included a reference to Bresnahan, but some details differed from Fogel's version: "Dooin said that he, along with infielders William 'Kitty' Bransfield, Mickey Doolan, Otto Knabe, and outfielder Sherwood Magee, and other players were offered $40,000 to throw the games in New York and Philadelphia, September 28–October 3. 'In fact,' Dooin added, 'the money was placed in my lap by a noted catcher of the New York Giants while I was in a railroad station.' Asked why he hadn't reported the matter at the time, Dooin explained that 'the other players and myself believed it would be in the best interest of baseball not to say anything, as none of us accepted the bribes.'"[25]

Fogel had earlier joined Charles Murphy in accusing Bresnahan of throwing games against the Giants late in the 1911 season.[26] He also insinuated that the 1912

National League pennant race was fixed in favor of the Giants, and that President Lynch and his umpires were party to that.[27] All this led to his being disbarred and "forever excluded from participation in the counsels of this league...."[28]

Though Bresnahan's name cropped up several times in connection with bribery, fixing and tampering, he was never formally implicated or charged and his suggested connections to misconduct of this kind has been forgotten.

* * *

Adeleen's divorce suit came to the Lucas County, Ohio, Court of Common Pleas on November 19, 1920. Judge Curtis Johnson heard the testimony of Mrs. Bresnahan who said for the first couple of years of their marriage "everything went along lovely" and that they "corresponded every day" when he was on the road. "I thought he was the best man in the world until 1905, when he became a member of a championship ball club, then he changed."[29] She alleged a number of hurtful things Roger said and did beginning in 1905, but the focus of couple's troubles centered on a number of letters from other women she found in November 1912 which "almost broke her heart."[30] She recounted, "One time he said my sweet eyes were dead to him and asked me to get a divorce.... When I promised to do so he put out his hand and asked me to shake on it."[31]

When Roger took the stand, he disputed several of Adeleen's accusations and added a complaint of his own: "I wanted to be a father—have some children running around the place—but Mrs. Bresnahan didn't want them."[32] Phil Bresnahan also testified in support of his brother, recalling that Adeleen "took one of my youngsters on her lap and said it was the greatest regret of her life that she didn't have children." Her stated reason was "she was afraid it would spoil her beauty."[33]

Upon the trial's conclusion, Judge Johnson ruled, "As both parties want the divorce dissension appears to be over alimony, I will leave it up to you people to reach some agreement."[34] That having been done, the judge proclaimed his decree on January 25, 1921, awarding Adeleen an absolute divorce, full title to their home and $10,000 alimony, payable at $1,000 per year.[35]

* * *

Hoping to continue the success Bresnahan—now flush with funds—set about rebuilding his team for the 1921 season. Since he "rather enjoyed presidenting the team instead of managing it," he hired Bill Clymer, a veteran minor-league manager, to direct the team on the field.[36] The hiring was considered a coup because of Clymer's "brilliant success."[37] Clymer had managed 20 seasons, which included 12 in American Association cities where he won four pennants and finished second four times.

Roger severed his relationship with the New York Yankees and formed a new one with the Detroit Tigers. He retained the ability to buy and sell players on the open market but would give Detroit the first opportunity to buy and the Tigers would offer their excess players for development to Toledo.[38] Toledo also developed what would become a fruitful relationship with the New York Giants through John McGraw's agent and former Bresnahan mate at St. Louis, Dick Kinsella.[39]

Chief among Roger's player acquisitions were several proven veterans—Jim Thorpe, Hugh Bedient and Fred Luderus. Thorpe was purchased from Akron.[40] Former Mud Hen Bedient returned from retirement.[41] Luderus was bought following a stellar career with the Philadelphia Phillies.[42] An all-around athlete and Olympic champion, Thorpe also excelled at football. He and Roger planned to bring professional football to Toledo's Swayne Field in the fall with Thorpe playing and managing but the deal never materialized.[43]

Manager Clymer gathered his players for spring practice at Augusta, Georgia. A staggered start was used with battery men beginning practice March 5 and position players a week later.[44]

The "first real game of the season" was a festive St. Patrick's Day affair in which the Regulars trimmed the Yannigans, 7–2. Seen by about 1,000 fans, the game was played for the benefit of the destitute of Ireland and raised more than $1,000. Roger appeared behind the bat—the first time in two years. He caught the entire game and "almost convinced himself he is still as good as he used to be."[45]

An expanded schedule of a dozen pre-season games with outside teams followed. Winning 10 of those likely boosted confidence but did not take into account the lesser level of competition. Roger felt this was the "best team he ever had."[46] He added the team "will start well, because it is in fine condition, and will continue high in the race because it has class."[47]

Despite Roger's optimism, the Mud Hens had just a fair start in the field as they compiled a 7–10 record following their initial road games and 10 games at home. But their start at the gate was outstanding as they won the league's Opening Day attendance trophy for the second straight year and drew 52,471 fans to Swayne Field for their homestand.[48]

Because Roger was unable to secure a front-line catcher and those he had retained for the backup role failed or were unavailable, Manager Bill Clymer found himself without a serviceable catcher during an early May road trip. The 40-year-old Mud Hens' owner-president journeyed to Milwaukee and jumped into the fray. Roger caught five games while the only catcher on the Toledo roster recovered from an injury. In the first game, Milwaukee stole six bases, but the Duke drove in two runs with a single in a 6–5 Toledo victory.[49] The next day he threw out the only runner that attempted to steal, had another hit, and the Hens won again.[50] Moving to Kansas City on Saturday, May 14, Roger caught his third straight complete game, had three hits including a winning rally starter, and stole two bases. The *Kansas City Star* reported Bresnahan "was behind the bat and he cut up like a frolicsome recruit cutting into the big show with a wiz bang."[51] On Sunday he started as catcher but retired after being caught in a rundown with "ankles sore and swollen."[52] He left the game early the next day when Toledo fell hopelessly behind.[53] On both occasions he was relieved by Outfielder Harry Manush. Catching help in the form of Clyde Manion was then sent by the Detroit Tigers allowing Roger to finally "retire."[54] He had batted .417 during his emergency service.[55]

At the end of May, the Mud Hens stood fifth in the American Association standings with a 20–20 record but slipped to seventh at 31–39 on June 30. Toledo won a doubleheader on July's first day. A meeting followed the twin win during which Bill Clymer resigned as manager. Roger immediately appointed Fred Luderus as his replacement. The Bresnahan-Clymer relationship had been strained all season.[56]

The pair had been at odds since clashing over training methods at spring practice. Roger contended that Clymer "failed to instill fight" into the team and "is lacking in aggressive baseball." Clymer countered that Bresnahan "is still the actual manager" and that he, Clymer, is "merely a foreman."[57] Knowing Roger's uncompromising stance on aggressive play and desire to win, it was virtually impossible for him to be "hands off" and the change was inevitable.

Luderus continued his fine play at first base, batted .323 and piloted the Hens to a 47–49 record the rest of the way. Toledo finished in seventh place at 80–88. The season's results certainly did not live up to expectations, but the seventh-place finish was just three games removed from the first division and attendance was 198,498.[58] Financially, "very little, if any, money was made."[59]

Bresnahan was highly pleased with Ludy's management of the team and indicated that had he been at the helm for the entire season the Hens would have been "flying high in the American Association struggle." He signed Luderus to manage the Mud Hens in 1922.[60]

* * *

Just before the season ended, Roger had one more game to play—a benefit for his former teammate and friend Christy Mathewson who was ill with tuberculosis. The combatants were the current Giants and former players who were hosted at the Polo Grounds on September 30. Roger was invited to play by Art Devlin, captain of the veteran squad, who inserted him as catcher batting in the leadoff position just as he was in his heyday as a Giant.[61] All of the great pitcher's former associates "received [an] uproarious welcome, with especial emphasis that greeted Matty's famous old backstop.... Bresnahan was wildly cheered when he strode to the plate to open the game. In consideration of matters of embonpoint, he declined to over-exert and took a base on balls."[62] "Roger had left a sick bed in Toledo to come and catch two innings and caught a train right back."[63] The event netted about $45,000 for Mathewson.[64]

The Hall-of-Fame battery was together with the Giants for seven seasons and remained friends until Matty finally succumbed to his disease on October 7, 1925. Over those intervening years their paths crossed many times.

Roger caught in 97 of Matty's starts, 15 of his shutouts and the three World's Series shutouts of 1905.[65] Mathewson said Bresnahan was "as brainy as he is tough."[66] He added that his help was "invaluable" that he "was quick to see signs of tiring ...

Roger Bresnahan and more than 20 former New York Giants returned on September 30, 1921, to play for the benefit of Christy Mathewson who was dying of tuberculosis. Roger proudly displays his Toledo Mud Hens' uniform. Seated: Bill Dahlen, Hans Lobert, Hooks Wiltse, Art Devlin, Moose McCormick, Joe Hornung, Joe Hornung III (mascot), Red Murray, Fred Tenney. Standing: Trainer Mackall, Amos Rusie, Roger Bresnahan, Jesse Burkett, Larry Doyle, Kelly, Jack Warner, Jeff Tesreau, Fred Merkle, Ed Holly. The event netted $40,000 (courtesy Sue Baxter/National Baseball Hall of Fame and Museum).

and gave fake signals when a pitcher began to weaken. The pitcher would shake his head negatively upon seeing Bresnahan's signs and thus have time to recover his poise."[67] He described Roger as an "aggressive player" who was "always coaching the other fielders holding the team together." Because "he was in a position to see which man would be able to make the play," he would give loud and clear advice to the pitchers and infielders by calling out whose ball it was.[68]

Matty said of his former mate in 1922, "Bresnahan certainly was a wonder.... I don't believe I disagreed with him over a half dozen times as what was the best style delivery to use on some strong batter in a pinch. Even better I do recall that every time I shook him off the batsman invariably came through with a base hit...."[69]

When comparing pitching monarchs, Bresnahan simply said "the game has only one king. He's my old pal, Christy Mathewson."[70] Because he knew Matty's delivery so well and the pitcher's control was so fine, Roger exclaimed that "he could sit in a rocking chair and catch when Mathewson is in the box."[71] Roger told Billy Evans in 1923, "The greatest pitcher, to my way of thinking, is Mathewson. I caught him when he was at his best and no one has a better idea of his greatness. Matty didn't have a single weakness."[72]

In an era when it was considered poor form for a player to banter with an opponent, Bresnahan and Mathewson did it anyway but neither let up during play. The pair talked for 20 minutes in 1914 before Mathewson and the Giants met Bresnahan's Cubs in Chicago. "When the Cub backstop came to bat, he yelled for Matty to duck as soon as he threw the ball if he wanted to keep on pitching. 'You could not hit .100

in the Kitty League,' Mathewson shot back, and proceeded to get his ex-mate on a foul fly to the catcher."[73]

* * *

The *Toledo News-Bee* published a biographical sketch of native son Roger Bresnahan on February 15, 1922. Richard J. "Dick" Meade, sporting editor extraordinaire for the newspaper, was close to the Toledo baseball operation and extremely knowledgeable of its history. He began writing sports with the paper in 1903 and continued until 1934, except for 1926–1928 while he was president of the Toledo club.[74] He most certainly had a hand in the Bresnahan biography and likely wrote it. Noted baseball historian Bill James suggested, "Almost every paragraph written about him included the adjective 'fiery.'"[75] Excerpts from the *Toledo News-Bee* regarding Roger Bresnahan's persona:

Former New York Giant battery mates, Hall of Famers, World's Series heroes and friends Christy Mathewson and Roger Bresnahan were reunited in this 1922 photograph. Roger related that the pitcher's "control was so fine he could sit in a rocking chair and catch him" while Christy said that Roger was "as brainy as he was tough" and that his help was "invaluable" (courtesy Roger M. Bresnahan).

> Highly strung and almost abnormally emotional.... Soft-hearted indeed ... and while he is hasty in his accusations, he is quick to forgive. It is said of him that during his career as a baseball manager in the National League and with the Toledo club, he has fined more players and taken less money from them than any leader in the game.
>
> His gravest fault, aside from his quick temper, is his lack of tact. That has been his constant enemy, and while it did not handicap him as a player, it has nullified his baseball intelligence as a manager.
>
> Tactless, he naturally had difficulty handling men, and while he would give them every dollar in his pocket off the field [Bresnahan's teams were the highest paid in the American Association],[76] he would not give them an inch on the diamond.
>
> A swift thinker himself and possessed of that strange commodity they call "baseball sense" he has no patience or sympathy for those whose brain does not rapidly respond to thought, or those who do not automatically perform in an emergency the plays that are out of the customary diamond routine.
>
> He is as temperamental as a prima donna. Victory is an obsession with him. Combine the two when defeat is in sight, and he rises to great heights of emotional anger.

> He manifests his disappointment in so marked a way upon the field of play that his expression of disgust and his gestures of despair have a chilling effect upon the spectators in his own town and hostile agitation in foreign cities.[77]

Ed Konetchy played four seasons for Roger and concurred his boss possessed a quick temper and was also generous with his money—"Tis his sense of values; he'd pay $10 for a bottle of beer and give a down and outer a hundred-dollar bill if he happened to have it."[78]

The Toledo newspaper also commented on Bresnahan's play, stating that "he became the greatest backstop ever known."[79]

* * *

Because he had kept only a few key players, Bresnahan was faced with his seemingly annual team rebuild for 1922. Manager Ty Cobb of Detroit added complexity to Roger's task when he broke his club's working agreement with Toledo, causing Roger to admit he "did not really know where his next season's ball club is coming from."[80]

Toledo formed a relationship with the New York Giants that would develop and become increasingly important as a result. Roger worked alongside returning Manager Fred Luderus during the Mud Hens' spring practice at Bristol, Tennessee, beginning on March 2.[81] His recruiting efforts resulted with a mixture of untried young players and veterans joining the several returning Mud Hens. Among the new men were Ed Konetchy and Slim Sallee both of whom were mainstays on Roger's former Cardinals teams.[82]

The camp was hindered by rainy weather, but work progressed in a tobacco warehouse dubbed "the house of nicotine" by *News-Bee* writer Earl Aiken.[83] A month's stay at Bristol ended when the team broke camp on April 4 to play their way to Toledo for the season's Opening Day on April 12. In all, the Mud Hens played 11 exhibition games, winning all which they well should have as 10 were against amateur teams. Meade wrote that no other club of Roger's "looked so good on paper" and "it is hard to figure how the crew can be kept out of the first flight."[84] Bresnahan was "confident the Hens will be with the pacemaker or be making the pace from the time the flag drops…."[85]

Fred Luderus led his untried Toledo Mud Hens into the 1922 American Association season at Toledo's Swayne Field and lost to Columbus 5–4. Though 9,578 watched in "benumbing dampness."[86]

The losing continued and reached inexplicably epic proportions. On May 9 the Hens' record stood at 3–19 and heads rolled when Roger asked for waivers on seven players including Sallee and Manager Luderus.[87] He installed Outfielder Al Wickland as interim manager.[88] Then, following John McGraw's suggestion, signed George "Possum" Whitted as field boss.[89] To fill the void, Roger claimed Second Baseman Frank Murphy off waivers from Louisville[90] and McGraw sent Shortstop Bill Black.[91] With Konetchy replacing Luderus at first base and Whitted taking over third base, Toledo had an all-new infield. McGraw also sent two future Hall-of-Fame players—Pitcher Bill Terry and 16-year-old Infielder Freddie Lindstrom.[92] Terry "showed considerable class" as a pitcher but was converted to a first baseman because of his potent bat.[93] Lindstrom did not join the team until he completed the school year. All this helped the Hens post a 62–82 record the rest of the way and enabled them to crawl out of a very deep hole and finish in seventh place.[94]

The conversion of Bill Terry from pitcher to first baseman proved to be an incredibly wise decision. John McGraw had seen his new signee working out at the Polo Grounds and was not impressed with his pitching but immediately recognized his potential as a hitter. He sent him to Toledo to develop that potential and learn to be a first baseman.[95] Toledo was in desperate need of effective left-handed pitching and initially utilized him on the mound.[96] Bresnahan and Manager Whitted noticed Terry could hit and McGraw may have reminded them of his vision for Terry's future as a Giant, resulting in the change to first base where he blossomed. Terry hit .337 in 1922, never pitched again and followed in 1923 with a .377 average and 15 home runs. The next year he assumed the first-base position for the Giants, which he held for 12 seasons and compiled a .341 career batting average.

The New York Giants had established a solid working arrangement with Toledo "whereby the Giants will get the pick of Toledo's graduates and in turn will give Bresnahan first choice of any players the Giants pass back."[97] Following, a flow of players from New York to Toledo commenced and Giants' owner Charles Stoneham visited Toledo.[98] The Giants cemented their financial intentions when Edgar P. Feeley, a Giants' attorney, purchased Swayne Field, Toledo's ballpark, and began acquiring the Toledo club's stock.[99] Bresnahan aided the Giants in the latter effort by acting as their agent and buying stock for them.[100] Meade accurately predicted, "It is presumed the owners of the New York Giants will be further interested financially in the club, and there may be some interesting news proclaimed before the winter is over."[101]

* * *

Meade's prediction was confirmed in early March of 1923: "James McGraw, brother of John McGraw, has been appointed a sort of business manager and advisor to Roger Bresnahan. He will look after the financial interests of John McGraw and Charles A. Stoneham in the Toledo Club. Roger Bresnahan, when it comes to business acumen, isn't exactly a John D. Rockefeller and the club has suffered financially as a result."[102]

Armed with financial backing and the promise of players from the Giants, Roger began building his 1923 team immediately following the 1922 season. The potential roster was reviewed, and changes were planned by the triumvirate of Bresnahan, Whitted and McGraw. The shakeup began by cleaning the house of four 1922 regulars including Ed Konetchy, a favorite of Roger's. There was no place for the hard-hitting first baseman in the lineup because of the ongoing conversion of Bill Terry from pitcher to first baseman. On the acquisition side, Roger made several outright purchases. Two of these, both veteran major-league players from the Boston Braves, were expensive but proved to be beneficial.[103] Walt Barbare played 161 games at third base replacing Whitted, who planned to manage from the bench, and Fred Nicholson appeared in 167 games in the outfield.[104]

These transactions were completed by mid–December 1922 prompting Meade to opine, "Right now the Mud Hens appear to be a fair team. The club is practically set except for pitchers and catchers."[105]

Bresnahan and Whitted took the 33 players to spring training at Greenwood, Mississippi.[106] Early March weather was favorable and allowed players to get "in much better shape than a year ago."[107] However, rains came during the last half of the month disrupting the games schedule before the Hens broke camp on April 1.[108] Final preparations for Opening Day on April 19 included games with the Giants' second team which would join with the Mud Hens as opponents on their trek home and allowed Bresnahan and Whitted to evaluate potential Toledo players.[109] Two of those games were played at the Hens' Swayne Field home with the Giants' Casey Stengel in the lineup. Stengel was destined to become a legendary manager at that park.[110] Toledo won six of the nine spring exhibition games played.

The "Fan Night" celebration and pep rally which had previously been held on the eve of the season's first home game was cancelled because of dismal ticket sales likely influenced by the opinion of American Association critics who picked the Hens to finish seventh or eighth in the standings.[111] Nonetheless, 12,556 paid their way into the season's initial contest and were rewarded with a fine game but disappointed with a loss—3–2 to Columbus in 10 innings.[112] The next day the Mud Hens scored three times in the bottom of the ninth to win 10–9 over the same Senators. Thanks to some lusty hitting the Hens won half of their first 18 games all against the league's weaker east division of Columbus, Indianapolis, and Louisville. Finishing a nearly month-long road trip they went 2–9 on a swing through the western cities of Kansas City, Milwaukee, Minneapolis and St. Paul and limped home with an 11–20 mark. The culprit was poor pitching that gave up over nine runs per game in the losses out west.

The losing continued at home aided by the losses of three regulars to injuries. On the plus side, McGraw was able to smuggle some player aid by returning several Giants to their former teams, who, in turn, released them and enabled Roger to sign them as free agents.

Despite these efforts, the rate of losing increased, as did the financial losses and the fans stayed away. Rumors of Roger retiring and the Giants taking over abounded but "the Duke, without question the hardest loser in baseball," hung on.[113]

The Mud Hens' team defense was particularly good and hitting continued to be strong but on June 18 the Mud Hens fell into the American Association's cellar—never to exit.[114]

Following the game of July 31, Manager Possum Whitted added to Roger's woes when, without warning, he submitted his resignation. "He said there were no hard feelings, and that the reason for his resigning was because he felt that he could accomplish no results with the team in view of the pitching staff he had to work with." President Bresnahan appointed 24-year-old Bill Terry as his replacement.[115] Terry, unable to work magic, compiled a slightly worse record than his predecessor. He was called from the team because of the death of his father and did not return because he was "sold," along with Freddie Lindstrom and Pitcher Pat Malone, to the Giants.[116] Walt Barbare finished the season at the Mud Hens' helm and presided over a final, colossal collapse—the Mud Hens lost 24 of their final 28 games which included 16 consecutive at one point.[117] Fan support nearly vanished—one game drew just 70 paying customers—and Swayne Field was dubbed "Potter's Field."[118] The team finished a distant last with a 54–114 record.[119] No Toledo team has ever lost more.[120]

Immediately following the close of the season, Roger spent some time in New York where he was the guest of the Giants for the World's Series and likely talked business with his associates there.[121] Following up on his mid-season hints of retirement, Roger had made it perfectly clear before going to New York, that he "was ready to dispose of his holdings in the Toledo club."[122] Though he pursued the rebuilding of his roster for the 1924 season, his primary focus was the sale of his interest in the Toledo Mud Hens.[123] Several negotiations failed because of Roger's asking price.[124]

Just after the arrival of 1924, Meade reported of Roger's plans for the upcoming season—he intended to manage himself and was considering a Florida spring training camp in order to be near McGraw and the Giants.[125] Meade also commented on the January 1 annual meeting of the stockholders of the Toledo Base Ball Company where James McGraw was elected a director—"the first official recognition of the McGraw interests."[126] Now confident of forthcoming help from the Giants, Roger began a flurry dealing his underperforming 1923 holdovers.

Quietly, Roger continued to pursue a sale of the Mud Hens. He solicited an offer from his longtime friend, Garry Herrmann of Cincinnati. He wrote the Reds president on January 7, 1924, "I feel that I have outlived my usefulness in this city and have other plans, should I sell."[127] Then, without forewarning, he accepted an offer on January 22, 1924—controlling interest of the Toledo Mud Hens would pass to Joseph D. O'Brien of New York on February 1, 1924. The price to be paid Roger for 532 of the 750 shares was not revealed but said by O'Brien to be "the largest ever given for a club in the American Association." Mr. O'Brien was formerly president of the American Association (1905–1910), business manager of the New York Giants (1911–1912) and secretary of the Giants (1919–1922). Along with his purchase announcement O'Brien volunteered that "the Giants no longer had any interest in the franchise."[128] However, the Giants retained ownership of Toledo's ballpark and sold O'Brien a player even before his purchase deal was closed.[129] Further, not only did he retain James McGraw, but he also made him business manager, secretary, and director. It seems Mr. O'Brien misspoke when he discounted the Giants' and John McGraw's—"whom he characterized as one of his closest friends"—interest in Toledo.[130]

Thirty-One

"I Didn't Have a Thing" (1924–1945)[1]

Roger Bresnahan's tumultuous eight-year reign as president and controlling owner of the Toledo Base Ball Co. ended on February 1, 1924. His time was marked by frustration, financial stresses, and losses on the field.

His frustration and likely some sadness were due to his failure to realize his long-held ambition to deliver a pennant to his hometown.

"He lost a fortune then made another out of the club" and lost that one too.[2] His financial failure was partly due to forces over which he had no control such as World War I and the Spanish flu pandemic but also due to his limited financial acumen—notably, he often paid top dollar for players and was very generous with the salaries he paid. He was constantly scouring for funds to keep his head above water, but as he did on the field, he never gave up.

Roger changed his team-building approach from signing and developing young players as he had espoused with the Cardinals and Cubs to largely signing veteran players to one-year deals. His teams' losses mounted in large part by his annual tearing down and rebuilding his season-opening teams when they did not perform as hoped.[3] In addition, the focus of his players was constantly disrupted by his micro-managing and sparring with his field generals, causing three to quit in midseason.

His attributes of a vast network of baseball friends, detailed understanding of how the game should be played, and his tenacity were not enough to overcome his shortcomings and make him a consistent winner.

In the end he accomplished a good deal with his sale. He realized the value of his asset, set his price high and stuck with it. He dickered with numerous potential buyers without success and resolved to forge ahead with the 1924 season. His patience was rewarded with the acceptance of his demands, and he was rewarded with a payday said to be about $150,000.[4]

* * *

After 27 years of professional baseball during which he participated in all aspects of the game (though he never umpired), Roger Bresnahan found himself well-fixed financially, prompting him to say, "It looked like I could hunt, fish and loaf the rest of my life."[5] Within days of closing the deal, he invested in a new $53,000 house in the Westmoreland neighborhood, just west of Toledo, and less than a mile from his boyhood home where he had been living with his mother.[6]

Roger Bresnahan and Gertrude E. Norenberg married in Toledo on November 29, 1924. The couple remained together until Roger's 1944 death. Gertrude died in 1968 (courtesy Roger M. Bresnahan).

The new home was the venue for Roger's marriage on November 29, 1924. His bride was Gertrude E. Norenberg, 41, a native Toledoan, described as a "society belle."[7] She was formerly a world-traveled opera performer and, in recent years, a retail salesperson.[8] She had not been previously married and would be with Roger for the rest of his life.

Several Bresnahan family members have mistakenly expressed that Gertrude Norenberg from New York City was Roger's only wife—not being aware of Roger's first wife and that Gertrude was a native Toledoan. Gertrude was born in Toledo on July 6, 1883, and was living in her parents' home in 1899.[9] According to the 1900 Federal Census, she was living in a Providence, Rhode Island, hotel as an employed actress. In 1901 the 18-year-old embarked on a three-year, around-the-world tour with the Josephine Stanton Opera Company which presented "comic opera and musical burlesque."[10] The tour played in the western United States, Hawaii, Japan and New Zealand before folding while playing in Australia in 1902.[11] Miss Norenberg then joined George Musgrove's Royal Comic Opera Company and played various roles while touring Australia and New Zealand.[12] She departed Sydney for San Francisco on January 11, 1904, and finally returned to Toledo in 1908.[13]

The following summer Roger became an orphan. Mary O'Donohue Bresnahan died at her home at about age 84 on June 17, 1925.[14]

Roger's "retirement" from baseball lasted a scant two years—old pal John McGraw put his former player back into a New York Giants uniform after an absence of 18 years. Roger signed as coach for pitchers.[15] Over the next three seasons he would also serve as assistant manager, third base coach and handy man.[16] He was *the* Giants' manager for 13 games in 1926 and 44 more in 1928.[17]

It is likely that Roger enjoyed returning to the scene of his greatest triumphs.

He was well remembered in the city that was always alive and even more so during the Roaring Twenties. "It was a case of the long-lost son back home. The Duke was still a hero in New York."[18] Following his signing, he attended the National League's Golden Jubilee at the Hotel Astor.[19] Gertrude accompanied him, part of the time, both in the city and at spring training.[20] In the wake of the death of Christy Mathewson, he joined with mates from his heyday in benefit games at Boston and the Polo Grounds to laud the great pitcher and raise money for his charities.[21]

Rebuilding his team, McGraw traded with the Cardinals for Rogers Hornsby, the defending World's Series champion manager and second baseman.[22] McGraw made his new addition team captain for 1927 and deferred to him, instead of Roger, as his temporary replacement. Though his prominence was diminished somewhat by Hornsby's presence, Roger was again made assistant manager and continued coaching pitchers and at third base. New York's *Daily News* described him as "a most capable coach of pitchers and an able baseball man generally," and said, "His return to the Giants is a good thing for the club."[23]

It is impossible to know the extent of Roger Bresnahan's influence on the development of the pitchers he managed or coached but we know he was reputed to be an excellent handler and teacher of pitchers. Some became effective after encountering Roger early in their career and others blossomed suddenly after being exposed to Roger following lackluster career beginnings. Some in the first category include (with career major league seasons and won-lost record) Bob Harmon (13, 108–133), Slim Sallee (14, 174–143), Carl Hubbell (16, 253–154) and Schoolboy Rowe (15, 158–101). Among those who experienced new-found success were Fred Toney (12, 139–102), Hippo Vaughn (13, 178–137), Freddie Fitzsimmons (19, 217–146) and Larry Benton (13, 128–128). Countless others—including Hall of Famers Christy Mathewson and Joe McGinnity—benefited from his direction from behind the bat.

Roger experienced another homecoming when the Giants made their then annual exhibition stop in Toledo on June 6, 1927. Roger was welcomed and presented with gifts of a watch, a shotgun, and a young pointer dog by Dick Meade, now president of the club.[24] The Mud Hens had been purchased from O'Brien by a local group but were still associated with the Giants. Under Manager Casey Stengel and were destined to be Toledo's best-ever team.[25] The Giants also did well in 1927 and finished in third place, just two and a half games behind Pittsburgh and St. Louis. During the season John McGraw was feted at the Polo Grounds on his silver anniversary as manager of the Giants. Roger, who was there with McGraw 25 years before, "gave his chief a silver service—the gift of the Giant players."[26]

Roger returned to the Giants for the 1928 season as McGraw's lieutenant, but Hornsby did not—he had been traded to the Boston Braves. Bresnahan twice filled in as manager, once for an extended period from May 14 through June 30 when McGraw was sidelined because of an injury suffered in an automobile accident. Once again, the Giants were in the hunt but finished in second place, two games behind the Cardinals.

John McGraw is flanked by Roger Bresnahan, on the left, and Rogers Hornsby. The three Hall of Famers were together as Giants only in 1927. Manager McGraw traded for Hornsby, installed him at second base, and made him team captain. The returning Bresnahan was assistant manager, pitching coach, and third base coach. However, McGraw chose Hornsby over Bresnahan as his temporary replacement, traded Hornsby following the season, and kept Bresnahan on his staff in 1928 (courtesy Roger M. Bresnahan).

John McGraw told the *New York Times* on November 12, 1928, that Bresnahan "was stepping out," and had been given his release.[27] Other reports were equally vague—"he has a chance to take a better place," "he had something better in view," and according to Blanche McGraw, John's wife, "he left to enter business in Ohio."[28] Historian Charles C. Alexander has suggested Roger was simply "tired of the stresses of being the Giants' part-time manager, [and] decided to remain in his native Toledo," where he continued as a stockholder of the Toledo Mud Hens.[29]

His reason for leaving the Giants is lost to us—unless his purpose was to retire which he appeared to embrace. Though he said he wanted to "continue in baseball," he was out of the game in 1929.[30] In August he gave an interview while in nearby Detroit to watch the Tigers and Athletics play and it may be that he was there for more than the game.[31] On September 16 the *Brooklyn Daily Eagle* suggested that Roger would "probably replace George McBride as [Bucky] Harris' first lieutenant."[32] The *Sporting News* confirmed that the Tigers had indeed lured Bresnahan from retirement to be in charge of its battery men. "Detroit desired Bresnahan because of his reputed knack of handling pitchers" and Harris planned to rely on him to select the staff in the spring and pitchers for daily duty.[33]

While Roger's employment negotiations were being conducted the nation's economy was in turmoil and all Americans and the world were soon to be affected. The timing of Roger's new employment would prove to be fortunate for him as the stock market crash affected him profoundly. He told the *Sporting News* how he was so suddenly devastated:

> "I'll never forget—how could I?—that year of 1929," ... I had a good chunk of Libbey-Owens-Ford and other stocks all wrapped up and paid for and my friends, well informed, influential men, and myself had gone into Electric Auto Light on the margin.... I had a paper profit of $173,000 on Auto Light and we had a little meeting, just to see what the other fellows planned to do. After a few rounds of good cheer, we all decided to sell when I could cash in for $200,000.
>
> Well, I went up in Michigan hunting for a few days and when I got back, I was told that I had to get $30,000 right away to cover. I plastered a mortgage for that amount on my home. The next day further demands to cover wiped out the house entirely and I was forced to sell my Libby-Owens-Ford to try to save myself.... In less than ten days I didn't have a thing, no home, no nothing.[34]

Roger Bresnahan (left) was lured out of retirement by the Detroit Tigers following the 1929 season to be Manager Bucky Harris's assistant and pitching coach. He was released following the 1931 season and found himself needing work at a difficult economic time (courtesy the Ernie Harwell Sports Collection, Detroit Public Library).

But he had a job.

* * *

Roger greeted Detroit's pitchers and catchers at the Tigers' spring camp in Tampa, Florida, on February 24, 1930.[35] Joining him as a coach was Jean Dubuc, his former player and substitute manager at Toledo.[36] Though 50, Roger was still active behind the plate—he caught his pitchers in warm-ups. He also appeared in several exhibition games. The Tigers improved slightly by winning five more games than in 1929. The 75–79 record moved them up one spot to fifth in the American League. Roger was invited back for 1931.

Spring practice was an adventure for the Tigers, but the season was not. Bresnahan and Dubuc took the mound staff to Richardson Springs, California, for two weeks work before joining the rest of the squad at Sacramento for exhibition play against Pacific Coast League teams.[37] The wheels came off during the 1931 season and the Tigers fell to a distant seventh place at 61–93. Bresnahan and Dubuc were both relieved of their duties.[38]

Roger's time in Detroit must have been different than his coaching experience with the Giants. But even with a new generation of ballplayers and in a different league, Roger found friends to whom he was connected through baseball. He had signed Frank Gilhooley, Sr.—who went on to a 20-year professional career—to his first major league contract at St. Louis in 1911. Frank was a lifelong Toledoan, as Roger was, and once drove Roger on his commute to Detroit for a game with the Yankees. Along for the ride was Frank Gilhooley, Jr., who became a beloved sportscaster in Toledo. Young Frank was 12 or 13 years old and shared some events of that day. Frank Sr. and Yankee Manager Joe McCarthy had been roommates at Buffalo. McCarthy sat with the two Franks for a half hour before the game. Roger was warming up a big, tall prospect in the bullpen and they thought the guy would kill Roger because he was so wild. Roger took a real beating. But the prospect learned how to get the ball over the plate and became a Tiger two years later—he was Schoolboy Rowe. Young Frank said Roger was a nice man, a funny guy, a great storyteller, and a solid person and added that his father loved and had the utmost respect for him.[39]

* * *

Roger Bresnahan's release by the Tigers launched him and Gertrude into a three-year period of financial hardship. The Great Depression was in full swing and work in baseball was not forthcoming in 1932 or thereafter. He obtained petitions for candidacy for Lucas County Sheriff as a Democrat, but did not survive the primary election in May of 1932.[40] About a year after leaving baseball, he found work as a turnkey at the City of Toledo House of Corrections but lost that when the city's administration changed a year later. His salary as a jailer was $100 a month.[41] He next worked for the Civilian Work Administration with pick and shovel, but that program was curtailed early in 1934.[42] Then it was on to Dyer's Chop House, an elite restaurant in downtown, as their "genial cashier."[43] He was likely a patron there in days past. The end of 1934 saw him find a sales position with the Buckeye Brewing Company with responsibility for the iconic Toledo brewer's sales in Ohio, Michigan, and West Virginia.[44] His salary was $200 a month and he was with Buckeye for the remainder of his life.[45]

Toledo's city directories for the years 1931–1934 do not include an occupation for Roger's entries. The directories do reveal he changed residences several times and landed at 2145 Mellwood Court in Toledo—his last home.[46]

* * *

During his financial turmoil Roger lost a dear friend, his mentor and one he admired and whose friendship he treasured—John Joseph McGraw died on February

25, 1934. Arthur Daley, sports columnist for the *New York Times* for 48 years, who had observed the pair working together penned, "There were no two closer friends in baseball than Bresnahan and McGraw."[47] Roger was shocked and could not restrain tears when he heard the news. He said: "I am as grief stricken as though a member of my family had passed. John McGraw was the finest friend a man could have. To him I owe whatever success I enjoyed in the game. He was the spirit of our national game, its greatest manager and strategist. I am heart-broken."[48]

A quarter of a century earlier—the year following his being traded to St. Louis (1909)—Roger had learned to respect McGraw because of the respect he had for his players. He described the leadership style of his former boss: "There isn't a manager in baseball today who is better to or more lenient with his players than McGraw, and as far as standing behind them is concerned, he is the peer of them all.... McGraw has been spoken of as a hard task master, but as a matter of fact, a player can get away with more stuff on the New York club than any other team in the league. McGraw will stand for more than any other manager I know. There are no rules on the New York team. Mac puts it up to the player. He places one on his honor ... as long as you deliver on the field he is satisfied."[49]

In McGraw's mind, Roger was set apart from other fine catchers by his quick thinking and baseball brains which added to his value. "He never had to be told twice. Once we had discovered a weak spot in the opposition and had discussed a plan for attacking it, I could depend on Bresnahan to carry it out. He did not forget. His whole mind was concentrated on winning that particular game and it was rarely that he overlooked anything."[50] McGraw intimated that he allowed only Roger to call pitches and that "He pulled out the best qualities a pitcher had, never let him relax, and himself was one of the stars of the game."[51]

John McGraw never stood in the way of his players advancing their careers and the business deal he made to send Roger to St. Louis benefited both of them, though he said, "I shall miss him, both as a catcher and a companion."[52]

Obviously, they were very close friends who had nearly identical personalities and their baseball careers were similar as well.

Born in Toledo Never in Politics Before

35 Years in Baseball Always Gave His Best

PLAY BALL WITH

X | ROGER BRESNAHAN

FOR SHERIFF

DEMOCRATIC TICKET

Don't You Think We Need New Blood In Our County Politics?

Roger Bresnahan's business card promoted his campaign for Sheriff of Lucas County, Ohio, in 1932. He hoped to emulate his long-time friend Bob Ewing who served as Sheriff of Auglaize County, Ohio, following his baseball career and to earn a regular paycheck during the Great Depression. Disappointingly, he lost in the Democratic primary by finishing fourth among the seven candidates (courtesy Roger M. Bresnahan).

When McGraw moved to New York, the Giants were a seventh-place team with some core players and Mac brought some key players with him to add to the mix. When Bresnahan moved to St. Louis, the Cardinals were a last-place team and had given up four of their best players for Roger. McGraw had nearly complete control for his years with the Giants and won a National League pennant in just two years. Roger also had complete control in St. Louis but only for a while. After three years, the Cardinals had their first winning record in a decade, but his autonomy was lost when his club's ownership changed, and others assumed much of the control. If Stanley Robison had not died, Roger's teams may have continued their upward trajectory emulating McGraw's experience.

* * *

The Great Depression eased, and Roger settled into his work for the brewery when he and Gertrude added to their family. Marian Patricia Norenberg came to live with them on October 14, 1937. Marian was the four-year-old daughter of Gertrude's brother, Clifford, and his wife, Ella. Roger and Gertrude proceeded to adopt Marian. The couple's worthiness was investigated by the probate court and its investigator was none other than Lillian Joss, the widow of the great pitcher Addie Joss. Mrs. Joss gave a glowing report of Roger and the home he and Gertrude provided: "Roger Bresnahan smokes, takes an occasional drink, has good moral character and disposition, is a salesman earning $200 a month, has an eighth-grade education, regularly attends Blessed Sacrament Catholic Church, pays bills promptly, has no fraternal connections and owns an automobile. She reported that the house was in good condition, clean, orderly, and valued at $6,000." Mrs. Joss also sought input from five references, one of whom was the Rev. Francis Gosser who said, "This child could not find a better home."[53]

The data revealed that Roger had recovered from his near ruin of 1929. His $2,400 income compared to the median income for a man of $956.[54] The wage, however, pales when compared to his former baseball earnings.

* * *

For his remaining years, Roger was devoted to his family, his dogs, and his work, but he maintained his connection to baseball in various ways. There was a time when Roger Bresnahan was in newspapers across the nation on a near daily basis. Now he was sometimes mentioned in a historical context and occasionally still made news. A few of those stories follow.

On a 1938 summer day when the Minneapolis Millers were visiting Toledo to play the Mud Hens, a 19-year-old Ted Williams found an opportunity to talk with Roger. While the pair sat in Roger's car, Williams "asked a few questions" and received a whole lot of advice in return:

- "...from the time you come out on the field with your uniform on until the game is over and you're back in the locker room, don't do a thing which you wouldn't do in a World Series game. By this I mean to hit in batting practice, every time you swing, as if the game depended on it. In fielding practice play every ball like you were trying to prevent the winning run from scoring in a pennant scoring game.

- ...never hit at a bad ball. Even if you have two strikes on you, and you think the next one is an inch outside the plate, let it go. I know you may be called out on strikes once in a while, but it's worth it in the long run. It's worth it because, when the umpires realize you are careful about the balls you hit, and really know a ball from a strike, will be careful too. But you can't blame an umpire for calling one that just misses the plate a strike, when just before that you've swung at one you couldn't reach with a fish pole.
- A left hander's curve ball may worry you, just as it worries most left-hand batters. The only southpaw curve you need to worry about is one that looks as if it's going to hit you somewhere above the knees. That's the one which can break over the plate, so follow it all the way.... When you swing at a wide curve ball and miss it, try this: Just after the catcher gets the ball, before he throws it back to the pitcher, just sort of look where the ball came in and move up to the plate a bit, as if you were getting ready to hit the same thing the next time. The catcher and pitcher will both notice this. Then you lay back for the fast one inside. It's pretty sure to come when they see you crowding the plate."[55]

Roger preached what he had practiced and "Williams seems to have taken the advice to heart."[56] We can never know if Bresnahan's words were heard or applied by Williams, but he did practice what Bresnahan preached.

Like ball players of all generations, Roger Bresnahan compared the game of his era to the one of the present days. After watching a 1920 World's Series game he, "bemoaned that his heyday was 20 years ago.... He'd like to get in on some of the 'big money' of present day players."[57] After watching a couple of 1940 World Series games in Detroit he commented, "I actually saw infielders in the series who didn't know how to stand properly when fielding a grounder.... Those are fundamentals, and I guess they're not teaching them anymore."[58] On another occasion he lamented "that players were much better and tougher in his day and that modern baseball lacks strategy. Inside baseball, as practiced by the old-timers, is missing from the game today. In the old days, ball teams were always trying to out-guess and out-smart the opponents.... Today most teams are just so many individual ballplayers."[59]

On January 20, 1943, Roger Bresnahan set the record straight when he registered his own birth with the Probate Court of Lucas County, Ohio. In doing so he corrected errors that had been embedded in baseball's record and newspaper files for years—with his encouragement. He made it clear that his birthplace was Toledo and not Tralee, County Kerry, Ireland; his middle name was Philip and not Patrick; and his birth date was June 11, 1879, and not 1880.[60] Grandnephew Roger Michael

A family group, from left to right: Roger's sister Margaret Henige, wife Gertrude, and daughter Marian with Roger, likely during the summer of 1944 (courtesy Roger M. Bresnahan).

Bresnahan suggests his namesake "wanted to honor his mother and did not want to die in a lie."[61] Dave Bresnahan, a distant relative, added that he "wanted to die with his slate clean."[62]

Bresnahan suited up as a Giant the final time on August 26, 1943. The occasion was a war bond all-star game of magnanimous proportions at the Polo Grounds—Hall of Famers and stars of yesteryear abounded. Admission tickets were available only to bond purchasers who invested an incredible $800 million. The 40,000 who attended were delighted by the whole affair and especially enjoyed the game's highlight in which Roger played a small part.[63] He was the catcher when Babe Ruth stepped to the plate to face Walter Johnson. Roger instructed the pitcher, "'Keep them high, Walter. I can't bend for those low ones anymore.' Ruth lofted one into the upper right field stands." It was a setup—it came on the 18th pitch to the Babe.[64]

Roger tossed his hat into the political ring when he was on the ballot for Lucas County commissioner as a Democrat on November 7, 1944. He missed election by just 263 votes of the 214,232 cast.[65] He must have been bitterly disappointed as he had said after winning his party's May primary election, "I've seen a lot of things on the ball diamond, I've had a lot of thrills and been in and come out of many a tough spot, but winning the nomination is to me the greatest thrill of all."[66]

A testimonial dinner for Billy Southworth, manager of the World Champion St. Louis Cardinals, may have been Roger's final public appearance. He spoke in Kenton, Ohio, on November 14, 1944, and singled out an old friend from his audience. He told a story of an embarrassing day he once experienced—"That was the day when I struck out four times, for the only time in my life. And the Cincinnati Red who struck me out four times is right here in the crowd tonight. Long Bob Ewing from Wapakoneta, Ohio. You wouldn't take a bow for it that day, Bob, you rascal, but you're going to take a bow for it tonight."[67]

"Perhaps Bresnahan's memory was flawed after more than 40 years, or perhaps he was embellishing the story a bit for Ewing's benefit. The reference was clearly to the game of August 13, 1903, when Ewing shut out the Giants on one hit, fanning Bresnahan three times. In any case, Ewing stood up and took a bow, smiling broadly."[68]

Some of Roger's later-life baseball stories were mainly told in pictures.

* * *

Less than a month following his failed election bid, Roger "died unexpectedly, of a heart attack." He had been bedfast for a week and collapsed when getting out of bed shortly before noon on Monday, December 4, 1944, at age 65. He "was dead when a physician arrived."[69] His funeral was officiated by the Rev. Francis X. Gosser, Roger's friend and priest, on the following Thursday at Blessed Sacrament Catholic Church in Toledo. "The church was filled with public figures, friends, and old-time ball players...." Gosser's eulogy included: "Roger Bresnahan deserved a niche in the hall of fame as a great baseball player and in the hall of life as a nobleman and a thoroughbred. He could be as hard as nails, and

In Roger's bid to become a commissioner for Lucas County, Ohio, in 1944, he missed election by only 263 votes of the 214,232 cast. He died less than a month after the election (courtesy the *Toledo Blade*).

he could be as tender as a woman. He was sincere and honest in everything he did. We honor him as much for his contributions to life as for his contributions to baseball. Life is a baseball game with the diamond and the rules laid out by the Great Coach. Each player must follow all the rules, or he is out. The main object is to get to the home plate safely."[70]

Roger Bresnahan made a point to University of Toledo's legendary baseball coach, Dave Connelly, in 1932. Connelly headed the Rockets' team from 1931 through 1950 (courtesy the *Toledo Blade*).

Competition was keen among the parish's altar boys wanting to serve during Bresnahan's Requiem Mass. Jim Silk was selected to toll the church bell and recalled "the excitement when the funeral was going on" and seeing "famous people" there.[71]

Floral tributes from the Toledo Baseball Club, Detroit Tigers, New York Giants, Baseball Writers Association of America and its New York Chapter, Buckeye Brewing Company, and the American League were among the five-dozen received and over 500 mourners signed the guest register.[72] Burial was at Calvary Cemetery in Toledo.[73]

Willard B. "Bill" Mason was a grandson of Roger's sister, Margaret. The grandnephew was 12 years old when Roger died. Bill related that Roger "always wanted a son" and that he "filled that role." Bill spent considerable time at Roger's Mellwood Court home and helped care for Roger's Irish setters and hunting dogs. He had about a dozen dogs, some of which he "showed." Roger taught Bill baseball, which he played in high school and at Michigan State University. He offered Bill advice—"you can't play baseball if you have a temper you can't control." Roger told Bill "he regretted his temper, and it got him in an awful lot of trouble and cost him dearly."[74]

* * *

Less than five months following Roger's passing he was selected to be enshrined in the National Baseball Hall of Fame.[75] The Hall of Fame had inducted its first class in 1936 and by the end of 1944 just 17 players had gained membership. The institution was meant to be an exclusive club—it was and still is. Originally, electors were exclusively members of the Baseball Writers Association of America, and it was required that nominees garner support from 75 percent of the voters.[76] As intended, the standard was very high but proved to be too high because some, considered worthy by many, went unelected. Consequently, other methods for election were devised. Baseball Commissioner Kenesaw Mountain Landis announced one such method on August 4, 1944, when he revealed that he and others had appointed a committee which was empowered to elevate "figures whose standout contributions were started before 1900."[77] This group, now known as the Old-Timers Committee, named 10 honorees on April 25, 1945—including Roger.[78]

Roger's election did not exactly come out of nowhere. He had been on all six ballots to date. Earlier in 1945, the writers voted on a ballot that had contained 95 names—none were elected, but Roger advanced farther up the list than any other nominee and finished fifth.

Though elected, Roger and the others in his class—Jimmy Collins, Fred Clarke, Wilbert Robinson, Dan Brouthers, Ed Delahanty, Jim O'Rourke, King Kelly, Hugh Duffy, and Hugh Jennings—were not enshrined with an induction ceremony. A duplicate of the plaque that was hung in the Hall of Fame was sent to the family in 1949.[79] After being invited many times,[80] Roger's widow Gertrude attended the ceremony in 1955 with two of Roger's grandnephews—David Henige, 15, and Roger

Roger Bresnahan (left) and Casey Stengel at Toledo's Swayne Field in 1929, dated by Stengel's distinctive cap. Stengel managed the Toledo Mud Hens for six seasons, 1926–1931. Toledo's greatest team, the 1927 edition, won Toledo's first American Association pennant (courtesy the *Toledo Blade*).

These baseball and boxing notables were at Swayne Field to commemorate the 20th anniversary of the Willard-Dempsey heavyweight boxing match held in Toledo, on July 4, 1919. The gentlemen from the left are Vice-Mayor Jon Carey, "Two-Ton" Toney Galento (who had just lost to Joe Louis), Roger Bresnahan, Cy Young and Jess Willard. Jack Dempsey could not attend because of appendicitis. The ladies, Virginia Vaughn and Cleo Saville, presented the flowers (courtesy the *Toledo Blade*).

M. Bresnahan, 15.[81] Shirley Povich, president of the Baseball Writers Association of America and the master of ceremonies, recognized her.[82]

Finally on June 28, 2013, the 1945 class was formally inducted. Jane Forbes Clark, Chairman of the Board of Directors of The National Baseball Hall of Fame and Museum, honored the class of 1945 saying, "these men are living legends as they define character, integrity and sportsmanship all within incredible baseball careers." Carlton Fisk, also a Hall of Fame catcher, read Roger's plaque at the event.[83]

Some are critical of the inclusion of Bresnahan as he was elected not by the stringent original rules but the subjective opinions of people who had seen or known of how he played the game and contributed to it. Bill James—the influential and prolific writer, statistician, and historian—wrote that Bresnahan has "no damn business" being in the Hall of Fame.[84] However, the Old-Timers Committee members who put him in recognized that Bresnahan was no ordinary player. Understandably, questions arise when Bresnahan's career is measured by today's advanced metrics.

At that time, those charged with electing knew the simpler, traditional statistical measures and what they had seen for themselves to aid their decision-making. The fact remains that comparing players across eras, even with modern analytical tools, is difficult, and does not include the subjective reasoning utilized by the voters of 1945. Intangibles affected voters' choices then and still do. Such outstanding performers as Barry Bonds, Mark McGwire, Roger Clemens, have been excluded from the Hall of Fame due to subjective reasoning.

Perhaps a simple comparison of a few traditional statistics of Roger Bresnahan to a more recent player like Johnny Bench will show that Roger may not be unworthy. Bench's batting average was .267 over his 17 big league seasons while Bresnahan's was .279 over a like period. Measured against their peers, Bench's average was 13 points above his league's average and Bresnahan was plus 23. Bench hit 389 home runs while Bresnahan had 26 but *nobody* that played during the Deadball Era hit home runs at Bench's rate. Bench stole 68 bases while Bresnahan's total was 212—the highest ever for a player whose primary position was catcher.[85] These measures seem crude by today's standard, but they do mean something and hint that Roger did play the game well—a game that featured far different strategies and equipment.

This Roger Bresnahan photograph was made by the *Sporting News* to accompany a feature article for its November 14, 1940, issue. The story was based on a Bresnahan interview and told how he was fighting back from the stock market crash of 1929 (author's collection).

One modem metric that attempts to quantify a player's ability to get on base and hit for power is OPS+ which normalizes the sum of slugging and batting averages so that the league average is 100 and is comparable across eras. Bench and Bresnahan have identical career OPS+ of 126 making them 26% better than the average batter.

The previous discussion focuses on the statistical record of ball players which is a major factor in a player getting on the ballot and for judging the relative merit of those elected or not elected. But the voters are charged to base their vote on far more—"Voting shall be based upon the player's record, playing ability, integrity, sportsmanship, character, and contributions to the team(s) on which the player played."[86]

Those that saw him play thought he did so well and *also* contributed to those other areas of the voting criteria—that is why he was elected.

Roger Bresnahan gave tips to youngsters during the 1943 Mud Hens clinic. Said the *Toledo Times*: "Despite ill health, the Duke of Tralee spent many of his leisure hours teaching the youngsters the fundamentals of the game and was constantly on the lookout for talent..." (courtesy the *Toledo Blade*).

Even though the timing of Roger's death did project his name before the Old-Timers Committee just as their members prepared to vote, Bresnahan's election was more than "sympathy."[87] Notables such as Grantland Rice and Arthur Daley had lobbied for his inclusion before his passing.[88] Honus Wagner who observed Bresnahan as an opponent for 15 years said the following about his former adversary in 1943:

> "Supposing we were choosing up sides for two all-time baseball teams and I had first pick. I wouldn't have to look far because the first man I'd select would be Roge.
>
> Here's why: He could do anything. He could catch, play the infield, or play the outfield. He could hit, throw, and run. I'd say he was the most talented and versatile player in the history of the sport."[89]

John Sheridan, writing in the *Sporting News*, expressed his thoughts in 1926: "...no man, except perhaps Cobb, exerted so great an individual force in a ball game, either behind the bat, at the bat, or on the bases as Bresnahan."[90]

Epilogue

Gertrude Norenberg Bresnahan. Following Roger's death, Gertrude sold their family home, moved with her adopted daughter Marian to a rental house and obtained employment as a Deputy County Recorder. By 1950 she purchased a home which she gave up for an apartment, presumably when Marian left the nest. In the late 1950s she bought another house which she shared for an indeterminate number of years with Marian, her son-in-law and two granddaughters.[1] She lived for an extended period in the Colonial Nursing Home in Toledo where she died at age 84 on January 19, 1968. Services were held at Toledo's Rosary Cathedral, and she was buried at Calvary Cemetery alongside Roger.[2]

Gertrude was remembered by Margaret Bresnahan (wife of Gertrude's grandnephew Roger M. Bresnahan) from her days in the nursing home as "elegant, loving, sweet, and quiet. I liked her a lot; she was a very nice lady."[3]

Marian Patricia Bresnahan. Roger and Gertrude's adopted daughter was 11 years old when Roger died. She attended Central Catholic High School and married William Knepper, Jr., as an 18-year-old in 1951.[4] Following their divorce, she married Roy Childers in 1955.[5] The couple had two daughters—Linda Lee died as an infant in 1961 and Dorothy Marie who married Marvin Nowak and had four children. Marian died at age 67 on April 21, 2000.[6]

Marian's recollections of Roger Bresnahan: "He was a good-hearted man, was good to me and helped people with money. He was bothered by rheumatism in his hips. He enjoyed hunting and fishing. He kept many dogs in a kennel at his Mellwood Court home."[7]

Adeleen Lidke Bresnahan. At least a year before Adeleen and Roger's divorce was finalized Adeleen left *her* home of about 15 years—hers because two years after he purchased the property in 1904, Roger had transferred the title to her.[8] She rented living accommodations and would do so for the rest of her life. She also became a landlord of her former home until May 1925 when she sold it. Her alimony, rental income and house sale funds appear to have served her well as no record of employment for her has been found. The 1940 United States Census Records show she had income from "other sources" but not from employment. She died at Maumee Valley Hospital in Toledo, Ohio, at age 70 on March 1, 1951.[9] Her services and interment at Woodlawn Cemetery were private.[10]

Helene Hathaway Robison Britton. Mrs. Britton owned the St. Louis Cardinals for six seasons—1911–1916. She functioned as the club's president for the first two years, attending and taking part in the National League's previously all-male meetings. Her husband, Schuyler Britton, succeeded her as president and represented the club before the National League but as a figurehead only—Mrs. Britton maintained control. Miller Huggins, whom she had appointed to succeed Bresnahan, remained with her for the remaining four years of her tenure. Her National League finishes in order were fifth, sixth, eighth, third, sixth and seventh. She sold the club and ballpark, which she had inherited, early in 1917 for $350,000.[11]

Appendix 1. Roger Bresnahan's Team Associations

Year	*Age*	*Team*	*League*	*Position*
1896	16	Toledo, Ohio	Amateur	player
1897	17	Toledo, Ohio	Amateur	player
1897	17	Bryan, Ohio	Independent	player
1897	17	Lima, Ohio	Independent	player
1897	18	Washington Senators	National League	player
1898	19	Toledo Mud Hens	Inter-State League	player
1898	19	Minneapolis Millers	Western League	player
1899	20	Minneapolis Millers	Western League	player
1899	20	Buffalo Bisons	Western League	player
1899	20	Manistee	Independent	player
1900	21	Manistee	Independent	player
1900	21	Chicago Orphans	National League	player
1901	22	Baltimore Orioles	American League	player
1902	23	Baltimore Orioles	American League	player
1902	23	New York Giants	National League	player
1903	24	New York Giants	National League	player
1904	25	New York Giants	National League	player
1905	26	New York Giants	National League	player
1906	27	New York Giants	National League	player
1907	28	New York Giants	National League	player
1908	29	New York Giants	National League	player
1909	30	St. Louis Cardinals	National League	manager, player
1910	31	St. Louis Cardinals	National League	manager, player
1911	32	St. Louis Cardinals	National League	manager, player
1912	33	St. Louis Cardinals	National League	manager, player
1913	34	Chicago Cubs	National League	player

Year	*Age*	*Team*	*League*	*Position*
1914	35	Chicago Cubs	National League	player
1915	36	Chicago Cubs	National League	manager, player
1916	37	Toledo Iron Men	American Association	owner, president, manager, player
1917	38	Toledo Iron Men	American Association	owner, president, manager, player
1918	39	Toledo Iron Men	American Association	owner, president, manager, player
1919	40	Toledo Mud Hens	American Association	owner, president, manager
1920	41	Toledo Mud Hens	American Association	owner, president, manager
1921	42	Toledo Mud Hens	American Association	owner, president, manager, player
1922	43	Toledo Mud Hens	American Association	owner, president
1923	44	Toledo Mud Hens	American Association	owner, president
1926	47	New York Giants	National League	manager, coach
1927	48	New York Giants	National League	coach
1928	49	New York Giants	National League	manager, coach
1930	51	Detroit Tigers	American League	coach
1931	52	Detroit Tigers	American League	coach

Appendix 2. Positions Played by Bresnahan in Major Leagues

Year	*Team*	*LG*	*Games*	*P*	*C*	*1B*	*2B*	*3B*	*SS*	*LF*	*CF*	*RF*	*PH*	*PR*
1897	Washington	NL	6	6	0	0	0	0	0	0	1	0	0	0
1900	Chicago	NL	2	0	1	0	0	0	0	0	0	0	0	1
1901	Baltimore	AL	86	2	69	0	2	4	0	7	0	1	2	0
1902	Baltimore	AL	65	0	22	0	0	30	0	0	15	0	1	0
1902	New York	NL	51	0	16	4	0	1	4	0	0	27	1	0
1903	New York	NL	113	0	11	13	0	4	0	4	81	1	1	1
1904	New York	NL	109	0	0	12	1	1	4	6	82	5	4	0
1905	New York	NL	104	0	88	0	1	0	0	0	4	5	9	0
1906	New York	NL	123	0	83	0	0	0	0	0	40	3	0	0
1907	New York	NL	110	0	95	6	0	1	0	0	2	0	7	0
1908	New York	NL	140	0	139	0	0	0	0	0	0	0	1	0
1909	St. Louis	NL	73	0	54	0	9	2	0	0	5	0	3	1
1910	St. Louis	NL	88	1	77	0	0	0	0	1	1	0	8	2
1911	St. Louis	NL	81	0	77	0	2	0	0	0	0	0	3	0
1912	St. Louis	NL	49	0	29	0	0	0	0	0	0	0	21	0
1913	Chicago	NL	69	0	58	0	0	0	0	0	0	0	11	0
1914	Chicago	NL	101	0	85	0	7	0	0	0	1	0	10	0
1915	Chicago	NL	77	0	68	0	0	0	0	0	0	0	9	0
Totals			1447	9	972	35	22	43	8	18	232	42	91	5

Appendix 3. Toledo in the American Association During Bresnahan's Ownership

Year	*Name*	*POS*	*Assoc*	*Manager*	*Fans*	*W*	*L*	*Pct*
1916	Iron Men	6		Bresnahan	124,363	78	86	.476
1917	Iron Men	8		Bresnahan	98,921	57	95	.375
1918	Iron Men	8	Yankees	Bresnahan		23	54	.299
1919	Mud Hens	7	Yankees	Rollie Zeider, Bresnahan	89,712	59	91	.393
1920	Mud Hens	3	Yankees	Bresnahan	241,718	87	79	.524
1921	Mud Hens	7	Tigers	Bill Clymer, Bresnahan, Fred Luderus	198,148	80	88	.476
1922	Mud Hens	7	Giants	Luderus, George Whitted	155,631	65	101	.392
1923	Mud Hens	8	Giants	Whitted, Bill Terry, Walt Barbare	98,694	54	114	.321
						508	708	.415

Appendix 4. Bresnahan's Playing Record at Toledo

	Batting									Pitching				
Year	*G*	*AB*	*R*	*H*	*2B*	*3B*	*HR*	*Avg*	*SB*	*W*	*L*	*IP*	*SO*	*BB*
1898	4	12	2	5	3	0	0	.417	0	2	2	33	11	8
1916	44	120	19	29	4	1	2	.242	4					
1917	40	80	10	22	5	0	0	.275	1					
1918	19	52	4	12	2	0	1	.230	0					
1921	5	12	0	5	0	0	0	.417	2					
	112	276	35	73	14	1	3	.264	7	2	2	33	11	8

Source: Lin Weber, Ralph Elliott, *The Toledo Baseball Guide of the Mud Hens 1883–1943*. Rossford, OH: Baseball Research Bureau, 1944.

Appendix 5. Roger Bresnahan's Major League Career Numbers

Batting													
Year	*Age*	*Team*	*LG*	*G*	*AB*	*R*	*H*	*2B*	*3B*	*HR*	*RBI*	*SB*	*BA*
1897	18	Washington	NL	6	16	1	6	0	0	0	3	0	.375
1900	21	Chicago	NL	2	2	0	0	0	0	0	0	0	.000
1901	22	Baltimore	AL	86	295	40	79	9	9	1	32	10	.268
1902	23	Baltimore	AL	65	235	30	64	8	6	4	34	12	.272
1902	23	New York	NL	51	178	16	51	9	3	1	22	6	.287
1903	24	New York	NL	113	406	87	142	30	8	4	55	34	.350
1904	25	New York	NL	109	402	81	114	22	7	5	33	13	.284
1905	26	New York	NL	104	331	58	100	18	3	0	46	11	.302
1906	27	New York	NL	124	405	69	114	22	4	0	43	25	.281
1907	28	New York	NL	110	328	57	83	9	7	4	38	15	.253
1908	29	New York	NL	140	449	70	127	25	3	1	54	14	.283
1909	30	St. Louis	NL	72	234	27	57	4	1	0	23	11	.244
1910	31	St. Louis	NL	88	234	35	65	15	3	0	27	13	.278
1911	32	St. Louis	NL	81	227	22	63	17	8	3	41	4	.278
1912	33	St. Louis	NL	48	108	8	36	7	2	1	15	4	.333
1913	34	Chicago	NL	69	162	20	37	5	2	1	21	7	.228
1914	35	Chicago	NL	101	248	42	69	10	4	0	24	14	.278
1915	36	Chicago	NL	77	221	19	45	8	1	1	19	19	.204
		Totals		1446	4481	682	1252	218	71	26	530	212	.279

World's Series Batting													
1905	26	New York	NL	5	16	3	5	2	0	0	1	1	.313

Pitching				*G*	*W*	*L*	*ERA*	*IP*	*R*	*ER*	*BB*	*K*	
1897	18	Washington	NL	6	4	0	3.95	41.0	21	18	10	12	
1901	22	Baltimore	AL	2	0	1	6.00	6.0	8	4	4	3	

Pitching				*G*	*W*	*L*	*ERA*	*IP*	*R*	*ER*	*BB*	*K*	
1910	31	St. Louis	NL	1	0	0	0.00	3.1	1	0	1	0	
		Totals		9	4	1	3.93	50.1	30	22	15	15	

Managing				*G*	*W*	*L*	*POS*	*%*
1909	30	St. Louis	NL	154	54	98	7	.355
1910	31	St. Louis	NL	153	63	90	7	.412
1911	32	St. Louis	NL	158	75	74	5	.503
1912	33	St. Louis	NL	153	63	90	6	.412
1915	36	Chicago	NL	157	73	80	4	.477
1926	47	New York	NL	13	5	8	5	.385
1928	49	New York	NL	44	24	19	2	.545
		Totals		832	357	459		.429

Coaching		
1926	47	New York NL
1927	48	New York NL
1928	49	New York NL
1930	51	Detroit AL
1931	52	Detroit AL

Appendix 6. Honors

National Baseball Hall of Fame and Museum, elected 1945.—National Baseball Hall of Fame and Library, "Roger Bresnahan," http://baseballhall.org/hof/bresnahan-roger.

Ohio Baseball Hall of Fame, inducted August 24, 1985.—*Toledo Blade*, August 23, 1985.

Toledo Baseball Hall of Fame, inducted February 7, 1955.—*Toledo Blade*, February 8, 1955.

All-Time Franchise Team (through 1987) New York/San Francisco Giants as catcher.—Eugene McCaffrey and Roger McCaffrey, *Players' Choice* (New York:Facts on File, 1987), 199.

John McGraw's best battery with Mathewson and best catcher.—*Sporting News*, February 8, 1934.

New York Telegram, Catcher for "Greatest Nine in Big Leagues," February 10, 1928.—National Baseball Hall of Fame and Library, Babe Ruth Personal Scrapbook, Vol. 9, Part 1, 1928, 18.

Bill James' All-Star Team 1900–1909, catcher.—Bill James, *The New Bill James Historical Baseball Abstract* (New York: Free Press, 2011), 83.

Fred Lieb's All-Time All-Star Team 1932, catcher.—*Sporting News*, February 28, 1932.

Honus Wagner's All-Time National League Team 1937, catcher.—*Sporting News*, December 9, 1937.

1905 National League and American League All-Star Teams, NL catcher.—*Courier-Journal* (Louisville, KY), October 22, 1905.

John McGraw's All-American Team, catcher.—John McGraw, *My 30 Years in Baseball* (New York: Boni and Liveright, 1923), 212.

Chapter Notes

The author has not cited basic data from baseball's magnificent statistical record because it is readily available to anyone. The principal sources utilized herein were retrosheet.org and baseball-reference.com for league, team, and individual records such as schedules, standings, game box scores, and exhaustive individual records including demographic information.

Epigraph

1. John B. Sheridan, "Back of the Home Plate," *Sporting News*, February 11, 1926.

Preface

1. Mike Lackey, email message to author, April 4, 2013.
2. Mike Lackey, email message to author, August 16, 2015.
3. Larson, *Dead Wake*, 359.
4. World's Series is an early term for World Series. "The modern term 'World Series,' without the apostrophe 's' after 'World,' did not come into general use until the 1930s."—Spatz, *Bad Bill Dahlen*, 228. In this work the term "World's Series" is used.

Chapter One

1. *Cincinnati Enquirer*, June 19, 1907.
2. *Sporting Life*, July 6, 1907. *Washington Post* reported on March 15, 1908, that Ganzel fielded the ball on the bound.
3. Early twentieth century sportswriters capitalized titles and occupations when preceding a name. Their lead is followed in this work.
4. Grayson, *They Played the Game*, 83.
5. *Sporting News*, August 31, 1907.
6. "In 1890, the United States Board of Geographic Names, which was created to bring consistency to the spellings of locations throughout the country, deemed that all cities ending in 'burgh' must drop the 'h' in the spirit of uniformity... Eventually, a special meeting of the U.S. Board of Geographic Names was arranged. On July 19, 1911, the board met. A preponderance of evidence citing Pittsburgh spelled with the 'h' over the decades convinced the board to reinstate the final letter."—Positively Pittsburg, "What's in an H?" http://popularpittsburgh.com/whatsinanh/
7. Lackey, *Spitballing*, 183.
8. Morris, *Catcher*, 230.
9. "A pitch that breaks, or otherwise has a pronounced movement, toward the batter, but not as sharp as a curve"—Dickson, *Dickson Baseball Dictionary*, 454.
10. *Cincinnati Enquirer*, June 19, 1907.
11. *Cincinnati Commercial Tribune*, June 19, 1907.
12. *Cincinnati Enquirer*, June 19, 1907.
13. McGraw's appearance was discovered by the author and is now included in his record increasing his major league seasons played to 17.
14. *Cincinnati Enquirer*, June 19, 1907.
15. *New York American*, June 19, 1907.
16. *New York Herald*, June 19, 1907.

Chapter Two

1. Skipper, *Baseball Nicknames*, 30.
2. *Washington Post*, December 22, 1912.
3. Byrne, *Ireland and the Americas*, 87.
4. Harvey Woodruff, "Life and Career of Roger Bresnahan," *Chicago Tribune*, February 2, 1913.
5. Fleitz, *The Irish in Baseball*, 135.
6. Fleitz, *The Irish in Baseball*, 135.
7. Fleitz, *The Irish in Baseball*, 135.
8. Thorn, *Five Books You Should Know*.
9. Roger M. Bresnahan, "Death Claims Widely Known Resident Here," unidentified news clip.
10. Kerryman's Protective and Benevolent Association, letter to Mrs. Roger Bresnahan, June 11, 1956.
11. Lucas County Ohio Probate Court Death Records, volume 5, page 13.
12. *Evening Star* (Washington, DC), August 30, 1897.
13. The author has searched for records of Roger's education to no avail. No records of attendance

have been found from the schools that existed at the time, public or parochial.

14. *Pittsburg Press*, June 18, 1909.
15. *Washington Post*, April 11, 1909.
16. Lin Weber, *Toledo Baseball Guide*, 137, 141, 143.
17. Establishing Roger Bresnahan's family genealogy is difficult because of the many Bresnahans and O'Donohues, with variant spellings, concentrated in County Kerry. Additional difficulties included being limited to public records and the remarkable inconsistencies contained in them. For example, United States census data for Roger's father's birth year for 1880 is 1823, 1900 is 1840 and 1910 is 1835, while his newspaper obituary and death certificate show 1822. His surname for those censuses is Busnahan, Bresnan and Bresnahan. Among the numerous sources of biographical information for this work are ancestry.com, newspapers, a Bresnahan family scrapbook and familysearch.org which include census records, marriage records, death records and address and occupation data from city directories.
18. *Toledo Bee*, May 24, 1896.
19. *Toledo Bee*, June 10, 1896.
20. *Toledo Bee*, June 26, 1896.
21. *Toledo Bee*, July 29, 1896.
22. *Toledo Bee*, September 27, 1896.

Chapter Three

1. *Toledo Bee*, May 10, 1897.
2. *Washington Post*, August 28, 1897.
3. Determined by the author from baseball-reference.com data. The study of this question included all major league pitchers dating back to 1876.
4. *Toledo Bee*, May 16, 1897.
5. *Toledo Bee*, May 17, 1897.
6. *Bryan Press* (OH), May 20, 1897.
7. *Toledo Bee*, May 24, 1897.
8. *Times-Democrat* (Lima, OH), June 4, 1897.
9. *Toledo Bee*, May 27, 1897.
10. *Times-Democrat* (Lima, OH), May 28, 1897.
11. *Toledo Bee*, June 16, 1897.
12. *Times-Democrat* (Lima, OH), June 19, 1897.
13. *Times-Democrat* (Lima, OH), June 21, 1897.
14. *Times-Democrat* (Lima, OH), June 25, 1897.
15. *Toledo Bee*, June 26, 1897.
16. *Times-Democrat* (Lima, OH), July 17, 1897.
17. *Toledo Bee*, July 23, 1897.
18. *Toledo Bee*, July 26, 1897.
19. *Times-Democrat* (Lima, OH), August 10, 1897.
20. *Times-Democrat* (Lima, OH), August 11, 1897.
21. *Times-Democrat* (Lima, OH), August 10, 1897.
22. Roger P. Bresnahan, *Roger's Scrapbook*, 40.
23. *Toledo Bee*, August 21, 1897.
24. *Washington Post*, August 16, 1897.
25. *Washington Post*, August 16, 1897.
26. The incorrect spelling, Bresnehan, was often used in Roger's career.
27. *Evening Star* (Washington, DC), August 27, 1897.
28. *Washington Post*, October 26, 1897.
29. *Washington Post*, August 28, 1897.
30. *Washington Post*, September 3, 1897.
31. *Washington Post*, September 7, 1897.
32. *Washington Post*, September 12, 1897.
33. *Washington Post*, September 19, 1897.
34. *Sporting News*, October 9, 1897, 2.
35. *Washington Post*, October 3, 1897.
36. *Washington Post*, October 3, 1897.
37. Lammers, *The Best Circuit You Never Heard Of*, 90.
38. *Toledo Bee*, October 7, 1897.

Chapter Four

1. *Toledo Bee*, August 27, 1898.
2. *Washington Post*, May 23, 1898.
3. *Baltimore Sun*, October 7, 1897.
4. *Washington Post*, March 3, 1898.
5. Scribner, *Memoirs of Lucas County*, 375.
6. Roger P. Bresnahan, *Roger's Scrapbook*, 38.
7. *Washington Post*, March 30, 1898.
8. *Washington Post*, April 2, 1898.
9. *Sporting Life*, April 9, 1898.
10. *Washington Post*, May 11, 1898.
11. *Sporting Life*, April 9, 1898.
12. *Dayton Press*, June 6, 1898.
13. *Sporting Life*, June 4, 1898.
14. *Dayton Press*, June 6, 1898, and *Courier Journal* (Louisville), June 3, 1898.
15. James, *The New Bill James Historical Baseball Abstract*, 377–379.
16. *Toledo Bee*, May 21, 1898.
17. *St. Louis Post-Dispatch*, June 3, 1898, 7.
18. *Toledo Bee*, May 24, 1898;
19. *Dayton Press*, June 6, 1898.

Toledo Blade, May 28, 1898.

20. *Dayton Herald*, May 31, 1898.
21. *Dayton Press*, June 1, 1898.
22. *Toledo Blade*, June 8, 1898.
23. *Minneapolis Tribune*, July 24, 1898.
24. *Minneapolis Tribune*, July 26, 1898.
25. *Minneapolis Tribune*, July 31, 1898.
26. *Minneapolis Tribune*, August 3, 1898.
27. *Minneapolis Tribune*, August 3, 1898.
28. *Toledo Bee*, August 26, 1898.
29. *Toledo Bee*, August 27, 1898.
30. *Toledo Bee*, August 31, 1898.
31. *Sporting Life*, October 15, 1898.

Chapter Five

1. *Manistee Daily News* (MI), August 16, 1899.
2. *Mansfield News* (OH), January 8, 1899.
3. *Upper Des Moines* (Algona, Iowa), January 4, 1899.
4. *Minneapolis Tribune*, April 14, 1899.
5. *Minneapolis Tribune*, April 16, 1899.
6. *Minneapolis Tribune*, April 23, 1899.

7. *Minneapolis Tribune*, April 29, 1899.
8. *Minneapolis Tribune*, May 3, 1899.
9. *Minneapolis Tribune*, May 12, 1899.
10. *Minneapolis Tribune*, June 15, 1899.
11. *Detroit Free Press*, June 19, 1899.
12. *Detroit Free Press*, June 20, 1899, and June 22, 1899.
13. *Detroit Free Press*, June 23, 1899.
14. The City of Manistee, Michigan, "History of Manistee," April 8, 2016, http://www.manisteemi.gov/248/History-of-Manistee.
15. *Sporting News*, December 7, 1944.
16. *Sporting News* (TSN) was the authoritative source for baseball news for more than a century and "is the oldest sporting publication in the United States. A weekly from its debut in 1886 until 2008, it was for decades known informally as "The Bible of Baseball" and was essential reading for players, officials, and fans."—Society for American Baseball Research, "The Sporting News, *https://sabr.org/bioproj/topic/sporting-news. Sporting News* contract cards are basic records collection of "214,000 index cards *Sporting News* maintained on virtually every professional baseball player from the early 1900s through the mid-1990s. The cards contain player biographical data, details of year-by-year contract signings, player trades and assignments.—Society for American Baseball Research, "'The Sporting News' donates two special resource collections to SABR," *https://sabr.org/latest/sporting-news-donates-two-special-resource-collections-sabr.* In Roger's case the first three teams entered are Manistee, Mich.; Lima, O.; and South Bend, Ind. These entries are undated and Roger's card, noted Manistee as the initial entry and simply assigned a year that fit the chronology of his major league service.
17. *Detroit Free Press* reported Manistee results under the heading "Amateur Baseball."
18. *Muskegon Chronicle* (MI), August 25, 1899.
19. *Muskegon Chronicle* (MI), August 25, 1899.
20. *Manistee Daily News* (MI), July 31, 1899.
21. *Manistee Daily News* (MI), August 1, 1899.
22. *Manistee Daily News* (MI), August 2, 1899.
23. *Manistee Daily News* (MI), August 3, 1899.
24. *Muskegon Chronicle* (MI), August 14, 1899.
25. *Manistee Daily News* (MI), September 18, 1899.
26. *Muskegon Chronicle* (MI), July 25, 1900. His batting average for 1900 at Manistee was. 312—*Baltimore Sun*, April 22, 1901.
27. *Detroit Free Press*, August 18, 1900.
28. *Sporting Life*, July 30, 1898.
29. *Sporting Life*, August 25, 1900.
30. *Chicago Tribune*, August 29, 1900.
31. *Inter Ocean* (Chicago), August 29, 1900.
32. *Chicago Tribune*, September 1, 1900.
33. *Chicago Tribune*, September 2, 1900.

Chapter Six

1. *Washington Post*, January 20, 1901.
2. *Washington Post*, January 27, 1901. This announcement may have been premature as the *Courier-Journal* (Louisville) reported on March 14, 1901, that Bresnahan had signed a Baltimore contract. This was followed by confirming reports by a rash of newspapers over the next few days.
3. *Baltimore Sun*, March 15, 1901.
4. *Baltimore Sun*, April 22, 1901.
5. Don Jensen, "John McGraw," *Society for American Baseball Research, Baseball Biography Project*, https://sabr.org/bioproj/person/john-mcgraw-2/.
6. *Baltimore Sun*, April 3, 1901.
7. Compiled by the author from *Baltimore Sun* game accounts.
8. *Baltimore Sun*, May 1, 1901.
9. *Baltimore Sun*, May 1, 1901.
10. *Baltimore Sun*, May 2, 1901.
11. Richard McCann, "The Payoff," *Sayre* (PA) *Evening Times*, May 26, 1937.
12. John McGraw, *My Thirty Years in Baseball*, 214.
13. *Baltimore Sun*, May 13, 1901.
14. *Baltimore Sun*, May 16, 1901.
15. *Sporting Life*, May 25, 1901.
16. *Baltimore Sun*, May 29, 1901, and *Detroit Free Press*, June 1, 1901.
17. *Baltimore Sun*, May 29, 1901.
18. *Detroit Free Press*, June 1, 1901.
19. Roger I. Abrams, *The First World Series and the Baseball Fanatics of 1903*, 47.
20. *Baltimore Sun*, June 11, 1901.
21. *Baltimore Sun*, June 8, 1901.
22. *Baltimore Sun*, June 11, 1901.
23. *Baltimore Sun*, June 12, 1901.
24. *Baltimore Sun*, July 13, 1901.
25. *Baltimore Sun*, August 26, 1901.
26. *Baltimore Sun*, July 18, 1901.
27. *Baltimore Sun*, July 19, 1901.
28. *Baltimore Sun*, August 20, 1901.
29. *Toledo Bee*, July 24, 1901.
30. *Cincinnati Enquirer*, July 26, 1901.
31. *Baltimore Sun*, August 19, 1901.
32. *Baltimore Sun*, September 17, 1901.
33. *Baltimore Sun*, August 28, 1901.
34. *Baltimore Sun*, September 13, 1901.
35. *Times-Democrat* (Lima, OH), October 5, 1901.
36. *Worcester Daily Spy*, October 2, 1901.
37. *Toledo Bee*, October 8, 1901.
38. *Toledo Bee*, October 8, 1901.
39. *Times-Democrat* (Lima, OH), October 9, 1901, *Cincinnati Enquirer*, October 17, 1901, and *New Orleans Item*, October 22 and 28, 1901.
40. *Dallas Morning News*, November 1, 1901.
41. *Pittsburg Press*, December 6, 1901.
42. *Cincinnati Enquirer*, October 31, 1901.
43. Joe S. Jackson, "Sporting Facts and Fantasies," *Detroit Free Press*, December 6, 1901.
44. *New Orleans Item*, December 6, 1901.
45. *Boston Herald*, December 4, 1901.
46. *Pittsburg Press*, December 28, 1901.
47. *Washington Post*, January 2, 1902.

Chapter Seven

1. J.R. Cummings, "Gossip of the Game," *Washington Post*, August 24, 1902.
2. J.R. Cummings, "Gossip of the Game," *Washington Post*, August 24, 1902.
3. *Sporting Life*, February 8, 1902, 7.
4. *South Bend Tribune* (IN), February 17, 1902.
5. *Baltimore Sun*, April 7, 1902.
6. *Baltimore Sun*, March 23, 1902.
7. *Baltimore Sun*, March 26, 1902.
8. *Baltimore Sun*, March 26, 1902.
9. *Baltimore Sun*, March 27, 1902.
10. *Baltimore Sun*, April 3, 1902.
11. Yannigan defined: "A rookie, not a regular player, a player on the second team in a spring training camp game"—Dickson, *Dickson Baseball Dictionary*, 951.
12. *Baltimore Sun*, April 11, 1902.
13. *Baltimore Sun*, April 20, 1902.
14. *Baltimore Sun*, May 2, 1902.
15. *Baltimore Sun*, May 3, 1902.
16. *Baltimore Sun*, May 4, 1902.
17. *Baltimore Sun*, April 28, 1902.
18. *Baltimore Sun*, May 9, 1902.
19. *Baltimore Sun*, May 21, 1902.
20. *Baltimore Sun*, May 6, 1902.
21. *Baltimore Sun*, May 25, 1902.
22. *Baltimore Sun*, June 29, 1902. McGraw's injury was incurred in a game against Detroit on May 24 and was described by the *Baltimore Sun* (May 25, 1902). "In the first inning Harley made a good hit, got second on Barrett's hit and tried a double steal with Barrett. Bresnahan [catching] threw to McGraw at third and Harley was out a mile. Harley slid to the base feet first. His spikes landed square on McGraw's leg at the knee, cutting three gashes in the flesh." The injury led to the end of McGraw's playing career.
23. *Toledo Bee*, June 13, 1902.
24. *Baltimore Sun*, May 7, 1902.
25. *Baltimore Sun*, May 16, 1902.
26. Walter Scott "Steve" Brodie, center fielder of the Baltimore Orioles of the 1890s.
27. *Baltimore Sun*, May 18, 1902.
28. *Baltimore Sun*, May 19, 1902.
29. *Baltimore Sun*, May 30, 1902.
30. *Baltimore Sun*, May 30, 1902.
31. *Baltimore Sun*, May 31, 1902.
32. *Baltimore Sun*, June 3, 1902.
33. *Baltimore Sun*, June 27, 1902.
34. *Baltimore Sun*, July 3, 1902.
35. *Baltimore Sun*, July 10, 1902.
36. *Baltimore Sun*, July 8, 1902.
37. *Baltimore Sun*, July 9, 1902.
38. *Baltimore Sun*, July 20, 1902.
39. Fleitz, *The Irish in Baseball*, 138.
40. Alexander, *John McGraw*, 91.
41. *Sporting Life*, August 9, 1902.
42. *New York Times*, August 12, 1902.
43. *New York Times*, August 22, 1902.
44. *World* (New York), August 29, 1902.
45. *Lima News* (OH), September 1, 1902.
46. *Detroit Free Press*, September 4, 1902.
47. *World* (New York), September 5, 1902.
48. *World* (New York), September 8, 1902.
49. *World* (New York), September 12, 1902.
50. *New York Times*, August 17, 1902.
51. *Toledo Bee*, October 22, 1902.
52. *Toledo Bee*, October 20, 1902.
53. *Toledo Bee*, October 23, 1902.
54. *Sentinel* (Bowling Green, OH), October 27, 1902.
55. *Sentinel* (Bowling Green, OH), October 27, 1902.
56. *Toledo Times*, October 24, 1902.
57. *Toledo Bee*, October 24, 1902.
58. *Cincinnati Enquirer*, November 17, 1902.
59. *Fort Wayne News* (IN), December 12, 1902.
60. *Fort Wayne News* (IN), December 19, 1902.
61. *Scranton Republican* (PA), December 27, 1902.
62. *Evening Journal* (Wilmington, DE), January 21, 1903.
63. *Boston Herald*, February 1, 1903.
64. Several variant spellings of Miss Lidke's given name are found in the records. Among them are Adaleen, Adeline, and Adalene but Adeleen appears most often and in the most recent records.
65. *Chicago Tribune*, January 23, 1903.
66. *Toledo Blade*, February 4, 1903.
67. *Toledo Daily Blade*, February 19, 1903.

Chapter Eight

1. *Lima News* (OH), May 25, 1903.
2. *New York Times*, March 15, 1903.
3. Rich Wittish, "Recalling Savannah's History as a Spring Training Site," *Savannah Morning News*, February 16, 2011.
4. *New York Times*, April 9, 1903.
5. www.sportsencyclopedia.com
6. *Wichita Daily Eagle*, March 2, 1911.
7. *World* (New York), March 24, 1903.
8. Rich Wittish, "Recalling Savannah's History as a Spring Training Site," *Savannah Morning News*, February 16, 2011.
9. *New York Times*, March 28, 1903.
10. *Atlanta Constitution*, March 29, 1903.
11. *Nashville American*, March 31, 1903.
12. *Courier-Journal* (Louisville), April 2, 1903.
13. *Columbus Dispatch*, April 6, 1903.
14. *Columbus Dispatch*, April 7, 1903.
15. *New York Times*, April 11, 1903.
16. *New York Times*, April 12, and April 14, 1903.
17. *New-York Tribune*, April 19, 1903.
18. *Baltimore Sun*, May 13, 1901.
19. Graham, New York Giants, 40.
20. *World* (New York), April 23, 1903.
21. *New York Times*, May 1, 1903.
22. *New York Times*, April 21, 1903.
23. *Sporting Life*, May 23, 1903.
24. *Washington Post*, May 19, 1903.
25. Roger P. Bresnahan, *Roger's Scrapbook*, 40.

26. Roger P. Bresnahan, *Roger's Scrapbook*, 40.
27. *New York Times*, April 13, 1903.
28. *Sun* (New York), May 17, 1903.
29. *Lima News* (OH), May 25, 1903.
30. *St. Louis Republic*, May 31, 1903.
31. *Sporting Life*, June 6, 1903.
32. *St. Louis Republic*, July 5, 1903.
33. *New York Times*, June 14, 1903.
34. *New York Times*, July 2, 1903.
35. *Evening Star* (Washington, DC), January 16, 1904.
36. Society for American Baseball Research, "SABR Triple Plays Database," sabr.org/tripleplays.
37. *Wilkes-Barre Record* (PA), July 3, 1903.
38. *Democrat and Chronicle* (Rochester, NY), July 4, 1903.
39. *Chicago Tribune*, July 5, 1903.
40. *World* (New York), July 4, 1903.
41. Roger P. Bresnahan, *Roger's Scrapbook*, 40.
42. *New York Times*, July 6, 1903.
43. *Courier-Journal* (Louisville), July 13, 1903.
44. *Detroit Free Press*, July 30, 1903.
45. *Detroit Free Press*, July 7, 1903.
46. *World* (New York), July 13, 1903.
47. *World* (New York), July 14, 1903.
48. *Scranton Republican* (PA), July 18, 1903.
49. *Detroit Free Press*, July 21, 1903.
50. *Washington Post*, September 20, 1903.
51. *Washington Post*, March 29, 1903.

Chapter Nine

1. Roger P. Bresnahan, "The Secret of Batting Explained by a Master." *The Illustrated Sporting News*, August 22, 1903, 6–7.
2. *Pittsburg Press*, August 24, 1903.
3. *Pittsburg Press*, August 24, 1903.
4. Bresnahan ranks 249th on the all-time career list.
5. James, *New Bill James Historical Baseball Abstract*, 377–379.
6. The most ejected major league players are Johnny Evers 45, Bill Dahlen 33, Gary Sheffield 33, Larry Doyle 31, Heinie Zimmerman 31, Bresnahan 30 and Jimmy Piersall 28.—David Vincent, email message to author, December 1, 2012.
7. *New York Times*, August 18, 1903.
8. *Sporting Life*, August 1, 1903.
9. *Boston Post*, January 10, 1904.
10. *Boston Herald*, September 16, 1903.
11. Leo Fischer, "Rough, Ready 'Rajah' Passes," *Chicago Herald American*, December 5, 1944.
12. *Wilkes-Barre Record* (PA), August 27, 1903.
13. *Detroit Free Press*, November 10, 1903.
14. *Pittsburgh Press*, March 24, 1904.
15. *Sporting Life*, October 10, 1903, 7.
16. *Cincinnati Enquirer*, October 11, 1903.
17. *Chicago Tribune*, October 18, 1903.
18. *Baltimore Sun*, October 19, 1903.
19. *World* (New York), October 27, 1903.
20. *Toledo News-Bee*, October 24, 1903.
21. *Indianapolis News*, December 3, 1903.
22. *Pittsburg Press*, November 25, 1903.
23. *Courier-Journal* (Louisville), December 9, 1903.
24. *Pittsburg Press*, December 4, 1903.
25. *Indianapolis Star*, October 30, 1903.

Chapter Ten

1. *Toledo News-Bee*, April 14, 1904.
2. *Indianapolis News*, February 15, 1904.
3. baseball-reference.com
4. *Wilkes-Barre Record* (PA), January 25, 1904.
5. *Pittsburg Press*, February 21, 1904.
6. *Pittsburg Press*, February 27, 1904.
7. *New York Times*, March 13, 1904.
8. *Pittsburg Press*, March 12, 1904.
9. Johnson and Wolff, *Encyclopedia of Minor League Baseball*, 194.
10. Statistics compiled by the author.
11. *Boston Post*, March 19, 1904.
12. *Arkansas Gazette* (Little Rock), March 31 and April 1, 1904; *Tennessean* (Nashville), April 2, and 3, 1904; *New York Times*, April 5, and 6, 1904.
13. Statistics compiled by the author.
14. *Sporting Life*, April 9, 1904.
15. *Pittsburg Press*, April 16, 1904.
16. *Wilkes-Barre Record* (PA), April 16, 1904.
17. *Sporting Life*, October 7, 1905.
18. *Toledo News-Bee*, April 14, 1904.
19. *World* (New York), May 3, 1904.
20. *Boston Post*, April 13, 1904.
21. *Sun* (New York), April 15, 1904.
22. *New York Times*, April 15, 1904.
23. *Sun* (New York), April 15, 1904.
24. *World* (New York), May 2, 1904.
25. *Sandusky Star-Journal* (OH), April 30, 1904.
26. *Democrat and Chronicle* (Rochester, NY), April 30, 1904.
27. *Sporting Life*, May 7, 1904.
28. *Pittsburg Press*, May 3, 1904.
29. *New York Times*, May 12, 1904.
30. *New York Times*, May 13, 1904.
31. *New York Times*, May 15, 1904.
32. *New York Times*, May 16, 1904.
33. *Pittsburg Post*, May 18, 1904.
34. *New York Times*, March 13, 1904.
35. *Sporting Life*, May 30, 1904.
36. *Washington Post*, May 23, 1904.
37. *World* (New York), June 6, 1904.
38. *New York Times*, June 7, 1904.
39. *St. Louis Post-Dispatch*, July 10, 1904.
40. *Toledo News-Bee*, July 13, 1904.
41. *Toledo News-Bee*, July 18, 1904.
42. *New York Times*, July 22, 1904.
43. *Baltimore Sun*, July 23, 1904.
44. *Toledo News-Bee*, July 30, 1904.
45. *Baltimore American*, August 15, 1904.
46. *New York Times*, September 23, 1904.
47. *Toledo News-Bee*, September 27, 1904.
48. Robert Sandomir, "The Series That Never Was," *New York Times*, September 11, 1994.
49. *Washington Post*, September 24, 1904.

50. Lucas County, Ohio Auditor's Office Deed Record, Volume 297, page 83.
51. *Dayton Daily News*, October 7, 1904.
52. Lucas County, Ohio Auditor's Office Deed Record, Volume 307, page 204.
53. *Toledo News-Bee*, September 28, 1904.
54. *Toledo News-Bee*, October 3, 1904.
55. *Sporting Life*, December 24, 1904.
56. *Toledo News-Bee*, November 15, 1904, and *Courier-Journal* (Louisville), November 16, 1904.
57. *New-York Tribune*, December 30, 1904.
58. *Baltimore Sun*, December 30, 1904.
59. *New-York Tribune*, December 30, 1904.
60. *Toledo News-Bee*, March 28, 1905.
61. *Toledo News-Bee*, January 9, 1932.
62. *Cleveland Leader*, December 22, 1904.

Chapter Eleven

1. *Sporting Life*, March 3, 1905.
2. *New York Times*, January 3, 1905.
3. *Inter Ocean* (Chicago), March 5, 1905.
4. *New York Times*, March 11, 1905.
5. *Toledo News-Bee*, March 2, 1905.
6. J.M. Cummings, "Gossip of the Game," *Washington Post*, August 24, 1902.
7. Bozeman Bulger, "Sunshine Brings the Giants Back to Form," *World* (New York), March 15, 1905.
8. Chest protector.—Dickson, *Dickson Baseball Dictionary*, 936.
9. *New York Times*, March 27, 1905.
10. *Evening Star* (Washington, DC), April 28, 1905.
11. *New York Times*, April 2, 3, 4, 5, and 6, 1905.
12. *New York Times*, April 6, 1905.
13. *New York Times*, April 14, 1905.
14. *New York Times*, April 14, 1905.
15. *Philadelphia Inquirer*, April 23, 1905.
16. *Pittsburg Press*, April 25, 1905.
17. *Philadelphia Inquirer*, April 23, 1905.
18. *Muncie Morning Star* (IN), May 17, 1905.
19. *Baltimore Sun*, April 25, 1905.
20. *Baltimore Sun*, April 25, 1905.
21. *Philadelphia Inquirer*, April 26, 1905.
22. *Pittsburg Post*, May 28, 1905, and *Washington Post*, June 6, 1905.
23. *Cincinnati Enquirer*, June 20, 1905.
24. *Toledo News-Bee*, June 20, 1905.
25. *Detroit Free Press*, July 5, 1905.
26. Bozeman Bulger, "Sunshine Brings the Giants Back to Form," *World* (New York), March 15, 1905.
27. *Sporting Life*, July 15, 1905.
28. *Sporting Life*, July 22, 1903.
29. *Plain Dealer* (Cleveland), July 13, 1905.
30. *New York Times*, May 26, 1905.
31. *New York Times*, May 28, 1905.
32. Lucas County, Ohio, Probate Court, Registration of Birth for Roger Philip Bresnahan, January 20, 1943.
33. *New York Times*, June 30, 1905.
34. *Detroit Free Press*, July 14, 1905.
35. *New York Times*, July 21, 1905.
36. *New-York Tribune*, August 19, 1905.
37. Bozeman Bulger, "Giants Win Two Games from Reds," *World* (New York), August 27, 1905.
38. *New York Times*, September 14, 1905.
39. *New York Times*, September 20, 1905.
40. *Post-Crescent* (Appleton, WI), September 16, 1905.
41. *Indianapolis Star*, October 3, 1905.
42. *Scranton Truth* (Scranton, PA), October 4, 1905.
43. *Toledo News-Bee*, October 4, 1905.
44. *Courier-Journal* (Louisville), October 9, 1905.

Chapter Twelve

1. *Burlington Free Press* (VT), October 20, 1905.
2. Allen Sangree, "Final Game Is Triumph for Great Pitcher," *World* (New York), October 14, 1905.
3. *Washington Times* (Washington, DC), October 9, 1905.
4. Macht, *Connie Mack and the Early Years of Baseball*, 352.
5. Dan O'Brien, "Rube Waddell," *Society for American Baseball Research, Baseball Biography Project*, https://sabr.org/bioproj/person/rube-waddell/.
6. *Inter Ocean* (Chicago), October 9, 1905.
7. *Washington Times* (Washington, DC), October 9, 1905.
8. Francis C. Richter, "Result of Battle of the Major Giants," *Sporting Life*, October 21, 1905.
9. *Washington Times* (Washington, DC), October 9, 1905.
10. Macht, *Connie Mack and the Early Years of Baseball*, 355.
11. *New-York Tribune*, October 10, 1905.
12. Bozeman Bulger, "Game in Detail Shows How Giants Out Classed Rivals," *World* (New York), October 9, 1905.
13. Two catchers have batted first in the order in post season play, both in the American League Championship Series—Jason Kendall of Oakland in 2006 and John Jaso for Oakland in 2010.
14. *Evening Star* (Washington, DC), October 16, 1905.
15. *Toledo News-Bee*, October 26, 1905.
16. *Sporting News*, October 21, 1905.
17. *Washington Times*, October 16, 1905.
18. *Burlington Free Press* (VT), October 20, 1905.
19. *Washington Times*, October 16, 1905.
20. *New York Times*, September 23, 1905.
21. Francis C. Richter, "Result of Battle of the Major Giants," *Sporting Life*, October 21, 1905.
22. *New York Times*, December 24, 1905.
23. Spatz, 2004, *Bad Bill Dahlen*, 147.
24. Francis C. Richter, "Result of Battle of the Major Giants," *Sporting Life*, October 21, 1905.
25. *Evening Star* (Washington, DC), October 22, 1905.

26. John McGraw, *My Thirty Years in Baseball*, 159.

27. *Toledo News*, February 4, 1903.

28. Roger P. Bresnahan, *Roger's Scrapbook*, 35.

29. *Washington Post*, October 18, 1905.

30. *Washington Times*, October 21, 1905.

31. *New York Times*, November 15, 1905.

32. *New York Times*, November 15, 1905.

33. *Star-Independent* (Harrisburg, PA), November 20, 1905.

Chapter Thirteen

1. *St. Louis Post-Dispatch*, May 26, 1906.

2. *Indianapolis Star*, January 18, 1906.

3. *Sporting News* contract cards, a collection of 214,000 index cards *Sporting News* maintained on virtually every professional baseball player from the early 1900s through the mid–1990s. The cards contain player biographical data, details of contracts, trades, and assignments.—https://sabr.org/latest/sporting-news-donates-two-special-resource-collections-sabr

4. Cappy Cagnon, email message to author, February 2, 2017. Gagnon is a former president of the Society for American Baseball Research, a Notre Dame alumnus now retired from his alma mater. He has been attempting to verify the connection between Bresnahan and Notre Dame since the middle 1970s. He fears that Bresnahan's attendance may have been an oral tradition, possibly related to having visited the campus while playing pro ball in the area.

5. *New York Times*, December 19, 1905, and *World* (New York), February 28, 1906.

6. *St. Louis Post-Dispatch*, March 2, 1906.

7. *World* (New York), February 28, 1906.

8. *Evening Star* (Washington, DC), March 6, 1906.

9. Johnson and Wolff, *Encyclopedia of Minor League Baseball*, 202.

10. *New York Times*, March 28, 1906; *Times* (Shreveport), March 30, 1906; *Lima News* (OH), March 28, 1906, and *Cincinnati Post*, March 30, 1906.

11. Johnson and Wolff, *Encyclopedia of Minor League Baseball*, 197.

12. *New York Times*, April 7, 1906.

13. Graham, *McGraw of the Giants*, 37.

14. *Philadelphia Enquirer*, April 13, 1906.

15. *New York Times*, April 13, 1906.

16. *Brooklyn Daily Eagle*, April 19, 1906.

17. *Sun* (New York), April 21, 1906.

18. *World* (New York), April 20, 1906.

19. *Brooklyn Daily Eagle*, April 21, 1906.

20. *New York Times*, April 26, 1906.

21. *New-York Tribune*, April 29, 1906.

22. *New York Times*, May 1, 1906.

23. J.C. Morse, "Hub Happenings," *Sporting Life*, May 12, 1906.

24. To upset the umpire by making uncomplimentary remarks to him—Dickson, *Dickson Baseball Dictionary*, 45.

25. T.H. Murnane, "Gossip on the Game," *Washington Post*, May 6, 1906.

26. *New York Times*, May 3, 1906.

27. *New-York Tribune*, May 5, 1906.

28. *Cincinnati Enquirer*, May 3, 1906, and *New York Times*, May 3, 1906.

29. *New York Times*, May 1, 1906.

30. *New York Times*, May 13, 1906.

31. *New York Times*, May 15, 1906.

32. *Cincinnati Enquirer*, May 16, 1906.

33. Bozeman Bulger, "Pirates Shut Out Giants; Score, 11 To 0," *World* (New York), May 16, 1906.

34. *Pittsburg Post*, May 18, 1906.

35. *New York Times*, May 20, 1906.

36. *New York Times*, May 21, 1906.

37. *St. Louis Post-Dispatch*, May 26, 1906.

38. Bozeman Bulger, "Cold Helps the Cardinals Beat Giants," *World* (New York), May 28, 1906.

39. Bozeman Bulger, "Giants Take Second Game in Brooklyn," *World* (New York), May 30, 1906.

40. *Sporting Life*, June 9, 1906.

41. *New York Times*, June 6, 1906.

42. *New York Times*, June 7, 1906.

43. *Washington Post*, June 8, 1906.

44. *Sun* (New York), July 8, 1906.

45. *Sporting Life*, July 21, 1906.

46. *Washington Post*, July 22, 1906.

47. *New York Times*, June 13, 1906.

48. *New York Times*, August 8, 1906.

49. *New-York Tribune*, August 19, 1906.

50. *Pittsburg Post*, August 14, 1906.

51. *Courier-News* (Bridgewater, NJ), August 24, 1906.

52. *Pittsburg Press*, August 23, 1906.

53. *Press and Sun Bulletin* (Binghamton, NY), October 10, 1906.

54. Blanche McGraw, *Real McGraw*, 213.

55. *Pittsburg Press*, August 25, 1906.

Chapter Fourteen

1. *Washington Post*, February 2, 1907.

2. *Courier-Journal* (Louisville), February 9, 1907.

3. *Rocky Mountain News* (Denver), February 24, 1907.

4. *Toledo News-Bee*, February 20, 1907.

5. *Chicago Tribune*, February 24, 1907.

6. *Chicago Tribune*, February 24, 1907.

7. Len Edgren, "Split in Giants' Ranks," *World* (New York), February 26, 1907.

8. Len Edgren, "Giants in California at Last," *World* (New York), February 28, 1907.

9. Len Edgren, "Danny Shay a Full-Fledged Giant," *World* (New York), March 1, 1907.

10. *Rocky Mountain News* (Denver), February 24, 1907.

11. Len Edgren, "Giants Get on the Job," *World* (New York), March 2, 1907.

12. *Los Angeles Times*, March 1, 1907.

13. A style of play characterized by lively,

scrappy, and aggressive tactics—Dickson, *Dickson Baseball Dictionary*, 721.

14. *Los Angeles Times*, March 1, 1907.

15. *New York Times*, March 4, 1907.

16. *New York Times*, March 11, and 15, 1907.

17. *New York Times*, March 10, 1907.

18. *New York Times*, March 8, March 9, and March 14, 1907.

19. Len Edgren, "Tully Against Giants," *World* (New York), March 7, 1907.

20. *San Francisco Call Bulletin*, March 16, 1907.

21. Harry Smith, "Baseball Opens at New Grounds," *San Francisco Chronicle*, March 16, 1907.

22. Len Edgren, "Giants in 'Frisco Ready for Series with Coast Club," *World* (New York), March 16, 1907.

23. The Giants' Secretary Frank Knowles estimated an out-of-pocket loss for the San Francisco trip of at least $3500 [$95,454]—*New York Times*, April 6, 1907.

24. *Philadelphia Enquirer*, March 20, 1907.

25. *World* (New York), March 20, 1907.

26. https://thebolditalic.com/don-t-call-it-frisco-the-history-of-san-francisco-s-nicknames-the-bold-italic-san-francisco-5c14348d49c

27. Len Edgren, "Giants Reach San Antonio Like a Dry Sponge Bunch," *World* (New York), March 22, 1907.

28. Len Edgren, "Giants Jubilant Over Return to Fold of Donlin," *World* (New York), March 23, 1907.

29. *New York Times*, March 28, 1907.

30. *New York Times*, March 29, 1907.

31. *New York Times*, March 29, 1907.

32. *New York Times*, March 30, 1907.

33. *New York Times*, April 1, 1907.

34. *Sporting Life*, November 23, 1907.

35. *New York Times*, April 2, 1907.

36. *New York Times*, April 3, 1907.

37. *New York Times*, April 4, 1907.

38. *New York Times*, April 5, 1907.

39. *New York Times*, April 6, 1907.

40. *Toledo News-Bee*, April 6, 1907.

41. *New York Times*, April 7, 1907.

42. *New York Times*, April 8, 1907.

43. *New York Times*, April 6, 1907.

44. *Courier-Journal* (Louisville), February 9, 1907.

45. *New York Times*, April 12, 1907.

46. *World* (New York), April 12, 1907.

47. *New York Times*, April 12, 1907.

48. *New York Times*, April 12, 1907.

49. *New-York Tribune*, April 12, 1907.

50. *Sporting Life*, April 6, 1907.

51. *Sporting Life*, April 20, 1907.

52. Morris, *Catcher*, 348.

53. Honig, *Greatest Catchers of All Time*, 5.

54. Examples of baseball players possibly wearing shin guards, most likely under their clothing, before Bresnahan: Dave Zearfoss, New York Giants rookie catcher, wore a cricket shield on his left leg to prevent being spiked—*Austin Daily Statesman*, April 26, 1896; Henry P. Dodge claimed to have worn shin guards while catching Roger Bresnahan in Toledo area amateur play in the 1890s—*Toledo Blade*, May 2, 1945; Fox, catcher for Mansfield in the Ohio and Pennsylvania League, wore shin guards under his stockings in 1906—*Sporting Life*, May 25, 1907; Ferd Thompson, amateur pitcher for East Abington, Massachusetts, wore high-legged boots with his trousers tucked inside for shin protection in 1871—Morris, *A Game of Inches, the Game on the Field*, 439; Frank Grant and Bud Fowler, nineteenth-century black infielders, wore primitive shin guards because they were spiked so often by vindictive white players—Morris, *A Game of Inches, the Game on the Field*, 439; Harry Seinfeldt, third baseman for Detroit's Western League team, wore shin guards in 1897—Tom Shieber e-mail to author August 5, 2004; Mike Kahoe claimed that he wore shin guards while catching for the Chicago Cubs in 1901—Morris, *A Game of Inches, the Game on the Field*, 440; Tom Needham, Boston Nationals catcher, wore a guard to protect a spike wound on his shin in 1904. Morris, *A Game of Inches, the Game on the Field*, 440; Nig Clark, Cleveland catcher, claimed that he wore football guards in 1905—Morris, *A Game of Inches, the Game on the Field*, 440.

55. Macht, *Charles Sebastian "Red" Dooin*, 189–90.

56. *Sporting Life*, June 1, 1907.

Chapter Fifteen

1. *New York American*, June 19, 1907.

2. *New York Times*, April 16, 1907.

3. *Brooklyn Daily Eagle*, April 17, 1907.

4. *Brooklyn Daily Eagle*, April 19, 1907.

5. *Boston Herald*, April 21, 1907.

6. *Boston Herald*, April 22, 1907.

7. *New York Times*, May 2, 1907.

8. *New York Times*, May 4, 1907.

9. *New York Times*, May 6, 1907.

10. *Buffalo Evening News*, May 14, 1907.

11. *Washington Post*, May 16, 1907.

12. *Sporting Life*, June 1, 1907.

13. *New York Times*, May 18, 1907.

14. *New York Times*, May 19, 1907.

15. *New York Times*, May 21, 1907.

16. F.H. Koelsch, "New York News," *Sporting Life*, May 25, 1907.

17. *World* (New York), May 21, 1907.

18. *New York Times*, May 22, 1907.

19. *New York Times*, May 22, 1907.

20. J. Ed Grillo, "Sporting Comment," *Washington Post*, May 26, 1907.

21. *Sporting Life*, June 1, 1907.

22. *New York Times*, May 25, 26, 29, and May 30, 1907.

23. Charles Dryden, "Cubs Take First from Giants, 8–2," *Chicago Daily Tribune*, June 6, 1907.

24. *Altoona Times* (PA), June 6, 1907.

25. *New York Times*, June 10, 1908.

26. *World* (New York), June10, 1907.
27. *Washington Herald*, June 16, 1907.
28. *Pittsburg Press*, June 15, 1907.
29. *Cincinnati Enquirer*, June 18, 1907.
30. *Cincinnati Commercial Tribune*, June 18, 1907.
31. *New York American*, June 19, 1907.
32. *New York Times*, June 19, 1907.
33. *Cincinnati Enquirer*, June 19, 1907.
34. *New York American*, June 19, 1907.
35. *Cincinnati Enquirer*, June 19, 1907.
36. *Cincinnati Times-Star*, June 20, 1907.
37. *Cincinnati Post*, June 19, 1907.
38. *Cincinnati Enquirer*, June 19, 1907.
39. *Cincinnati Commercial Tribune*, June 21, 1907.
40. *Cincinnati Commercial Tribune*, June 22, 1907.
41. *Toledo News-Bee*, June 25, 1907.
42. *Cincinnati Post*, June 28, 1907.
43. *Cincinnati Enquirer*, June 29, 1907.
44. *Toledo News-Bee*, July 8, 1907.
45. *Sporting Life*, July 20, 1907.
46. *Cincinnati Enquirer*, July 8, 1907.
47. *New York Journal*, July 12, 1907.
48. *New York Times*, July 13, 1907.
49. Sam Crane, "Bresnahan Plays with Giants," *New York Journal*, July 13, 1907.
50. *Cincinnati Times-Star*, June 19, 1907.
51. Roger P. Bresnahan, *Roger's Scrapbook*, 33.
52. *Cincinnati Enquirer*, July 26, 1907.
53. *Wilkes-Barre Times* (PA), September 28, 1907.
54. *Sporting Life*, November 9, 1907.
55. J. Ed Grillo, "Sporting Comment," *Washington Post*, November 12, 1907.
56. *Sporting Life*, December 7, 1907.
57. *Sporting Life*, December 14, 1907.
58. *Sporting Life*, December 7, 1907.
59. *Sporting Life*, December 28, 1907.
60. *Washington Post*, December 29, 1907.
61. J. Ed Grillo, "Sporting Comment," *Washington Post*, January 10, 1908.
62. *World* (New York), January 9, 1908.

Chapter Sixteen

1. *Sporting Life*, December 14, 1907.
2. Cait Murphy, *Crazy '08*, 29.
3. Fleming, *Unforgettable Season*, 7.
4. Bozeman Bulger, "New York Teams Gladden Hearts of Followers," *World* (New York), April 11, 1908.
5. Wm. W.F. Koelsch, "Metropolitan Mention," *Sporting Life*, January 11, 1908.
6. *New York Times*, February 4, 1908.
7. *Washington Post*, February 17, 1908.
8. *St. Louis Post-Dispatch*, February 17, 1908.
9. *New York Times*, February 21, 1908.
10. *New York Times*, February 22, 1908.
11. *New York Times*, February 23, 1908.
12. *New York Times*, February 22, 1908.
13. *New York Times*, February 23, 1908.
14. *New York Times*, March 1, 1908.
15. *New York Times*, March 2, 1908.
16. *New York Times*, March 4, 1908.
17. *New York Times*, March 8, 1908.
18. *New York Times*, April 4, 1908.
19. *New York Times*, March 24, 1908.
20. *Toledo News-Bee*, April 8, 1908.
21. *Toledo News-Bee*, April 8, 1908.
22. *Toledo News-Bee*, April 8, 1908.
23. *New York Times*, April 14, 1908.
24. *Sporting Life*, December 14, 1907.
25. *Pittsburg Press*, February 17, 1908.
26. *Washington Post*, February 17, 1908.
27. *Toledo News-Bee*, May 20, 1908.
28. Fleming, *Unforgettable Season*, 76.
29. I.E. Sanborn, "One Timely Blow Serves Dual End," *Chicago Daily Tribune*, May 26, 1908.
30. *Indianapolis News*, May 28, 1908.
31. *Decatur Herald* (IL), June 5, 1908.
32. *Washington Herald*, June 5, 1908.
33. R. Edgren, "R. Edgren's Column," *World* (New York), June 3, 1908.
34. Macht, *Charles Sebastian "Red" Dooin*, 349.
35. *World* (New York), June 12, 1908.
36. *Pittsburg Press*, June 13, 1908.
37. *New-York Tribune*, June 13, 1908.
38. Fleming, *Unforgettable Season*, 94.
39. Fleming, *Unforgettable Season*, 101.
40. Fleming, *Unforgettable Season*, 104.
41. *Toledo Blade*, August 3, 1908.
42. *Washington Post*, August 2, 1908.
43. Fleming, *Unforgettable Season*, 108.
44. *New-York Tribune*, July 16, 1908.
45. *New York Times*, August 5, 1908.
46. *New York Times*, August 11, 1908.
47. Fleming, *Unforgettable Season*, 170.
48. *New-York Tribune*, August 21, 1908.

Chapter Seventeen

1. *Toledo News-Bee*, December 8, 1908.
2. Fleming, *Unforgettable Season*, 182.
3. Fleming, *Unforgettable Season*, 186.
4. *New York Times*, September 19, 1908.
5. Fleming, *Unforgettable Season*, 243.
6. Dickson, *Dickson Baseball Dictionary*, 542.
7. *Boston Herald*, February 2, 1907.
8. Daley, *Times at Bat*, 33.
9. Klein, *Stealing Games*, 90.
10. *New-York Tribune*, September 26, 1908.
11. *World* (New York), September 25, 1908.
12. *New York Times*, September 29, 1908.
13. *Philadelphia Inquirer*, September 30, 1908.
14. Fleming, *Unforgettable Season*, 271.
15. *Toledo News-Bee*, September 30, 1908.
16. *Philadelphia Inquirer*, September 30, 1908.
17. *St. Louis Post-Dispatch*, October 2, 1908.
18. Bozeman Bulger, "Donlin, Crippled, Keeps Giants on Top in Race," *World* (New York), October 2, 1908.
19. *New-York Tribune*, October 3, 1908.

20. Klein, *Stealing Games*, 92.
21. *World* (New York), October 10, 1908.
22. *New-York Tribune*, October 5, 1908.
23. *Sun* (New York), October 7, 1908.
24. *Sporting Life*, October 17, 1908.
25. Cait Murphy, *Crazy '08*, 254.
26. Klein, *Stealing Games*, 93.
27. Fleming, *Unforgettable Season*, 300.
28. Cait Murphy, *Crazy '08*, 269.
29. Klein, *Stealing Games*, 103, 107.
30. Evers, *Touching Second*, 207–208.
31. Evers, *Touching Second*, 208.
32. Steinberg, *The World Series in the Deadball Era*, 40–41.
33. Cait Murphy, *Crazy '08*, 273.
34. *New York Times*, October 19, 1908.
35. The record for games caught in a season before 1908 was 133 by Deacon McGuire. Roger eclipsed his former mate's mark but could not claim the record because George Gibson of Pittsburg caught 140 that same year.
36. *World* (New York), October 1, 1908.
37. *World* (New York), October 13, 1908.
38. *Toledo News-Bee*, October 13, 1908.
39. *Toledo News-Bee*, October 26, 1908.
40. *Washington Post*, October 29, 1908.
41. *Washington Post*, November 2, 1908.
42. *Sporting Life*, November 28, 1908.
43. *Toledo News-Bee*, December 8, 1908.
44. *Sporting Life*, December 12, 1980.
45. *St. Louis Post-Dispatch*, October 12, 1908.
46. *St. Louis Post-Dispatch*, December 17, 1908.
47. *Courier-Journal* (Louisville), January 3, 1909.
48. Lieb, *St. Louis Cardinals*, 38.
49. *St. Louis Post-Dispatch*, December 14, 1908.

Chapter Eighteen

1. John E. Wray, "Nine Reasons to Think the Browns Best," *St. Louis Post-Dispatch*, March 7, 1909.
2. James Crusinberry, "Robison Can Be a Plunger Without Fear," *St. Louis Post-Dispatch*, December 12, 1908.
3. *Chicago Tribune*, December 22, 1908.
4. *Courier-Journal* (Louisville), January 10, 1909.
5. *Sporting Life*, January 2, 1909.
6. *Sporting Life*, December 26, 1908.
7. *Toledo News-Bee*, December 29, 1908.
8. *Toledo News-Bee*, February 8, 1909.
9. *Washington Post*, February 15, 1909.
10. Blanche McGraw, *Real McGraw*, 242.
11. James Crusinberry, "Cardinals See a Future with Roger at the Helm," *St. Louis Post-Dispatch*, February 28, 1909.
12. *Washington Post*, January 22, 1909.
13. *Christian Science Monitor* (Boston), January 19, 1909.
14. *Toledo News-Bee*, December 17, 1908.
15. *St. Louis Post-Dispatch*, December 21, 1908.
16. *New York Times*, January 1, 1909.
17. James Crusinberry, "Fans Waiting for Cardinals New Players," *St. Louis Post-Dispatch*, January 10, 1909.
18. *St. Louis Post-Dispatch*, December 18, 1908.
19. *New York Times*, January 15, 1909.
20. *St. Louis Post-Dispatch*, January 17, 1909.
21. *St. Louis Post-Dispatch*, January 16, 1909.
22. *Detroit Free Press*, January 18, 1909.
23. *Cincinnati Enquirer*, February 16, 1909.
24. *Cincinnati Enquirer*, January 3, 1909.
25. *Cincinnati Enquirer*, February 4, 1909. Waivers defined: A system by which all teams have a chance to bid on a player about to be released or included in a trade. Before a player can be released, waivers must be granted by all teams in reverse order of their standings. If the rights to that player are claimed (not waived) by one of those teams, his contract must be sold at the standard waiver price—$1,500 ($40,062) in 1909—Dickson, *Dickson Baseball Dictionary*, 918.
26. *Detroit Free Press*, February 1, 1909.
27. *Arkansas Democrat* (Little Rock), February 28, 1909.
28. *St. Louis Post-Dispatch*, March 2, 1909.
29. *Arkansas Democrat* (Little Rock), March 2, 1909.
30. *St. Louis Post-Dispatch*, March 2, 1909.
31. James Crusinberry, "Bresnahan Is Real Manager on Ball Field," *St. Louis Post-Dispatch*, March 3, 1909.
32. James Crusinberry, "No Peace for the Weary at Camp Cardinal," *St. Lous Post Dispatch*, March 4, 1909.
33. *St. Louis Post-Dispatch*, March 14, 1909.
34. *St. Louis Post-Dispatch*, March 9, 1909.
35. *St. Louis Post-Dispatch*, March 5 and 9, 1909.
36. *St. Louis Post-Dispatch*, March 10, 1909, and *Arkansas Gazette* (Little Rock), March 9, 1909.
37. *St. Louis Post-Dispatch*, March 24, 1909.
38. *St. Louis Post-Dispatch*, March 25, 1909.
39. *St. Louis Post-Dispatch*, March 26, 1909.
40. *St. Louis Post-Dispatch*, March 30, 1909.
41. *St. Louis Post-Dispatch*, March 29, 1909.
42. *Sporting Life*, March 6, 1909.
43. *St. Louis Post-Dispatch*, March 31, 1909.
44. James Crusinberry, "Bresnahan Working Hard to Build Up Cardinals," *St. Louis Post Dispatch*, April 4, 1909.
45. *Arkansas Democrat* (Little Rock), April 1, 1909.
46. *St. Louis Post-Dispatch*, April 1, 1909.
47. *Paducah Evening Sun* (KY), April 2, 1909, and *St. Louis Post-Dispatch*, April 3, 1909.
48. James Crusinberry, "Roger's Youths Find Paducah Farmers Easy," *St. Louis Post-Dispatch*, April 4, 1919, and *Paducah Evening Sun* (KY), April 5, 1909.
49. *St. Louis Post-Dispatch*, April 6, 1909.
50. *Inter Ocean* (Chicago), April 7, 1910.
51. *Inter Ocean* (Chicago), April 8, 1910.
52. *Dayton Herald*, April 9, 1909.
53. Johnson and Wolff, *Encyclopedia of Minor League Baseball*, 218.

54. *Courier-Journal* (Louisville), April 11 and 12, 1909.
55. Jerry Winters, "No Ginger in Play of Toledo," *Toledo Daily Blade*, April 13, 1909.
56. *Toledo Blade*, April 12, 1909.
57. *Toledo Blade*, April 13, 1909.
58. John E. Wray, "Nine Reasons to Think the Browns Best," *St. Louis Post-Dispatch*, March 7, 1909.

Chapter Nineteen

1. *Democrat and Chronicle* (Rochester, NY), June 23, 1909.
2. *Inter Ocean* (Chicago), April 15, 1909.
3. I.E. Sanborn, "Cubs Land on Top in Second Game," *Chicago Tribune*, April 16, 1909.
4. Lieb, *St. Louis Cardinals*, 39.
5. *St. Louis Post-Dispatch*, April 17 and 18, 1909.
6. *St. Louis Post-Dispatch*, April 17, 1909.
7. Jack Ryder, "Cardinals Not So Easy as Pirates," *Cincinnati Enquirer*, April 19, 1909.
8. *Cincinnati Enquirer*, April 20, 1909.
9. *Cincinnati Enquirer*, April 21, 1909.
10. Accounts of attendance vary: 10,000—*Chicago Tribune*, April 23, 1909; 12,000—*St. Louis Post-Dispatch*, April 23, 1909, and 15,000—baseball-reference.com.
11. I.E. Sanborn, "Cubs Flatten Out Perky Cardinals," *Chicago Tribune*, April 23, 1909.
12. *Pittsburgh Post*, April 27, 1909.
13. *Brooklyn Daily Eagle*, April 30, 1909.
14. *St. Louis Globe-Democrat*, April 27, 1909.
15. *St. Louis Post-Dispatch*, April 27, 1909.
16. Gazette Times (Pittsburg, PA), April 28, 1909.
17. *Courier-Journal* (Louisville), April 30, 1909.
18. John E. Wray, "Cardinals Bat More Pitchers to the Bench," *St. Louis Post-Dispatch*, May 3, 1909.
19. *Brooklyn Daily Eagle*, May 13, 1909.
20. *New York Times*, May 25, 1909.
21. *St. Louis Post-Dispatch*, May 25, 1909.
22. *New-York Tribune*, May 25, 1909.
23. *New York Times*, May 25, 1909.
24. Harold W. Lanigan, "Players Were Beau Brummells in the Gay 90s," *Sporting News*, November 7, 1940.
25. Gaines, *Christy Mathewson, the Christian Gentleman*, 225.
26. *New York Times*, May 25, 1909.
27. Roger M. Bresnahan, email message to author, January 17, 2015.
28. Confidential author's source.
29. *New York Times*, May 26, 1909.
30. *Cincinnati Enquirer*, May 31, 1909.
31. *Pittsburg Post*, June 2, 1909.
32. *St. Louis Post-Dispatch*, June 2, 1909.
33. *Sporting Life*, June 19, 1909, 7.
34. James Crusinberry, "Hit-And-Run Is Game Roger Has Mastered," *St. Louis Post Dispatch*, June 3, 1909.
35. *Sporting Life*, June 5, 1909.
36. *Boston Globe*, April 15, 1909.
37. *Sporting Life*, May 15, 1909.
38. *Sporting Life*, May 22, 1909.
39. *Sporting Life*, June 5, 1909.
40. E.H. Simmons, "New York Nuggets," *Sporting Life*, May 22, 1909.
41. *Sporting Life*, June 12, 1909.
42. *Atchison Daily Globe* (KS), June 25, 1909.
43. *Sporting Life*, June 5, 1909, 6.
44. *New York Times*, June 6, 1909.
45. *St. Louis Post-Dispatch*, June 8, 1909.
46. *New-York Tribune*, June 9, 1909.
47. *Democrat and Chronicle* (Rochester, NY), June 23, 1909.
48. The Three-I League was Class B and named for Iowa, Illinois, and Indiana from which its teams hailed.
49. *Daily Review* (Decatur, IL), June 11, 1909.
50. *Chicago Tribune*, June 19, 1909.
51. *Shreveport Times*, June 20, 1907.
52. *St. Louis Post-Dispatch*, July 3, 1909.
53. *Chicago Tribune*, July 7, 1909.
54. *Sporting Life*, July 17, 1909, 3.
55. *Chicago Tribune*, January 31, 1910.
56. *St. Louis Post-Dispatch*, July 17, 1909.
57. *Evening Star* (Washington, DC), July 28, 1909.
58. *St. Louis Post-Dispatch*, July 22, 1909.
59. *New York Times*, July 20, 1909.
60. E.H. Simmons, "New York News," *Sporting Life*, July 31, 1909.
61. *Buffalo Evening News*, August 14, 1909.
62. *St. Louis Post-Dispatch*, August 9, 1909.
63. James Crusinberry, "Hit-And-Run Is Game Roger Has Mastered," *St. Louis Post-Dispatch*, June 3, 1909.
64. *Morning Tribune* (Altoona, PA), August 21, 1909.
65. *Evening News* (Wilkes Barre, PA), September 13, 1909.
66. The length of his suspension during the July 8–12 series in Boston is not known.
67. *Boston Daily Globe*, July 9, 1909.
68. *Oakland Tribune*, September 12, 1909.
69. James Crusinberry, "Roger's Task Next Season No Sinecure," *St. Louis Post-Dispatch*, September 28, 1909.
70. *St. Louis Post-Dispatch*, August 22, 1909.
71. *Wilkes-Barre Times-Leader* (PA), August 26, 1909.
72. James Crusinberry, "Overwrought Cardinals in Need of Rest," *St. Louis Post-Dispatch*, August 12, 1909.
73. *Democrat and Chronicle* (Rochester, NY), June 23, 1909.
74. *St. Louis Post-Dispatch*, September 4, 1909.
75. *Salt Lake Telegram*, August 23, 1909.
76. *Courier-Journal* (Louisville), July 25, 1909.
77. *St. Louis Post-Dispatch*, August 28, 1909.
78. R.H. Lanigan, "Bresnahan's Methods," *Sporting Life*, October 23, 1909.
79. *The Buffalo Enquirer*, September 27, 1909.
80. *St. Louis Post-Dispatch*, October 7, 1909.

81. *Fort Wayne News* (IN), July 1, 1909.
82. *St. Louis Post-Dispatch*, October 17, 1909.
83. *Sporting Life*, October 16, 1909.
84. *Sporting Life*, October 16, 1909.

Chapter Twenty

1. *St. Louis Post-Dispatch*, August 20, 1910.
2. *St. Louis Post-Dispatch*, March 17, 1910.
3. James Crusinberry, "Baseball War Is Averted by a Compromise," *St. Louis Post-Dispatch*, December 19, 1909.
4. *Sporting Life*, November 6, 1909, 5.
5. James Crusinberry, "Bresnahan and Robison May Force a Good Trade from Other Magnates," *St. Louis Post-Dispatch*, December 10, 1909.
6. James Crusinberry, "Baseball War Is Averted by a Compromise," *St. Louis Post-Dispatch*, December 19, 1909.
7. *Washington Post*, December 31, 1909.
8. *Buffalo Evening News*, January 3, 1910.
9. *Toledo Blade*, January 18, 1910.
10. *St. Louis Post-Dispatch*, February 4, 1910.
11. *St. Louis Post-Dispatch*, February 15, 1910.
12. *St. Louis Post-Dispatch*, March 9, 1910.
13. *St. Louis Post-Dispatch*, March 8, 1910.
14. *St. Louis Post-Dispatch*, January 17, 1910.
15. *St. Louis Star*, February 20, 1910.
16. *St. Louis Post-Dispatch*, February 23, 1910.
17. Nickname coined by Writer JLL—*St. Louis Star*, March 16, 1910.
18. *St. Louis Post-Dispatch*, March 8, 1910.
19. *Arkansas Democrat* (Little Rock), March 10, 1910.
20. *St. Louis Post-Dispatch*, March 12, 1910.
21. *St. Louis Star*, March 14, 1910.
22. *St. Louis Post-Dispatch*, March 20, 1910.
23. *St. Louis Post-Dispatch*, January 17, 1910.
24. *St. Louis Post-Dispatch*, March 24, and 25, 1910 and *Arkansas Democrat* (Little Rock), March 26, 1910.
25. *St. Louis Post-Dispatch*, March 27, 1910.
26. *St. Louis Post-Dispatch*, March 28, 1910.
27. *St. Louis Post-Dispatch*, April 3, and 4, 1910.
28. *St. Louis Post-Dispatch*, April 9, 1910.
29. *St. Louis Star*, April 9, 1910.
30. *St. Louis Post-Dispatch*, April 10, 1910.
31. *St. Louis Post-Dispatch*, April 11, 1910.
32. *St. Louis Post-Dispatch*, April 10, 1910.
33. *New Castle Herald* (PA), April 9, 1910.
34. *St. Louis Post-Dispatch*, April 12, 1910.
35. *St. Louis Star*, April 9, 1910.
36. *Pittsburg* Press, April 14, 1910.
37. *St. Louis Star*, April 15, 1910.
38. *Pittsburg Post*, April 16, 1910.
39. *St. Louis Post-Dispatch*, April 21, 1910.
40. *Pittsburg* Press, April 23, 1910. DTs—Delirium tremens is a rapid onset of confusion usually caused by withdrawal from alcohol.
41. R.W. Lardner, "Cubs in Bad Fix," *Chicago Tribune*, April 21, 1910.
42. *St. Louis Post-Dispatch*, April 22, 1910.
43. Lynch was elected as a compromise candidate by the Board of Directors on December 18, 1909—*New York Times*, December 19, 1909.
44. *St. Louis Star*, May 3, 1910.
45. Jack Ryder, "Sixteen Cardinals in the Game," *Cincinnati Enquirer*, May 3, 1910.
46. *Cincinnati Enquirer*, May 3, 1910.
47. *Chicago Tribune*, May 3, 1910.
48. *St. Louis Star*, May 6, 1910.
49. *Chicago Tribune*, May 3, 1910.
50. *Cincinnati Enquirer*, May 7, 1910.
51. *St. Louis Post-Dispatch*, May 8, 1910.
52. *Sporting Life*, May 14, 1910.
53. *St. Louis Post-Dispatch*, May 5, 1910.
54. *St. Louis Post-Dispatch*, May 14, 1910.
55. *St. Louis Post-Dispatch*, May 15, 1910.
56. *New-York Tribune*, May 16, 1910.
57. *St. Louis Post-Dispatch*, May 16, 1910.
58. *St. Louis Star*, May 16, 1910.
59. *St. Louis Post-Dispatch*, May 17, 1910.
60. *St. Louis Post-Dispatch*, May 17, 1910.
61. *Washington Post* (Washington, DC), July 7, 1910.
62. *St. Louis Post-Dispatch*, July 10, 1910.
63. Meryl Baer, "The History of American Income," September 26, 2017, https://bizfluent.com/info-7769323-history-american-income.html.
64. *St. Louis Post-Dispatch*, May 28, 1910.
65. *St. Louis Post-Dispatch*, May 31, 1910.
66. *St. Louis Post-Dispatch*, May 21, 1910.
67. *St. Louis Post-Dispatch*, July 23, 1910.
68. *St. Louis Star*, July 25, 1910.
69. *St. Louis Post-Dispatch*, June 23, 1910.
70. The *Pittsburgh Post*, *Pittsburg Press*, *St. Louis Post-Dispatch* and *St Louis Star* of June 22, 1910, were consulted.
71. *St. Louis Post-Dispatch*, June 23, 1910.
72. *St. Louis Post-Dispatch*, June 22, 1910.
73. *St. Louis Post-Dispatch*, September 11, 1910.
74. Brice Hoskins, "Bresnahan Performs in Splendid Style," *St. Louis Star*, July 22, 1910.
75. *St. Louis Post-Dispatch*, August 20, 1910.
76. *Brooklyn Daily Eagle*, August 4, 1910.
77. *St. Louis Star*, August 23, 1910.
78. *St. Louis Post-Dispatch*, August 27, 1910.
79. John E. Wray, "Wray's Column," *St. Louis Post-Dispatch*, December 8, 1910.
80. *St. Louis Post-Dispatch*, October 5, 1910.
81. *St. Louis Post-Dispatch*, April 4, 1911.
82. *St. Louis Post-Dispatch*, August 27, 1910.

Chapter Twenty-One

1. *St. Louis Post-Dispatch*, November 9, 1910.
2. *St. Louis Post-Dispatch*, November 10, 1910.
3. *St. Louis Post-Dispatch*, November 17, 1910.
4. *Cincinnati Enquirer*, November 23, 1910.
5. *St. Louis Post-Dispatch*, November 23, 1910.
6. *St. Louis Post-Dispatch*, November 21, 1910.
7. *Cincinnati Enquirer*, November 23, 1910.
8. *St. Louis Star*, December 12, 1910.
9. *Daily Review* (Decatur, IL), December 13, 1910.

10. *St. Louis Post-Dispatch*, December 14, 1910.
11. *St. Louis Post-Dispatch*, December 18, 1910.
12. *St. Louis Post-Dispatch*, December 16, 1910.
13. *St. Louis Star*, August 29, 1910.
14. *St. Louis Post-Dispatch*, December 21, 1910.
15. *St. Louis Post-Dispatch*, March 27, 1911.
16. *Sporting Life*, January 23, 1915.
17. Buck Weaver, "'Buck' Weaver Writes of Baseball Oddities," *Our Paper* (Concord, MA), August 28, 1915.
18. *St. Louis Post-Dispatch*, January 16, 1910.
19. *Plain Dealer* (Cleveland), March 25, 1911.
20. *Plain Dealer* (Cleveland), April 6, 1911.
21. *St. Louis Post-Dispatch*, January 21, 1911.
22. *St. Louis Post-Dispatch*, March 28, 1911.
23. *St. Louis Post-Dispatch*, February 18, 1911.
24. *St. Louis Post-Dispatch*, March 9, 1911.
25. *St. Louis Post-Dispatch*, February 21, 1911.
26. *St. Louis Post-Dispatch*, March 15, 1911.
27. *St. Louis Post-Dispatch*, March 19 and 20, 1911.
28. *St. Louis Post-Dispatch*, March 15, 1911.
29. *St. Louis Post-Dispatch*, March 4, 1911.
30. *St. Louis Post-Dispatch*, March 24, 1911.
31. Thomas, *Baseball's First Lady*, 49.
32. *Plain Dealer* (Cleveland), March 25, 1911.
33. *St. Louis Post-Dispatch*, March 24, 1911, 2.
34. *St. Louis Post-Dispatch*, March 26, 1911, 33.
35. *St. Louis Post-Dispatch*, March 26, 1911, 33.
36. Thomas, *Baseball's First Lady*, 52.
37. *St. Louis Post-Dispatch*, March 29, 1911.
38. Thomas, *Baseball's First Lady*, 52–53.
39. *St. Louis Star*, March 28, 1911.
40. *Detroit Free Press*, March 27, 1911.
41. *St. Louis Star*, March 25, 1911.
42. Thomas, *Baseball's First Lady*, 53.
43. *St. Louis Post-Dispatch*, March 29, 1911.
44. Thomas, *Baseball's First Lady*, 55.
45. *St. Louis Post-Dispatch*, April 2 and 3, 1911.
46. *St. Louis Post-Dispatch*, April 4, 1911.
47. *St. Louis Post-Dispatch*, April 7, 1911.
48. *St. Louis Post-Dispatch*, April 5, 1911.
49. *St. Louis Star*, April 21, 1911.
50. *St. Louis Post-Dispatch*, April 7, 1911.
51. *Plain Dealer* (Cleveland), March 30, 1911.
52. *St. Louis Post-Dispatch*, July 11, 1911.
53. *St. Louis Post-Dispatch*, July 8, 1911.
54. *St. Louis Post-Dispatch*, April 8, 1911.
55. Ray Webster, "Cardinals 7 Brownies 1," *St. Louis Star*, April 9, 1911 and *St. Louis Post-Dispatch*, April 10, 1911.
56. *St. Louis Post-Dispatch*, April 10, 1911.
57. *St. Louis Post-Dispatch*, April 12, 1911.
58. *St. Louis Post-Dispatch*, April 13, 1911.
59. *Chicago Tribune*, April 14, 1911.
60. *St. Louis Post-Dispatch*, April 14, 1911.
61. *St. Louis Post-Dispatch*, April 16, 1911.
62. *Cincinnati Enquirer*, April 19, 1911.
63. Jack Ryder, "Roger Hurried to a Dentist," *Cincinnati Enquirer*, April 20, 1911.
64. *St. Louis Star*, April 19, 1911.
65. Jack Ryder, "Roger Hurried to a Dentist," *Cincinnati Enquirer*, April 20, 1911.
66. *St. Louis Post-Dispatch*, April 23, 1911.
67. *St. Louis Post-Dispatch*, April 23 and 26, 1911.
68. *St. Louis Post-Dispatch*, April 25, 1915.
69. Henry P. Edwards, "Live Sport Talks," *Plain Dealer* (Cleveland), April 26, 1911.
70. Gertrude Gordon, "Woman Owner Watches Her Ball Team Lose a Game at Forbes Field," *Pittsburg Press*, May 4, 1911.
71. *St. Louis Star*, May 14, 1911.
72. *Democrat & Chronicle* (Rochester, NY), May 17, 1911.
73. *St. Louis Post-Dispatch*, May 29, 1911.
74. *St. Louis Post-Dispatch*, June 1, 1911.
75. John E. Wray, "Wray's Column," *St. Louis Post-Dispatch*, June 2, 1911.
76. Ray Webster, "*Roger's 'Wrecking Crew' Smashes Reds*," St. Louis Star, June 2, 1911.
77. *Cincinnati Enquirer*, June 1, 1911.
78. John E. Wray, "Wray's Column," *St. Louis Post-Dispatch*, May 25, 1911.
79. John E. Wray, "Wray's Column," *St. Louis Post-Dispatch*, May 7, 1911.
80. *St. Louis Star*, June 21, 1911.
81. *St. Louis Post-Dispatch*, June 8, 1911.
82. *Sporting Life*, July 1, 1911.
83. *St. Louis Post-Dispatch*, June 12, 1911.
84. *St. Louis Post-Dispatch*, June 11, 1911.
85. *St. Louis Post-Dispatch*, June 14, 1911.
86. *St. Louis Post-Dispatch*, June 16, 1911.
87. *St. Louis Star*, June 16, 1911.
88. *New York Times*, June 24, 1911.
89. *Cincinnati Enquirer*, June 24, 1911.
90. *St. Louis Post-Dispatch*, June 24, 1911.
91. *St. Louis Post-Dispatch*, June 26, 1911.
92. *St. Louis Post-Dispatch*, June 26, 1911.
93. *Sporting Life*, July 8, 1911.
94. *Sporting Life*, July 8, 1911.
95. *St. Louis Post-Dispatch*, June 27, 1911.
96. *Sporting Life*, July 8, 1911.
97. *St. Louis Post-Dispatch*, June 24, 1911.
98. *St. Louis Post-Dispatch*, June 29, 1911.
99. *St. Louis Post-Dispatch*, July 2, 1911.
100. *Pittsburgh Post*, July 1, 1911.

Chapter Twenty-Two

1. *Washington Post*, July 13, 1911.
2. H.W. Belnap, "Report of H.W. Belnap," 187.
3. H.W. Belnap, "Report of H.W. Belnap," 187.
4. *Boston Daily Globe*, July 11, 1911.
5. *Bridgeport Evening Farmer* (CT), July 11, 1911.
6. *St. Louis Post-Dispatch*, July 11, 1911.
7. *Plainfield Courier-News* (NJ), July 12, 1911.
8. *St. Louis Post-Dispatch*, July 11, 1911.
9. *Bridgeport Evening Farmer* (CT), July 11, 1911.
10. *Boston Daily Globe*, July 11, 1911.
11. H.W. Belnap, "Report of H.W. Belnap," 187.
12. *Buffalo Commercial*, July 11, 1911.
13. *St. Louis Post-Dispatch*, July 11, 1911.
14. *World* (New York), July 11, 1911.
15. Dom Amore, "Heroes Off the Field: In 1911,

the St. Louis Cardinals Became First Responders in Bridgeport Train Wreck," *Hartford Courant*, July 9, 2011.

16. *St. Louis Post-Dispatch*, July 11, 1911.
17. F.C. Lane, "The Heroes of the Bridgeport Wreck," *Baseball Magazine*, September 17, 1911, 37.
18. *Gazette Times* (Pittsburg), July 12, 1911.
19. *Bridgeport Evening Farmer* (CT), July 11, 1911.
20. *Bridgeport Evening Farmer* (CT), July 11, 1911.
21. *St. Louis Post-Dispatch*, July 11, 1911.
22. *St. Louis Post-Dispatch*, July 11, 1911; *Pittsburg Press*, July 11, 1911, and F.C. Lane, "The Heroes of the Bridgeport Wreck," *Baseball Magazine*, September 17, 1911, 36.
23. *New York Times*, July 12, 1911.
24. *Sporting Life*, July 22, 1911.
25. *New York Times*, July 12, 1911.
26. Dom Amore, "Heroes Off the Field: In 1911, the St. Louis Cardinals Became First Responders in Bridgeport Train Wreck," *Hartford Courant*, July 9, 2011.
27. Fred Schuld, "Railroad Accidents and Baseball in the Early 20th Century," (Unpublished manuscript, June 21, 1997), paper copy.
28. *Buffalo Courier*, July 18, 1911.
29. *Boston Daily Glo*be, August 19, 1911.
30. H.W. Belnap, "Report of H.W. Belnap," 187.
31. F.C. Lane, "The Heroes of the Bridgeport Wreck," *Baseball Magazine*, September 17, 1911, 38.
32. *Sporting Life*, July 22, 1911.
33. *Bridgeport Evening Farmer* (CT), July 12, 1911.
34. *St. Louis Post-Dispatch*, July 11, 1911.
35. F.C. Lane, "The Heroes of the Bridgeport Wreck," *Baseball Magazine*, September 17, 1911, 37.
36. *Washington Post*, July 13, 1911.
37. *St. Louis Post-Dispatch*, July 15, 1911.
38. *St. Louis Post-Dispatch*, July 25, 1911.
39. *St. Louis Post-Dispatch*, August 8, 1911.
40. *St. Louis Post-Dispatch*, July 24, 1911.
41. *St. Louis Post-Dispatch*, August 6, 1911.
42. *St. Louis Post-Dispatch*, August 1, 1911.
43. *Pittsburg Press* (Pittsburgh, PA), July 25, 1911.
44. *St. Louis Post-Dispatch*, August 11, 1911.
45. *St. Louis Star*, August 11, 1911.
46. *St. Louis Post-Dispatch*, August 12, 1911.
47. *St. Louis Post-Dispatch*, August 13, 1911.
48. The U.S. Board of Geographic Names restored the *h* in Pittsburgh on July 19, 1911.
49. *St. Louis Star*, August 15, 1911.
50. *St. Louis Globe-Democrat*, August 17, 1911.
51. *Philadelphia Inquirer*, July 27, 1911.
52. *St. Louis Post-Dispatch*, August 17, 1911.
53. *St. Louis Star*, August 21, 1911.
54. *St. Louis Star*, August 25, 1911.
55. *St. Louis Post-Dispatch*, August 28, 1911.
56. *St. Louis Globe-Democrat*, *St. Louis Star*, and *St. Louis Post-Dispatch*, all of August 3, 1911.
57. *St. Louis Post-Dispatch*, August 30, 1911.
58. *St. Louis Post-Dispatch*, August 30, 1911.
59. *St. Louis Post-Dispatch*, September 10, 1911.
60. *St. Louis Post-Dispatch*, September 11, 1911.
61. Lowenfish, *Branch Rickey*, 85.
62. Lieb, *St. Louis Cardinals*, 44.
63. *St. Louis Post-Dispatch*, September 13, 1911, 8.
64. Lieb, *St. Louis Cardinals*, 46.
65. Bresnahan's three-year contract called for $30,000—not $25,000 "as has been generally supposed since he was signed by the late M.S. Robison..."—*St. Louis Post-Dispatch*, September 8, 1911.
66. Lieb, *St. Louis Cardinals*, 46.
67. *St. Louis Post-Dispatch*, October 1, 1911.
68. *St. Louis Post-Dispatch*, September 23, 1911.
69. *St. Louis Post-Dispatch*, October 4, 1911.
70. *St. Louis Star*, September 23, 1911.
71. *St. Louis Post-Dispatch*, October 10, 1911.
72. *St. Louis Post-Dispatch*, October 19, 1911.
73. Lieb, *St. Louis Cardinals*, 44.
74. *St. Louis Star*, July 11, 1911.
75. *St. Louis Post-Dispatch*, July 11, 1911.

Chapter Twenty-Three

1. Clarence Lloyd, "Mr. Old Timer in Annual Fear of 'Going Back,'" *St. Louis Post-Dispatch*, December 29, 1911.
2. *St. Louis Post-Dispatch*, October 28, 1911.
3. Sid Keener, "Roger Ready to Buy," *St. Louis Star*, November 27, 1911.
4. *St. Louis Post-Dispatch*, November 18, 1911.
5. *St. Louis Star*, November 22, 1911.
6. *St. Louis Post-Dispatch*, December 12, 1911.
7. *St. Louis Post-Dispatch*, December 22 and 24, 1911.
8. Clarence F. Lloyd, "Mr. Old Timer in Annual Fear of 'Going Back,'" *St. Louis Post-Dispatch*, December 29, 1911.
9. L.C. Davis, "Sport Salad," *St. Louis Post-Dispatch*, January 29, 1912.
10. *St. Louis Globe-Democrat*, December 13, 1911.
11. Jack Ryder, "Roger Bresnahan and Charles 'Cub' Murphy Almost Come to Blows Over Player Saier," *Cincinnati Enquirer*, December 16, 1911.
12. Roger Bresnahan, letter to August Herrmann, December 18, 1911—August "Garry" Herrmann papers, National Baseball Hall of Fame Library BA-MSS-12 (hereafter cited as HOF).
13. *St. Louis Globe-Democrat*, December 12, 1911.
14. *Pittsburgh Daily Post*, February 14, 1912.
15. *St. Louis Post-Dispatch*, February 18, 1912.
16. *St. Louis Post-Dispatch*, March 1, 1912.
17. *St. Louis Globe-Democrat*, March 2, 1912.
18. *St. Louis Post-Dispatch*, March 3, 1912.
19. *St. Louis Globe-Democrat*, March 4, 1912.
20. *St. Louis Star*, March 9, 1912.
21. *St. Louis Globe-Democrat*, March 9, 1912.
22. W.J. O'Connor, "Cardinals Quit Jackson After a One Day Tryout," *St. Louis Post-Dispatch*, March 11, 1912.
23. W.J. O'Connor, "Cardinals Halt at Jackson, Mississippi to Test Climate," *St. Louis Post-Dispatch*, March 12, 1912.
24. *Jackson Daily News* (MS), March 12, 1912.
25. Frederick Sullens, "Cardinals Settle Down to Work," *Jackson Daily News* (MS), March 13, 1912.

26. W.J. O'Connor, "Cardinals Halt at Jackson, Mississippi to Test Climate," *St. Louis Post-Dispatch*, March 12, 1912.
27. *St. Louis Post-Dispatch*, March 13, 1912.
28. *St. Louis Globe-Democrat*, March 14, 1912.
29. *St. Louis Post-Dispatch*, March 14 and 17, 1912 and *Jackson Daily News* (MS), March 17, 1912.
30. W.J. O'Connor, "Condition Gives Cardinals Edge in Spring Series," *St. Louis Post-Dispatch*, March 19, 1912.
31. *St. Louis Post-Dispatch*, March 21, 1912.
32. *St. Louis Post-Dispatch*, March 21, 1912.
33. Clarence Lloyd, "Cardinals Face Double Workout Despite Weather," *St. Louis Post-Dispatch*, March 22, 1912.
34. *Jackson Daily News* (MS), March 18, 1912.
35. *St. Louis Post-Dispatch*, March 22, 1911.
36. *St. Louis Globe-Democrat*, March 25, 1912.
37. *St. Louis Globe-Democrat*, March 2, 1912.
38. *St. Louis Globe-Democrat*, March 25, 1912.
39. *St. Louis Globe-Democrat*, March 27, 1912.
40. Clarence Lloyd, "Mowery Told to Report Here for Work with Cards," *St. Louis Post-Dispatch*, March 26, 1912.
41. *St. Louis Globe-Democrat*, April 1, 1912, 14.
42. Clarence Lloyd, "Mowery Told to Report Here for Work with Cards," *St. Louis Post-Dispatch*, March 26, 1912.
43. *St. Louis Post-Dispatch*, March 28, 1912, and *St. Louis Globe-Democrat*, March 31, 1912.
44. *St. Louis Post-Dispatch*, April 5, 1911.
45. Smith, *Baseball's Famous First Basemen*, 83–84. In his subsequent book, Smith added the month to the time of the event.
46. Lieb, *St. Louis Cardinals*, 44–5.
47. *St. Louis Star*, February 17, 1911.
48. *St. Louis Globe-Democrat*, March 25, 1912.
49. Clarence Lloyd, "Not a Cardinal Hurler Ready to Go Derby Route," *St. Louis Post-Dispatch*, March 28, 1912.
50. *St. Louis Globe-Democrat*, March 31, 1912.
51. *St. Louis Post-Dispatch*, April 1 and 4, 1911.
52. *Daily Review* (Decatur, IL), April 6, 1912.
53. *St. Louis Globe-Democrat*, April 5, 1912, and *Cincinnati Enquirer*, April 6, 1912.
54. *St. Louis Star*, April 6, 1912.
55. *St. Louis Post-Dispatch*, April 7, 1911.

Chapter Twenty-Four

1. *St. Louis Post-Dispatch*, April 11, 1912.
2. W.J. O'Connor, "Roger Promises Fans a Pennant Within 5 Years," *St. Louis Post-Dispatch*, April 21, 1912.
3. *St. Louis Post-Dispatch*, April 11, 1912.
4. W.J. O'Connor, "Bresnahan Only Cardinal Still in the Hospital," *St. Louis Post Dispatch*, May 3, 1912.
5. Frankie Noel, "Cards Now Where Browns Should Be," *St. Louis Star*, May 12, 1912.
6. *St. Louis Post-Dispatch*, April 22, 1912.
7. *St. Louis Post-Dispatch*, March 21, 1912.
8. *St. Louis Post-Dispatch*, April 11, 1912.
9. *St. Louis Star*, April 12, 1912.
10. *St. Louis Post-Dispatch*, April 14, 1912.
11. W.J. O'Connor, "Bresnahan Only Cardinal Still in the Hospital," *St. Louis Post Dispatch*, May 3, 1912.
12. *St. Louis Globe-Democrat*, May 7, 1912.
13. W.J. O'Connor, "Battered Cards Show Signs of Coming to Life," *St. Louis Post-Dispatch*, May 8, 1912.
14. W.J. O'Connor, "Injuries Bench Five Cardinals," *St. Louis Post-Dispatch*, May 9, 1912.
15. *St. Louis Globe-Democrat*, April 13, 1912, and W.J. O'Connor, "Bob Ewing Signs With Cardinals," *St. Louis Post-Dispatch*, April 13, 1912.
16. *St. Louis Post-Dispatch*, April 11, 1912.
17. *St. Louis Post-Dispatch*, April 14, 1912.
18. *St. Louis Star*, April 21, 1912.
19. *St. Louis Post-Dispatch*, May 3, 1912.
20. *St. Louis Star*, April 20, 1912.
21. *St. Louis Post-Dispatch*, May 3, 1912.
22. *St. Louis Post-Dispatch*, May 21, 1912.
23. *St. Louis Globe-Democrat*, May 17, 1912.
24. *St. Louis Post-Dispatch*, May 21, 1912.
25. *Washington Post*, May 23, 1912.
26. *St. Louis Star*, May 22, 1912.
27. *St. Louis Post-Dispatch*, May 18, 1912.
28. *Washington Post*, May 23, 1912.
29. W.J. O'Connor, "Cards Expect to Return Home in Second Position," *St. Louis Post-Dispatch*, May 27, 1912.
30. W.J. O'Connor, "Bresnahan Sees Only the Giants in Pennant Path," *St. Louis Post-Dispatch*, May 29, 1912.
31. Sam Crane, "Cardinals Took Game from Giants," *Buffalo Enquirer*, June 1, 1912.
32. W.J. O'Connor, "Bresnahan Planning to Bench Himself," *St. Louis Post-Dispatch*, June 13, 1912.
33. *St. Louis Post-Dispatch*, June 19, 1912.
34. W.J. O'Connor, "Roger to Catch No More Except in Emergencies," *St. Louis Post Dispatch*, June 11, 1912.
35. W.J. O'Connor, "Boston Stands Collapse," *St. Louis Post-Dispatch*, June 14, 1912.
36. *St. Louis Post-Dispatch*, June 14, 1912.
37. *St. Louis Post-Dispatch*, June 18, 1912.
38. *St. Louis Star*, June 15, 1912.
39. *St. Louis Post-Dispatch*, June 18, 1912.
40. W.J. O'Connor, "Bresnahan Wants Only Fleet Men to Build Cards," *St. Louis Post-Dispatch*, June 17, 1912.
41. *St. Louis Post-Dispatch*, May 22, 1912.
42. *St. Louis Post-Dispatch*, June 4, 1912.
43. *St. Louis Globe-Democrat*, June 5, 1912.
44. James C. Jones, letter to August Herrmann, September 25, 1912—HOF.
45. *St. Louis Post-Dispatch*, June 4, 1912.
46. Ray Webster, "What Is the Matter with the Cardinals," *St. Louis Star*, June 20, 1912.
47. Billy Murphy "What Other People Think About You," *St. Louis Star*, June 21, 1912.

48. August Herrmann, letter to Roger Bresnahan, June 29, 1912—HOF.
49. Ray Webster, "Who 'Balked' Big Deal with August Herrmann?," *St. Louis Star*, July 20, 1912.
50. W.J. O'Connor, "Many Cardinal Trades Fail" *St. Louis Post-Dispatch*, July 19, 1912.
51. W.J. O'Connor, "Many Cardinal Trades Fail" *St. Louis Post-Dispatch*, July 19, 1912.
52. H.R. Britton, letter to August Herrmann, July 15, 1912—HOF.
53. Roger Bresnahan, letter to August Herrmann, July 24, 1912—HOF.
54. August Herrmann, letter to Roger Bresnahan, July 28, 1912—HOF.
55. *St. Louis Globe-Democrat,* July 26, 1912.
56. Max Fleischmann, telegram to August Herrmann, August 10, 1912—HOF.
57. Max Fleischmann, Private Wire Telegram to August Herrmann, August 12, 1912—HOF.
58. August Herrmann, telegram to Max Fleischmann, August 12, 1912—HOF.
59. Julius Fleischmann, Private Wire Telegram to August Herrmann, August 13, 1912—HOF.
60. Julius Fleischmann, Private Wire Telegram to August Herrmann, August 13, 1912—HOF.
61. August Herrmann, telegram to Max Fleischmann, August 13, 1912—HOF.
62. Max Fleischmann, Private Wire Telegram to August Herrmann, August 14, 1912—HOF.
63. Max Fleischmann, letter to August Herrmann, August 14, 1912—HOF.
64. Roger Bresnahan, telegram to August Herrmann, August 14, 1912—HOF.
65. *St. Louis Globe-Democrat,* August 16, 1912.
66. *St. Louis Globe-Democrat,* August 16, 1912.
67. *Cincinnati Enquirer*, August 16, 1912.
68. *St. Louis Globe-Democrat,* August 16, 1912.
69. *St. Louis Globe-Democrat,* August 16, 1912.
70. *St. Louis Post-Dispatch*, October 22, 1912.
71. *St. Louis Post-Dispatch*, July 30, 1912.
72. *St. Louis Post-Dispatch*, August 23, 1912.
73. *St. Louis Globe-Democrat,* August 24, 1912.
74. *St. Louis Post-Dispatch*, August 23, 1912.
75. *St. Louis Globe-Democrat,* August 24, 1912.
76. *St. Louis Post-Dispatch*, August 23, 1912.
77. *Pittsburgh Gazette Times*, August 27, 1912.
78. *St. Louis Globe-Democrat,* September 4, 1912.
79. August Herrmann, letter to Max Fleischmann, August 16, 1912—HOF.
80. W.J. O'Connor, "Roger Positively Will Be Leader of Cards in 1913," *St.Louis Post-Dispatch*, September 6, 1912.
81. W.J. O'Connor, "Roger Positively Will Be Leader of Cards in 1913," *St. Louis Post-Dispatch*, September 6, 1912.
82. W.J. O'Connor, "Cardinals Play Out Season Seven More Games at Home," *St. Louis Post-Dispatch*, September 5, 1912).
83. *St. Louis Post-Dispatch*, October 17, 1912.
84. *St. Louis Globe-Democrat,* October 23, 1912.
85. *St. Louis Post-Dispatch*, October 19, 1912.
86. *St. Louis Post-Dispatch*, October 22, 1912.

Chapter Twenty-Five

1. *New York Times*, October 24, 1912.
2. *Los Angeles Express*, October 22, 1912, and *Birmingham News* (AL), October 22, 1912.
3. *St. Louis Post-Dispatch*, October 22, 1912.
4. *New York Times*, October 23, 1912.
5. *St. Louis Globe-Democrat*, October 23, 1912.
6. *St. Louis Globe-Democrat*, October 23, 1912.
7. Roger Bresnahan, letter to Board of Directors of National League of Baseball Clubs, November 5, 1912—HOF.
8. *St. Louis Globe-Democrat*, October 23, 1912.
9. *New York Times*, October 24, 1912.
10. *St. Louis Post-Dispatch*, November 8, 1912.
11. *St. Louis Post-Dispatch*, November 13, 1912.
12. *St. Louis Globe-Democrat*, November 8, 1912.
13. W.J. O'Connor, "Bresnahan Free to Accept Berth in Either League," *St. Louis Post-Dispatch*, November 6, 1912.
14. *St. Louis Globe-Democrat*, December 8, 1912.
15. *St. Louis Post-Dispatch*, November 10, October 25, November 18, and November 12, 1912.
16. *St. Louis Post-Dispatch*, November 20, and December 4, 1912.
17. *St. Louis Globe-Democrat*, November 5, 1912.
18. *St. Louis Post-Dispatch*, January 17, 1913.
19. Letter from Roger Bresnahan to Board of Directors of National League of Baseball Clubs, November 5, 1912—HOF.
20. *New York Times*, December 11, 1912.
21. John Wray, "Wray's Column," *St. Louis Post-Dispatch*, December 6, 1912.
22. *St. Louis Post-Dispatch*, December 8, 1912.
23. *St. Louis Star*, October 31, 1912.
24. Bozeman Bulger, "Decision in Bresnahan Case To-Night Will Affect All Future Contracts," *World* (New York) December 9, 1912.
25. James C. Jones, letter to Thomas Lynch, December 4, 1912—HOF.
26. Bozeman Bulger, "Decision in Bresnahan Case To-Night Will Affect All Future Contracts," *World* (New York), December 9, 1912.
27. *New-York Tribune*, December 10, 1912.
28. John Wray, "Wray's Column," *St. Louis Post-Dispatch*, December 6, 1912.
29. *St. Louis Globe-Democrat*, December 10, 1912.
30. *New-York Tribune*, December 10, 1912.
31. *Sporting News*, December 12, 1912.
32. *New-York Tribune*, December 11, 1912.
33. *New-York Tribune*, December 10, 1912.
34. *St. Louis Globe-Democrat*, December 13, 1912, and *St. Louis Post-Dispatch*, December 26, 1912.
35. *St. Louis Star*, December 20, 1912.
36. *Sporting News*, December 12, 1912.
37. *St. Louis Globe-Democrat*, December 21, 1912.
38. August Herrmann, to Roger Bresnahan, December 26, 1912—HOF.
39. *St. Louis Globe-Democrat*, December 27, 1912.
40. *St. Louis Post-Dispatch*, December 28, 1912.
41. *St. Louis Post-Dispatch*, December 15, 1912.

42. *St. Louis Post-Dispatch*, December 21, 1912.
43. *St. Louis Post-Dispatch*, January 2, 1913.
44. *St. Louis Star*, January 4, 1913.
45. W.J. O'Connor, "Roger Settles Claim Against Cardinal Club," *St. Louis Post-Dispatch*, January 5, 1912.
46. John Wray, "Bresnahan Received $9000 [$234,650]," *St. Louis Post-Dispatch*, January 11, 1913.
47. *St. Louis Post-Dispatch*, January 5, 1913.
48. Harold Lanigan, "Stove League Fuel," *Sporting News*, December 26, 1912.
49. W.J. O'Connor, "Bresnahan Sees $40,000 Pay for 3-Year Contract," *St. Louis Post-Dispatch*, January 7, 1913.

Chapter Twenty-Six

1. *Day Book* (Chicago), June 24, 1913.
2. *St. Louis Globe-Democrat*, January 8, 1913.
3. *St. Louis Globe-Democrat*, January 8, 1913.
4. W.J. O'Connor, "Bresnahan Sees $40,000 Pay for 3-Year Contract," *St. Louis Post-Dispatch*, January 7, 1913.
5. Sam Weller, "McGraw of Giants Booster for Cubs," *Chicago Tribune*, January 14, 1913, and *Day Book* (Chicago), February 20, 1913.
6. Harvey Woodruff, "Life and Career of Roger Bresnahan," *Chicago Tribune*, February 2, 1913.
7. *Day Book* (Chicago), February 20, 1913.
8. *Inter Ocean* (Chicago), March 16, 1913.
9. Hy Low, "Northbound Cubs Today Lie Over in Jacksonville," *Inter Ocean* (Chicago), March 19, 1913; and *Chicago Tribune*, February 16, 1913.
10. *Chicago Tribune*, March 31, 1913.
11. *Day Book* (Chicago), March 26, 1913.
12. I.E. Sanborn, "Rain Threatens to Balk Trojans in Opener Today," *Chicago Tribune*, April 10, 1913.
13. *Inter Ocean* (Chicago), April 13, 1913.
14. *St. Louis Post-Dispatch*, April 17, 1913.
15. *Chicago Tribune*, April 19, 1913.
16. *Inter Ocean* (Chicago), April 13, 1913.
17. *Inter Ocean* (Chicago), June 14, 1913.
18. *Day Book* (Chicago), June 17, 1913.
19. *Day Book* (Chicago), June 24 and 19, 1913.
20. *Day Book* (Chicago), July 9, 1913.
21. *Chicago Tribune*, July 23, 1913.
22. *St. Louis Post-Dispatch*, February 13, 1914.
23. *Day Book* (Chicago), July 28, 1913.
24. *Day Book* (Chicago), September 3, 1913.
25. *Chicago Tribune*, October 14, 1913.
26. *Day Book* (Chicago), October 21, 1913, and *Inter Ocean* (Chicago), October 23, 1913.
27. *Dayton Herald*, December 15, 1913, *St. Louis Globe-Democrat*, December 25, 1913, and *Chicago Tribune*, February 15, 1914.
28. *St. Louis Post-Dispatch*, October 21, 1913, and *Inter Ocean* (Chicago), October 24, 1913.
29. *Cincinnati Enquirer*, November 28, 1913.
30. *St. Louis Star*, December 5, 1913.
31. *Akron Beacon Journal* (OH), December 10, 1913.
32. *Cincinnati Enquirer*, November 28, 1913.
33. *Chicago Tribune*, February 11, 1914.
34. W.J. O'Connor, "Failure of Roger to Succeed Evers Is Puzzling Fans," *St. Louis Post-Dispatch*, February 13, 1914.

Chapter Twenty-Seven

1. *Day Book* (Chicago), November 21, 1914.
2. *Chicago Tribune*, February 21, 1914.
3. Henry Edwards, "Toledo A.A. Franchise Is Transferred to Cleveland," *Plain Dealer* (Cleveland), February 17, 1914.
4. *Plain Dealer* (Cleveland), February 22, 1914.
5. *Day Book* (Chicago), March 2, 1914.
6. *St. Louis Post-Dispatch*, February 28, 1914.
7. *Chicago Tribune*, February 21, 1914.
8. Daniel Ginsburg, "John Tener," *Society for American Baseball Research, Baseball Biography Project*, https://sabr.org/bioproj/person/john-tener/.
9. *Cincinnati Enquirer*, February 21, 1914.
10. *Chicago Tribune*, February 22, 1914.
11. *Moline Daily Dispatch* (IL), February 21, 1914.
12. *Chicago Tribune*, February 21, 1914.
13. *Moline Daily Dispatch* (IL), February 21, 1914.
14. *Chicago Tribune*, February 22, 1914.
15. *Chicago Tribune*, February 22, 1914.
16. *Chicago Tribune*, February 25, 1914.
17. *Day Book* (Chicago) March 2, 1914.
18. *Inter Ocean* (Chicago), March 19, 1914.
19. *Day Book* (Chicago) March 2, 1914, and *Chicago Tribune*, April 2, 1914.
20. *Chicago Tribune*, April 12, 1914.
21. *Chicago Tribune*, April 12, 1914.
22. *St. Louis Post-Dispatch*, April 21, 1914.
23. *St. Louis Star*, April 22, 1914.
24. *St. Louis Post-Dispatch*, April 22, 1914.
25. *Chicago Tribune*, April 12, 1914.
26. *Chicago Tribune*, May 12, 1914.
27. *Chicago Tribune*, May 29, 1914.
28. *Day Book* (Chicago), May 29, 1914.
29. *Chicago Tribune*, June 7, 1914, and *Day Book* (Chicago), June 9, 1914.
30. *Chicago Tribune*, June 9, 1914, *Day Book* (Chicago), June 9, 1914, and *Daily Tribune*, June 10, 1914.
31. *Chicago Tribune*, June 10, 1914.
32. *Chicago Tribune*, June 24, 1914.
33. *Chicago Tribune*, June 25, 1914.
34. *Chicago Eagle*, July 4, 1914.
35. *Day Book* (Chicago), July 23, 1914.
36. *Day Book* (Chicago Illinois), August 18, 1914.
37. *Day Book* (Chicago), July 16, 1914.
38. *Chicago Tribune*, July 15, 1914.
39. *Chicago Tribune*, July 16, 1914.
40. *Chicago Tribune*, July 24, 1914, and *Day Book* (Chicago), July 25, 1914.
41. *Day Book* (Chicago), August 18, 1914.
42. *Chicago Tribune*, August 26, 1914.
43. *Chicago Tribune*, September 29, 1914.

44. *Chicago Tribune*, October 12, 1914.
45. *Chicago Tribune*, October 16, 1914.
46. *Sporting Life*, July 25, 1914.
47. *Chicago Tribune*, July 20, 1914.
48. *Day Book* (Chicago), October 23, 1914.
49. *Chicago Tribune*, October 25, 1914.
50. *Chicago Tribune*, December 15, 1914.
51. *New York Times*, October 24, 1914.
52. Sam Weller, "Cubs to Tackle Central Stags," *Chicago Tribune*, June 4, 1915.
53. *Chicago Tribune*, December 10, 1914.
54. U.S. News, "A Glimpse at Your Expenses 100 Years Ago,' January 2, 2015, https://money.usnews.com/money/personal-finance/articles/2015/01/02/a-glimpse-at-your-expenses-100-years-ago#:~:text=1915.,year%2C%20according%20to%20the%20Census.
55. *Chicago Tribune*, October 29, 1914.
56. Noah H. Swayne, letter to George B. Wild, October 6, 1914—Wisconsin Historical Society, "Robert Wild Family Papers," http://digital.library.wisc.edu/1711.dl/wiarchives.uw-whs-mil000cj.
57. *Day Book* (Chicago), November 19, 1914.
58. *Chicago Tribune*, November 20, 1914.
59. *Chicago Eagle*, January 2, 1915.
60. *Chicago Tribune*, November 21, 1914.
61. *Day Book* (Chicago), November 21, 1914.
62. *Day Book* (Chicago), February 19, 1914.
63. *Chicago Tribune*, December 15, 1914.
64. *Day Book* (Chicago), February 11, 1914.
65. *Chicago Tribune*, December 15, 1914.
66. *Chicago Tribune*, December 25 and 29, 1914.
67. *Day Book* (Chicago), January 14, 1915.
68. James Crusinberry, "Cubs Release Tommy Leach and 3 Others," *Chicago Tribune*, February 14, 1915.

Chapter Twenty-Eight

1. *Day Book* (Chicago), July 23, 1915.
2. I.E. Sanborn, "Bresnahan Leads Cubs to Tampa for Spring Work," *Chicago Tribune*, March 1, 1915 and "Can These Men Win That Flag for Boss Roger?," *Chicago Tribune*, March 16, 1915.
3. *Day Book* (Chicago), March 4, 1915.
4. I.E. Sanborn, "Cub Collegian Spikes Himself," *Chicago Tribune*, March 3, 1915.
5. *Chicago Tribune*, March 6, 1915.
6. *Day Book* (Chicago), March 8, 1915.
7. *Day Book* (Chicago), March 31, 1915.
8. I.E. Sanborn, "Cubs Start Trip Back from Camp in Great Shape," *Chicago Tribune*, April 1, 1915.
9. I.E. Sanborn, "Lookouts Beat Bresnahans 3–2 by Rally in 9th," *Chicago Tribune*. April 6, 1915.
10. *Day Book* (Chicago), April 8, 1915.
11. I.E. Sanborn, "Three Clouts, Two in Eighth, Bring Victory," *Chicago Tribune*, April 3, 1915 and "Single by Zim Scores Three in Last Round," *Chicago Tribune*, April 5, 1915.
12. I.E. Sanborn, "Two Cub Errors Give Victory to Memphis 6 to 5," *Chicago Tribune*, April 9, 1915.
13. *Day Book* (Chicago), April 9, 1915.
14. *Day Book* (Chicago), April 14, 1915.
15. *Chicago Tribune*, April 11, 1915.
16. *Day Book* (Chicago), March 16, 1915.
17. *Chicago Tribune*, April 11, 1915.
18. I.E. Sanborn, "Fighting Spirit Makes Catcher of Bresnahan, Once a Pitcher," *Chicago Tribune*, April 11, 1915.
19. *Day Book* (Chicago), April 13, 1915.
20. Handy Andy, "Thomas Dopes Cubs for Flag Winners," *Chicago Tribune*, March 18, 1915.
21. Bozeman Bulger, "Vote of Players Favors Red Sox and the Giants," *St. Louis Post-Dispatch*, April 13, 1915.
22. Grantland Rice, "The Sportlight," *New-York Tribune*, April 13, 1915.
23. *Day Book* (Chicago), April 14, 1915.
24. *Day Book* (Chicago), April 14, 1915.
25. *Day Book* (Chicago), April 19, 1915.
26. I.E. Sanborn, "Three Tallies in 8th Frame Sew Up Game," *Chicago Tribune*, May 6, 1915.
27. I.E. Sanborn, "Hostile Hits Rout Vaughn in Five Rounds," *Chicago Tribune*, May 8, 1915.
28. I.E. Sanborn, "Rogers Win 1–0," *Chicago Tribune*, May 19, 1915.
29. I.E. Sanborn, "Cubs Blanked by Giants," *Chicago Tribune*, June 5, 1915.
30. I.E. Sanborn, "Cincy Rain Jolts Cubs' Game Off Bill," *Chicago Tribune*, June 30, 1915.
31. *Cincinnati Enquirer*, June 29, 1915.
32. Jack Ryder, "Third Straight Win for Toney," *Cincinnati Enquirer*, June 29, 1915.
33. I.E. Sanborn, "Lavender Loses Two Hit Game," *Chicago Tribune*, July 1, 1915.
34. James Crusinberry, "Reds Beat Cubs in Two Clashes Full of Turmoil," *Chicago Tribune*, July 6, 1915.
35. *Cincinnati Enquirer*, July 7, 1915.
36. retrosheet.org and John R. Husman
37. James Crusinberry, "Cheney Halts Drop of Cubs After Giants Take Opener," *Chicago Tribune*, July 15, 1915.
38. Heywood Broun, "Giants Defeat Cubs Then Taste Defeat," *New-York Tribune*, July 15, 1915.
39. *day book* (Chicago), July 16, 1915.
40. Marks Sternman, "The Last Day Best Day," *The National Pastime: Baseball in Chicago*, 2015.
41. James Crusinberry, "Try New Stuff to Make Cubs' Tour a Success," *Chicago Tribune*, July 19, 1915.
42. James Crusinberry, "Freak Home Run Helps Phillies Beat Cubs, 5–4," *Chicago Tribune*, July 20, 1915.
43. *Day Book* (Chicago), July 21, 1915.
44. James Crusinberry, "Cub Misfits Lose to Braves in Eleven Round Game, 2–1, *Chicago Tribune*, July 24, 1915.
45. James Crusinberry, "Cub Misfits Lose to Braves in Eleven Round Game, 2–1, *Chicago Tribune*, July 24, 1915.
46. *Chicago Tribune*, July 24, 1915.
47. James Crusinberry, "Cubs Sign Boy Who Tried for 'Tribune' Trip," *Chicago Tribune*, July 25, 1915.

48. James Crusinberry, "Cub Misfits Lose to Braves in Eleven Round Game, 2–1, *Chicago Tribune*, July 24, 1915.

49. James Crusinberry, "Cubs Back Home with Only Coin to Offset Woe," *Chicago Tribune*, July 28, 1915.

50. James Crusinberry, "Shakeup Coming Unless Cubs Get Heart in Game," *Chicago Tribune*, July 26, 1915.

51. James Crusinberry, "Cub Manager Plans to Reconstruct Nine if Veterans Weaken," *Chicago Tribune*, July 29, 1915.

52. *Chicago Tribune*, July 31, 1915.

53. Ritter, *The Glory of Their Times*, 241–242.

54. *Toledo News-Bee*, August 16, 1915, and James Crusinberry, "'Trib' Amateur a Cub," *Chicago Tribune*, August 17, 1915.

55. *Day Book* (Chicago), July 23, 1915.

56. James Crusinberry, "'Trib' Amateur a Cub," *Chicago Tribune*, August 17, 1915.

57. *Chicago Tribune*, August 30, 1915.

58. J.J. Alcock, "Whales Win Pennant as 34,000 Fans Cheer," *Chicago Tribune*, October 4, 1915.

59. Includes the 1871 through 1968 seasons.

60. *Chicago Tribune*, October 4, 1915.

61. *Chicago Tribune*, October 7, 1915.

62. *Chicago Tribune*, October 8, 1915.

63. *Chicago Tribune*, October 11, 1915.

64. James Crusinberry, "Thomas Takes Roger Along on Still Hunt," *Chicago Tribune*, October 16, 1915.

65. James Crusinberry, "Bresnahan Gloomy," *Chicago Tribune*, October 12, 1915.

66. James Crusinberry, "Thomas Takes Roger Along on Still Hunt," *Chicago Tribune*, October 16, 1915.

67. James Crusinberry, "Cubs Out for Stars, and Coin No Object," *Chicago Tribune*, October 13, 1915.

68. *Chicago Tribune*, October 20, 1915.

69. *Chicago Tribune*, November 4, 1915.

Chapter Twenty-Nine

1. J.J. Alcock, "Cub Leader Departs for League Session in Swapping Mood," *Chicago Tribune*, December 10, 1915.

2. *Chicago Tribune*, December 15, 1915, and James Crusinberry, "J. Ogden Armour Reported Cubs Purchaser," *Chicago Tribune*, December 18, 1915.

3. James Crusinberry, "Bresnahan Gloomy," *Chicago Tribune*, October 12, 1915.

4. James Crusinberry, "Peace Pact Signed by Baseball Magnates," *Chicago Tribune*, December 23, 1915.

5. James Crusinberry, "Bresnahan Gloomy," *Chicago Tribune*, October 12, 1915.

6. James Crusinberry, "Peace Pact Signed by Baseball Magnates," *Chicago Tribune*, December 23, 1915.

7. *Sandusky Register* (OH), December 18, 1915.

8. *Plain Dealer* (Cleveland), January 23, 1916.

9. *Chicago Tribune*, March 5, 1916.

10. *Plain Dealer* (Cleveland), March 9, 1916.

11. *Toledo Blade*, April 18, 1916.

12. *Chicago Tribune*, March 7, 1916.

13. *Washington Post*, November 29, 1903.

14. J.J. Alcock, "Roger Gets Toledo Franchise in A.A.," *Chicago Tribune*, March 7, 1916.

15. *Plain Dealer* (Cleveland), March 8, 1916.

16. *Toledo News-Bee*, April 12, 1916.

17. Dick Meade, "Ten—Count 'Em—Ten Players to Be Turned Over to Bresnahan When Spiders Are Mud Hens," *Toledo News-Bee*, March 1, 1916.

18. Dick Meade, "How George Stovall Was Bagged for Hens by Roger Bresnahan," *Toledo News-Bee*, March 16, 1916.

19. Wiggins, *The Federal League of Baseball Clubs*, 10, 17.

20. *Plain Dealer* (Cleveland), April 16, 1916, and Harry Dix Cole, "New York News," *Sporting Life*, June 15, 1912.

21. *Toledo News-Bee*, March 20, and April 7, 1916.

22. Dick Meade, "New Title for Club," *Toledo News-Bee*, April 11, 1916.

23. *Toledo Blade*, April 17, 1916.

24. *Toledo News-Bee*, April 18, 1916.

25. Dick Meade, "Five American Association Cities Figure They Have Flag Chance," *Toledo News-Bee*, April 17, 1916.

26. *Toledo News-Bee*, April 18, 1916.

27. *Toledo News-Bee*, April 19, 1916.

28. *Toledo News-Bee*, April 19, 1916.

29. *Toledo News-Bee*, March 21, 1917.

30. United States, "Study of Monopoly Power," 1963, https://babel.hathitrust.org/cgi/pt?id=umn.31951d03669259b&view=1up&seq=1963.

31. *Sporting Life*, January 7, 1917.

32. *Toledo News-Bee*, October 16, 1916.

33. *Toledo News-Bee*, February 28, and March 13, 1917.

34. Mitchell Woodbury "Wind Prevents a Toledo Victory," *Toledo News-Bee*, March 29, 1917.

35. Mitchell Woodbury, "Iron Men Start for the North," *Toledo News-Bee*, April 4, 1917.

36. Dick Meade, "Kansas City and Louisville Look Like the Most Complete A.A. Teams," *Toledo News-Bee*, April 2, 1917.

37. Dick Meade, "Toledo Team Returns Home to Face the Boston Red Sox This Afternoon," *Toledo News-Bee*, April 7, 1917.

38. Lin Weber, *Toledo Baseball Guide*, 133.

39. Mitchell Woodbury, "Iron Men Are Trimmed by the Indians," *Toledo News-Bee*, April 11, 1917.

40. Dick Meade, "Iron Men Open with Hoosiers," *Toledo News-Bee*, April 11, 1917.

41. *Toledo News-Bee*, April 20, 1917.

42. *Toledo News-Bee*, September 20, 1917.

43. (Meade, April 9, 1917) and https://babel.hathitrust.org/cgi/pt?id=umn.31951d03669259b&view=1up&seq=1963

44. Alexander, *John McGraw*, 196.

45. Dick Meade, "World Champs Get Eight Hits in Two Days Off Four Toledo Pitchers," *Toledo News-Bee*, April 9, 1917.

46. Dick Meade, "Bailey's One Round Spasm Gives Tiges Enough Runs to Win," *Toledo News-Bee*, April 10, 1917.

47. *Toledo News-Bee*, January 4, 1918.

48. *Toledo News-Bee*, April 1, 1918.

49. *Toledo News-Bee*, March 1, 1918.

50. Dick Meade, "Toledo's Experimental Training Session Opens at Swayne Field Today," *Toledo News-Bee*, April 1, 1918.

51. *Toledo News-Bee*, May 1, and April 30, 1918.

52. Dick Meade, "American Association Baseball Season Back for Another Year of Strif," *Toledo News-Bee*, May 1, 1918.

53. Lin Weber, *Toledo Baseball Guide*, 134.

54. *Toledo News-Bee*, July 22, 1918.

55. Dick Meade, "Duke Is About Thru," *Toledo News-Bee*, April 16, 1918.

56. Lin Weber, *Toledo Baseball Guide*, 135.

57. *Toledo News-Bee*, July 22, 1918.

58. Lin Weber, *Toledo Baseball Guide*, 136.

59. *Toledo News-Bee*, June 1, 1918.

60. *Toledo News-Bee*, April 25, 1918.

61. *Cincinnati Enquirer*, August 14, 1918.

62. Dick Meade, "Random Shots," *Toledo News-Bee*, January 21, 1919.

63. Dick Meade, "Roger Bresnahan to Have a Suprise for the Fans," *Toledo News-Bee*, January 30, 1919.

64. *Toledo News-Bee*, April 10, 1919.

65. *Toledo News-Bee*, March 11, 1919.

66. *Toledo News-Bee*, January 29, and March 20, 1919.

67. Dick Meade, "Sweeney's Sale Biggest Deal of Winter," *Toledo News-Bee*, March 22, 1919.

68. Dick Meade, "Wont [sic] Get Players If Bresnahan Isn't Boss," *Toledo News-Bee*, April 3, 1919.

69. *Fort Wayne Journal-Gazette* (IN), July 26, 1918. Another report from midseason 1919 offered further confirmation that Roger had lost his entire investment in the Toledo venture and was $25,000 [$376,127] in debt—*Fort Wayne News and Sentinel* (IN), July 19, 1919.

70. Dick Meade, "Deal to Finance Toledo Club May Be Settled Today," *Toledo News-Bee*, April 8, 1919 and "Order Toledo Players to Start at Once to City," *Toledo News-Bee*, April 10, 1919.

71. Dick Meade, "How the Toledo Ball Team Will Look on Opening Day," *Toledo News-Bee*, April 16, 1919.

72. Lin Weber, *Toledo Baseball Guide*, 137.

73. Dick Meade, "*Toledo Players Go Into Action for the First Time Today*," *Toledo News-Bee*, April 17, 1919.

74. *Toledo News-Bee*, May 7, 1919, and June 10, 1919.

75. *Toledo News-Bee*, May 6, 1919. Although Mud Hens was used occasionally by out-of-town newspapers the *Toledo News Bee* used neither Iron Men nor Mud Hens until May 6 when Mud Hens suddenly appeared without explanation.

76. *Toledo News-Bee*, April 28, 1919.

77. *Toledo News-Bee*, June 7, 1919.

78. *Toledo News-Bee*, June 13, 1919.

79. *Toledo News-Bee*, July 15, 1919.

80. Lin Weber, *Toledo Baseball Guide*, 137.

81. United States, "Study of Monopoly Power," 1963, https://babel.hathitrust.org/cgi/pt?id=umn.31951d03669259b&view=1up&seq=1963.

82. *Toledo News-Bee*, July 5, 1919.

83. *Louisville Courier-Journal*, October 26, 1919.

84. Mitchell Woodbury, "Hens Drawing Well on the Road, *Toledo News-Bee*, August 6, 1919.

85. *Toledo News-Bee*, September 18, 1919.

86. *Toledo News-Bee*, September 16, 1919.

87. *Louisville Courier-Journal*, October 26, 1919, and *Indianapolis Star*, November 26, December 21, 22 and 28, 1919.

88. *Indianapolis Star*, September 5, 1919.

89. *St. Louis Post-Dispatch*, September 6, 1919.

90. *News-Messenger* (Fremont, OH), November 11, 1919.

91. Lucas County, Ohio, Court of Common Pleas, Case #80969.

Chapter Thirty

1. Dick Meade, "Same Leaders Will Handle A.A. Ball Teams," *Toledo News-Bee*, October 7, 1920.

2. Dick Meade, "Hens Start South on March 15," Toledo News-Bee, March 5, 1920.

3. *Toledo News-Bee*, January 6, 1920.

4. *Toledo News-Bee*, January 8 and 31, 1920, Dick Meade, "Cheery News—Al Wickland Signs His Toledo Contract," *Toledo News-Bee, March 11, 1920* and *Toledo News- Bee* March 22, 1920.

5. *Toledo News-Bee*, January 2, 1920, and *Baltimore Sun*, March 21, 1920.

6. Louis Silverthorne, "Baseball Outlook Seems Brighter for Mud Hens," *Indianapolis Star*, February 15, 1920, and *Sporting News*, February 26, 1920.

7. Dick Meade, "Spends Big Money for Toledo Players," *Toledo News-Bee*, March 24, 1920.

8. *Toledo News-Bee*, April 15, 1920.

9. *Toledo News-Bee*, April 29, 1920.

10. *Rock Island Argus* (IL), January 16, 1920.

11. *Toledo News-Bee*, April 29, 1920.

12. Dick Meade, "Dubuc Is New Field Captain," *Toledo News-Bee*, July 30, 1920.

13. Dick Meade, "Same Leaders Will Handle A.A. Ball Teams," *Toledo News-Bee*, October 7, 1920.

14. Lin Weber, *Toledo Baseball Guide*, 140.

15. Dick Meade, "Toledo Leads All A.A. Cities in Season's Attendance," *Toledo News-Bee*, October 4, 1920 and United States, "Study of Monopoly Power," 1963, https://babel.hathitrust.org/cgi/pt?id=umn.31951d03669259b&view=1up&seq=1963.

16. *Sporting News*, December 2, 1920, and Dick Meade, "Goodby Baseball Season Tomorrow," *Toledo News-Bee*, October 2, 1920.

17. *New-York Tribune*, September 16, 1920.

18. *Detroit Free Press*, September 27, 1920.
19. Dick Meade, "Reason Why Dubuc Has Not Been Signed to Boss Hens," *Toledo News-Bee*, October 26, 1920.
20. *Evening Review* (East Liverpool, OH), October 19, 1920.
21. *Toledo News-Bee*, October 6, 1920.
22. *Akron Evening Times* (OH), October 19, 1920.
23. Dick Meade, "Jean Dubuc, Mud Hen Leader, Is Given Outright Release," *Toledo News-Bee*, December 4, 1920.
24. *Philadelphia Inquirer*, September 30, 1920.
25. Alexander, *John McGraw*, 135.
26. *Cincinnati Enquirer*, August 19, 1912.
27. *Philadelphia Inquirer*, November 27, 1912.
28. Phil Williams, "Horace Fogel," *Society for American Baseball Research, Baseball Biography Project*, https://sabr.org/bioproj/person/horace-fogel/#sdendnote54sym
29. *Cincinnati Enquirer*, November 20, 1920.
30. *Toledo Blade*, November 20, 1920.
31. *Toledo News-Bee*, November 20, 1920.
32. *Toledo Times*, November 20, 1920.
33. *Toledo News-Bee*, November 20, 1920.
34. *Toledo News-Bee*, November 20, 1920.
35. Lucas County, Ohio, Court of Common Pleas, Case #80969.
36. Dick Meade, "Same Leaders Will Handle A.A. Ball Teams," *Toledo News-Bee*, October 7, 1920.
37. Dick Meade, "Now You'll Have Your Old Friend Bill Clymer for 1921," *Toledo News-Bee*, December 16, 1920.
38. Dick Meade, "Two More Players Lost to Mud Hens," *Toledo News-Bee*, December 2, 1920.
39. *Toledo News-Bee*, April 18, 1921.
40. *Toledo News-Bee*, January 12, 1921.
41. Dick Meade, "Hugh Bedient Coming Back to Mud Hens," *Toledo News-Bee*, January 3, 1921.
42. Dick Meade, "Toledo Buys Fred Luderus for First Base," *Toledo News-Bee*, February 22, 1921.
43. *Seattle Star*, February 23, 1921.
44. Dick Meade, "One Day More and Hens Will Be on the Way," *Toledo News-Bee*, March 4, 1921.
45. Dick Meade, "Regulars Trim Yans in First Real Game of Season," *Toledo News-Bee*, March 19, 1921.
46. *Toledo News-Bee*, April 15, 1921.
47. Dick Meade, "Duke Says Hens 50 Per Cent Stronger Than 1920 Club," *Toledo News-Bee*, March 25, 1921.
48. *Kansas City Star*, May 6, 1921.
49. *Toledo News-Bee*, May 12, 1921.
50. *Toledo News-Bee*, May 14, 1921.
51. *Kansas City Star*, May 15, 1921.
52. *Kansas City Times*, May 16, 1921.
53. *Kansas City Times*, May 17, 1921.
54. *Dayton Daily News*, June 14, 1921.
55. Lin Weber, *Toledo Baseball Guide*, 144.
56. Dick Meade, "Clymer Bows Out," *Toledo News-Bee*, July 2, 1921.
57. *Kansas City Star*, June 19, 1921.
58. Lin Weber, *Toledo Baseball Guide*, 143 and United States, "Study of Monopoly Power," 1963, https://babel.hathitrust.org/cgi/pt?id=umn.31951d03669259b&view=1up&seq=1963.
59. Dick Meade, "Random Shots,"February 10, 1922.
60. Dick Meade, "Fred Luderus to Again Manage the Mud Hens Next Year," *Toledo News-Bee*, September 30, 1921.
61. R.J. Kelly, "Double Defeat Puts Pirates Out of Running," *New-York Tribune*, September 30, 1921.
62. *New York Times*, October 1, 1921.
63. *Toledo News-Bee*, October 1, 1921.
64. *New York Times*, October 1, 1921.
65. Tripod, "Top 25 Catchers-1900s," http://members.tripod.com/bb_catchers/catchers/1900catchers.htm.
66. Honig, *The Greatest Catchers of All Time*, 4.
67. Edward Lyell Fox, "Baseball as the Players See It," *Outing Magazine*, May, 1911.
68. Mathewson, *Pitching in a Pinch*, 80.
69. Billy Evans, "Lively Ball Bad Thing for Game," *Charlotte Observer*, March 3, 1923.
70. *Evening Telegram* (Salt Lake City), April 23, 1909.
71. *Port Huron Daily Times* (MI), June 15, 1907.
72. Billy Evans, "Lively Ball Bad Thing for Game," *Charlotte Observer*, March 3, 1923.
73. *Sporting Life*, September 5, 1914.
74. *Toledo Blade*, December 10, 1935.
75. James, *The New Bill James Historical Baseball Abstract*, 377.
76. *Toledo News-Bee*, February 22, 1922.
77. *Toledo News-Bee*, February 15, 1922.
78. *Brooklyn Daily Eagle*, January 25, 1923.
79. *Toledo News-Bee*, February 15, 1922.
80. *Muncie Morning Star* (IN), December 30, 1921.
81. *Toledo News-Bee*, March 3, 1922.
82. Dick Meade, "Random Shots," *Toledo News-Bee*, February 23, 1922, and *Toledo News-Bee*, January 7, 1922.
83. Earl Aiken, "Cheerful News Is the Chilly Story from Bristol," *Toledo News-Bee*, March 8, 1922.
84. Dick Meade, "Random Shots," *Toledo News-Bee*, March 2, and April 4, 1922.
85. *Indianapolis News*, April 8, 1922.
86. Dick Meade, "Random Shots," *Toledo News-Bee*, April 13, 1922.
87. *Louisville Courier-Journal*, May 12, 1922.
88. *Toledo News-Bee*, May 16, 1922.
89. *Toledo News-Bee*, May 30, 1922.
90. *Toledo News-Bee*, May 20, 1922.
91. *Toledo News-Bee*, May 10, 1922.
92. *Toledo News-Bee*, May 20, 1922.
93. *Toledo News-Bee*, May 22, 1922.
94. Lin Weber, *Toledo Baseball Guide*, 146.
95. Graham, *McGraw of the Giants*, 154, and Blanche McGraw, The Real McGraw1953, 287.
96. *Williams. When the Giants Were Giants*, 46.
97. *St. Louis Star*, March 7, 1922.
98. *Cincinnati Enquirer*, April 18, 1922.
99. Lucas County, Ohio Auditor's Office Record of Deeds Volume 585, page 290.

100. Dick Meade, "Random Shots," *Toledo News-Bee*, June 3, 1922.
101. Dick Meade, "Random Shots," *Toledo News-Bee*, September 9, 1922.
102. *Sporting News*, March 15, 1923.
103. Dick Meade, "Random Shots," *Toledo News-Bee*, April 4, 1923.
104. Lin Weber, *Toledo Baseball Guide*, 150.
105. Dick Meade, "Random Shots," *Toledo News-Bee*, December 18, 1922.
106. *News-Democrat* (Paducah, Kentucky), March 15, 1923.
107. Dick Meade, "Random Shots," *Toledo News Bee*, March 19, 1923.
108. Dick Meade, "Random Shots," *Toledo News-Bee*, March 2, 1923.
109. Dick Meade, "Random Shots," *Toledo News-Bee*, March 20, 1923.
110. Stengel managed Toledo from 1926 through 1931 and won the city's only Junior World Series Championship in 1927—Lin Weber, *Toledo Baseball Guide*, 164.
111. *Toledo News-Bee*, April 18, 1923, and Dick Meade, "Random Shots," *Toledo News-Bee*, April 16, 1923.
112. Dick Meade, "Random Shots," *Toledo News-Bee*, April 20, 1923.
113. Dick Meade, "Random Shots," *Toledo News-Bee*, June 5, 1923.
114. Lin Weber, *Toledo Baseball Guide*, 151 and *Toledo News-Bee*, June 23, 1923. At mid–June four of the American Association's five top hitters were Mud Hens: Anderson .416, Smith .378, Terry .371, and Lamar .366.
115. *Toledo News-Bee*, August 1, 1923.
116. *Toledo News-Bee*, September 17, 1923, and *Sporting News*, September 27, 1923.
117. *Toledo News-Bee*, September 17, 1923.
118. *Toledo News-Bee*, September 22, 1923, and Earl Aiken, "Kelley's Warriors Make It Four Straight Against Hens," *Toledo News-Bee*, June 5, 1923.
119. Lin Weber, *Toledo Baseball Guide*, 149.
120. Toledo Mud Hens Media Guide.
121. *Bulletin* (Pomona, CA), October 12, 1923.
122. *Sporting News*, June 7, 1923, and *St. Louis Globe-Democrat*, October 2, 1923.
123. Dick Meade, "Random Shots," *Toledo News-Bee*, December 28, 1923.
124. *St. Louis Globe-Democrat*, October 2, 1923.
125. Dick Meade, "Random Shots," *Toledo News-Bee*, January 7, 1924.
126. Dick Meade, "Random Shots," *Toledo News-Bee*, January 12, 1924.
127. Roger Bresnahan, letter to August Herrmann, January 7, 1924—HOF.
128. Dick Meade, "Give Fancy Price for Toledo Team," *Toledo News-Bee*, January 22, 1924.
129. Moses Solomon was sold to Toledo—Dick Meade, "Random Shots," *Toledo News-Bee*, January 31, 1924.
130. Dick Meade, "Random Shots," *Toledo News-Bee*, February 2, 1924.

Chapter Thirty-One

1. Dick Farrington, "Bresnahan, Former Catching Star, Fighting Back at 60 from Crash That Turned His Wealth Into Want," *Sporting News*, November 14, 1940.
2. Dick Meade, "Random Shots," *Toledo News-Bee*, June 7, 1923.
3. Dick Meade, "Random Shots," *Toledo News-Bee*, June 13, 1922.
4. Dick Meade, "Random Shots," *Toledo News-Bee*, February 2, 1924.
5. *Sporting News*, November 14, 1940.
6. Lucas County, Ohio, Auditor's Office, transfer card for Parcel 16–14931 and Toledo, Ohio City Directories of various years.
7. *Altoona Tribune* (PA), December 4, 1924.
8. *Age* (Melbourne, Australia), May 20, 1902, and Toledo, Ohio City Directories of various years.
9. Toledo, Ohio City Directory 1899.
10. *Fielding Star* (Masterson, New Zealand), August 23, 1901.
11. *Anaconda Standard* (MT), April 4, 1901, *Hawaiian Star* (Honolulu), April 20, 1901, and *Japan Weekly Mail*, May 4, 1901, 475—books.google.com/books.
12. Theatre Heritage Australia, Inc., "One tenor," June 3, 2020, https://www.theatreheritage.org.au/on-stage-magazine/general-articles/item/636-one-tenor-fifty-years-four-continents-umpteen-countries-three-wives-two-fathers?fbclid=IwAR3r2VEESPdJR_GlS18ktuvFgPiKTps_okWtOfVgBW8p20kNTh72mV6Zd24
13. Ancestry.com—Ventura passenger list booked from Sydney to San Francisco via Japan and various Toledo, Ohio city directories.
14. State of Ohio, Department of Health, Division of Vital Statistics, Certificate of Death, File No. 36049. Her birth date on the certificate is likely misstated, making her 95 at death.
15. *New York Times*, February 4, 1926.
16. Henry Farrell, "Giants, with Much Improved Ball Club, Will Be Hard Combination to Beat," *Dayton Herald*, April 10, 1926; *Daily News* (New York), April 13, 1926, and *Pittsburgh Press*, February 20, 1926.
17. *Daily News* (New York), April 30, 1926. Bresnahan's service as manager of the New York Giants in 1926 and 1928 had not been included in baseball's record. Since this has been revealed through research for this work, it now is.
18. Dick Meade, "Random Shots," *Toledo News-Bee*, February 9, 1926.
19. *New York Times*, February 4, 1926.
20. *Daily News* (New York), August 15 and March 6, 1926.
21. *New York Times*, July 8, 1926.
22. *York Dispatch* (PA), December 21, 1926.
23. *Daily News* (New York), January 20, 1927.
24. *Toledo News-Bee*, June 7, 1927.
25. Toledo won the American Association pennant and defeated Buffalo of the International

League in the Junior World Series—Lin Weber, *Toledo Baseball Guide*, 161–174).

26. James P. Harrison, "Landis and Heydler Attend McGraw Jubilee," *Yonkers Herald* (NY), July 20, 1927.

27. *New York Times*, November 13, 1928, and *Detroit Free Press*, November 13, 1928.

28. *Charlotte Observer* (NC), November 13, 1928, Blanche McGraw, *The Real McGraw*, 318 and *Los Angeles Express*, November 13, 1928.

29. Alexander, *John McGraw*, 288.

30. *Cincinnati Enquirer*, November 28, 1928.

31. *Atlanta Constitution*, August 18, 1929.

32. *Brooklyn Daily Eagle*, September 16, 1929.

33. *Sporting News*, October 31, 1929.

34. Dick Farrington, "Bresnahan, Former Catching Star, Fighting Back at 60 from Crash That Turned His Wealth Into Want," *Sporting News*, November 14, 1940.

35. *Detroit Free Press*, January 28, 1930.

36. *Brooklyn Daily Eagle*, February 27, 1930.

37. *Detroit Free Press*, February 14, 1931.

38. *Sporting News*, October 22, 1931.

39. Frank Gilhooley, Jr., in discussion with the author, September 28, 2010.

40. *Toledo News-Bee*, January 23, 1932, and *Toledo Blade*, May 10, 1932.

41. John E.Wray, "Wray's Column," *St. Louis Post-Dispatch*, July 19, 1934.

42. *Sporting News*, November 14, 1940.

43. Lou Klewer, "Bresnahan Names Greatest Players He Has Ever Seen," *Toledo Blade*, July 9, 1934.

44. *Toledo Blade*, November 29, 1934.

45. Jack Puffenberger, in discussion with the author, February 18, 2021.

46. Toledo, Ohio City Directories of various years.

47. *New York Times*, January 4, 1974, and Arthur Daley, *Times at Bat*, 46.

48. *Detroit Free Press*, February 26, 1934.

49. *Toledo News-Bee*, February 10, 1909.

50. John J. McGraw, *My Thirty Years in Baseball*, 160.

51. *New-York Tribune*, November 5, 1922.

52. *Montgomery Times* (AL), April 27, 1909.

53. Jack Puffenberger, in discussion with the author, February 18, 2021. Coupled with the seventh-grade mention in Chapter Two, this eighth-grade notice confirms that Roger Bresnahan *did not* attend high school.

54. National Public Radio, "The 1940 Census," April 2, 2012, https://www.npr.org/2012/04/02/149575704/the-1940-census-72-year-old-secrets-revealed#:~:text=The%20median%20income%20for%20a,every%20dollar%20a%20man%20earned.

55. Bob French, "Mirrors of Sport," *Toledo Blade*, August 16, 1938.

56. Mike Lackey letter to the author, March 24, 2021.

57. *Elmira Star-Gazette* (NY), October 15, 1929.

58. Grayson, *They Played the Game*, 84.

59. Fleitz, *Ghosts in the Gallery at Cooperstown*, 42.

60. *Toledo Times*, January 20, 1943.

61. Roger M. Bresnahan, email message to author, April 30, 2021.

62. Dave Bresnahan, email message to author, June 24, 2016.

63. John Drebinger, "City's All-Stars Beat Gowdy Team," *New York Times*, August 27, 1943.

64. Arthur Daley, "The War Bond Game," *New York Times*, August 27, 1943.

65. *Toledo Blade*, November 7, 1944.

66. *Toledo Blade*, December 4, 1944.

67. Lackey, *Spitballing*, 292 and *Sporting News*, December 14, 1944.

68. Lackey, *Spitballing*, 292.

69. *Toledo Blade*, December 4, 1944.

70. *Toledo Blade*, December 7, 1944.

71. Jim Silk, in discussion with the author, October 17, 2012.

72. Roger M. Bresnahan, unidentified mortuary records for Roger P. Bresnahan.

73. *Toledo Blade*, December 7, 1944.

74. Willard B. "Bill" Mason, in discussion with the author, January 8, 2007.

75. Dan Daniel, "Hall of Fame Vote Ignores FDR, Griffith," *Sporting News*, May 3, 1945.

76. *Sporting News*, February 1, 1945.

77. Fred Lieb, *The St. Louis Cardinals*, 10.

78. Dan Daniel, "Hall of Fame Vote Ignores FDR, Griffith," *Sporting News*, May 3, 1945.

79. Larry Marthey, "Roger Bresnahan Hall of Fame Award Finally Here for Late Star's Family," *Toledo Blade*, June 26, 1949.

80. Tom Loomis, "Roger Bresnahan's Widow to Attend Hall of Fame Ceremonies Tomorrow," *Toledo Blade*, July 25, 1955.

81. Roger M. Bresnahan, email message to author, April 6, 2021.

82. *Sporting News*, August 3, 1995.

83. Jane Forbes Clark, "Hall of Fame Induction Ceremony Remarks," Cooperstown, NY, June 23, 2013.

84. James, *The Politics of Glory*, 42.

85. Roger Bresnahan's 212 stolen bases during his career are the most for any player whose primary position was catcher. He is followed by Jason Kendall (1996–2010) with 187 and Ray Schalk (1912–1929) with 177. The order changes when only games played at catcher are considered; Kendall 187, Schalk 177 and Bresnahan 146—Raw data from retrosheet.com and calculations by the author.

86. Baseball Writers' Association of America, "Hall of Fame Election Requirements," https://bbwaa.com/hof-elec-req/

87. James, *The Politics of Glory*, 42.

88. Roger M. Bresnahan, "Rog. Bresnahan Deserves Niche in Baseball Hall of Fame," unidentified news clip authored by Grantland Rice and Arthur Daley, "Knocking at the Door of the Hall of Fame," *New York Times*, August 31, 1943.

89. Arthur Daley, "In Tribute to the Duke of Tralee," *New York Times*, December 7, 1944.

90. John B. Sheridan, "Back of the Home Plate," *Sporting News*, February 11, 1926.

Epilogue

1. Toledo, Ohio City Directories of various years.
2. *Toledo Blade*, January 20, 1968.
3. Margaret Bresnahan, email messages to author, November 30 and December 2, 2015.
4. Toledo Central Catholic High School Centritetal (yearbook) 1949, 57 and Lucas County, Ohio, Probate Court, Marriage Record 192066, July 14, 1951.
5. Lucas County, Ohio, Probate Court, Marriage Record 216330, December 17, 1955.
6. *Toledo Blade*, September 7, 1961 and April 23, 2000.
7. Marian Bresnahan Childers, in discussion with the author, July 6, 1987.
8. Lucas County, Ohio, Auditor's Office, Record of Deeds; Volume 297, page 83, October 4, 1904, and Volume 307, page 204, October 24, 1906.
9. Toledo Lucas County Health Department, Death Certificate for Adeleen Bresnahan, October 1, 1951.
10. *Toledo Blade*, March 3, 1951.
11. Joan M. Thomas, "Helene Britton," *Society for American Baseball Research, Baseball Biography Project*, https://sabr.org/bioproj/person/helene-britton/

Bibliography

Main Sources

Abrams, Roger I. *The First World Series and the Baseball Fanatics of 1903.* Tampa: Book Production Resources, 2003.

Alexander, Charles C. *John McGraw.* Lincoln: University of Nebraska Press, 1988.

Belnap, H.W. *Report of H.W. Belnap, Chief Inspector of Safety Appliances Interstate Commerce Commission.* Committee on Rules, United States House of Representatives. Washington, D.C.: Government Printing Office, 1913.

Bresnahan, Roger M. *Personal Collection of Photographs and Unidentified Newspaper Clips.* Unpublished, not dated.

Bresnahan, Roger P. *Roger's Scrapbook.* Unpublished, not dated.

Byrne, James P., Philip Coleman, and Jason King, Editors. *Ireland and the Americas: Culture, Politics and History, Vol. 2.* Santa Barbara: ABC-CLIO, 2008.

Daley, Arthur. *Times at Bat: A Half Century of Baseball.* New York: Random House, 1950.

Dickson, Paul. *The Dickson Baseball Dictionary.* New York: W.W. Norton, 2009.

Evers, John J. *Touching Second.* London: Forgotten Books (1910) 2012.

Fisher, Claude S., and Michael Hart. *Century of Difference: How America Changed in the Last One Hundred Years.* New York: Russell Sage Foundation, 2006.

Fleitz, David L. *Ghosts in the Gallery at Cooperstown.* Jefferson, NC: McFarland, 2004.

______. *The Irish in Baseball.* Jefferson, NC: McFarland, 2009.

Fleming, Gordon H. *The Unforgettable Season.* New York: Fireside, 1981.

Gaines, Bob. *Christy Mathewson, the Christian Gentleman: How One Man's Faith and Fastball Forever Changed Baseball.* Lanham, MD: Rowman & Littlefield, 2015.

Graham, Frank. *McGraw of the Giants: An Informal Biography.* New York: Van Rees Press, 1944.

______. *The New York Giants: An Informal History of a Great Baseball Club.* Carbondale and Edwardsville, IL: Southern Illinois University Press, 2002.

Grayson, Harry. *They Played the Game: The Story of Baseball Greats.* New York: A.S. Barnes, 1944.

Honig, Donald. *The Greatest Catchers of All Time.* Dubuque, IA: William C. Brown, 1991.

James, Bill. *The New Bill James Historical Baseball Abstract.* New York: Free Press, 2001.

______. *The Politics of Glory: How Baseball's Hall of Fame Really Works.* New York: Macmillan, 1994.

Johnson, Lloyd, and Miles Wolff, eds. *The Encyclopedia of Minor League Baseball.* Durham, NC: Baseball America, 2007.

Klein, Maury. *Stealing Games: The Amazing 1911 New York Giants and Their World.* New York: Bloomsbury Press, 2016.

Lackey, Mike. *Spitballing: The Baseball Days of Long Bob Ewing.* Wilmington, OH: Orange Frazer Press, 2013.

Lammers, Craig. "The Best Circuit You Never Heard Of: The 1897 Wood County League." *Base Ball: A Journal of the Early Game.* Jefferson, NC: McFarland, Spring 2008.

Larson, Erik. *Dead Wake: The Last Crossing of the Lusitania.* New York: Crown Publishers, 2015.

Lieb, Frederick G. *The St. Louis Cardinals: The Story of a Great Baseball Club.* New York: G.P. Putnam's Sons, 1944.

Lin Weber, Ralph Elliott, ed. *The Toledo Baseball Guide of the Mud Hens 1883–1943.* Rossford, OH: Baseball Research Bureau, 1944.

Littlefield, Bill, and Richard A. Johnson. *Fall Classics: The Best Writing About the World Series' First 100 Years.* New York: Three Rivers, 2004.

Lowenfish, Lee. *Branch Rickey: Baseball's Ferocious Gentleman.* Lincoln: University of Nebraska Press, 2009.

Macht, Norman. "Charles Sebastian 'Red' Dooin." Tom Simon, ed. *Deadball Stars of the National League.* Dulles, VA: Brassey's, Inc., 2004.

______. *Connie Mack and the Early Years of Baseball.* Lincoln: University of Nebraska Press, 2007.

Mathewson, Christy. *Pitching in a Pinch.* New York: Penguin Books, 2013.

McCaffrey, Eugene, and Roger McCaffrey. *Players' Choice.* New York: Facts on File, 1987.

McGraw, Blanche Sindall. *The Real McGraw.* New York: Van Rees, 1953.

McGraw, John J. *My Thirty Years in Baseball.* New York: Boni and Liveright, 1923.

Morris, Peter. *Catcher: How the Man Behind the Plate Became an American Folk Hero.* Chicago: Ivan R. Dee, 2009.

______. *A Game of Inches, The Game on the Field.* Chicago: Ivan R. Dee, 2006.

Murphy, Cait. *Crazy '08: How a Cast of Cranks, Rogues, Boneheads and Magnates Created the Greatest Year in Baseball History.* New York: HarperCollins, 2007.

Ritter, Lawrence S. *The Glory of Their Times.* New York: Macmillan, 1966.

Scribner, Harvey, ed. *Memoirs of Lucas County and the City of Toledo.* Madison, WI: Western Historical Association, 1910.

Seymour, Harold. *Baseball: The Early Years.* New York: Oxford University Press, 1960.

______. *Baseball: The Golden Age.* New York: Oxford University Press, 1971.

Skipper, James K., Jr. *Baseball Nicknames: A Dictionary of Nicknames and Meanings.* Jefferson, NC: McFarland, 1992.

Smith, Ira L. *Baseball's Famous First Basemen.* New York: A.S. Barnes, 1956.

Spatz, Lyle. *Bad Bill Dahlen: The Rollicking Life and Times of an Early Baseball Star.* Jefferson, NC: McFarland, 2004.

Steinberg, Steve. *The World Series in the Deadball Era.* Haworth, NJ: St. Johann, 2018.

Thomas, Joan M. *Baseball's First Lady: Helene Hathaway Robison Britton and the St. Louis Cardinals.* St. Louis, MO: Reedy Press, 2010.

Thorn, John. "MLB/blogs." February 15, 2016. *Our Game.* http://ourgme.mlblogs.com/2016/02/15/five-books-you-should-know/.

Wiggins, Robert Peyton. *The Federal League of Baseball Clubs: The History of an Outlaw Major League, 1914–1915.* Jefferson, NC: McFarland, 2009.

Williams, Peter. *When the Giants Were Giants.* Chapel Hill, NC: Algonquin, 1944.

Newspapers Consulted

Age (Melbourne, Australia)
Akron Beacon Journal (OH)
Akron Evening Times (OH)
Altoona Times (PA)
Altoona Tribune (PA)
Anaconda Standard (MT)
Arkansas Democrat (Little Rock)
Arkansas Gazette (Little Rock)
Atchison Daily Globe (KS)
Atlanta Constitution
Austin Daily Statesman
Baltimore American
Baltimore Sun
Birmingham News (AL)
Boston Daily Globe
Boston Herald
Boston Post
Bridgeport Evening Farmer (CT)
Brooklyn Citizen
Brooklyn Daily Eagle
Bryan Press (OH)
Buffalo Commercial
Buffalo Courier
Buffalo Enquirer
Buffalo Evening News
Bulletin (Pomona, CA)
Burlington Free Press (VT)
Charlotte Observer (NC)
Chicago Eagle
Chicago Tribune
Christian Science Monitor
Cincinnati Commercial Tribune
Cincinnati Enquirer
Cincinnati Post
Cincinnati Times-Star
Cleveland Leader
Columbus Dispatch
Courier-Journal (Louisville)
Courier-News (Bridgewater, NJ)
Daily News (New York)
Daily Review (Decatur, IL)
Dallas Morning News
Day Book (Chicago)
Dayton Daily News
Dayton Herald
Dayton Press
Decatur Herald (IL)
Democrat and Chronicle (Rochester, NY)
Detroit Free Press
Elmira Star-Gazette (NY)
Evening Journal (Wilmington, DE)
Evening News (Wilkes-Barre, PA)
Evening Review (East Liverpool, OH)
Evening Star (Washington, D.C.)
Evening Telegram (Salt Lake City)
Fort Wayne Journal-Gazette (IN)
Fort Wayne News (IN)
Fort Wayne News and Sentinel (IN)
Gazette Times (Pittsburg)
Indianapolis News
Indianapolis Star
Inter Ocean (Chicago)
Jackson Daily News (MS)
Kansas City Star
Kansas City Times
Lima News (OH)
Los Angeles Express
Los Angeles Times
Louisville Courier Journal
Manistee Daily News (MI)
Mansfield News (OH)
Minneapolis Journal
Minneapolis Tribune
Moline Daily Dispatch (IL)
Montgomery Times (AL)
Morning Tribune (Altoona, PA)
Muncie Morning Star (IN)
Muskegon Chronicle (MI)
Nashville American
New Castle Herald (PA)
New Orleans Item
New York American
New York Herald
New York Journal
New York Times

New York World-Telegram
New-York Tribune
News-Messenger (Fremont, OH)
Oakland Tribune
Our Paper (Concord, MA)
Paducah Evening Sun (KY)
Philadelphia Inquirer
Pittsburg Post
Pittsburg Press
Pittsburgh Post
Pittsburgh Press
Plain Dealer (Cleveland)
Plainfield Courier-News (NJ)
Port Huron Daily Times (MI)
Post-Crescent (Appleton, WI)
Press and Sun Bulletin (Binghamton, NY)
Rock Island Argus (IL)
Rocky Mountain News (Denver)
St. Louis Globe-Democrat
St. Louis Post-Dispatch
St. Louis Republic
St. Louis Star
Salt Lake Telegram
San Francisco Call Bulletin
Sandusky Register (OH)
Sandusky Star-Journal (OH)
Scranton Republican (PA)
Scranton Truth (PA)
Seattle Star
Sentinel (Bowling Green, OH)
Shreveport Times
South Bend Tribune (IN)
Sporting Life (Philadelphia)
Sporting News (St. Louis)
Star-Independent (Harrisburg, PA)
Sun (New York)
Sun And The New York Herald
Tennessean (Nashville)
Times (Shreveport)
Times-Democrat (Lima, OH)
Toledo Bee
Toledo Blade
Toledo News
Toledo News-Bee
Toledo Times
Upper Des Moines (Algona, IA)
Washington Herald
Washington Post
Washington Times
Wichita Daily Eagle
Wilkes-Barre Record (PA)
Wilkes-Barre Times (PA)
Wilkes-Barre Times-Leader (PA)
Worcester Daily Spy
World (New York)
Yonkers Herald (NY)
York Dispatch (PA)

Index